Learning

Microsoft Office XP

(Revised and Enlarged Edition)

Ramesh Bangia
B.Sc., Dip. Comp. Sc.
Formerly: Managing Editor, Software Today
Formerly: Incharge Computer Centre, Hindustan Copper Ltd., New Delhi

KHANNA BOOK PUBLISHING CO. PVT. LTD.

Learning MS Office XP
Ramesh Bangia

ISBN : 81-87522577

First Edition : 2001
Second Edition : 2002
Reprint : 2003-13, **2014**

Published by:
KHANNA BOOK PUBLISHING CO. (P) LTD.
4C/4344, Ansari Road, Darya Ganj, New Delhi-110 002
Phone: 011-23244447, 23244448
Email: contact@khannabooks.com
Website: www.khannabooks.com

Regd. Off: 1694-95, Ist Floor, Nai Sarak, Delhi–110006
Phone: 011-23283211, 23256658

Printed in India
R-Tech Offset, Delhi

PREFACE

Learning of a software is both easy and difficult. It depends upto what level you are planning to learn. If you are learning only for the working use, then it is very easy. But, when you try to go deep into it, then you realise how difficult it is to master it.

Microsoft Office XP is such vast subjects that it will take a lot of time to understand it fully. This book has been written in mind to make you aware of the options available in the software and how they can be used. It is like telling the child about the steps and stairs. You are the one who is to climb the stair. This book will just guide you how to use the stairs.

I am indeed debited to my publishers Khanna Book Publishing Co. Pvt. Ltd., specially Vivek and Puneet for their suggestions and encouragement given in producing this book.

I would like to thank my family specially my wife Sadhna, kids Mayank and Samarth, for without their criticism this book would not have seen the day.

Suggestions for improvement of the book are indeed welcome.

Ramesh Bangia

CONTENTS

MICROSOFT OFFICE XP

MICROSOFT WORD 2002

Microsoft Excel 2002

MICROSOFT ACCESS 2002

MICROSOFT POWERPOINT 2002

MICROSOFT FRONT PAGE 2002

1

Introduction to Microsoft Office XP

Introduction

Microsoft Corporation which is the largest producer of software in the World, in the 90's introduced the concept of Office Suite. The idea behind was to provide all the possible software which a small office or home office would probably use. This concept was introduced first for Macintosh machines of Apple and was named Microsoft Office Suite. It was in 1990 that the first suite for Windows was introduced. Initially the software were stand-alone software but were sold as a bundle, as part of the marketing strategy. It was later on formed as an integrated package. The first in this line was Microsoft Office ver. 4.3 for Windows 3.1 followed by Microsoft Office 7.0 for Windows 95 and Microsoft Office 97 for Windows 95 and Microsoft Office 2000 for Windows 98. In this series the new software is called Microsoft Office XP.

Microsoft Office is a powerful combination of software which allows to you to write letters, prepare a presentation, keep database records, prepare a spreadsheet, publish a newsletter and many more applications. Integration of the various constituents is very useful because this was you can write a letter in Word 2002 and have figures from the database Microsoft Access in it and a spreadsheet in a tabular form from Microsoft Excel. It is this integration which makes the Microsoft Office as the number 1 selling software in the World. Various constituents of the suite are:

MICROSOFT WORD 2002

A word processing software which allows you to write letters, edit them and print them after formatting it according to your needs. It has all the possible options of a word processer in the form of font style and size; indents; line spacing; margins; spell checking and grammar checkers to name a few. A now you can speak you letter into the software using the new technique of Speech.

MICROSOFT EXCEL 2002

This spreadsheet program allows you to manipulate and present your data in almost any way you choose. It allows you to work on a tabular pad consisting of columns and rows where you can perform all your mathematic, financial and statistical calculations. These calculations can be as simple as totalling a row or column of values or as complex as figuring the rate of return on an investment under varying circumstances. It also allows you to make a graphical representation of all your data in the form of 2-dimensional or 3-dimensional graph or pie chart.

MICROSOFT ACCESS 2002

A software to take care of most of your database requirements. It allows you to store and organize information in sets of tables, which can be displayed in the form of columns and rows to look like a table or an index card. What's more it allows you to perform calculations and find for you simple statistics like totals and averages. It allows you to sort the data in any form and extract the required information based on the key given by you.

MICROSOFT POWERPOINT 2002

Want to make a presentation in a hurry! This is an ideal program fo

the same. Make sophisticated slide shows and professional looking electronic presentations. It also allows you to add charts, tables and pictures for make the presentation look alive.

Microsoft Outlook 2002

It is an electronic tool for managing appointments, addresses, e-mail, and notes.With lots of stress being given to the e-mail these days, it is an ideal software for sending and receiving e-mail.

Microsoft FrontPage 2002

A program which allows you to create you own Web site. With  FrontPage 2002, the knowledge of HTML programming language is no longer required. FrontPage 2002 carries out the programming for you in the background, allowing you to concentrate on the other features in your Web pages such as design, feel and functionality.

Microsoft Publisher 2002

It is Microsoft's answer to the various other publishing software available in the market like PageMaker. It allows you to create invitations, design business-cards, and letter-heads, make your own calenders, produce newsletter, etc.

Microsoft PhotoDraw 2002

It is used to create and enhance drawings and photgraphs. It is the newest member of the Microsoft Office Suite. With this software, even with little capabilities in graphic designing, you can create good looking graphics.

Microsoft Office Bar

With so many software and their options, does it not seem to an impossible task to master all of them. Well, No. Microsoft had this is mind when it decided on to have quite a number of similar commands for these software. Not only that their launch and opening has been integrated into a small toolbar called Microsoft Office Manager. When you install Office into your computer, this bar finds a place on your desktop. It is a rotating toolbar and can be moved anywhere on the screen and can be hidden if not needed.

Let us see what this toolbar has:

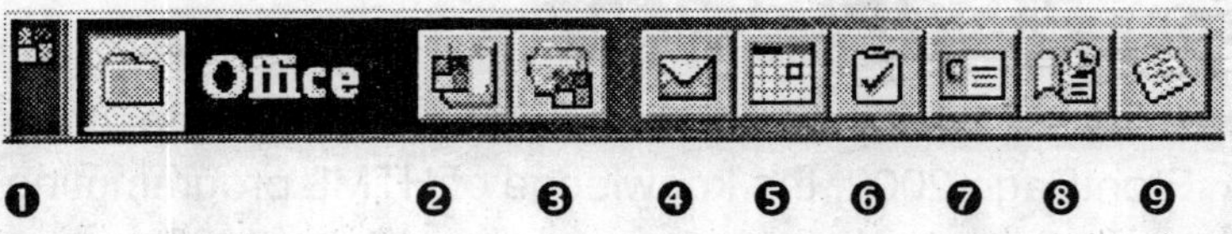

➊ ➋ ➌ ➍ ➎ ➏ ➐ ➑ ➒

➊ Close button	This button allows you to make toolbar icons smaller or bigger. You can even hide the toolbar using this button. You can also get information about Microsoft Office from this button.
➋ New Office Document	This button allows you to open a new office document from the dialog box which is produces after you click this button.
➌ Open Office Document	This button allows you to open an existing document from your computer.
➍ New Message	It allows you to compose a new message to be sent as e-mail.
➎ New Appointment	It allows you to set a aaappointment task in Microsoft Outlook.

❻ New Task	This button allows you to set a new task in Microsoft Outlook.
❼ New Contract	This button allows you to make a new contract in Microsoft Outlook.
❽ New Journal Entry	This button allows you to make a new journal entry in Microsoft Outlook.
❾ New Note	This button allows you make a new note in Microsoft Outlook.

❶ ❷ ❸ ❹ ❺ ❻

❶ Microsoft Word	This button opens Microsoft Word for you.
❷ Microsoft Excel	This button opens Microsoft Excel for you.
❸ Microsoft PowerPoint	This button opens Microsoft PowePoint for you.
❹ Microsoft Outlook	This button opens Microsoft Outlook for you.
❺ Microsoft Access	This button opens Microsoft Access for you.
❻ Microsoft FrontPage	This button opens the Microsoft FrontPage for you.

This toolbar is on the desktop looks like as shown on the next page.

Using the Mouse

Since most of the activities in Microsoft Office are done using the

mouse, it is very important to have the complete knowledge of working of mouse while using the constituents of Microsoft Office.

To click

1. Position the pointer on a menu, a button, or an icon and click the left mouse once.

To double-click

1. Position the pointer on an item and click the left mouse button twice in quick succession.

To select

1. Position the pointer on the first item to select.
2. Click and hold down the mouse button.
3. Move the mouse pointer across the items to select.

4. Release the mouse button.

To drag

1. Position the pointer on an item.
2. Click and hold down the left mouse button.
3. Move the mouse.
4. Release the mouse button.

To scroll

1. Drag the scroll button in the scroll bar up or down.

   Or

   Click a scroll arrow at either end of the scroll bar.

To choose from a menu

1. Click a menu name.
2. Click an item on a menu.

   Or

   If the item is followed by an arrow, position the mouse pointer on the item to open the submenu and then click an item on the submenu.

To move a window

1. Position the pointer on the window's titile bar and press and hold the mouse button as your drag the window.

To resize a window

1. Position the pointer on the window's corner and, when you see the diagonal pointer, drag to resize the window.

To minimize a window

1. Click the Minimize button.

To restore a minimized window

1. Click the button for the window on the taskbar.

To maximize a window

1. Click the Maximize button.

To switch windows

1. Click any visible part of the window

   Or

   Click the button for the window on the taskbar.

To close a window

1. Click the Close button on the window

   Or

   Right click the button for the window on the taskbar and choose Close from the shortcut menu.

Remember

1. Menus in Office programs might be collapsed to show only frequently used items. To view the complete menu, click the More icon at the bottom of the menu or pause with the pointer on any menu option.
2. Menu items that are grayed out are not currently available.
3. To display a tooltip, which is a description of a toolbar button, position the pointer on the button and pause for a moment without clicking.

4. To minimize all windows, you can rightclick the taskbar and then click Minimize All Windows from the shortcut menu.
5. If one window fills the screen, you might have to click its Restore button to return it to a partial-screen window. You will then be able to see and click other windows.

New Microsoft Office Features

Office task panes

The most common tasks in Microsoft Office are now organized in panes that display in place with your Office document. Continue working while you search for a file using the Search task pane, pick from a gallery of items to paste in the Office Clipboard task pane, and quickly create new documents or open files using the task pane that appears when you start an Office program. Other task panes vary per Office program.

New look

Microsoft Office XP has a cleaner, simpler look to its interface. Softer colors also contribute to this updated feel.

More convenient access to Help

Get the full power of the Answer Wizard in an unobtrusive package. When you enter a question about an Office program in the Ask a Question box on the menu bar, you can see a list of choices and read a Help topic whether you are running the Office Assistant or not.

Control paste options and automatic changes with smart tags

New in-place buttons called "smart tags" let you immediately adjust how information is pasted or how automatic changes occur in your

Office programs. For example, when you paste text from Microsoft Word into Microsoft PowerPoint, a button appears next to the text. Click the button to see a list of choices for fine-tuning the formatting of the pasted text. Smart tags and their associated choices vary per Office program.

Updated Clip Organizer

Hundreds of new clips, an easy task pane interface, as well as the same abilities to organize clips and find new digital art on the Web are part of the updated Clip Organizer (formerly Clip Gallery).

Conceptual diagrams

Word, Microsoft Excel, and PowerPoint include a new gallery of conceptual diagrams. Choose from diagrams such as Pyramid for showing the building blocks of a relationship, Radial for showing items in relation to a core element, and more.

Voice commands and dictation

In addition to mouse and keyboard methods, you can now select menu, toolbar, and dialog box items by speaking. You can also dictate text. This feature is available in the Simplified Chinese, English (U.S.), and Japanese language versions of Microsoft Office, and has some special hardware requirements.

Support for handwriting

You can use handwriting recognition to enter text into an Office document. You can write by using a handwriting input device—such as a graphics tablet or a tablet-PC — or you can write using your mouse. Your natural handwriting is converted to typed characters. In Word and Microsoft Outlook, you can also choose to leave text in handwritten form.

Improved fidelity of pictures and drawings

In Office XP, Word, Excel, PowerPoint, Microsoft FrontPage, and Microsoft Publisher are using an improved graphics system (GDI+). With this new graphics system, shapes and WordArt have smoother outlines and adjustable levels of transparency with true blending. Digital pictures stay sharper and clearer when you resize them.

Accessibility

Office XP programs support Microsoft Active Accessibility 2.0. This technology makes accessibility aids, such as screen readers or screen enlargers, more effective.

Find printers

If your organization uses Microsoft Windows 2000 and the Active Directory directory service, you can search for printers across your network from the Print dialog box in Office XP programs.

Storing documents with Microsoft Exchange Server 2000

You can store Microsoft Office documents on Exchange Server 2000 and access them through the File Open, File New, and File Save dialog boxes, as you would any other Office document.

SECURITY

Digital signatures

You can apply a digital signature to Microsoft Word, Microsoft Excel, and Microsoft PowerPoint files to confirm that the file has not been altered.

Increased protection against macro viruses

Network administrators can remove Microsoft Visual Basic for

Applications, the programming language of Microsoft Office, when deploying Office. This can decrease the possibility of viruses spreading via Office documents.

Web documents and Web sites

Target your Web publishing efforts

Save your Microsoft Office documents as Web pages for versions 3.0-6.0 of various Web browsers and give your readers the best possible viewing experience.

Share your Office documents over the Web

From any Office program, you can save documents to Web sites on MSN. This gives you an instant collaboration space where you can share files with other people.

Save a Web site as a single file

A special Web archive file format is available in Microsoft Access, Microsoft Excel, Microsoft PowerPoint, Microsoft Publisher, and Microsoft Word. This file format lets you save all the elements of a Web site, including text and graphics, into a single file.

Open Office Web pages for editing from the browser

Office programs recognize the HTML pages that they generate. You can open an Office document that you've saved as a Web page in the program it was created in, right from Microsoft Internet Explorer.

Language-specific features

If you are not using the specific language version of Microsoft Office for which one of these features is designed, then the feature is only available if you have installed the Microsoft Office XP Multilingual

User Interface Pack or Microsoft Office Proofing Tools for that language. In addition, you must enable support for the language through Microsoft Office Language Settings.

Improvements to changing the language of the user interface and Help

More components across Microsoft Office support changing the language of their user interface. In addition, terms on the interface match the terms in Help, even when the main text of Help is in a different language than the interface. This feature is only available with the Office XP MUI Pack and a volume licensing agreement.

Hangul/Hanja converter improvements

Over 20,000 new characters are supported by this converter for Korean language documents. The converter automatically uses new fonts that have the proper glyphs for the new characters.

Full support for Windows 2000 language features

Microsoft Office programs now support all the languages that Microsoft Windows 2000 does. Office also supports the latest extensions to Chinese character encoding via Unicode, including support for almost 70,000 Chinese characters.

East Asian character support on non-East Asian systems

Now you can enter characters from East Asian languages in all Office programs, even if your system software is a non-East Asian language version. (This was previously only supported in Microsoft Word and Microsoft Outlook, or on Windows 2000.) For example, on a computer running English (U.S.) Microsoft Windows 98, you can enter Japanese characters in Microsoft Excel.

ERROR PREVENTION AND RECOVERY

Document recovery and safer shutdown

Documents you are working on can be recovered if the program encounters an error or stops responding. The documents are displayed in the Document Recovery task pane the next time you open the program.

Office Safe Mode

Microsoft Office XP programs can detect and isolate startup problems. You can bypass the problem, run your Office program in safe mode, and keep getting your work done.

Office crash reporting tool

Diagnostic information about program crashes can be collected and sent to your company's information technology department or to Microsoft, allowing engineers to correct these problems so they don't interrupt you again.

Microsoft FrontPage 2002

Finally, this software is the ideal software for creating a Web page of your own, right from the blank screen to finally publishing your site.

2

SPEECH AND HANDWRITING

INTRODUCTION

Two of the very important additions in the Office XP suite are the ability of the software to recognize your handwriting and your speech. Now you can write anything on the screen and the computer will recognize it. Also, you can give the commands to the computer by the way of speaking.

These two options make very interesting propositions but how best you can use them is up to you.

SPEECH RECOGNITION

This feature is available in the Simplified Chinese, Traditional Chinese, English, Japanese, and Korean language versions of Microsoft Office.

Install handwriting recognition

1. On the Microsoft Windows **Start** menu, point to **Settings**, and then click **Control Panel**.
2. Double-click **Add/Remove Programs**.
3. Click **Change or Remove Programs**, select **Microsoft Office XP**, and then click **Change**.
4. Click **Add or Remove Features**, and then click **Next**.
5. Under Features to install, next to **Office Shared Features**, click .

6. Next to **Alternative User Input**, click **Handwriting**, and then select the type of installation you want.
7. Click Update

Using Handwriting Recognition

Write as you naturally do on a paper surface, using cursive style, printing, or a combination of both. As you write, enter entire words without pausing after each letter, and leave space between words.

1. Place the insertion point where you want to insert handwriting.
2. Select a writing area by doing one of the following:
    1. On the **Language** bar, click **Writing Pad**.

       If Writing Pad is not available, click **Handwriting** on the **Language** bar, and then select **Writing Pad**.
    2. To increase or decrease the size of the Writing Pad box, move the pointer to an outside edge of the box until it changes into a double-headed arrow, and then drag to the desired size.
    3. Move the insertion point into the **Writing Pad** box. When it changes to a pen, you're in an area of the screen that you can write in.

       You can move the Writing Pad box to different areas on the screen by dragging it.

       On the Language bar, click Write Anywhere.

       If Write Anywhere is not available, click Handwriting on the Language bar, and then select Write Anywhere.

       You can move the Write Anywhere toolbar to different areas on the screen by dragging it.
3. Select the type of input you want in the program. Do one of the following to insert:

Click Ink on the Writing Pad or Write Anywhere toolbar.

Example: *hello*

4. To write, use a handwriting input device, or move your mouse on your mouse pad to form words.

   If you use the Writing Pad box, write on the line, just as you would on lined notebook paper.

   Your handwriting is automatically recognized and entered at the insertion point in the program.

5. To close the handwriting box, click Close on the Writing Pad or Write Anywhere toolbar.

   * You can format writing inserted in handwritten form in Microsoft Word and Microsoft Outlook just as you do with typed text. For example, change font size and color, or apply other types of formatting, such as bold. You can also find and replace text in handwritten form in the same way you do with typed text.
   * To enter handwriting into an application immediately without waiting for a recognition delay, click Recognize Now on the Writing Pad or Write Anywhere toolbar.
   * You can turn automatic recognition on or off, and select options such as changing the rate at which handwriting is recognized, or change pen color and width. Click Options box or the Write Anywhere toolbar, and then click Options.

SPEECH RECOGNITION

As mentioned above this option allows you to speak anything to the computer and it will recognize it.

System Requirements

* A high quality close-talk (headset) microphone with gain

adjustment support (A universal serial bus (USB) microphone is recommended.)

* A **400 megahertz** (MHz) or faster computer
* **128 MB** or more of memory
* Windows 98 or later or Windows NT 4.0 or later
* Microsoft Internet Explorer 5 or later

Adjusting the Position of the Microphone

A high quality close-talk (headset) universal serial bus (USB) microphone with gain adjustment support is recommended.

Position the microphone so that:

* It is about an inch, or a thumb's width, to the side of your mouth.
* It is not directly in front of your mouth, and you are not breathing directly into it.

If you inadvertently move the microphone as you speak, remember to bring it back to the correct position.

Install and Train Speech Recognition

Speech recognition is installed in all Office programs by initially using the feature in Microsoft Word or by doing a custom installation.

After speech recognition is installed, you can increase speech recognition accuracy by taking a few minutes to train the computer to recognize how you speak.

Install and train by using Word

1. Open Microsoft Word.
2. On the **Tools** menu, click **Speech**.

   You're asked if you want to install the feature. Click **Yes**.

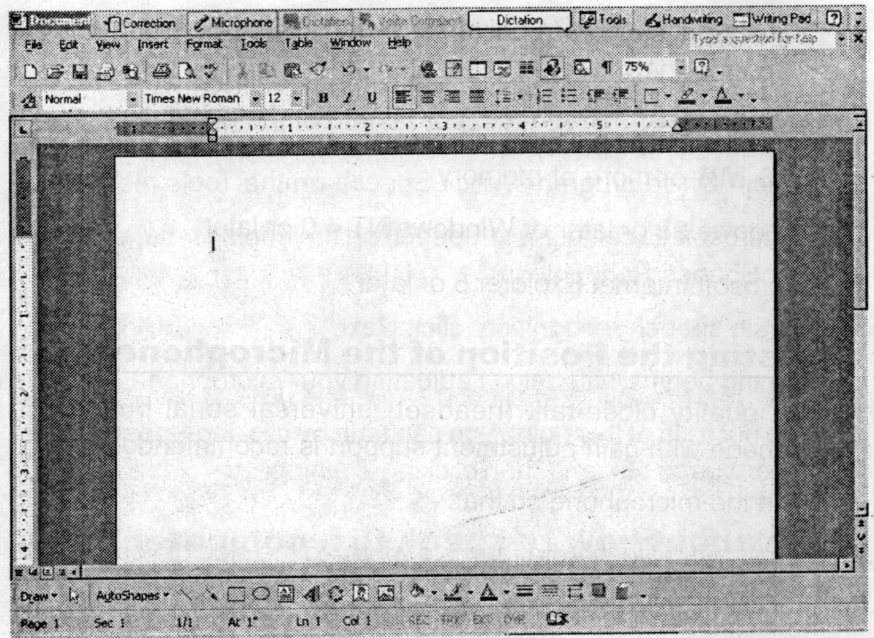

3. After the installation is complete, click **Next** to train speech recognition.

Training begins with help in adjusting your microphone.

Custom installation and training

1. On the Microsoft Windows **Start** menu, point to **Settings**, and then click **Control Panel**.
2. Double-click **Add/Remove Programs**.
3. Click **Change or Remove Programs**, select **Microsoft Office XP**, and then click Change.
4. Click Add or Remove Features, and then click **Next**.
5. Under **Features to install**, next to **Office Shared Features**, click .
6. Next to Alternative User Input, click **Speech**, and then select the type of installation you want.

7. Click **Update**.

After the custom installation is completed, you can train speech recognition.

1. In most Office programs, click Speech on the Tools menu.

   In Microsoft Excel, point to Speech on the Tools menu, and then click Speech Recognition.

2. To train speech recognition, click Next.

   Training begins with help in adjusting your microphone.

If you do not train at this point, you can train by clicking Speech Tools on the Language bar, and then clicking Training.

Learn about how to speak to a computer

When speaking to others, you're usually understood whether you whisper or shout, or talk fast or slow. However, a computer understands speech best when spoken to in a more predictable way.

* Speak in a consistent, level tone. Speaking too loudly or too softly makes it difficult for the computer to recognize what you've said.
* Use a consistent rate, without speeding up and slowing down.
* Speak without pausing between words; a phrase is easier for the computer to interpret than just one word.

  For example, the computer has a hard time understanding phrases such as, "This (pause) is (pause) another (pause) example (pause) sentence."

  Because we don't usually need to think about how to speak, it can seem a little awkward at first to speak to a computer. However, with a little practice, speaking to a computer will become more natural.

Speech recognition tips

* Start by working in a quiet environment so that the computer hears you instead of the sounds around you, and use a high quality close-talk (headset) microphone.

  If your work environment has a lot of noise or if the noise level varies during the day, try creating different speech recognition profiles for different times of day. If you work in several different environments, create different profiles for each environment.

* Keep the microphone in the same position; try not to move it around once it's adjusted.

* Train your computer to recognize your voice by reading aloud prepared training text in the training wizard. Additional training may increase may speech recognition accuracy.

* As you dictate, don't be concerned if you do not immediately see your words on the screen. Continue speaking and pause at the end of your thought. The computer will display the recognized text on the screen after it finishes processing your voice.

* Pronounce words clearly, but don't separate each syllable in a word. For example, sounding out each syllable in "e-nun-ci-ate" will make it harder for the computer to recognize what you've said.

* Remember to turn the microphone off when you are not using speech recognition. Speech recognition will continue to process sounds until the microphone is turned off.

Practice using speech recognition

You can use speech recognition by clicking buttons on the Language bar to switch between two modes — **Dictation** and **Voice Command**. The Language bar appears by default in the upper-right corner of the screen of any Office programs.

Language bar with text labels hidden

The Language bar shows text labels beside each button on the bar. You can hide or show the text labels by right-clicking the Language bar, and then clicking Text Labels.

You'll switch between Dictation mode and Voice Command mode less often and save time if you complete dictation first, review your file, and then format text or make corrections.

1. Position your microphone.
2. Click in the program in which you want to use speech recognition.

   If you open a Help topic while you're working or if a message appears on the screen, click again in the program to continue using speech recognition.
3. If the microphone is not already turned on, click Microphone on the Language bar.
4. Switch between Dictation and Voice Command modes as you work:

   Use Dictation mode

   To turn the words you speak into text, click Dictation on the Language bar.

   As you speak, you'll see a blue bar on the screen that means the computer is processing your voice. As your words are recognized, text is displayed on the screen.

   You can continue to speak while the computer processes your voice; you don't have to wait until the blue bar disappears to speak again.

   Use Voice Command mode

   To select menu, toolbar, dialog box (U.S. English only), and task pane (U.S. English only) items, click Voice Command on the Language bar.

For example, to change font format, you can say "font" to open the Font box on the Formatting toolbar, and then say a font name.

Or to format selected text, say "bold" or "underline."

If Voice Command is not on the Language bar, see the Speech recognition isn't working section on the Troubleshoot speech recognition Help topic.

5. Turn the microphone off when you are through speaking to the computer by clicking Microphone on the Language bar.

Tips

* You can also switch between Dictation and Voice Command modes by saying "dictation" or "voice command."
* In Microsoft Word, you can delete the last thing you said in Dictation mode by saying "scratch that."
* You can turn the microphone on and off by clicking Speech on

the Tools menu (in Microsoft Excel, point to Speech on the Tools menu, and then click Speech Recognition).

You can also turn the microphone off by saying "microphone."

Learn about things you can do and say with speech recognition

When you use Office speech recognition, you'll switch between working in Voice Command mode and Dictation mode by clicking buttons on the Language bar or by saying "voice command" or "dictation."

To select menu, toolbar, dialog box, and task pane items by using your voice, if the microphone is not already turned on, click Microphone on the Language bar, and then click Voice Command on the Language bar, or say "voice command."

For example, to change the font in any Office program by using your voice, do the following:

1. To open the Format menu, say "format."
2. To open the Font dialog box, say "font."
3. To change the font from Times New Roman to Verdana, say "Verdana."
4. To close the Font dialog box, say "OK."

You can also change font format without opening the Font dialog box. Say "font" to open the Font box on the Formatting toolbar, and then say a font name.

Other Voice Command mode examples

Do the following to select:

Toolbar buttons

* Say the name of the toolbar button. If you don't know the name,

rest the mouse pointer on the button to display a ScreenTip that shows you the name you can say.

For example, the ScreenTip for the Save button is “Save.” Say “save” to open the Save dialog box.

Menu and command items

* Say the name of the menu. For example, to open the Tools menu, say “tools” or “tools menu.”
* If all the commands you want to see on a menu are not visible, say “expand” or “more buttons.”
* To select a command on the Tools menu, say “options,” for example, which will open the Options dialog box.

Dialog box items

* To select different tabs in a dialog box, say the name of the tab. For example, in Microsoft Word, say “edit” or “tab edit” in the Options dialog box to select the Edit tab.
* Say the name of any dialog box option. For example, on the Edit tab in the Options dialog box in Word, say “prompt to update style” or “check prompt to update style” to select the Prompt to update style check box.
* To clear a dialog box option, say ”prompt to update style” again or say “uncheck prompt to update style.”
* In an Open dialog box, you can open a drop-down list by saying the name next to the list, if a name is available. For example, in Microsoft PowerPoint, to open the Tools menu, say “tools.” To select the Options command, say “options,” which opens the Options dialog box.
* To select a tab in the Options dialog box, say the name of the tab. For example, say “save” to open the Save tab.
* To see the items in the Save PowerPoint files list, say “save PowerPoint files as” or “drop save PowerPoint files as.”

Task pane items

To open the New File task pane in Office programs, do the following:

* Say "file" to open the File menu, and then say "new" to open the New File task pane.

To open a new blank file, say "new file."

* To say the name of a hyperlink in a task pane, say the name of the entire hyperlink. For example, to open Templates on Microsoft.com in the New File task pane, say "templates on Microsoft dot com."

Commands you can say

The following list is a sample of the commands you can say.

Navigation examples

The command you can say is shown first, followed by the keyboard or mouse equivalent for the command. For example:

(command you can say) (keyboard or mouse equivalent)

END	Press END	
Return	Enter	Press ENTER
Backspace	Delete	Press BACKSPACE
Back one word	Last word	Press Ctrl+Lelf Arrow
Space	Space Bar	Press the SPACEBAR
Escape	Cancel	Press ESC
Right-click	Context menu	Right-click menu
Right-click a menu		
Tab	Press TAB	
Shift Tab	Press SHIFT+TAB	
End	Go End	Press END
Home	Go Home	Press HOME
Up	Go Up	Press UP ARROW
Down	Go Down	Press DOWN ARROW

Left	Go Left	Press LEFT ARROW
Right	Go Right	Press RIGHT ARROW
Previous Page	Press CTRL+PAGE	
Next Page	Press CTRL+PAGE+DOWN ARROW	
Page Down	Press PAGE DOWN	
Page Up	Press PAGE UP	

Using Dictation mode

To dictate text into any Office program, if the microphone is not already turned on click Microphone on the Language bar, and then click Dictation on the Language bar, or say "dictation."

* You can dictate by spelling. Say "spelling mode," pause briefly, and then say "s-u-n."

* You can use Dictation mode to get help as you work. Place the insertion point into the Office Assistant or into the Ask a Question box, and then dictate your question.

The following lists tell you how to say some things as you dictate. What you can say is followed by what is inserted. For example:

	What you say	***What is inserted***
Period	Dot	.
	Comma	,
	Colon	:
	Semi-colon	;
	Question mark	?
	Exclamation point	!
	Ampersand	&
	Asterisk	*
	At sign	@
	Backslash	\
	Slash	/
	Vertical bar	|
	Hyphen	Dash -

	Double dash	—
	Equals	=
	Plus	Plus sign +
	Pound sign	#
	Percent	Percent sign %
	Dollar sign	$
	Underscore	_
	Tilde	~
	Ellipsis	...
	Greater than	>
	Less than	<
	Caret	^
	New line	Enter
	New paragraph	Enter twice
	Brackets	Bracket
	Left bracket	Open bracket [
	End bracket	Right bracket
	Close bracket	]
	Open brace	Curly brace
	Left brace	{
	Close brace	End curly brace
	Right brace	}
Open parenthesis	Left paren	(
Close parenthesis	Right paren	)
Quote	Open quote	“
	Close quote	“
Single quote	Open single quote	‘
	Close single quote	‘
Numbers	5	five
	21	21 (numbers greater than 20 are inserted as digits)
	first	first (ordinal numbers)

3

Creating Document in Word 2002

Introduction

The best way to learn about a new software is to use it. It is like jumping into the swimming pool to learn swimming. What we will do here is that we will type our document and learn the various commands side by side.

Starting Word 2002 is easy so I am not discussing that here. Let us start a new document here. This can again be done by three methods. *Firstly* from the **Start** button, opening a **New Office Document** and a **New Document** from the dialog box thus displayed, as shown on next page.

If you have opened Word 2002 from any other method, you can either click at **New** from the **File menu** or **New** from the **Task Pane**.

Supposing we have to create a document in the form of a letter written to the General Manager of Telephones complaining him of the inflated bills.

The final product has to look like the one shown on the next to next page. Now that you have opened a new document, do not worry about any typing mistakes or any formatting, just type the text as it is.

After typing, your screen will look like as shown on the subsequent page.

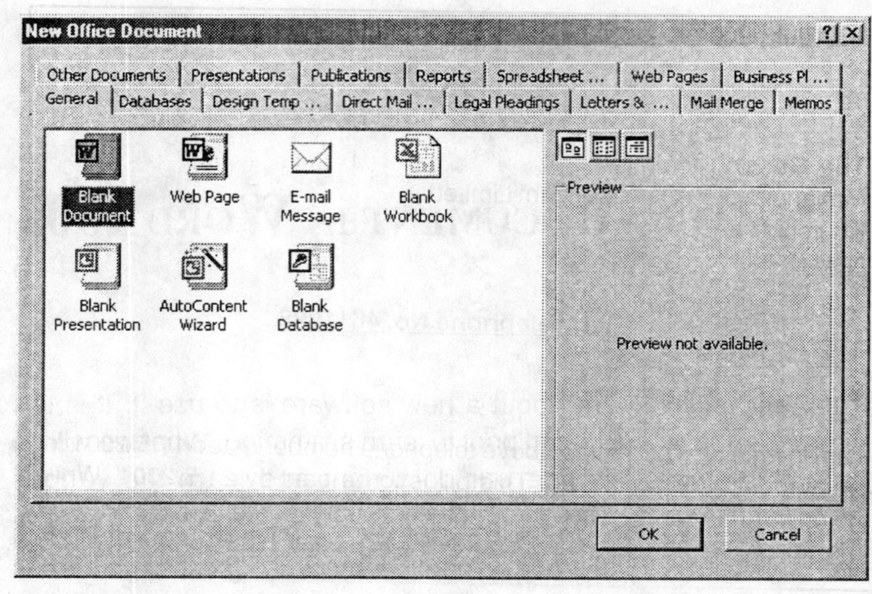
New Office Document
Other Documents
Presentations
Publications
Reports
Spreadsheet ...
Web Pages
Business Pl ...
General
Databases
Design Temp ...
Direct Mail ...
Legal Pleadings
Letters & ...
Mail Merge
Memos
Blank Document
Web Page
E-mail Message
Blank Workbook
Blank Presentation
AutoContent Wizard
Blank Database
Preview
Preview not available.
OK
Cancel

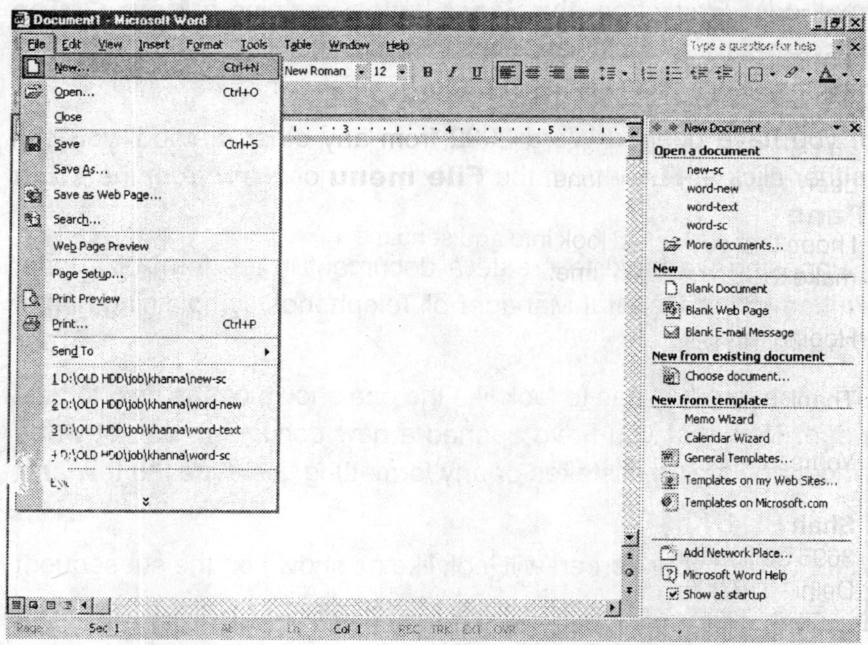
Document1 - Microsoft Word
File Edit View Insert Format Tools Table Window Help
Type a question for help
New... Ctrl+N
Open... Ctrl+O
Close
Save Ctrl+S
Save As...
Save as Web Page...
Search...
Web Page Preview
Page Setup...
Print Preview
Print... Ctrl+P
Send To
1 D:\OLD HDD\job\khanna\new-sc
2 D:\OLD HDD\job\khanna\word-new
3 D:\OLD HDD\job\khanna\word-text
4 D:\OLD HDD\job\khanna\word-sc
Exit
New Roman
12
New Document
Open a document
new-sc
word-new
word-text
word-sc
More documents...
New
Blank Document
Blank Web Page
Blank E-mail Message
New from existing document
Choose document...
New from template
Memo Wizard
Calendar Wizard
General Templates...
Templates on my Web Sites...
Templates on Microsoft.com
Add Network Place...
Microsoft Word Help
Show at startup
Sec 1
Col 1
REC TRK EXT OVR

13th July, 2001

To,

The General Manager
Mahanagar Telephones Nigam Limited
Khurshid Lal Bhawan
New Delhi - 110 001

Ref: Telephone No. 4611098

Sir,

I am in receipt of bill for the above telephone number dated 11.5.2001 for an amount of Rs. 4,678.90. This bill is to be paid by 21.5.2001. While going through the bill, I see that I have been charged at two accounts for the calls which have not been made by me. These enteries are:

Called Id	***Duration***	***Amount***
0017249873769	120	1,008.00
0013245934234	60	675.90

As you can notice that both these entries pertain to **International calls** and since my phone does not have this facility, these calls could not have been made from my phone.

I hope that you would look into and send me the revised bill, so that I can make the payment in time.

Hoping for an early action,

Thanking you,

Yours faithfully,

Shah Rukh Khan
3695 Ballimaran
Delhi - 110 006

* This letter has few errors, which will be corrected in Word 2001

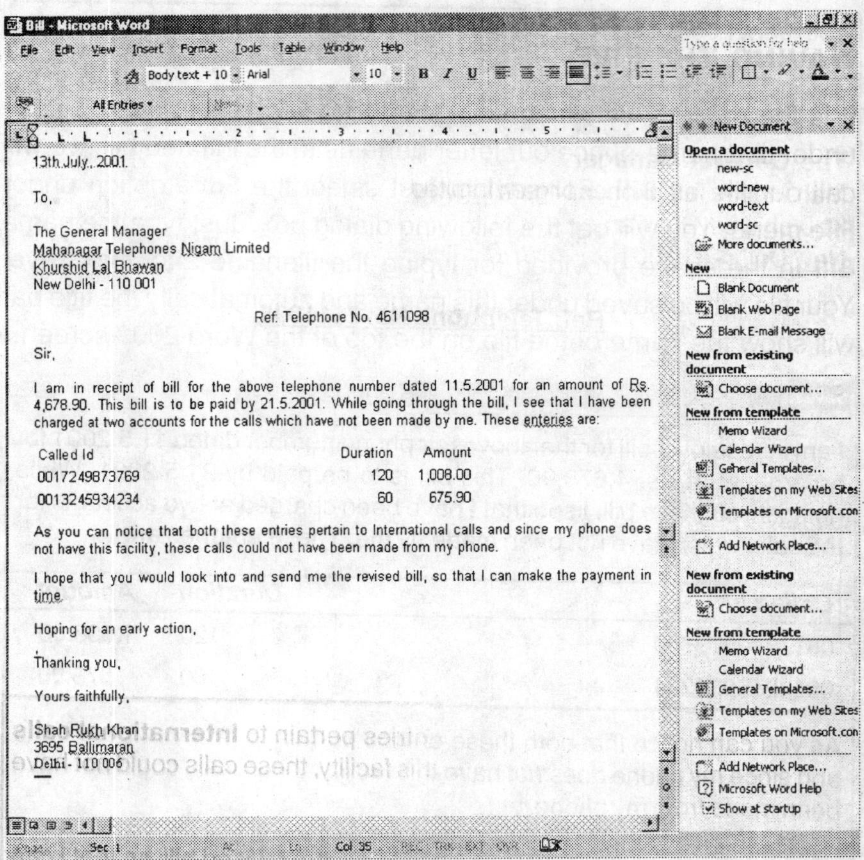

13th July, 2001

To,

The General Manager
Mahanagar Telephones Nigam Limited
Khurshid Lal Bhawan
New Delhi - 110 001

Ref: Telephone No. 4611098

Sir,

I am in receipt of bill for the above telephone number dated 11.5.2001 for an amount of Rs. 4,678.90. This bill is to be paid by 21.5.2001. While going through the bill, I see that I have been charged at two accounts for the calls which have not been made by me. These enteries are:

Called Id	Duration	Amount
0017249873769	120	1,008.00
0013245934234	60	675.90

As you can notice that both these entries pertain to International calls and since my phone does not have this facility, these calls could not have been made from my phone.

I hope that you would look into and send me the revised bill, so that I can make the payment in time.

Hoping for an early action,

Thanking you,

Yours faithfully,

Shah Rukh Khan
3695 Ballimaran
Delhi - 110 006

You may not see the full screen as shown, but the whole text, will look like this. As you must have noticed there are few red and green wavy lines. The red lines, show that the word is incorrectly typed as per the dictionary available with the system and the word/words under whom the green line is, show that the words are grammatically wrong. This is the opinion of the software, you may beg to differ from it. Since most of the proper names like Shah Rukh Khan, are shown as wrong.

This is just the raw text which has been typed. Now we have to do the formatting. But, before that, lest the file gets tangled in power failure or something, we must save the file.

Saving the File

It is the process by which you give the name to the file and save under that name. Since our letter pertains to the inflated bill, we will call our file as **Bill**. For saving, just select the **Save** option under **File** menu. You will get the following dialog box. Just type the name **Bill** in the space provided for typing the filename and click **Save**. Your file will be saved under this name and automatically the title bar will show the name of the file on the top of the Word 2002 screen.

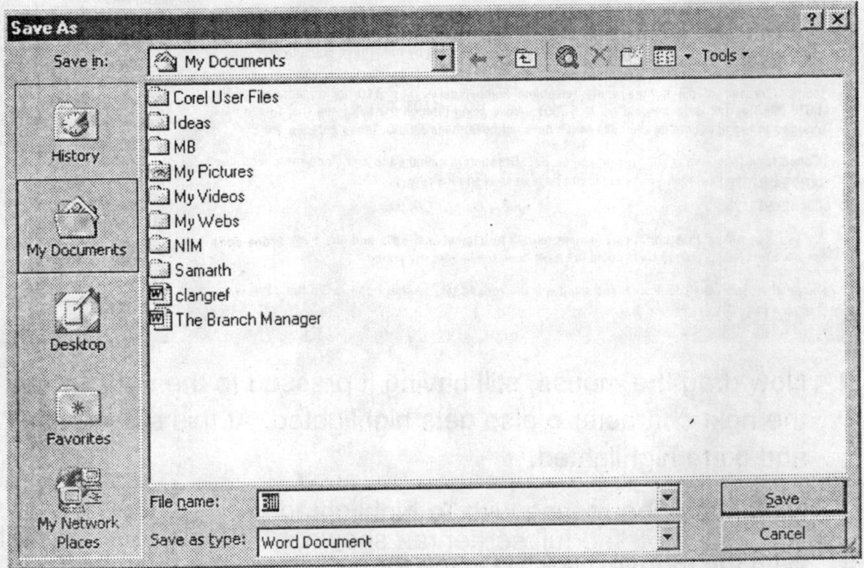

Now we come to other fomatting tools.

Formatting the Text

Let us now start our formatting from the top. The first line containing address has nothing to be done.

The second line containing **To**, has to be *italized.*

For this do the following:

1. Click the mouse button at the left of **T** of **To**.

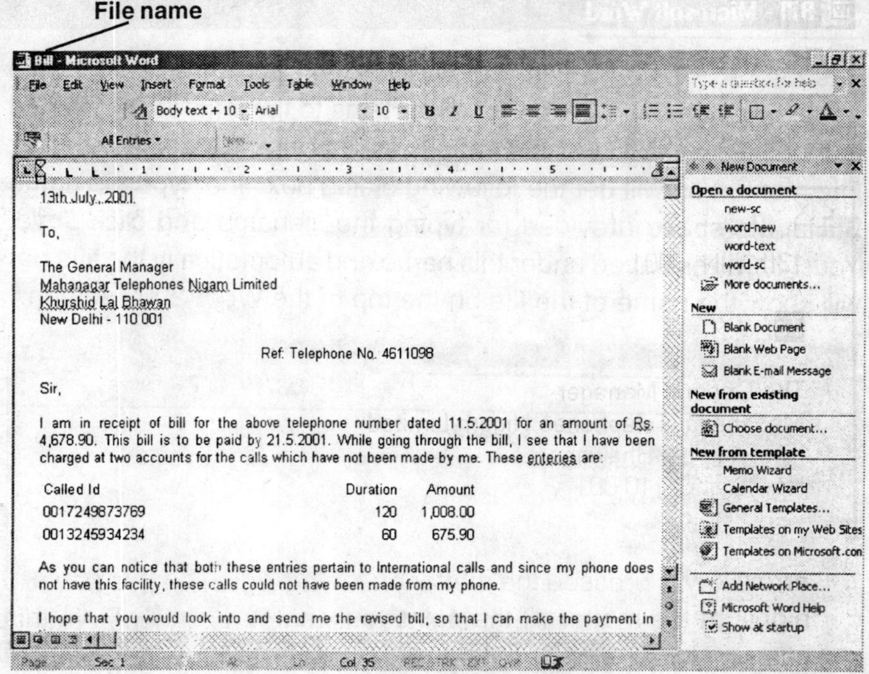

2. Now drag the mouse, still having it pressed to the right so that the next character **o** also gets highlighted. At this stage both **T** and **o** are highlighted.

3. Now leave the mouse with **To** highlighted.

4. With the mouse, click at **I** in the formatting toolbar to make To as *To.*

5. See how **To** looks in the figure.

Now we come to the line having **The General Manager**. This line has to be made bold. This is how we do it.

1. Click the mouse button at the left of **T** of **The General Manager**.

2. Since we had highlighted the matter using mouse in the case of **To**, we will use a different approach here. Press **Shift** key and start pressing right arrow key ⇨. You will see that as the right

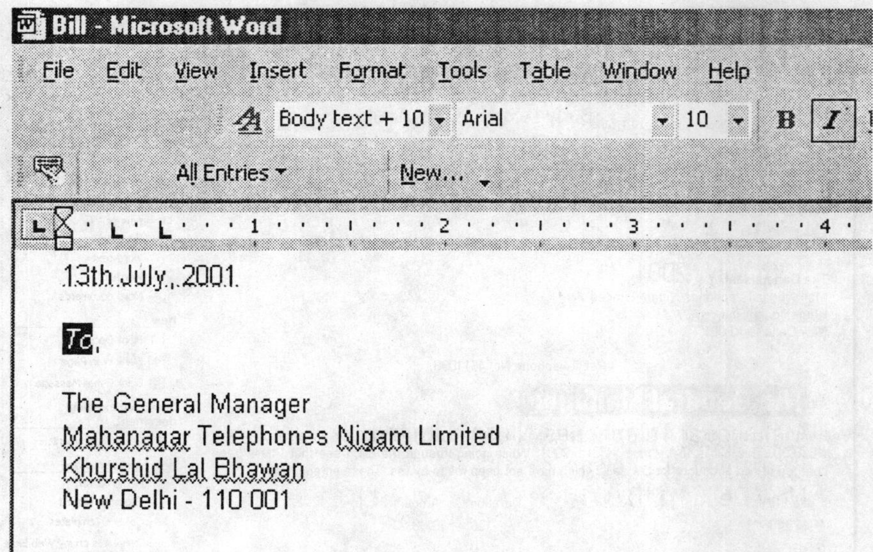

arrow key is pressed the matter on the right gets highlighted. So highlight the matter till the point you want it to highlight. In this case highlight till **r** of **Manager**.

3. Now leave the shift key.
4. With the mouse, click at **B** in the formatting toolbar to make the highlighted text as **Bold**.
5. In the figure on the next page, see how the text looks now.

Next in the line is the address, whose last line New Delhi - 110 001 has to be underlined. Word 2002 allows you the option of underlining the word with one or more lines. This option is available under **Font**. But for the time being, we will stick to single underline.

For this do the following:

1. Click the mouse button at the left of **N** of **New Delhi - 110 001**.
2. Using any of the two methods described above, highlight the text to be underlined.

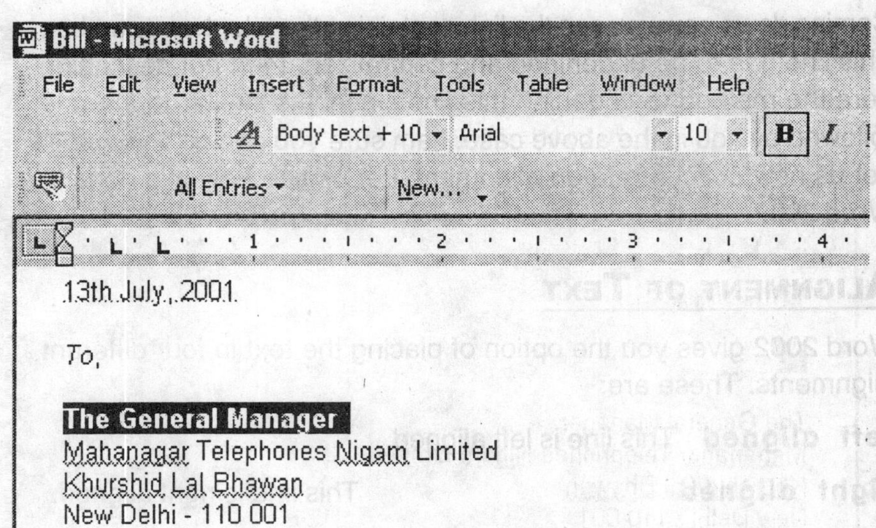

3. With the mouse, click at **U** in the formatting toolbar to make the highlighted text **Underlined**.
4. You can see the text underlined below.

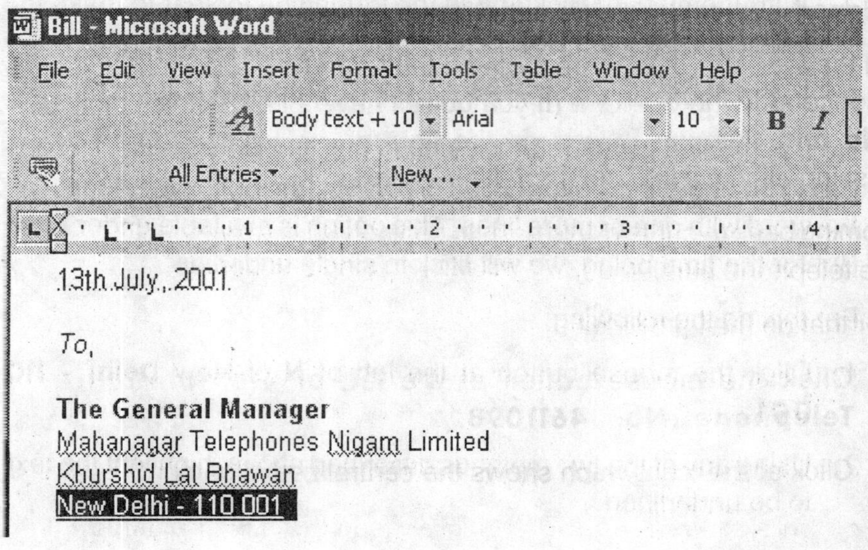

Coming down now you see the line containing the telephone number. This line has to be underlined and centralized. I am not describing here the method to underline this line since it is similar to the one followed by you in the above case. I am sure you can do it yourself. Let us now concentrate on alignment. Let us see how it is done in Word 2002.

ALIGNMENT OF TEXT

Word 2002 gives you the option of placing the text in four different alignments. These are:

Left aligned This line is left aligned.

Right aligned This line is right aligned.

Centralized This line is centrally aligned.

Justified This line has been justified.

You will not notice much of a difference here in left aligned text and justified text. This is so because the matter is small. Just notice the whole text of this book, it is justified, i.e., it aligns to the left and right both. Whereas this **particular paragraph is left aligned** and see the difference for yourself.

All the four alignments are there on the formatting toolbar. You can choose any one of them. (If you do not have all 4 of them, click at **Add and Remove button** on the right of the toolbar to add the missing alignment to the formatting toolbar.

Coming back to our text. We have to centrally align the line containing the telephone number.

For that do the following:

1. Click the mouse button at the left of **R** of **Reference: Telephone No. 4611098**.
2. Click at the icon which shows the centralized alignment.

3. Notice here that you do not have to highlight the text for alignment. This is so since the whole matter of the paragraph has to be aligned to the same alignment. It is not possible to align one word to one alignment and another word to another alignment.

4. You can see the text underlined and centralized aligned in the figure below.

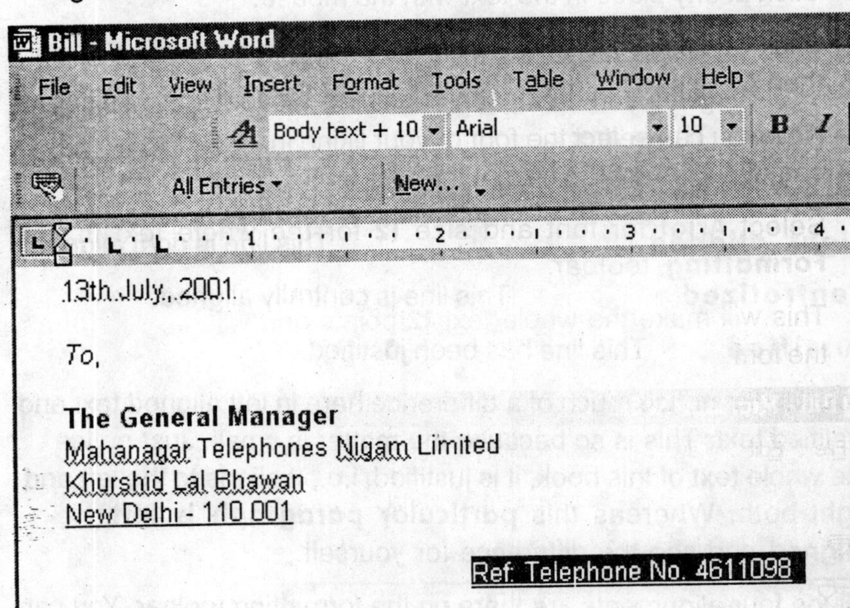
Bill - Microsoft Word

13th July, 2001.

To,

The General Manager
Mahanagar Telephones Nigam Limited
Khurshid Lal Bhawan
New Delhi - 110 001

Ref: Telephone No. 4611098

Now that the next lines have nothing much to be done, expect that International calls and Shah Rukh Khan have to be made bold. This I presume you will be able to do without any difficulty.

We are leaving the table to be done later when we read about the tables in a later chapter.

It is time to save the document again so as to make sure that the changes made by you are stored in the hard disk.

Next, let us try to put some fancy things on the text. First among them is **Font**.

Applying Fonts

It is upto you to select the same font for the whole text or have different fonts for different paragraphs.

Let us see how it is done.

1. Click at any place in the text with the mouse.
2. Click at **Select All** in the **Edit** menu or simply press **Ctrl** and then **A**. This will highlight the whole text in the document.
3. Now you can select the font of your liking in the whole text. You can also change the size of the font too.
4. Select **Arial** for font and size **12** for the whole text in the **Formatting** toolbar.
5. This will make the whole text **12** points and will have **Arial** as the font.

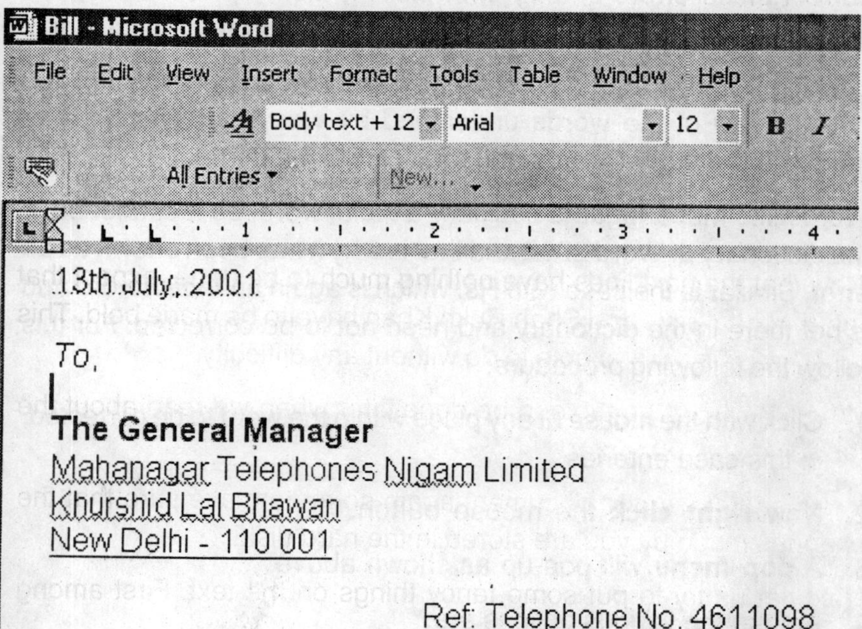

6. The previous changes made by you in terms of **Bold**, *Italics* will remain intact and will not be disturbed by doing this.
7. Now if you want you can change the font of particular items like address, etc., to make it more decorative.

Now that our letter is ready, we can just print it, but before that we must check the spelling in the document so as no typological errors remain in the document.

SPELL CHECKING

As was mentioned in the options, Word 2002 points out the spelling errors by underling the word/words with red wavy line. Since our document is just one page long. It is not difficult to pin point the errors.

There are two methods of correcting these errors. One method is to correct these errors one by one, picking them up. Secondly, you spell check the whole document. Let us do both on our document.

Looking from top to bottom of the text in the document file **Bill**, you will see few of the words underlined by **wavy red line**. Few of them are the proper words and thus cannot be corrected.

Words like Mahanagar is basically a *Hindi* word, so it cannot be in the dictionary of Word 2002 and that is why it has been shown as an error. Similar is the case with Rs. which is again an *Indian* word and is not there in the dictionary and need not to be corrected. For this follow the following procedure:

1. Click with the mouse at any place within the word to be corrected, in this case enteries.
2. Now **right click** the mouse button.
3. A **pop-menu** will pop-up as shown above.
4. Among the various options are:

   Alternative words Word 2002 displays few words

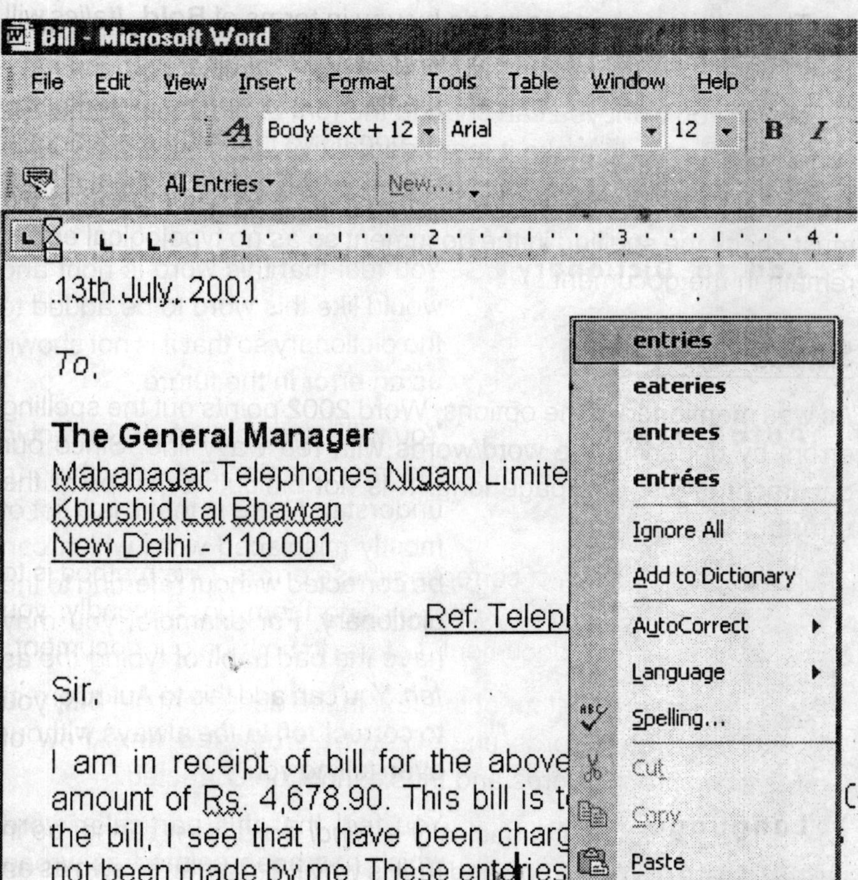

which are similar to the word in question with a hope that these may had been word in your mind while typing this word wrongly. You can choose any one of them, which you feel is the right word by just clicking and selecting that and leaving the mouse. The word will stand corrected with the new word and will replace the wrong word.

Ignore All	It is like over ruling the dictionary and saying that whatever you have typed is right and would like the dictionary to ignore this not only at this place but also at all other places within the document.
Add to Dictionary	You feel that this word is right and would like this word to be added to the dictionary so that it is not shown as an error in the future.
AutoCorrect	You will learn about AutoCorrect in the later chapter. But, only thing to understand here is that it is a list of mostly misplaced word which can be corrected without referring to the dictionary. For example, you may have the bad habit of typing *the* as *teh*. You can add this to AutoCorrect to correct *teh* to *the* always without even telling you.
Language	You feel that this particular word which has been pointed as wrong by the current dictionary would be available in other language dictionary. So mention here the name of the other dictionary where this word could be found. If you do not have a second dictionary loaded, just ignore this.
Spelling	By clicking at this, you can start the spell checking of the whole document from this point onward.
Cut, Copy and Paste	These can be used for transferring

the word to some other place in the document by cutting or copying it at this place and pasting it there.

5. In our case we will accept **entries** as the correct substitute for the wrong word **enteries**.

Since there is no other word which is to be corrected here. The corrected text would now look like the one shown below.

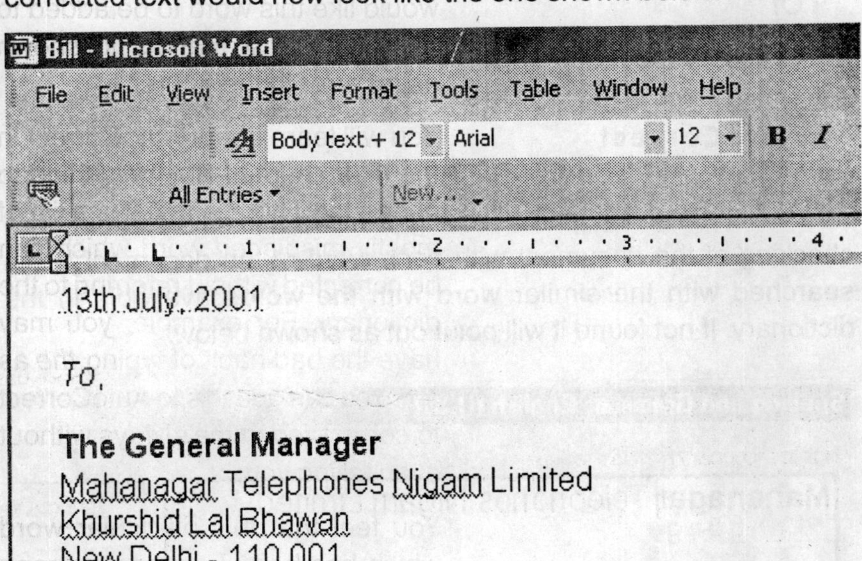

13th July, 2001

To,

The General Manager
Mahanagar Telephones Nigam Limited
Khurshid Lal Bhawan
New Delhi - 110 001

Ref: Telephone No. 4611098

Sir,

I am in receipt of bill for the above telephone number amount of Rs. 4,678.90. This bill is to be paid by 21.5.2C the bill, I see that I have been charged at two accounts not been made by me. These entries are:

Called Id	Duration	Amount
0017249873769	120	1,008.00

Now we come to the second way of spell checking which is checking the whole document. In this case place the cursor at the beginning of the text in the document. In our case we will place the cursor at the left of **1** of **13th July**.

From here do either of the following to start the spell checking.

1. Select **Spelling and Grammar** from the **Tools** menu.

   Or

2. Press **F7**

   Or

3. Click at **Spell Checking button** on the **Standard** toolbar.

This will initiate the spell checking process and will start the spell checking of the document with each word of the document being searched with the similar word with the words available in the dictionary. If not found it will point out as shown below.

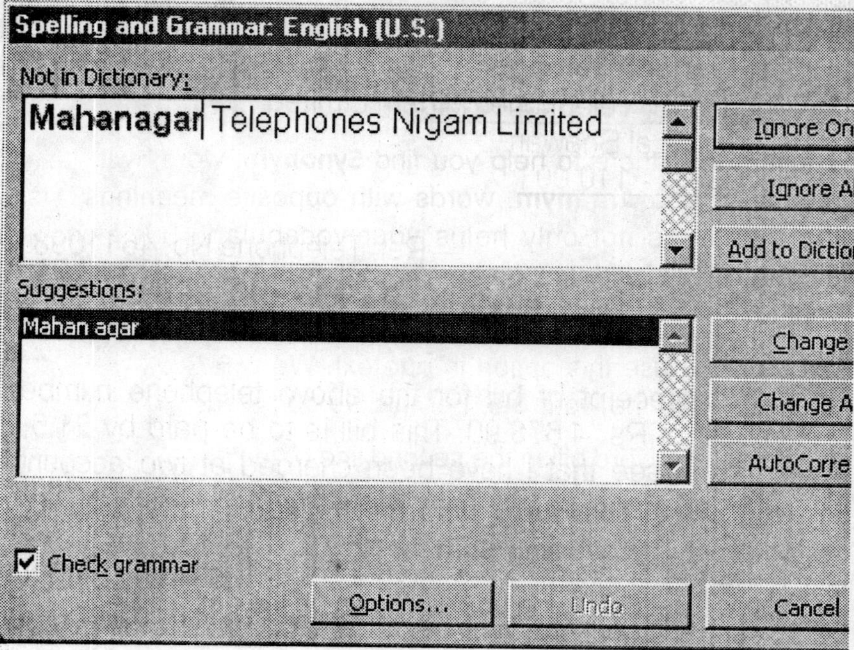

It selects *Mahanagar* of **Mahanagar Telephones Nigam Limited.** As was mentioned before it is a proper *Hindi* word, so it cannot be corrected. **Ignore** it to proceed further. Other words in the document are also correct. So keep clicking **Ignore** for all of them till you reach the end of the document and it stops checking the spelling of the document.

After this there is no other word to correct and the spell checking ends with a dialog box, saying that the spelling checking is complete.

Remember, you can spell check a portion of the text or a word by just highlighting it and then clicking at **Spell Checking Icon**.

Then there is another option called **Thesaurus**.

CONSULTING THESAURUS

Thesaurus is there to help you find **Synonym**, words with similar meanings and **Antonym**, words with opposite meanings. Using the thesaurus not only helps your vocabulary, but gives you alternatives to using the same word over and over again throughout your text.

Let us try to use this option in our text. We would like to see the alternatives to the word **Bill**. For this we do the following:

1. Select the word bill in the second line of the paragraph.
2. Now select **Thesaurus** from the **Tools** menu and **Language** or simply by pressing **Shift + F7**.
3. You will get the dialog box as shown on the next page.

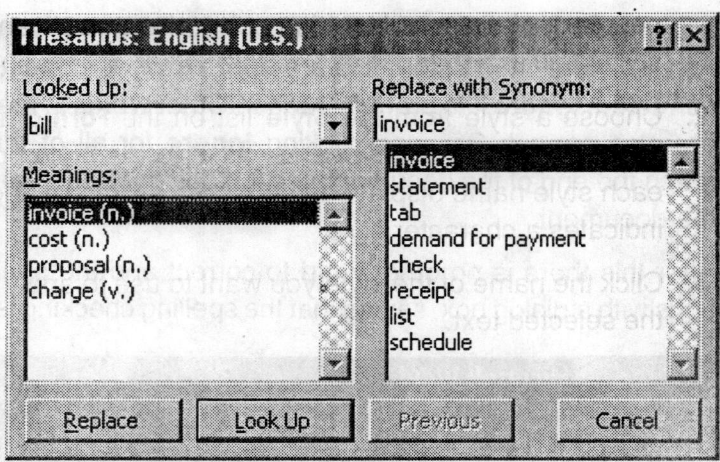

4. The options given here are **Invoice** as the main. But there are others too like statement, check, etc.
5. You have the option to select a new word Invoice or other or let the bill remain as it is.

Assign Character Styles

Styles are sets of formatting attributes that you can apply to text in your document. Typically styles are applied to whole paragraphs and allow you to use preset formatting for headings, captions, numbered paragraphs, and so forth. However, **Character styles** are useful when you find yourself using the Format Painter over and over again to apply character formatting.

Character styles add to the current formatting of text. For example, if the text is **12 point Arial** italics and your character style applies **bold** and **strikethrough**, the text to which you apply the character style will be **12 point Arial bold**, *italic*, and ~~*strikethrough*~~.

Assign a Character Style

1. To apply a style to existing text, select the text to which you want to assign the style. If you want to apply a style as your are entering

new text, place your insertion point where you want the newly styled text to appear.

2. Choose a style from the **Style** list on the **Formatting** toolbar. When you click the down arrow next to the **Style** box, you see each style name displayed in the style's font. An underlined "a" indicates a character style.

3. Click the name of the style you want to use to apply the style to the selected text.

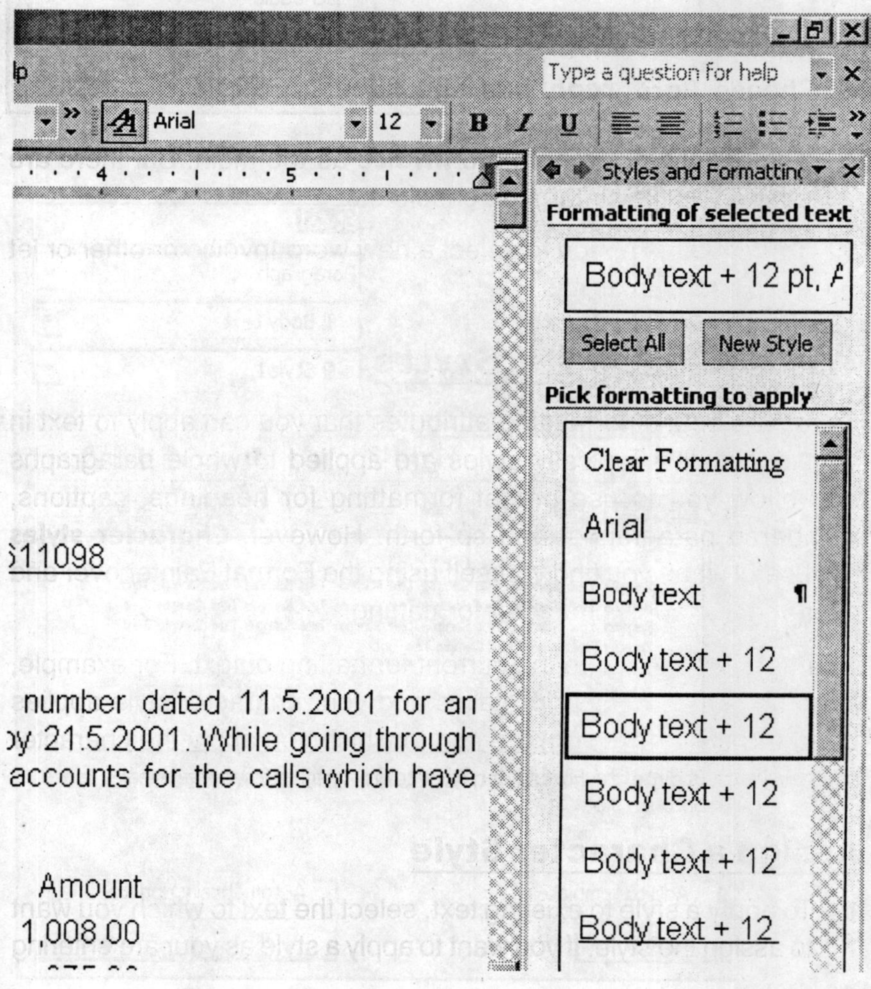

When you want to remove the character style from selected text, apply the character style **Default Paragraph Font**. The text reverts to the formatting defined in the paragraph style assigned to the paragraph in which the selected text is located.

Create a character style

1. Open the **Format** menu and choose **Style and Formatting.**
2. Choose **New Style.**
3. Type a name for the new style in the **Name** box.
4. Choose **Paragraph** from the **Style Type** box.

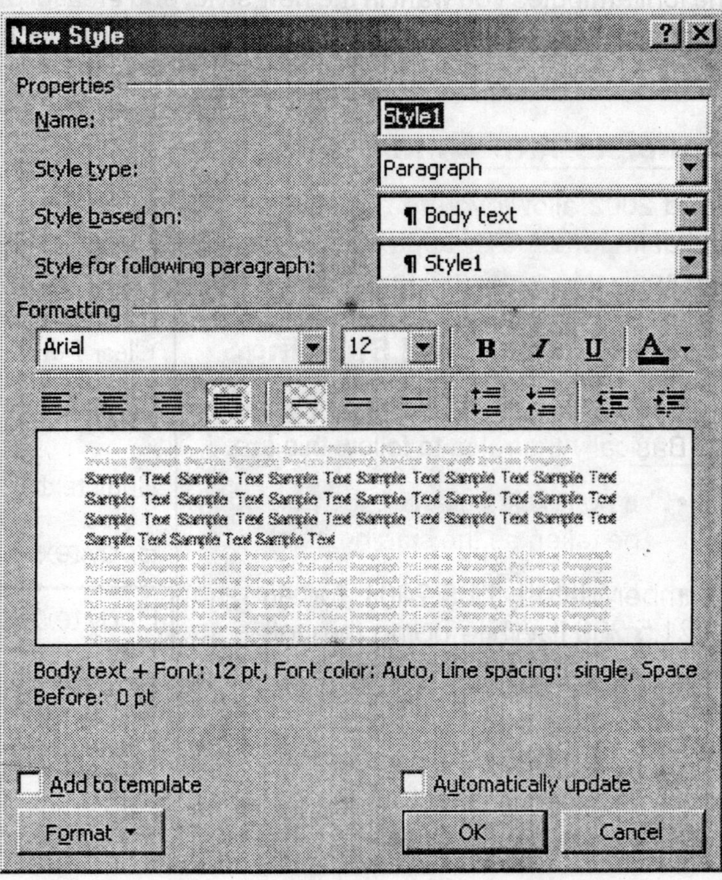

5. Choose **Format** then **Font** to set the style's attributes from the **Font** dialog box. Choose Ok.
6. To add a border or shading to the new character font, choose **Format** and then **Border** to open the **Borders and Shading** dialog box. Make your selections and then choose **OK**.
7. Choose Ok to close the **New Style** dialog box.
8. Choose **Apply** to apply the new style to current text. Choose **Close** to save the new style definition without assigning it to any text.

Creating a character style is easiest when you select text first, apply the font attributes you want in the new style, and then follow steps 1-5 above. You won't have to select any formatting, so skip to steps 7-8 to finish creating the style.

Borders and Shading

Word 2002 allows you to highlight headlines, captions, and other text of importance by applying a border or shading to that text. You can apply it to a piece of text or to the full text.

Apply Borders and Shading

1. Select the text on which you want to apply **Borders** or **Shading**. Basically the rules to follow this are:
   - If no text is selected, the paragraph where the cursor is, will be taken as the starting point.
   - If you select text within a single paragraph, but the paragraph mark itself is not included in the selection, the results affect only the selected text.
   - If you select text included in more than one paragraph (so that at lease one paragraph mark is included in the selection), the results affect all the paragraphs in which any of the selected text resides.

2. Open the **Format** menu, and select **Borders and Shading**.
3. Click **Borders** to work with options available under it.
   - Under **Setting**, click one of the preset border options.
   - Select **None** to remove all borders from the selected paragraph(s), **Box** to insert a box border around the selected paragraph(s), and **Shadow** to insert a box border around the selected paragraph(s) and apply preset shadow formatting to the border.
   - Select **3-D** to insert a box border around the selection and apply preset **3D** border formatting. Choose **Custom** to create a border using the options you click in the **Preview** window. When you choose any of these settings, the current selections in **Style**, **Colour**, and **Width** apply to the borders.

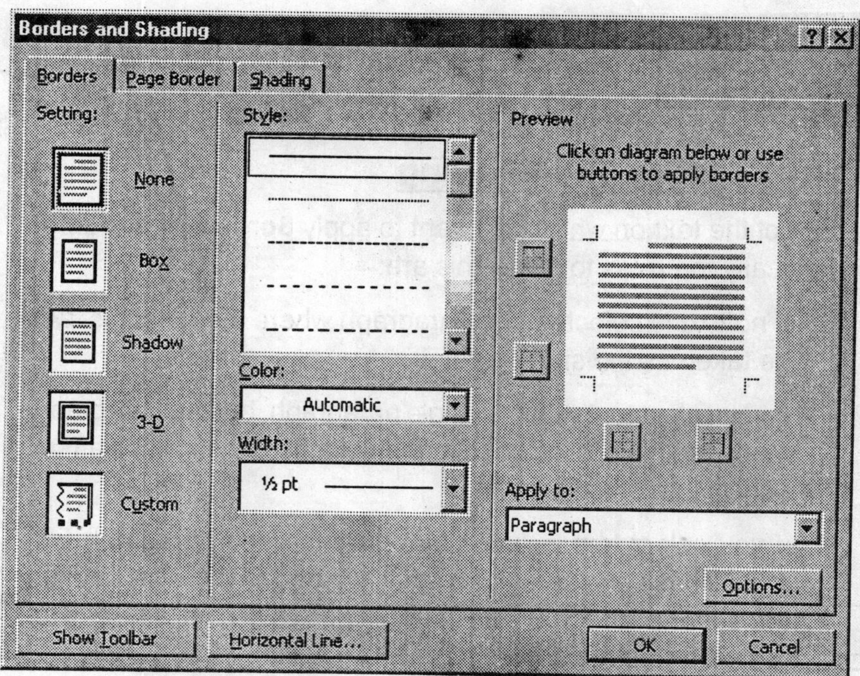

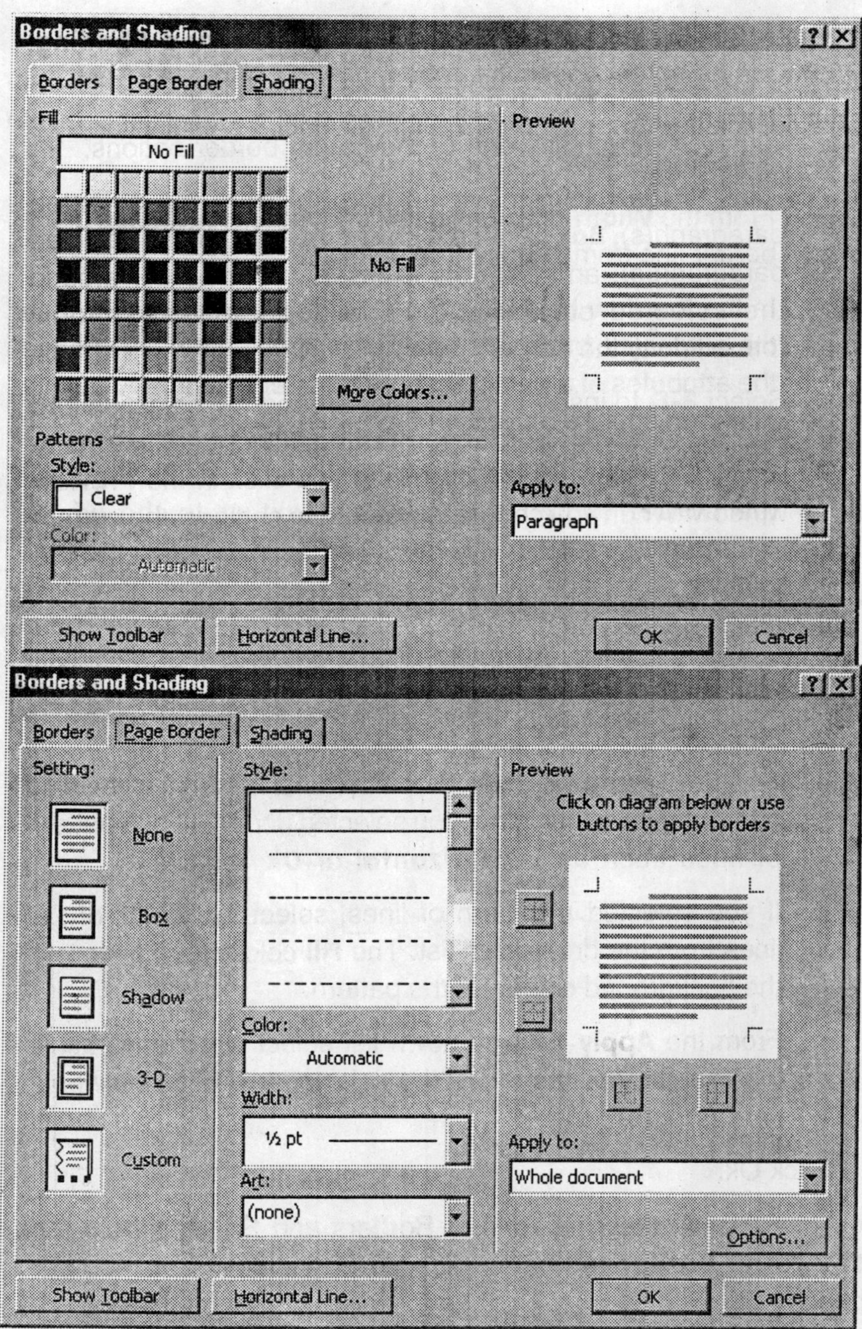

Borders and Shading
Borders
Page Border
Shading
Fill
No Fill
No Fill
More Colors...
Patterns
Style:
Clear
Color:
Automatic
Preview
Apply to:
Paragraph
Show Toolbar
Horizontal Line...
OK
Cancel
Borders and Shading
Borders
Page Border
Shading
Setting:
None
Box
Shadow
3-D
Custom
Style:
Color:
Automatic
Width:
½ pt
Art:
(none)
Preview
Click on diagram below or use buttons to apply borders
Apply to:
Whole document
Options...
Show Toolbar
Horizontal Line...
OK
Cancel

- From the **Style** list, select the type of line you want to use for the border, including *dotted*, *dashed*, and *wavy lines.*
- Click the **Color** drop-down list to select a colour to apply to the border.
- From the **Width** drop-down list, choose the thickness of the border line from ¼ point to 6 points.
- In the **Preview** box, click the individual border lines or use the border line buttons to apply or remove borders or change the attributes of a particular border (select the attributes first and then add the border).
- From the **Apply To** drop-down list, select whether to apply the border to just the selected text or to the whole paragraph(s).

4. Select **Shading** to choose shading options.
   - Under **Fill**, select the colour or shade of gray with which you want to fill the selection. Click **More Colors** to see a larger selection of colours.
   - From the **Patterns Style** drop-down list, choose a shading percentage for the colour you selected under **Fill** or a pattern of lines such as **Lt Horizontal** or **Dk Trellis**.
   - If you selected a pattern of lines, select the **Color** of the lines from the drop-down list. The **Fill** colour then becomes the background colour for the pattern.
   - From the **Apply To** drop-down list select whether to apply the shading options to just the selected text or to the whole paragraph(s).
5. Click Ok.

You can use all these options of Borders and Shading from the **Tables** and **Border** toolbar, which can be called from toolbar options.

This will allow you to select shading colours, border line styles, border line colours, and border line widths, etc.

Following are the button on the toolbar that apply to borders and shading.

Button	***Description***
Line Style	Sets the style of the border lines (dotted, dashed, wavy, double, and so on)
Line Weight	Sets the thickness of the border lines
Border Color	Sets the colour of the border lines
Borders	Specifies where the border appears (top, bottom, left, right, or box)
Shading Color	Sets the colour of the background shading for the paragraph (you cannot specify the percentage)

Since our letter is a formal one, we would not like to use any of these decorations. They have been told here so that they can be used at a later stage in another document.

Now that our letter is final. What we would do now is that we will close the file and then reopen and finally print. This is deliberately done so as to learn the concept of closing and opening of the file. If you want you can print the file as it is.

Closing of the File

As you would have noticed that there is no Close command in File menu. All you have to do is close the file using the ☒ button on the extreme right top of the word document. But don't forget to save the file before closing else the software will ask you to do so.

Save as option

Let us understand the difference between **Save** and **Save As**.

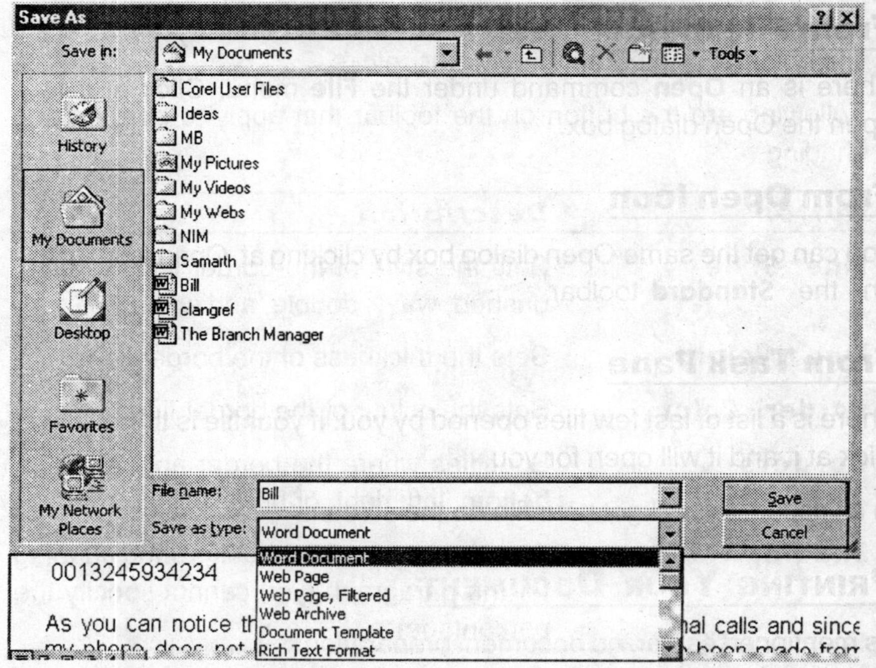

You save your document file as you save any other file. Save As option allows you to save with another name, maybe another format at another drive/directory. It is not that the system will not allow you to save the file with the same name under Save As option. It will ask you whether you want to overwrite the file which exists. This is just a precautionary option so that you do not overwrite a file with the same name accidentally.

Now suppose that you have closed the file after saving, the next option obviously is open this file.

Open File

Opening of the file can be done by 3 methods if you are already working under Word 2002.

From File menu

There is an **Open** command under the **File** menu. Click at it to open the Open dialog box.

From Open Icon

You can get the same Open dialog box by clicking at Open icon  on the **Standard** toolbar.

From Task Pane

There is a list of last few files opened by you. If your file is there, just click at it and it will open for you.

In all cases you will get your file on the screen.

Printing Your Document

As mentioned earlier, no document preparation process is complete without printing it. For this we have the **Print** option under the **File** menu.

Once clicked it gives rise to a dialog box as shown on the next page. The various options on the dialog box are as follows:

Printer Select the printer to which you want to send the printing. From the drop-down list, you can select one of the many printers which you may have installed under Windows.

Properties Clicking at it would lead to a dialog box having the properties of the selected printer. If some adjustments are to be made in the properties of the selected printer, they can be done here.

Print to file Sometimes it is possible that you may like to print the document to the printer which is not installed in your computer. In this case you will select this option and create a print file for that particular printer and copy the file and then print on that printer where it is installed.

Print range You may like to print few selective pages instead of printing the whole document. So either click **All**, for printing all pages of the document or **Pages**, for defining the pages you want to print. You can even print the current page, i.e., page on the screen.

Copies Word 2002 allows you to print multiple copies of the pages in the document. You can mention here the number of copies you want. What's more you can have the copies collated for you, if you select the **collate** option.

Print what Various options available here are Document, Document properties, Comments, Styles,

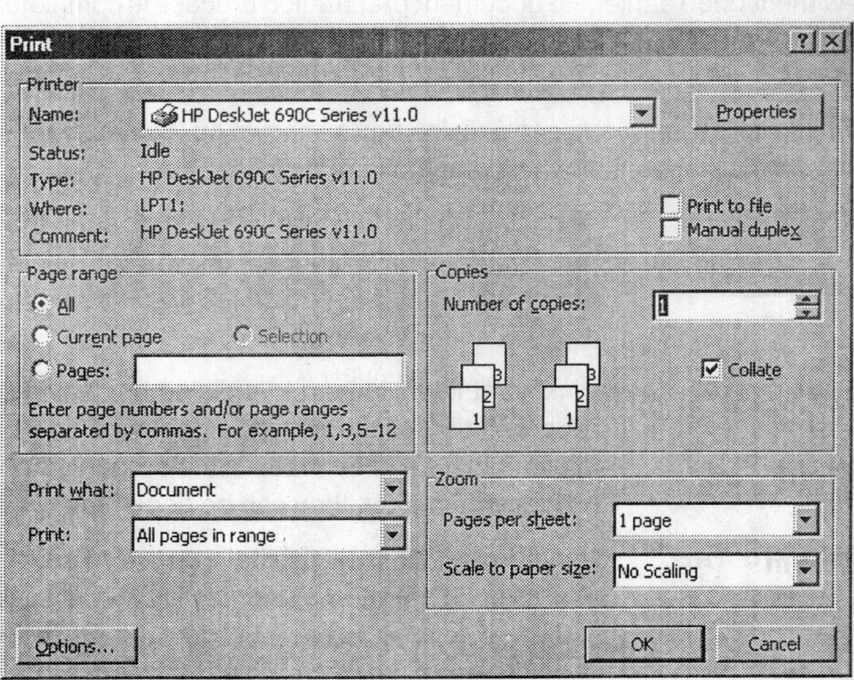

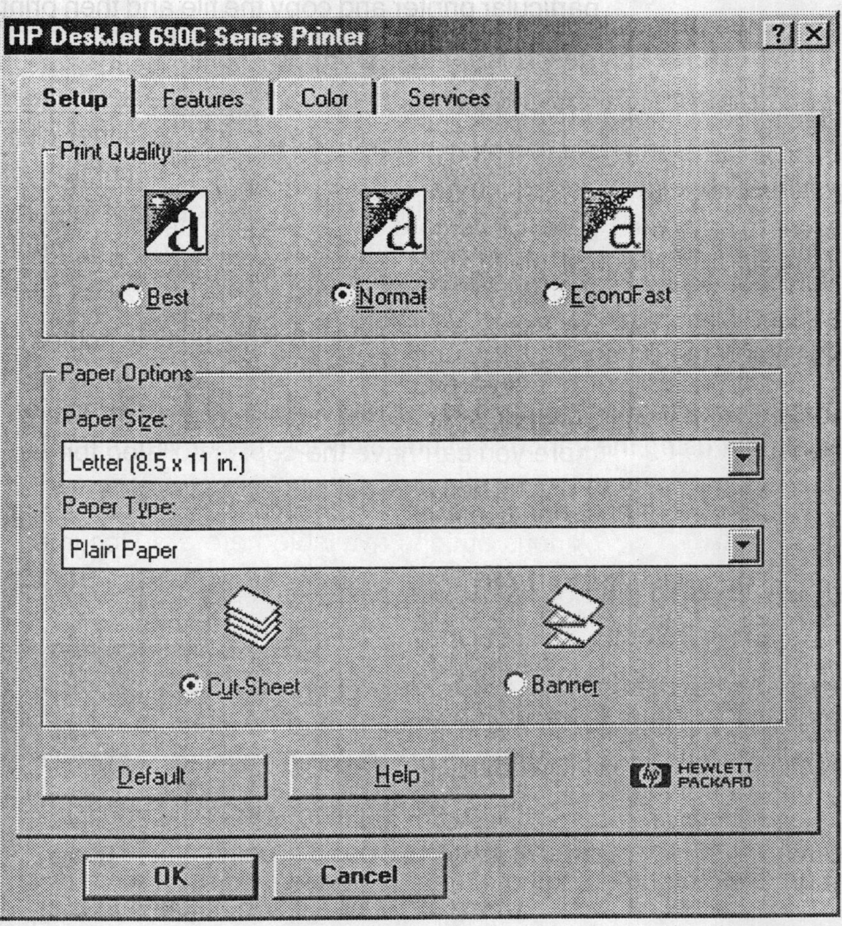

AutoText entries, Key assignments. But, most of the time you would be printing with Document option.

Print You have the option of printing all pages or all **odd pages** or all **even pages**.

Zoom Pages per sheet allows you to print 1 to 16 pages of the document on one sheet. Scaling allows you to scale your document to the various sizes of the paper.

Options This will lead to the print options, already described under **Options** and select the option of your choice.

Once you are sure that you have selected all the options required by you, just click Ok to for document to start printing. However, do not forget to have the Printer ON before giving the final print command.

I suggest you write a similar letter to another authority and try this process from creating the document to printing as an example, for practice.

In the next chapter, you will learn more skills of improving your document using the various options available under Word 2002.

Remember

1. **Footer** appear at the bottom of each page on the presentation.
2. You can skip the intermediatory steps by clicking at **Finish** in the first dialog box of the Wizard.
3. Each presentation is given a look which is preset. You can change this according to your liking.
4. Two level of text is given on the left hand side of the presentation. The one with the serial number is the heading of the slide. The second level of text is the text which appears as the part of the presentation.
5. You can change this text about which you will read later in the book.

4

Proofing Your Document

Introduction

Now that you have printed the document, you may want to either correct few words which you have realized that they do not look good in the letter. Even otherwise you may want to enhance the overall look of the letter. Besides this you would also learn how to do the tailor's job, i.e., Cut, Copy and Paste. There are other options too which may not be used in this letter but are quite useful overall for editing. Let us start with the proofing tools.

Editing Tools

Many editing functions are performed on selected text, such as cut, copy, move, and delete. There are various tools provided by Word to help you edit text:

Cut, Copy — Cutting and copying items places them on the Clipboard and you can paste these items anywhere in the document, wherever required. These items can be text, graphics, tables and any other object which is there in the word document. Cut and Copy can be performed using mouse and key strokes.

Paste — It is the command used to paste whatever is available on the Clipboard to paste it in the document. This is also done by the use of mouse and key strokes.

Move	It is an action associated with the mouse. However, if you cut and paste from one place to another, it can also be called move.
Insert Mode	It is the feature that adjusts spacing when you add new text to the document.
Overtype Mode	This option replaces the existing text with your new text.
Delete	It is an action you should reserve for text you want to permanently remove. Deleted text is not placed in the Clipboard. You can delete text with either mouse or key strokes.
Undo and Redo	Using these commands you can reverse the tasks performed earlier.

All these commands are available on the toolbars as icons too.

You can find them in the **Edit** menu too.

For either cutting or copying, you have to highlight the part of the text on which you want to perform this operation. All these commands have their keyboard strokes associated with them too.

They are:

Cut	Ctrl + X
Copy	Ctrl + C
Paste	Ctrl + V
Move	Ctrl + X and then Ctrl + V

Delete Backspace or Delete

Undo Ctrl + Z

Redo Ctrl + Y

Let us now learn few options of Word 2002 which help us in correcting our document with minimum efforts.

AutoCorrect

It is a handy feature of Word 2002 which automatically corrects common typing, capitalization, and spelling errors for you, as you type. It also enables you to type shortcuts that AutoCorrect replaces with the full text, such as typing BOMBAY and having AutoCorrect replace it with MUMBAI. This has been neccesiated due to the fact that the name of the city has been changed as thus. Although Word 2002 has a number of default AutoCorrect entries, you can add your own common misspellings and shortcuts.

It only checks whole words, so if you type TEH, Word won't replace it with THE until your press the spacebar, period, or some other key that indicates that the word is complete. It is also useful tool for applying formatting options. In a business letter, for example, you might want your company name to always appear in a certain font and size, regardless of the font you are using for the letter. By creating an AutoCorrect entry of your company name with formatting options, you eliminate the need to format while you type, or to run search and replace when you are finished with the letter.

Add AutoCorrect Entries Without Formatting

1. From the **Tools** menu, select **AutoCorrect** to open the AutoCorrect dialog box. Click AutoCorrect tab if it is not already selected.

2. Click **Replace Text as You Type** to place a check mark there, if it isn't already checked.

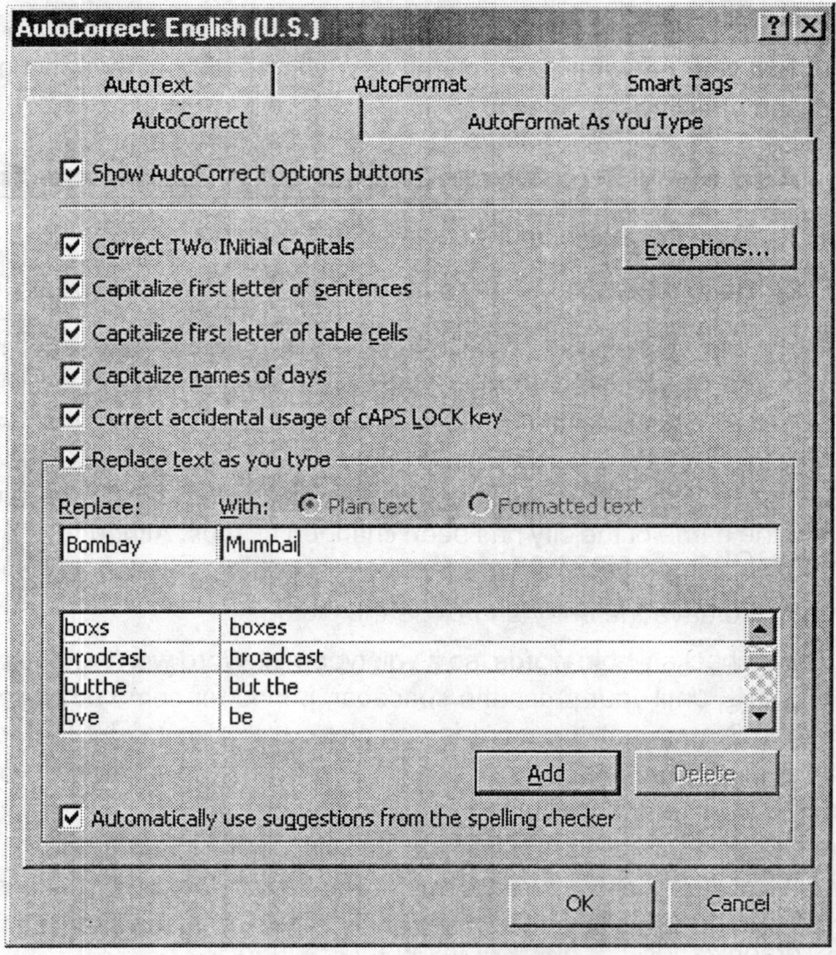

3. In the replace box, enter the text you want AutoCorrect to automatically replace for you, such as your initials or a word you commonly misspell.

4. Click **Plain Text** if it is not selected to inserted text without formatting options.

5. Choose **Add**. If the text in the **Replace** box is already listed, choose Replace to replace the existing replacement text with the text you entered in the **With** box.

6. Click Ok.

Text your new AutoCorrect entry by typing the word in a document and pressing the Spacebar.

Add New AutoCorrect Entries with Formatting

1. Type the text in your document and format it.
2. Select the text. To store paragraph formatting with your entry, include the paragraph mark at the end of the text, in your selection.
3. From the **Tools** menu, select **AutoCorrect**. The AutoCorrect dialog box appears.
4. In the **Replace** text box, type a name for the **AutoCorrect** entry (an abbreviation, or the entire word or phrase).
5. Click **Formatted Text**.
6. To save the entry and close the dialog box, click **Add**.

Another option available in Word 2002 is AutoText. Let us see how it works.

AutoText

AutoCorrect stores frequently used text or graphics that automatically replace designated text entries. **AutoText**, called the **Glossary** in older versions of Word, also keeps frequently used text and graphics for you but only inserts them in the document when you call for them—not automatically. For example, you could store your company logo as an Auto Text entry and insert it in your document when you press the appropriate keys. Auto Text is also useful for abbreviating entries of larger bodies of text, such as addresses for frequently used paragraphs.

Creating an AutoText Entry

1. Select whatever text and/or graphics you want to include in the

AutoText entry. Be sure to include the paragraph marker in the selection if you want the text's paragraph formatting to be part of the entry.

2. On the **Insert** menu, select **AutoText**. Then select the option **New**. You can also press **Alt + F3**, or choose **New** on the AutoText toolbar. The **Create Auto Text** dialog box appears.
3. Accept the entry name that automatically appears or enter your own in the **Please Name Your Auto Text Entry** text box.

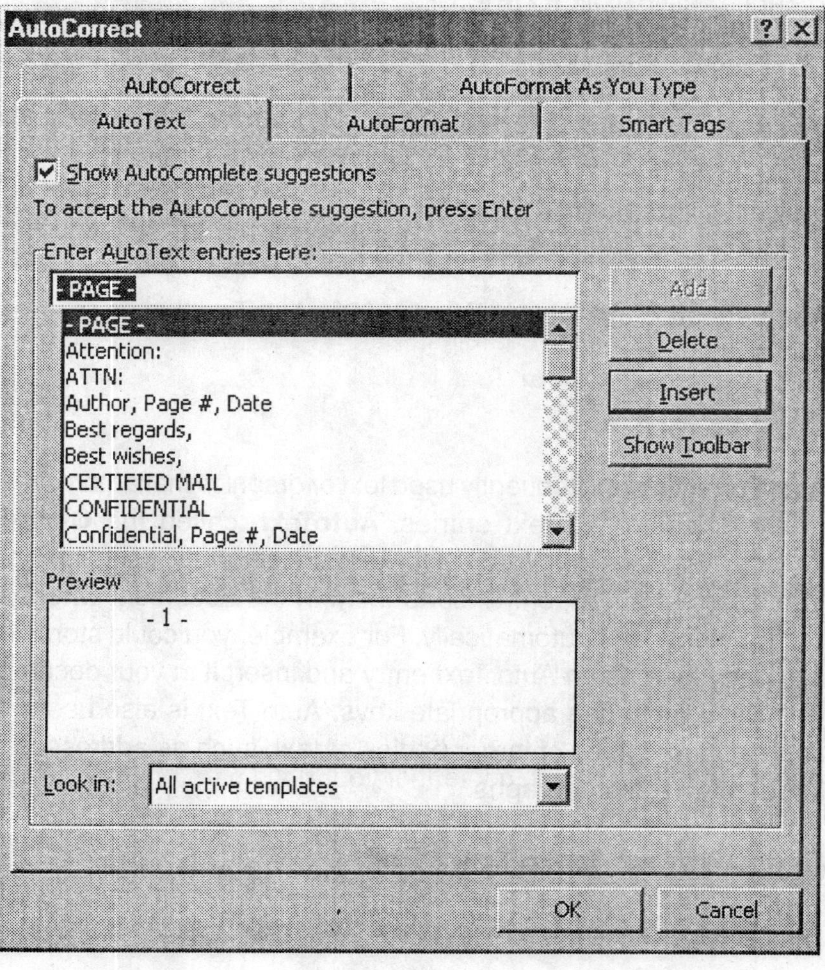

4. Click Ok.

AutoText entries can be inserted into your document in several different ways:

1. Type the name of the Auto Text entry and then press F3.
2. From the **Insert** menu, select **AutoText**. Then select the desired entry from the submenu.
3. Choose the middle button on the Auto Text toolbar to see a list of available Auto Text entries. If the current text style is Normal, this button is labelled **All Entries**. Otherwise, the button has the name of the current paragraph style. Then select the entry you want from the list that appears.
4. When **AutoComplete** is enabled, Word displays a matching Auto Text entry in a small pop-up menu next to the insertion point when you have typed enough of the Auto Text entry name to identify the entry. Press **F3** to insert the entire entry. To ignore it, keep typing.

To display all entries, regardless of style, hold down the **Shift** key while clicking the **Auto Text** toolbar or choose **Auto Text** from the **Insert** menu.

AutoFormat

Word 2002 has automated a lot of small, tedious chores that we had to do manually in older word processing programs. Many of these are formatting chores, and Word collects them under the term AutoFormat. You can control what formatting chores Word 2002 performs automatically in the AutoFormat panels of the AutoCorrect dialog box. The benefit of using AutoFormat is that you can concentrate more on the content of your document and less on the details of formatting.

AutoFormat works on two different ways—**as you type** or **on command**.

AutoFormat as You Type

Automatically formats headings, bulleted and numbered lists, borders, numbers, symbols, and so on, as you type.

AutoFormat on Command

Automatically formats selected text or the entire document in one pass.

You don't have to do anything to activate AutoFormat. By default, **AutoFormat as You Type** is enabled—you just enter text and Word formats it as you go. You can change the default to **AutoFormat on Command**, which allows you to manually run AutoFormat. This is similar to the way in which you can spell check a document—as you type, or manually, using the menu commands or toolbar icons.

AutoFormatting Text

1. To AutoFormat a block of text, select it. To AutoFormat the entire document, make sure that no text is selected.
2. From the **Format** menu, select **AutoFormat** to open the AutoFormat dialog box.

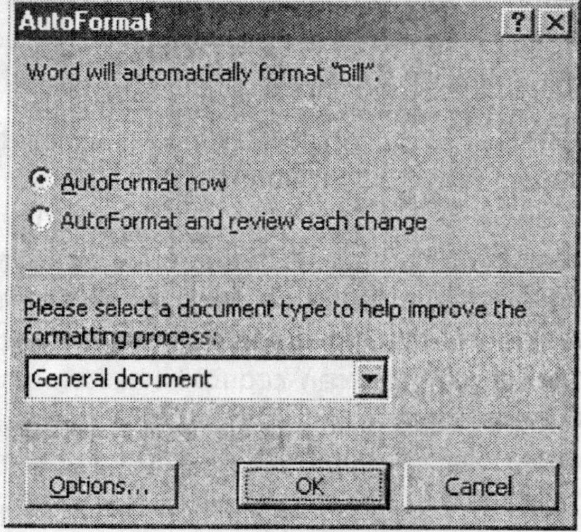

3. Click **AutoFormat Now** if you want Word 2002 to format the document without prompting you to review the changes.

4. Click **AutoFormat and Review Each Change** if you want the opportunity to accept or reject each change proposed by Word.
5. Choose the type of document you have created in the drop-down list labelled **Please Select a Document Type to Help Improve the Formatting Process**. This helps Word to AutoFormat the document properly.
6. If you want to limit the types of formatting Word does, choose the Options button to display the AutoFormat panel of the AutoCorrect dialog box. Make your selections and then click Ok to return to the AutoFormat dialog box.
7. Click Ok to begin the AutoFormat process.

If you choose AutoFormat Now, Word 2002 formats the document, and that's that. If you choose AutoFormat and Review Each Change, Word 2002 formats the document and then presents a new AutoFormat dialog box. This version of the document looks very different from the first version.

Find and Replace

Supposing you had prepared a thesis on the working of middle level managers in the city of Bombay. Naturally the word Bombay must have come in it quite a number of times. Then you hear that the Government of that State has decided to change the name of city from **Bombay** to **Mumbai.** What will you do? Will you be able to locate each occurrence of Bombay and physically change it to Mumbai? No! For this Word 2002 has an excellent option called **Find and Replace**. Once you give this command, Word 2002 will automatically search for Bombay and replace it with Mumbai.

You can use Find and Replace to do the following:

Text strings	Either strings of text embedded in words, or discrete words or whole phrases.

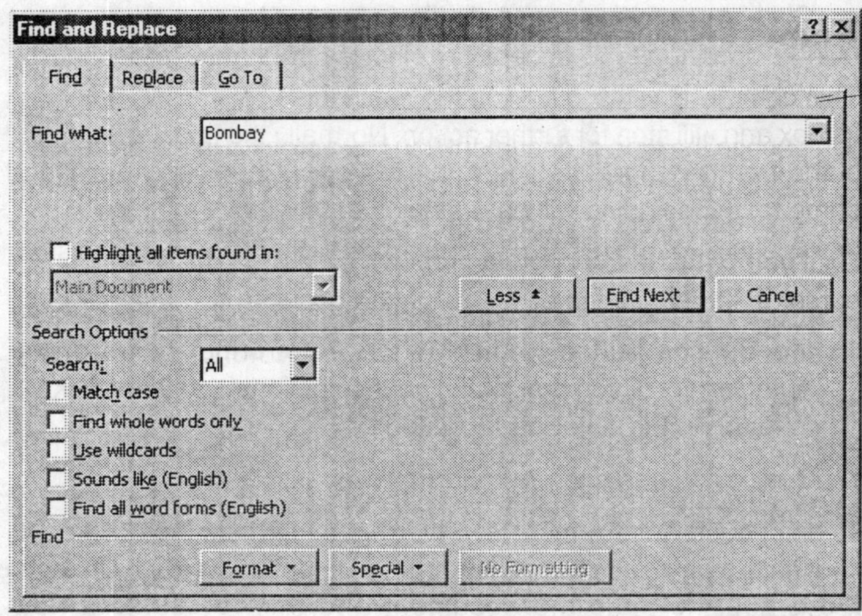

Text strings with formatting Strings of text that are formatted a particular way, such as Bold.

Formatting Font formatting options, such as underlining and bold, that are not necessarily associated with words or text.

Styles Find all instances of a named style or replace one named style with another.

Special characters Tab markers, forced line breaks, non-breaking spaces, non-breaking hyphens, whitespace, and so on.

This command is actually divided into 2 parts, **Find** and **Replace**. Let us see how the find command works first.

FIND

This command will find for you the exact text which is mentioned in its box and will stop for further action. Normally the finding of the text starts from the position where the cursor is. If you have selected some text, the finding will be restricted to that block of text only.

So if you have to select the entire text, then it is advised to put the cursor at the beginning of the text in the document.

To start the **Find** command, do any of the following:

1. Open the **Edit** menu and select **Find**.

   Or

2. Press **Ctrl + F**.

   Or

3. Click the **Find** icon, which is part of **Standard** toolbar. If it is not there you can add it on your toolbar from the Add and Remove buttons.

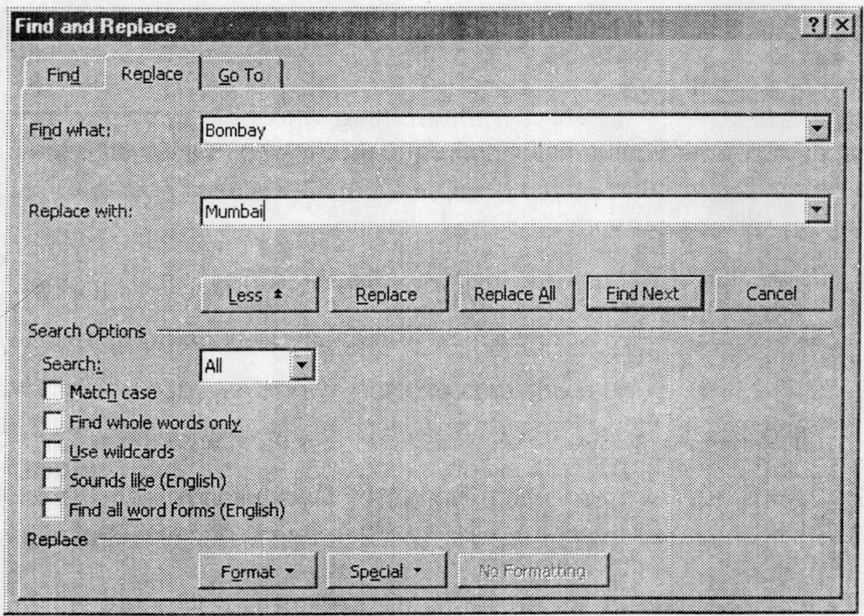

Find and Replace dialog box, as shown here will appear in each of the above cases.

This is how you will use the **Find** command.

1. Type the text that you are seeking in the **Find What?** text box. This word or phrase is also referred to as the search string.
2. Choose the **More** button (if necessary) to specify search options.
3. Choose **Find Next**. Find looks through the document for text that matches your search strings. When it finds matching text, Word highlights the text in the document and stops. The Find and Replace dialog box remains on screen.
4. Choose **Find Next** if you want to continue the search for another instance of the search string. Click **Cancel** or press **Esc** to close the dialog box and return to the document. The text in the document is still highlighted.

When Word finishes the entire document, or if it could not find the search string in the document, a dialog box displays a message to that effect. Choose Ok to continue working in the document.

Replace Text

Next step after finding the required text is to replace it with some other text. For this we would call the command called **Replace**. To get the replace command do the following.

1. Open the **Edit** menu and select **Replace**.

   Or

2. Press **Ctrl + H**.

   Or

3. Click the **Find** icon, which is part of **Standard** toolbar. If it is not there you can add it on your toolbar from the Add and Remove buttons.

Now on the Find and Replace dialog box click at the **Replace** panel and do the following:

1. Type the text you want to replace in the **Find What** text box (in this case, *Bombay*). You can leave this field blank if you have to search for a formatting only. However, you have to search for something.
2. Type the text you want to replace it with in the **Replace With** text box (in this case, *Mumbai*). If you search for text and leave this field blank, you are in effect telling Word to delete all instances of the search strings, because they would be replaced by a blank.
3. Choose the **More** button (if necessary) to specify search options.
4. Choose **Find Next** to locate and highlight the first occurence of text that matches your search string.
5. Then do one of the following:
    - Choose **Replace** to replace the text matching the search string with the replacement text and then locate the next occurrence of the search string in your document.
    - Choose **Find Next** to leave the text matching the search string unchanged and to locate the next occurence of the search string.
    - Choose **Replace All** to replace text in the entire document that matches the search string with the replacement text.
6. Choose **Cancel**. Alternatively, press **Esc** to close the **Find and Replace** dialog box and return to the your document.

When Word has finished searching through the document and has replaced all occurrences of the search text or can't find any further occurrences, a message box appears.

Click Ok to return to your document.

Page Numbering

Printed documents longer than one page should have page numbers. You can set up page numbering in two ways. Either insert a page number code while editing headers and footers, or insert page numbers from the **Insert** menu. Both methods insert a page number code in you documents' header or footer, but there are two differences.

Putting the page numbers through header and footer, we will learn that when we learn Header and Footer, later in the chapter. Otherwise you do the following:

1. Click the **Insert** menu and select **Page Numbers** to open the Page Numbers dialog box, as shown on the next page.
2. From the **Position** drop-down list, select the position on the page where you want your page numbers to appear. The options are:

   Top of the Page (Header)

   Bottom of the Page (Footer)
3. From the alignment drop-down list, select Left, Center, or Right to specify the horizontal position of the page number in relation to the right or left margins.
4. If you want the page number to appear on the first page, Show

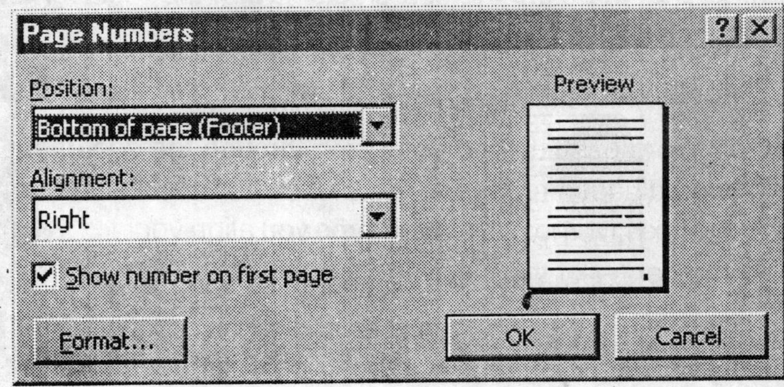

number on first page to place check mark there. Deselecting this option creates a separate header or footer for the first page.

5. Click Ok.

When you insert a page number, Word automatically switches you to Print Layout view so you can scroll to the portion of the page where the page number appears to check its appearance.

HEADER AND FOOTER

As you must be knowing that **Header** appears on the top of the page and **Footer** appears on the bottom of the page. Word 2002 allows you to put both of them on the document pages.

Headers and footers can vary within a document. Choices include:

1. The same header and footer on every page.
2. A different header and footer for the first page only
3. Different headers and footers for odd numbered pages than those on even numbered pages.
4. Different headers and footers for each section of the document.

Adding a Header or Footer in Your Document

1. Click the **View** menu and select **Header and Footer**. The document appears in the Print Layout view with the header area indicated by a nonprinting dashed line box, as shown on next page. Regular document text is gray, and the header and footer toolbar is displayed.
2. Type the header or footer text. Edit and format the text as you would anywhere else in the document. Both the header and the footer have two tabs set to help you align your text a centre tab at the center of the page and a right tab at the right margin.
3. Use the toolbar buttons, as shown on next page, to add page numbers, total page numbers, date, time, etc.

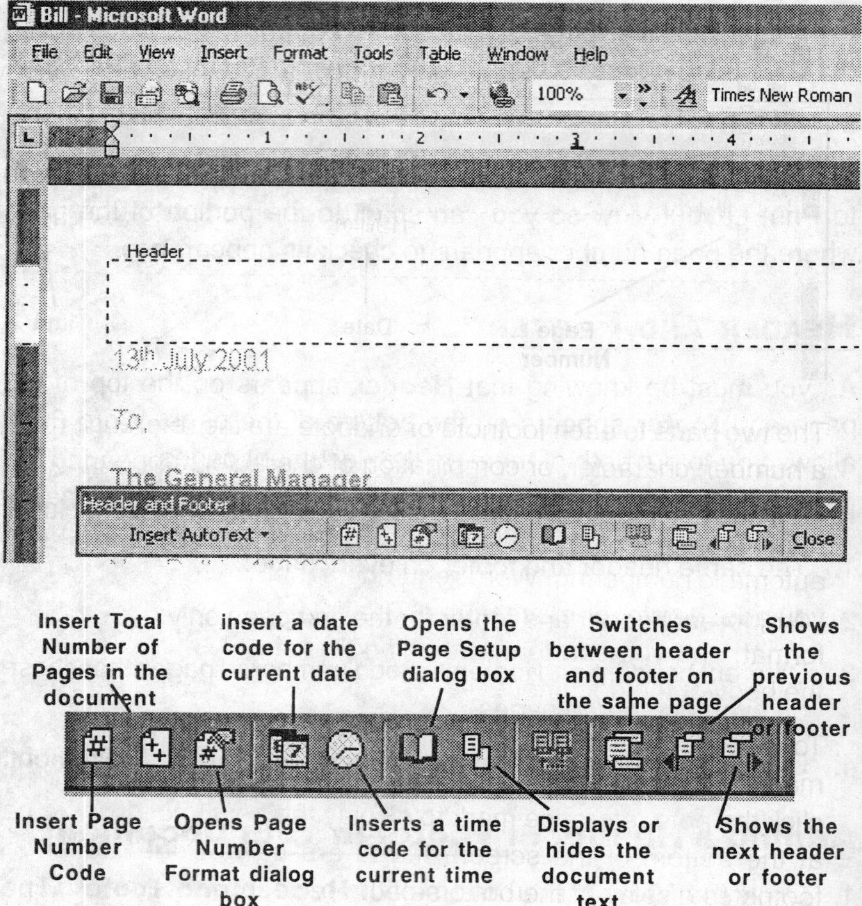

4. Choose Close on the Header and Footer toolbar to return to the document.
5. A header would like the one shown on the next page.

Footnotes and Endnotes

These are used in the documents to provide references to the source documents for the document text, to provide more detailed explanations and definitions that might otherwise distract the reader if left in the main body of the document.

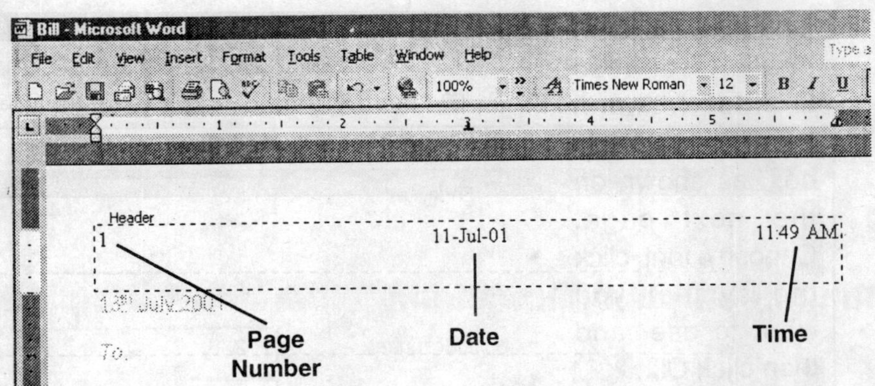

The two parts to each footnote or endnote are the reference mark—a number, character, or combination of characters appearing in the body of the document—and the note text. You may automatically number the marks or create your own custom marks. If you use the automatic numbering, Word renumbers the note reference marks if you add, delete, or move notes. The note can be of any length and format, and you can format the line that separates the notes from the body of the document.

To view the note text, rest the mouse pointer on the note reference mark. The note text appears in a pop-up box above the mark. Double-click the note reference mark to display the note text in a note pane at the bottom of the screen. If you are using Print Layout view, footnotes display at the bottom of the page, endnotes at the end of the document.

Add a Footnote or Endnote

1. Place curosr where you want the note reference mark to appear.
2. Choose the **Insert** menu and select **Reference and Footnote**. The Footnote and Endnote dialog box appears.
3. Select **Footnote** or **Endnote**.
4. Under **Numbering**, select **AutoNumber** or **Custom Mark**. If you choose Custom Mark, insert the symbol or symbols for

the reference mark or choose **Symbol** to open the Symbol dialog box, as shown on the next page. Choose a font, click the symbol you want to use, and then click Ok.

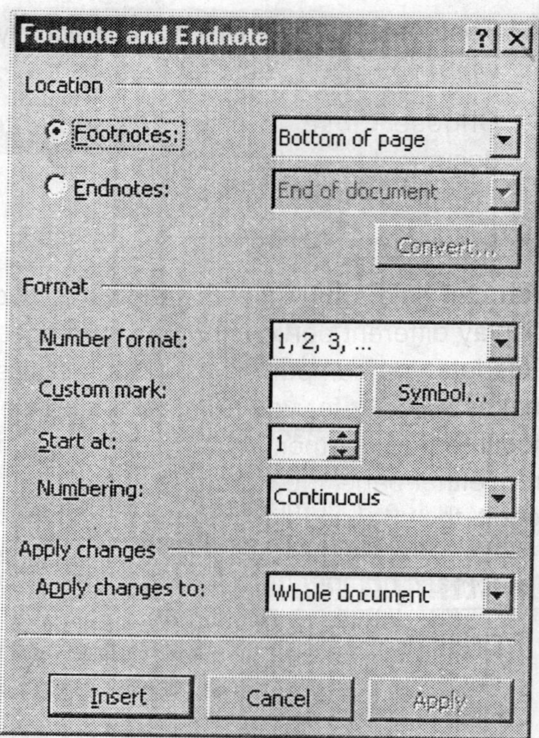

5. Choose Ok to close the Footnote and Endnote dialog box.
6. Type the note text in the footnote pane. Apply formatting as desired or, better yet, reformat the

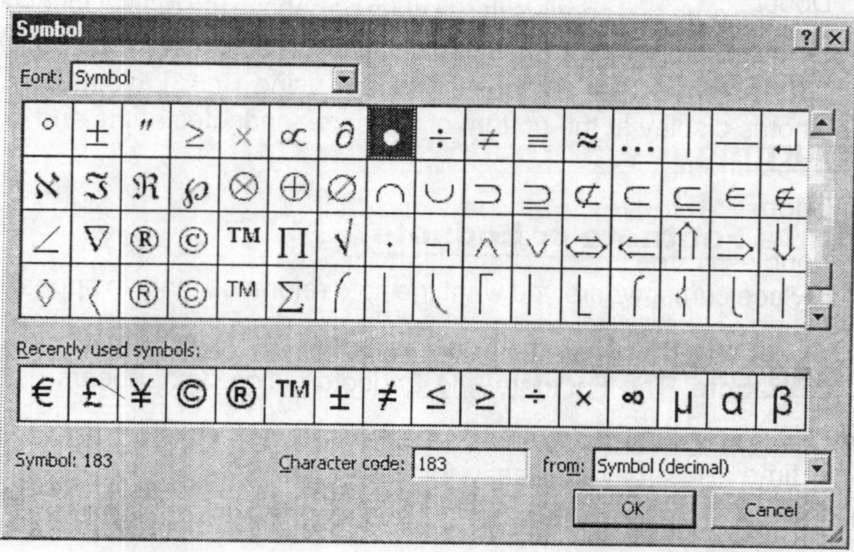

Footnote text style (which automatically appears in the Style list when you insert your first footnote).

7. Choose **Close** to close the footnote pane or click in the document to continue typing.

Splitting Panes

You can split a document window into two panes. Then, you can display different portions of the same document at the same time. This lets you compare two portions of a single document. It also makes it easier for you to move or copy text from one portion of a document to another. When you make a change to the document from either pane, the change is applied to the same document. As a result, the change can be found in both panes.

Splitting Document into Two Panes

1. Choose the **Split** command from the **Window** menu, drag the separator bar to where you want to split the window, and click the left mouse button.
2. Double click on the split bar that appears above the vertical scroll bar or drag the split bar down to where you want to split the window.

Returning to a Normal Window Option

1. Choose **Remove Split** command from the **Window** menu.
2. Double-click on the Split bar or drag the Split bar to the top of the document window.

Tiling of the Documents

With tiling you can display two or more different documents at the same time. This makes it easy for you to compare two or more documents, or to move and copy text from one document to another.

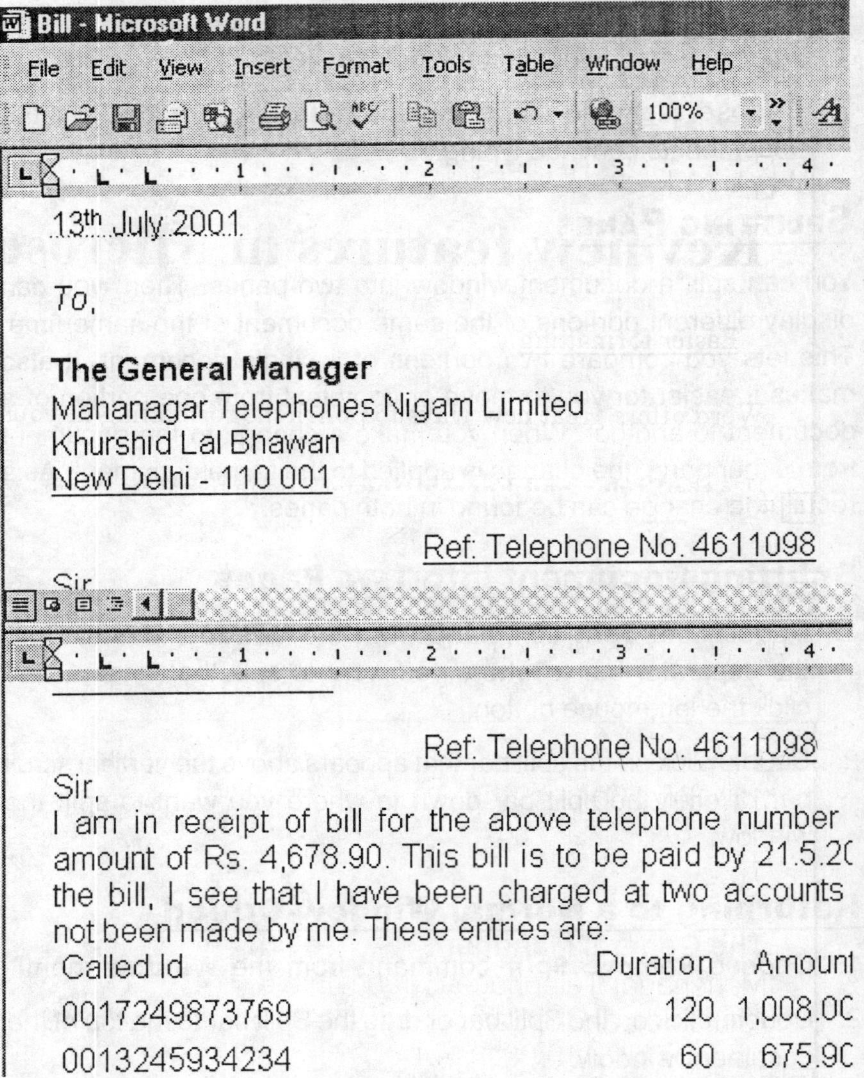

13th July 2001

To,

The General Manager
Mahanagar Telephones Nigam Limited
Khurshid Lal Bhawan
New Delhi - 110 001

Ref: Telephone No. 4611098

Sir

Ref: Telephone No. 4611098

Sir,
I am in receipt of bill for the above telephone number amount of Rs. 4,678.90. This bill is to be paid by 21.5.2(the bill, I see that I have been charged at two accounts not been made by me. These entries are:

Called Id	Duration	Amount
0017249873769	120	1,008.0(
0013245934234	60	675.9(

However, this works best when only two documents are open. Otherwise, the windows get too small for effective use. To return the display so only one window shows, just maximize the window that you want dispalyed.

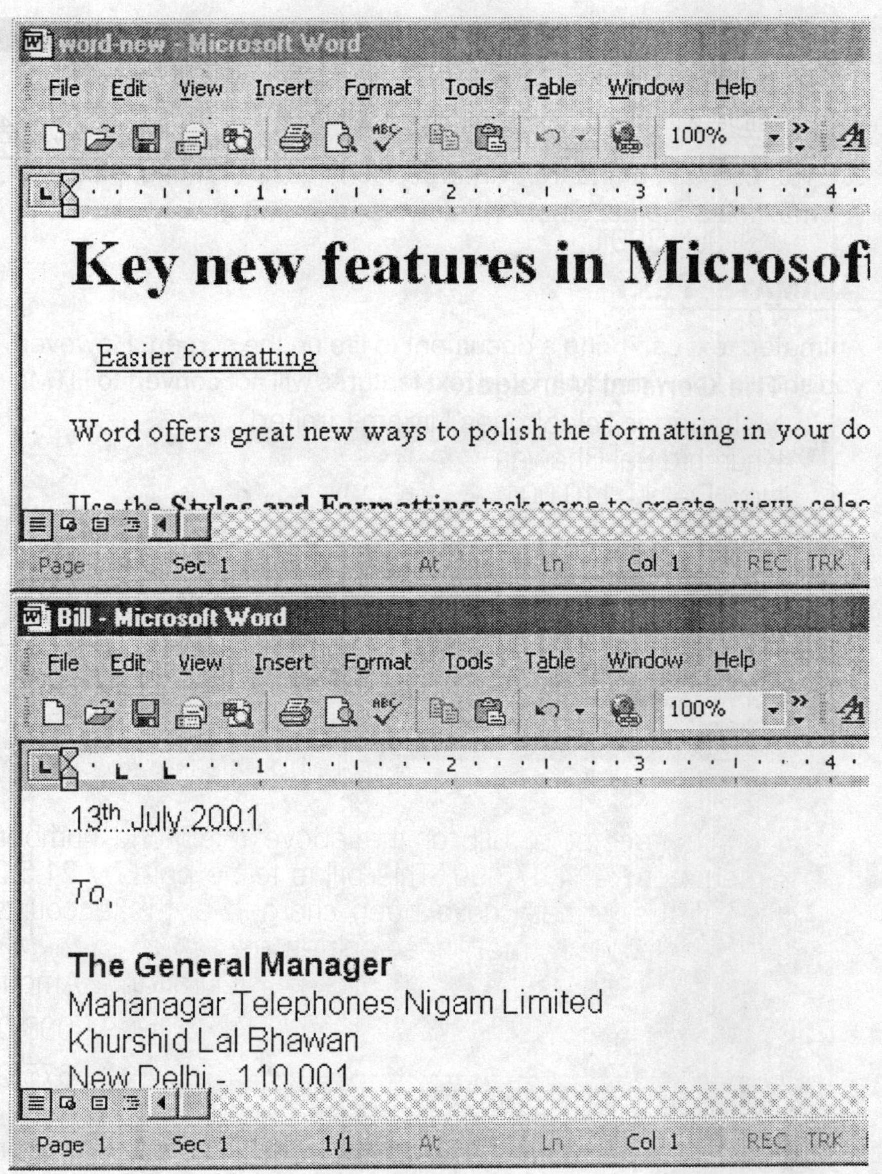

To Tile Open Document Window

1. Choose the **Arrange All** command from the **Window** menu.

2. The Arrange All command sizes the open documents windows so they are all the same height and so they are as wide as possible within Word's application window.

3. You can use standard Windows techniques to move, size and maximize the document windows and to switch between them.

Animate Text

Animated text can bring a document to life on the screen. However, you should know that animated text features will not convert to HTML

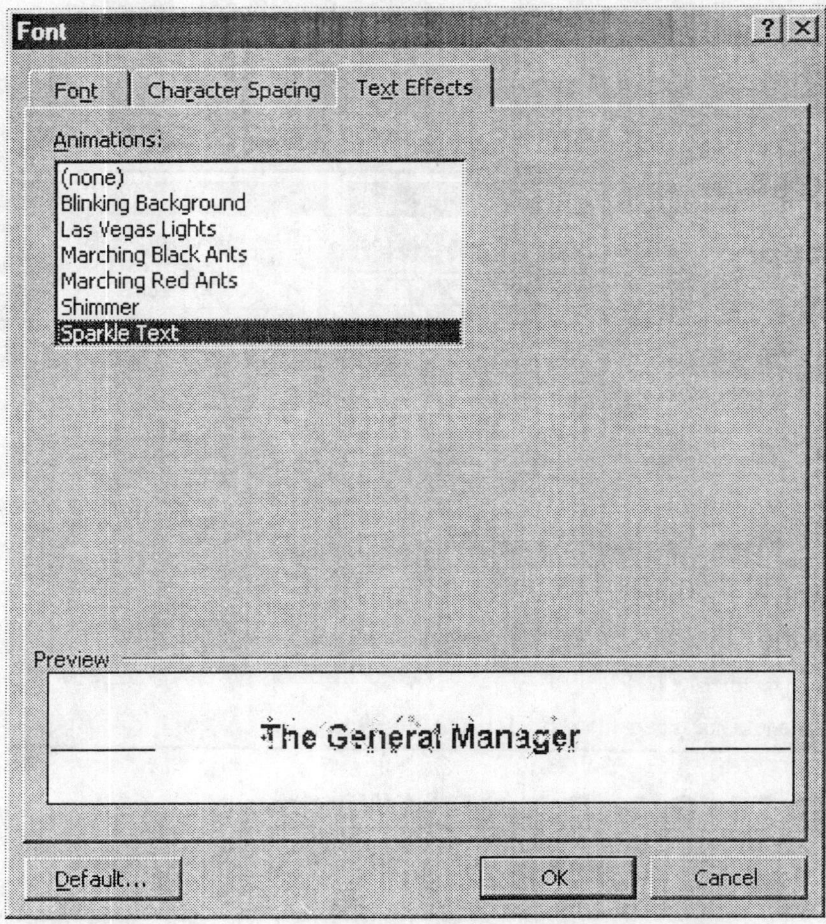

if you are creating a document for the Web. Of course, animated text can't translate to the printer, so text animation features should be reserved for documents that will be read online and in Word.

Applying Animated Text

1. Select the text you want to animate.
2. Right-click the text and choose **Font** from the pop-up menu.
3. The Font dialog box appears.
4. Choose an effect from the **Animation** list. Click Ok to close the dialog box and apply the animation effect to your text.

Reveal Formatting

This is a new feature in Word 2002. This when selected reveals the formatting of the text in the Task Pane.

Applying Reveal Formatting

1. Select the text whose formatting you want to know.
2. From the **Format** menu select the option of **Reveal Formatting**.
3. The Reveal Formatting appears in the **Task Pane**.
4. You can see the complete formatting of **The General Manager** on the next page.

With this ends the various options of proofing and changing the styles of the document.

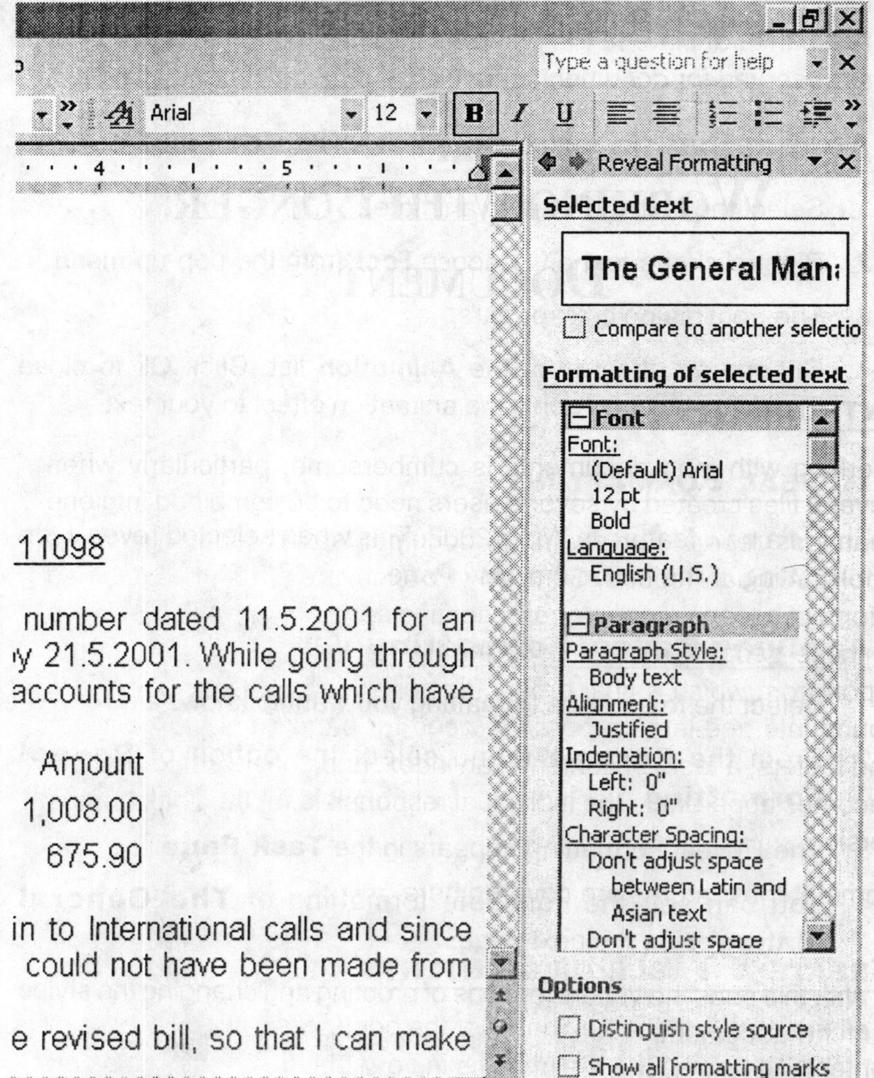
Type a question for help
Arial
12
Reveal Formatting
Selected text
The General Man
Compare to another selectio
Formatting of selected text
Font
Font:
(Default) Arial
12 pt
Bold
Language:
English (U.S.)
Paragraph
Paragraph Style:
Body text
Alignment:
Justified
Indentation:
Left: 0"
Right: 0"
Character Spacing:
Don't adjust space between Latin and Asian text
Don't adjust space
Options
Distinguish style source
Show all formatting marks
11098
number dated 11.5.2001 for an
y 21.5.2001. While going through
accounts for the calls which have
Amount
1,008.00
675.90
in to International calls and since
could not have been made from
e revised bill, so that I can make

5

Working with Longer Document

Introduction

Working with long documents is cumbersome, particularly when several files created by several users need to be combined into one seamless report. For example, documents and reports such as Books, Annual Reports, Company Policies, are often the combined efforts of a team of people representing several departments. Each of these people create a separate file for their contribution to the report from which a final product is generated. When the files are bound into one large report, the need for page numbers, headers and footers, a table of contents, an index, and consistent formatting becomes apparent to the individual responsible for the final, printed version.

Some of the features are covered here.

Create a Table of Contents

In all the books, in the beginning of the book, you will find a table of contents. It lists all the main topics in your document and notes on which page number each topic starts. Word helps you generate a table of contents for your document automatically. The easiest method for doing this is to assign one of Word's built-in heading styles (Heading 1 to Heading 9) to the headings you want to include in the table of contents. If you are not using Word's heading styles, you must assign a table of contents level to the styles you are using or mark text for inclusion in the table of contents.

Create a Table

1. Apply the built-in heading styles Heading 1 to Heading 9 to the headings in your document that you want to include in the table of contents.

2. Place the cursor in the document where you want the table of contents to appear. You may want to add a section or page break before your document text so the table of contents is on a separate page. You may also want to add a title for your page, such as "Table of Contents".

3. Click the **Insert** menu and select **Reference** and **Index and Tables**. The Index and Tables dialog box appears.

4. Select the **Table of Contents** tab if it is not already displayed.

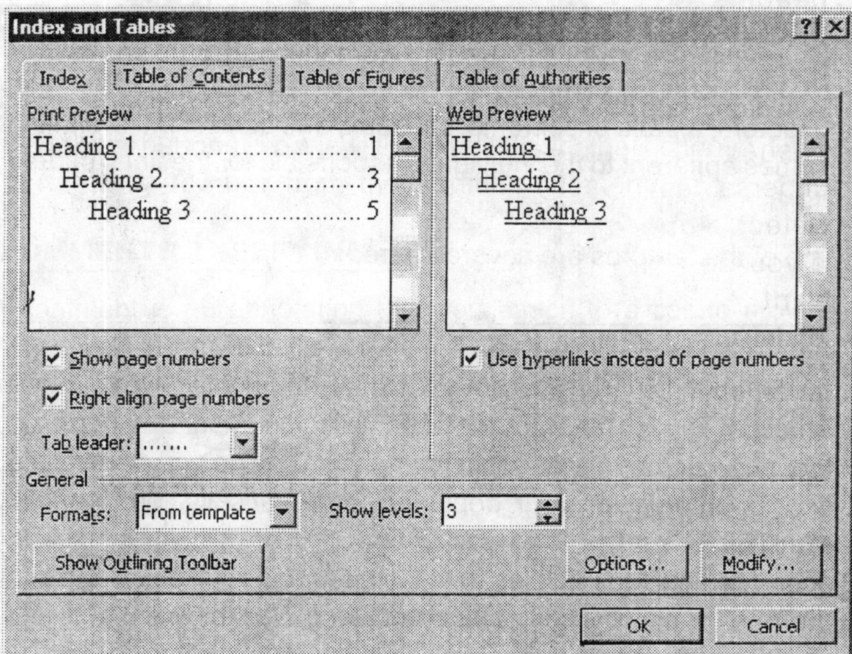

5. From the **Formats** drop-down list, select the format that you want to apply to the table of contents. As you click a format, a sample appears in the **Print Preview** window and in the **Web Preview** window.

6. If you want the page numbers to appear for each topic, click **Show Page Numbers** to enable that option. Click **Right Align Page Numbers** if you want the page numbers lined up on the right margin.

7. In the **Show Levels** box, enter the number of headings levels you want to appear in the table of contents, or use the up and down arrows to select the number.

8. From the **Tab Leader** drop-down list, select the repeat character (leader) you want to appear between the heading and the page number (it can be dots, dashes or underscores). Select **None** if you do not want any leaders.

9. If you want to change the format, choose **Modify** to open the Style dialog box.

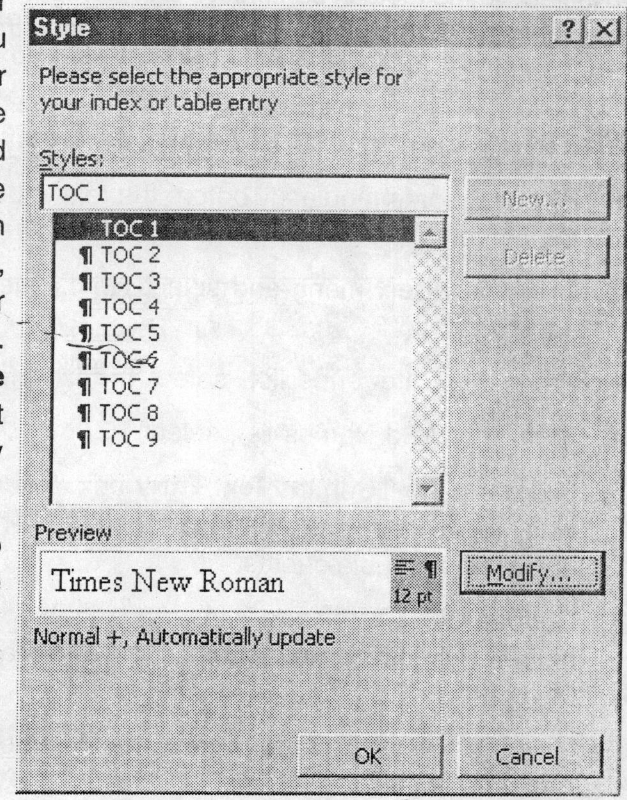

From the Styles box, select the heading level you want to change in the table of contents and then choose Modify to open the **Modify Style** dialog box. Choose **Format** to select the type of format you want to specify and then select the formatting options you desire. Choose Ok to return to the Style dialog box, and then choose **Apply**.

10. Choose Ok. Word generates the table of contents for your document.

MARKING TEXT FOR TABLE OF CONTENTS

Table of contents entries can be marked by field codes, marking each entry as you type. Use this method if you have items you want to include in the table of contents, but those items do not have styles associated with them. You can use this method in combination with creating tables of contents using styles.

Marking Entries of a Table of Contents

1. Place cursor immediately before the text you want to include in the contents.
2. Click the **Insert** menu and select **Field**. The Field dialog box appears.
3. From the Categories list, select **Index and Tables**.
4. From the Field Names list, select **TC**.
5. Following the TC in the **Text Entry** box, enter the text that you want to appear in the table of contents. The text should be enclosed in double quotes.
6. Choose Ok. A field code is inserted in the document text but is hidden. Choose **Show/Hide** on the Standard toolbar to see the code.

Perform the following steps to generate a table of contents from your marked entries.

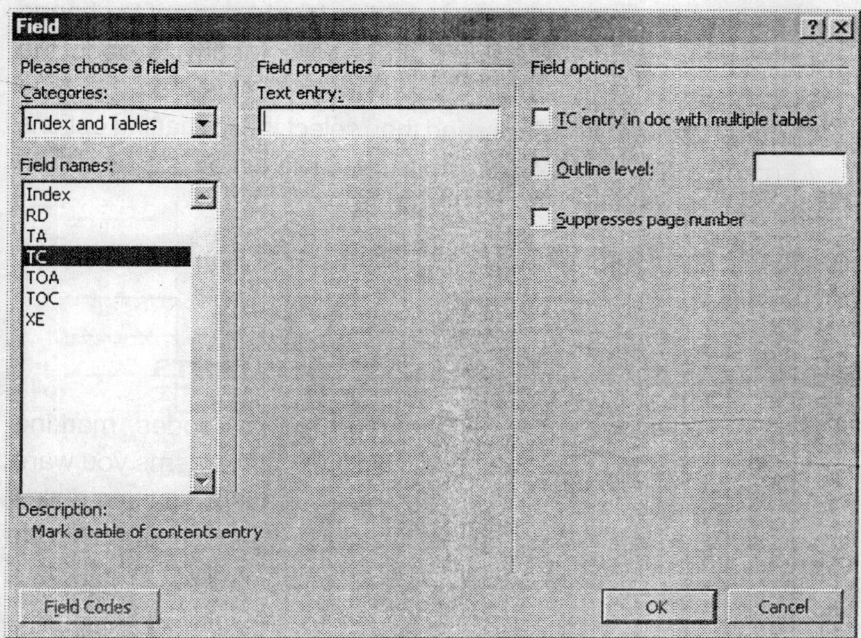

Generate a Table of Contents from Marked Entries

1. Place the insertion point where you want the table of contents to appear.
2. Click the **Insert** menu and select **Index and Tables**. The Index and Tables dialog box appears.
3. Select the **Table of Contents** tab if it is not already selected.
4. Choose **Options** to open the **Table of Contents Options** dialog box. Click **Table Entry Fields**. Choose Ok to return to the Index and Tables dialog box.
5. Choose Ok to generate the table of contents.

Create an Index

An index usually appears at the end of the book. It contains references

Table of Contents Options
Build table of contents from:
Styles
Available styles:
TOC level:
Body Text
Footer
Header
Heading 1
1
Heading 2
2
Heading 3
3
Outline levels
Table entry fields
Reset
OK
Cancel

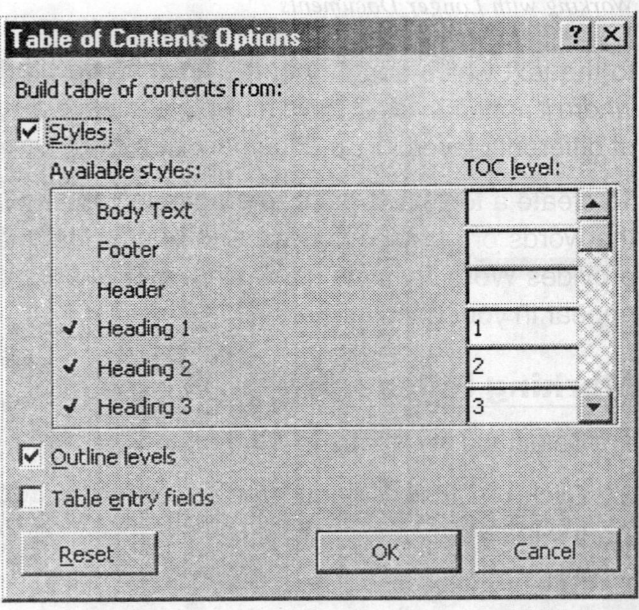

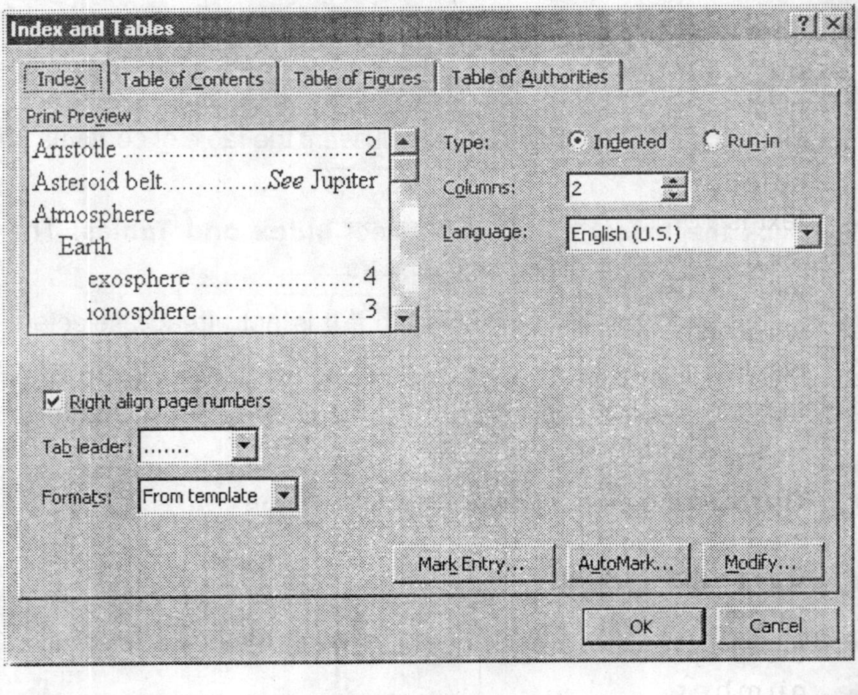

Index and Tables
Index
Table of Contents
Table of Figures
Table of Authorities
Print Preview
Aristotle 2
Asteroid belt................See Jupiter
Atmosphere
Earth
exosphere 4
ionosphere 3
Type:
Indented
Run-in
Columns:
2
Language:
English (U.S.)
Right align page numbers
Tab leader:
Formats:
From template
Mark Entry...
AutoMark...
Modify...
OK
Cancel

to the text which appears in the book alongwith the page number where it appears. It can have multiple entries, e.g., a word can appear at different places in the document at various pages.

To create a topic and page reference in your index, you must mark the words or phrases you want to appear in the index. Doing this provides Word a way to know what and where indexed references appear in your document.

Marking Index Entries

1. Select the text that you want for the index entry.
2. Click the **Insert** menu and select **Index and Tables** to open the Index and Tables dialog box.
3. Select the **Index** tab.
4. Choose **Mark Entry**. The Mark Index Entry box appears.
5. The selected text appears in the **Main Entry** box. Edit that text or enter new text if the selected text is not exactly what you want to display in the index.

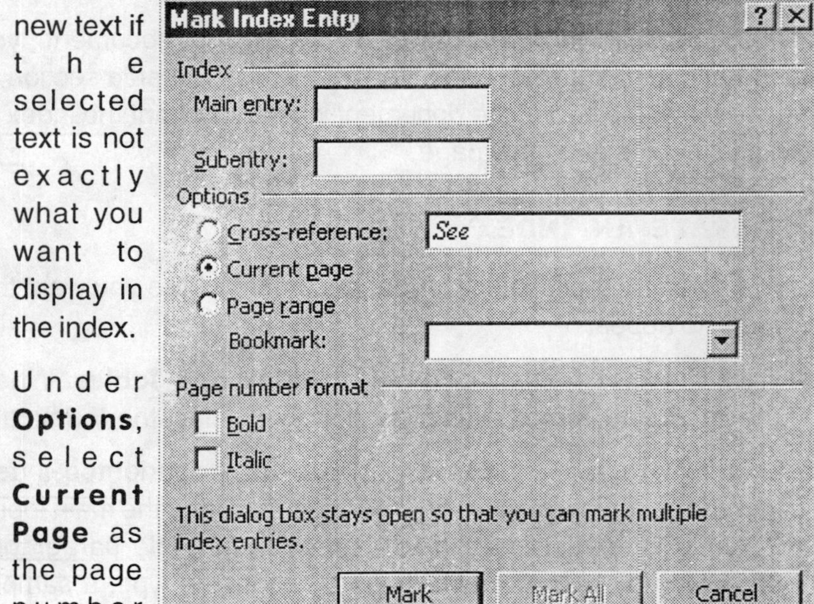

6. Under **Options**, select **Current Page** as the page number

you want cited in the index. If you want to add formatting to the page numbers as they appear in the index, click **Bold** or *Italics* under **Page Number Format**.

7. Choose **Mark** to mark the entry. Choose **Mark All** to mark the first occurrence in each paragraph of your document that exactly matches the text and case of the entry.
8. The dialog box remains open so you may make additional index entries. To make another entry click in the document to make it active, then select the text in the document or click immediately after it, click back in the **Mark Index Entry** dialog box to make it active, and repeat steps 5 to 7.
9. Repeat step 7 for each index entry you want to make in this session. Choose **Close** to close the Mark Index Entry dialog box.

Word marks each index entry by inserting a field immediately after the entry text in your document. If the field is not visible, choose **Show/Hide** on the **Standard** toolbar.

After you have all the index entries marked in your document., you are ready to generate the index. You may want to insert a section or page break at the end of the document where you want the index to start so it begins on a new page.

Generate an Index

1. Put cursor at the location in your document where you want the index to appear.
2. Click the **Insert** menu and select **Index and Tables**. When the Index and Tables dialog box appears, select the **Index** tab.
3. Under **Type**, click **Indented** or **Run-In**. An indented index lists the subentries as indented paragraphs under the main topic. A run-in index lists all the subentries in a single paragraph, separated by semicolons. When you choose a type, a sample appears in the Print Preview window.

4. To choose from the predefined index formats available in Word, select one from the **Formats** list. When you do, the **Print Preview** changes to show you an example of that format.

5. Because the index can be lengthy but the lines are short, you may want to set it up to run in columns. Enter the number of columns you want in the **Columns** box.

6. Page numbers in an index generally follow immediately after the topics. If you would rather have your numbers appear on the right side of the line, click **Right Align Page Numbers**. Choose a character from the **Tab Leader** drop-down list, if you want to join the entry text with the page number by a tap leader.

7. Choose Ok to generate the index.

USING BOOKMARKS

A bookmark is a location in your document or a selection of text that you name for reference purposes. After you place a bookmark, you can return to the same location again and again by selecting the bookmark when you use Word's **Go To** feature (pressing **Ctrl+G** or **F5**). Bookmarks are especially useful when you are modifying or editing a large document. Create a bookmark when you close the document so on opening it again, you

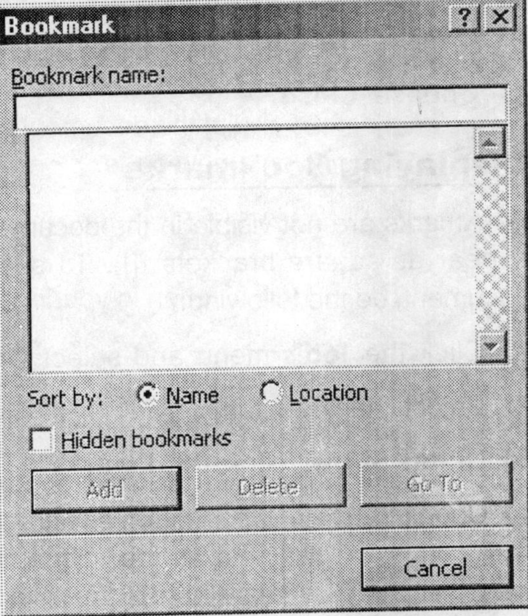

can find where you left. Bookmarks are also useful as reference points for cross-references, index entries, and macros.

Add a Bookmark

1. Place cursor where you want to insert the bookmark.
2. Click the **Insert** menu and select **Bookmark** to open the Bookmark dialog box.
3. Type a name for the bookmark in the **Bookmark Name** box (do not enter any spaces in the name) or select one from the list. If you select the name of an existing bookmark, it will move the bookmark location to the current position of your cursor.
4. Choose **Add**.

Deleting Bookmark

1. Click the **Insert** menu and select **Bookmark**.
2. Select the name of the bookmark you want to remove.
3. Choose **Delete**.
4. Choose **Close**.

Displaying Bookmarks

Bookmarks are not visible in the document. They can be made to appear as square brackets ([]). To see the bookmarks in your document, do the following:

1. Click the **Tools** menu and select **Options**.
2. Select the **View** tab.
3. Under **Show**, click **Bookmarks**.
4. Choose Ok.

6

Creating Documents using Wizards

Introduction

Wizards are there in any software to guide and create for you in a flash the document/output which you are trying to create using the software. These are there for like having fast food instead of having a good sit down dinner. Here everything is ready made and you have to just fill in the data and the document is ready for you. I will start with Fax wizard. This is how you will use it.

Using Fax Wizard

The Fax Wizard helps you in sending an electronic fax, merge several names to a fax, or print a cover sheet to send using a fax machine. The steps involved in running a fax wizard are:

1. Open the document you want to fax. Click the File menu and select New.
2. When the New dialog box opens select the Letters & Faxes tab.
3. Click the Fax Wizard icon to select it and then choose Ok.
4. The Fax Wizard dialog box appears. The left side of the dialog box has a progress chart.
5. Choose Next. The Fax Wizard asks "Which document do you want to send?" The name of the document that is currently open

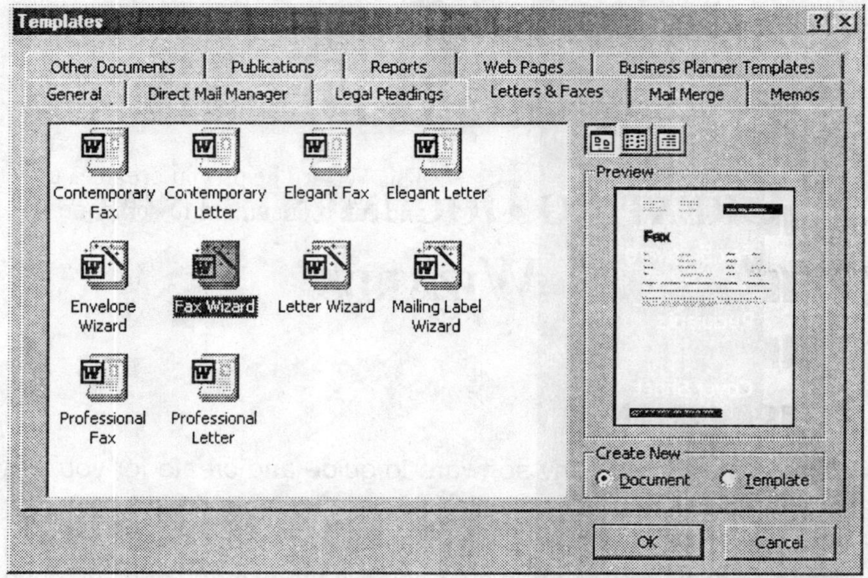

automatically appears in the drop-down list box under "The Following Document".

6. To send the current document, click "The Following Document" and leave the name of the current document in the box. To send a short message, you can include the message on the cover sheet and send it alone. To do this, click "Just a Cover Sheet with a Note".

7. If you are sending a document with your cover sheet, click "With a Cover Sheet" to send a cover sheet with the document you choose or "Click without a Cover Sheet" to send the document by itself.

8. Choose Next. The Fax Wizard asks you to identify the fax software you are going to use to send the fax. "Microsoft Fax" is one of the choice. If you have another fax program, click "A Different Fax Program Which is Installed on this System". Then select the name of your fax program from the drop-down list below "Which of the Following is Your Fax Program"

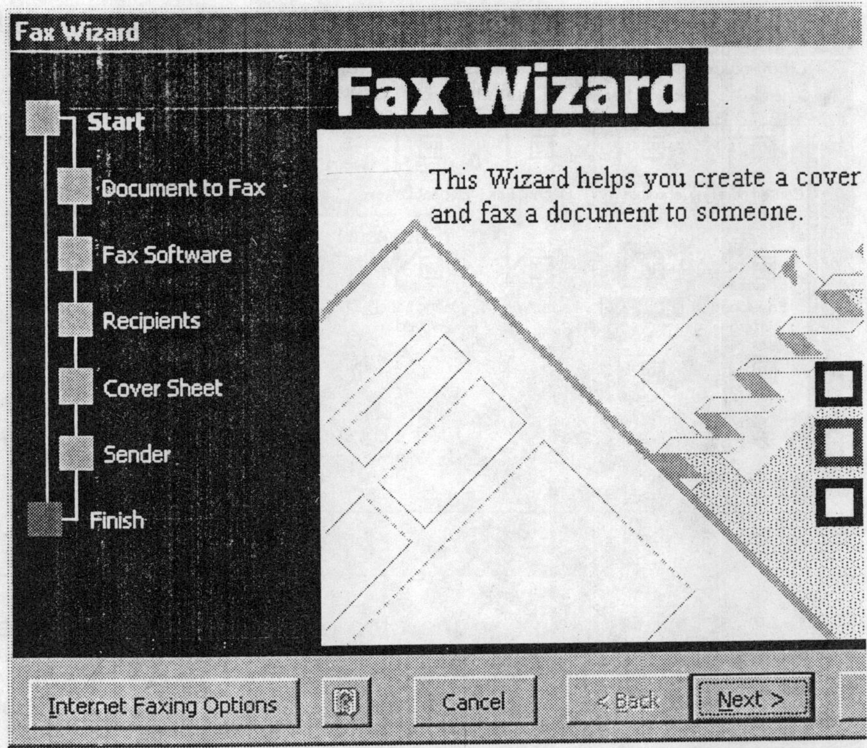

If you don't see your fax program listed, choose "Other" and select the name of your fax software. If you do not have fax software loaded on your system, click "I want to Print My Document so I Can Send it from a Separate Fax Machine".

9. Choose Next. The Fax Wizard asks you the names of the recipients of your fax. If you have used the Fax Wizard before, the names of recent recipients appear in the drop-down boxes and you can click a name to select it as a recipient.

   Or, you can click in a box and enter a name and then the corresponding fax telephone number (exactly as they should be dialed, including numbers your system requires to reach an outside line). If you use Microsoft Outlook, choose Address Book and select a name from your address book.

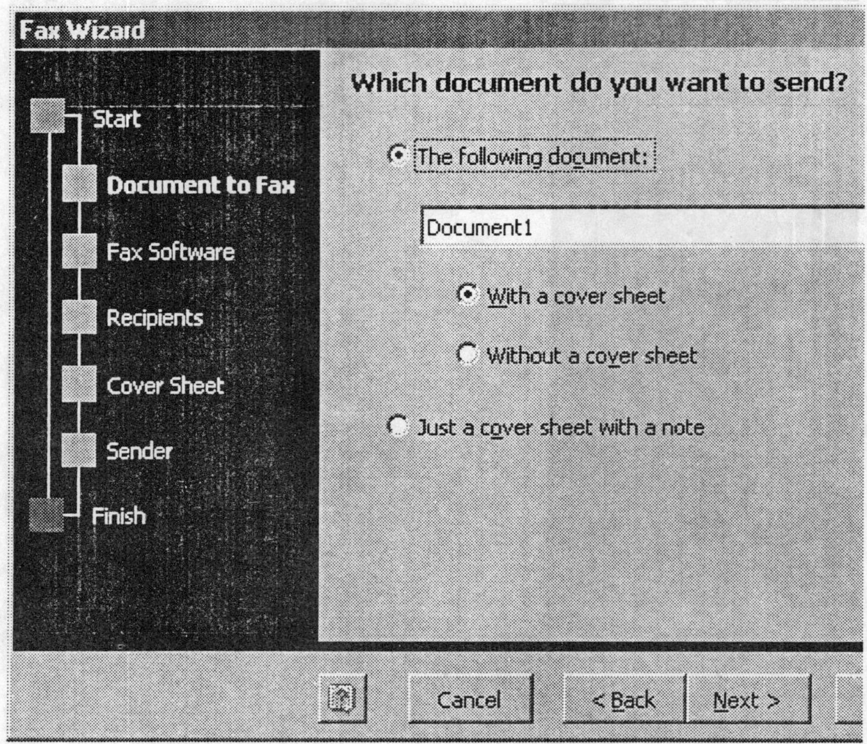

10. Choose Next. If you choose to create a cover sheet, the Fax Wizard lets you select one of the three styles of cover sheets it has it has available—Professional, contemporary, or Elegant. Click the style you want to use.

11. Choose Next. This screen asks who the fax is from. The Fax Wizard automatically pulls information from Word's User Information (click the Tools menu, select Options, and select the User Information tab to see what data is stored about you, and make any necessary changes).

    Enter or replace the information in the Name, Company, Mailing Address, Phone and Fax fields. Or, click Address Book and select information from your Outlook Address Book. If you elected not to use a cover sheet, you won't see this screen.

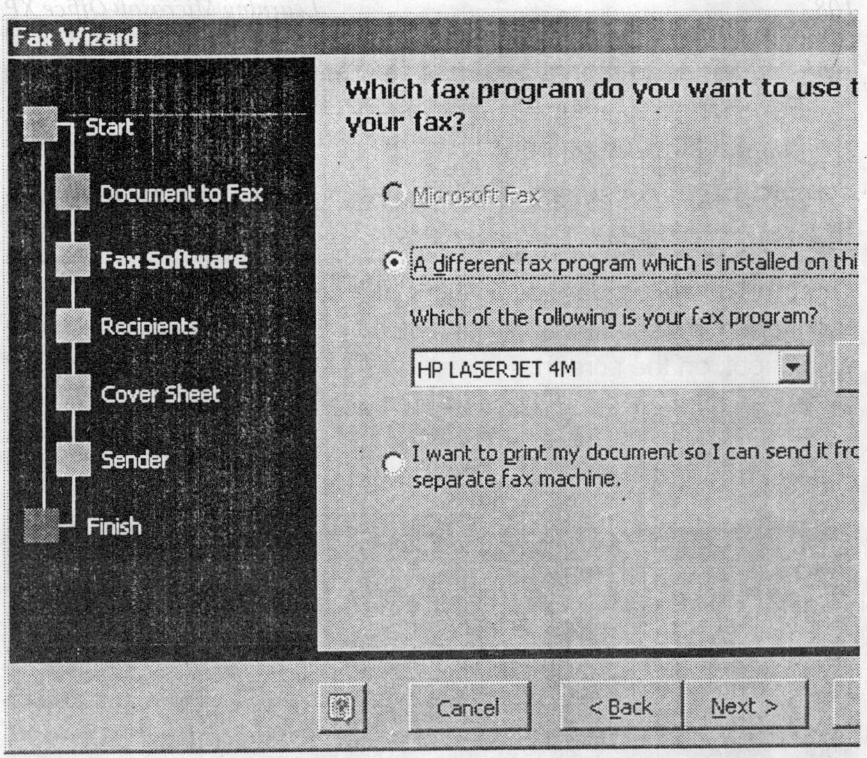

12. Choose Next. The final screen of the wizard reminds you to add any prefixes to the phone numbers that you need to access an outside line.
13. Choose Finish. The fax cover sheet document opens. Several "Click here and Type" fields appear. Click once on a field to select it and then enter the required information.

    Delete any fields that you don't want to appear on your fax cover sheet, and modify any other text as necessary.
14. Choose "Send Fax Now" on the Fax Wizard toolbar to send the fax. If you choose to send only a cover sheet with a note, click the field where it says "Click Here and Type Any Comments" and type your note.

The choose "Send Fax Now". If you are printing the fax so that you can send it on a separate fax machine, you won't see the Fax Wizard toolbar. For a fax addressed to a single recipient, just print the document.

For a fax addressed to multiple recipients, choose Merge to Printer on the Mail Merge toolbar.

On the following pages, you would see the various screens mentioned in the steps above, followed by the fax cover sheet as it would look on the screen.

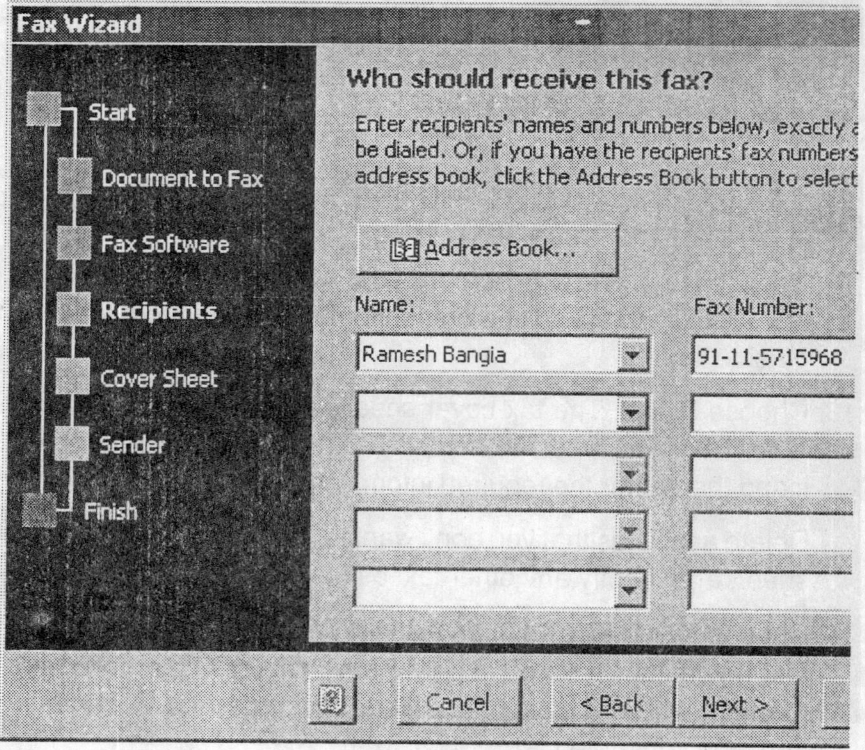

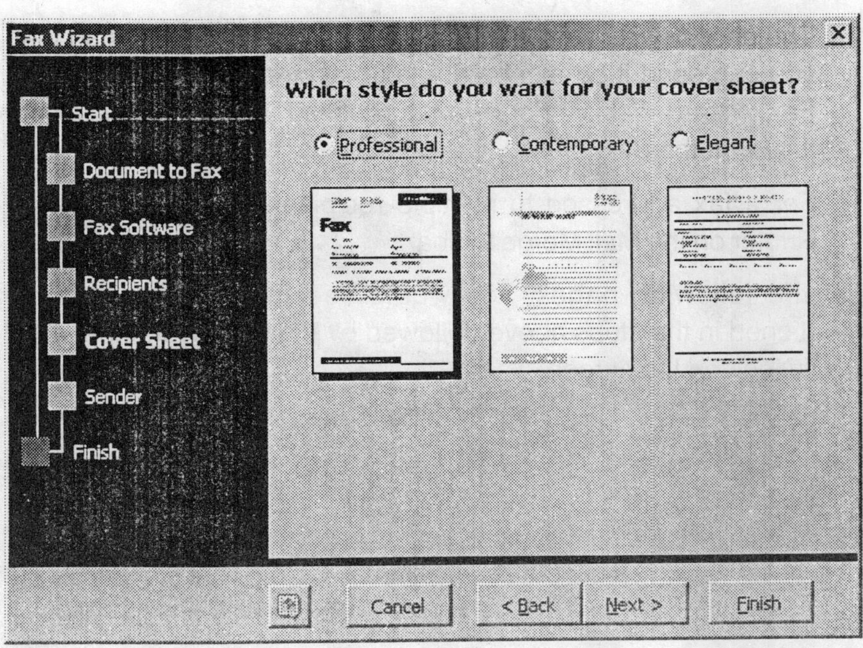
Fax Wizard
Start
Document to Fax
Fax Software
Recipients
Cover Sheet
Sender
Finish
Which style do you want for your cover sheet?
Professional
Contemporary
Elegant
Cancel
< Back
Next >
Finish

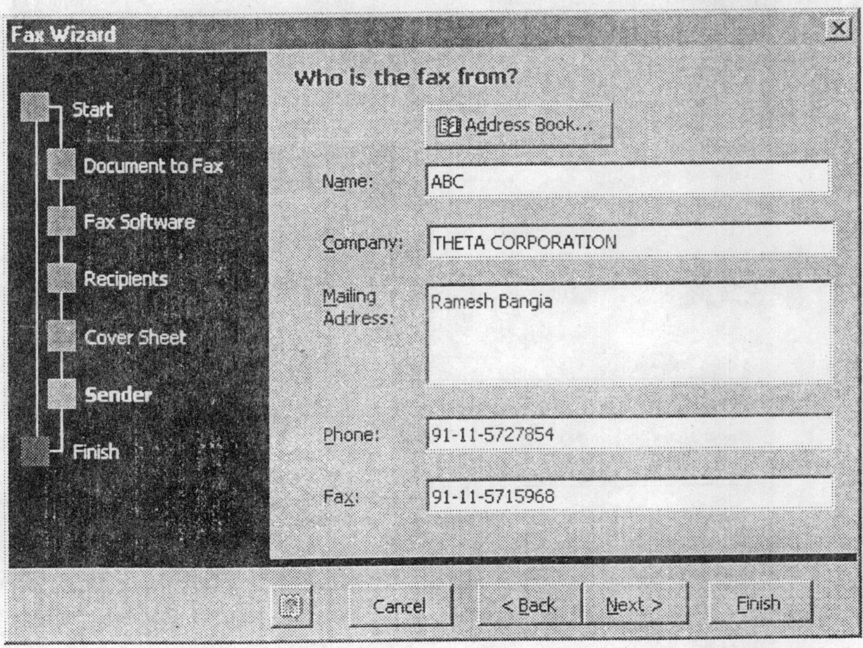
Fax Wizard
Start
Document to Fax
Fax Software
Recipients
Cover Sheet
Sender
Finish
Who is the fax from?
Address Book...
Name:
ABC
Company:
THETA CORPORATION
Mailing Address:
Ramesh Bangia
Phone:
91-11-5727854
Fax:
91-11-5715968
Cancel
< Back
Next >
Finish

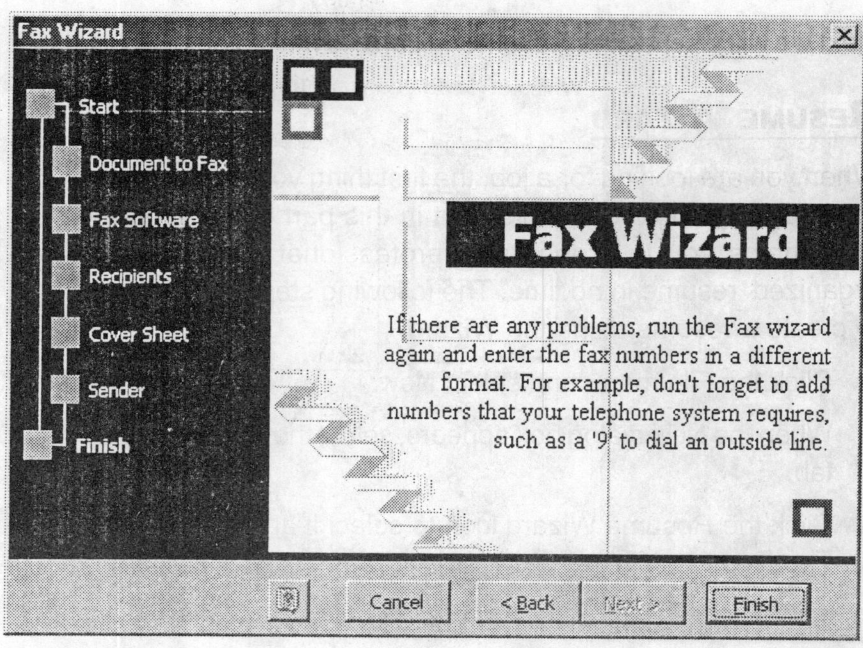
Fax Wizard
Start
Document to Fax
Fax Software
Recipients
Cover Sheet
Sender
Finish
Fax Wizard
If there are any problems, run the Fax wizard again and enter the fax numbers in a different format. For example, don't forget to add numbers that your telephone system requires, such as a '9' to dial an outside line.
Cancel
< Back
Next >
Finish

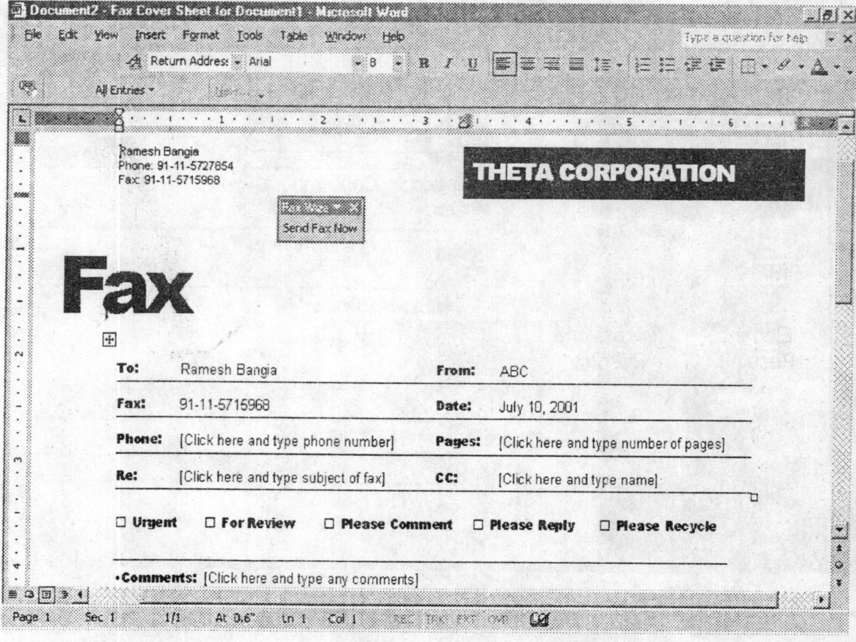
Document2 - Fax Cover Sheet for Document1 - Microsoft Word
File Edit View Insert Format Tools Table Window Help
Ramesh Bangia
Phone: 91-11-5727854
Fax: 91-11-5715968
THETA CORPORATION
Send Fax Now
Fax
To: Ramesh Bangia
From: ABC
Fax: 91-11-5715968
Date: July 10, 2001
Phone: [Click here and type phone number]
Pages: [Click here and type number of pages]
Re: [Click here and type subject of fax]
CC: [Click here and type name]
Urgent
For Review
Please Comment
Please Reply
Please Recycle
•Comments: [Click here and type any comments]

Next we will discuss the Resume Wizard, to make you own resume.

RESUME WIZARD

When you are looking for a job, the first thing you need a resume of yours or better known as Bio-data in this part of the World. Word 2002 helps you in preparing a professional looking, neat and organized resume in no time. The following steps you have to take to create a resume using the Wizard.

1. Click the File menu and select New.
2. When the New dialog box appears, select the "Other Documents" tab.
3. Click the Resume Wizard icon to select it and then choose Ok. The Resume Wizard dialog box appears.

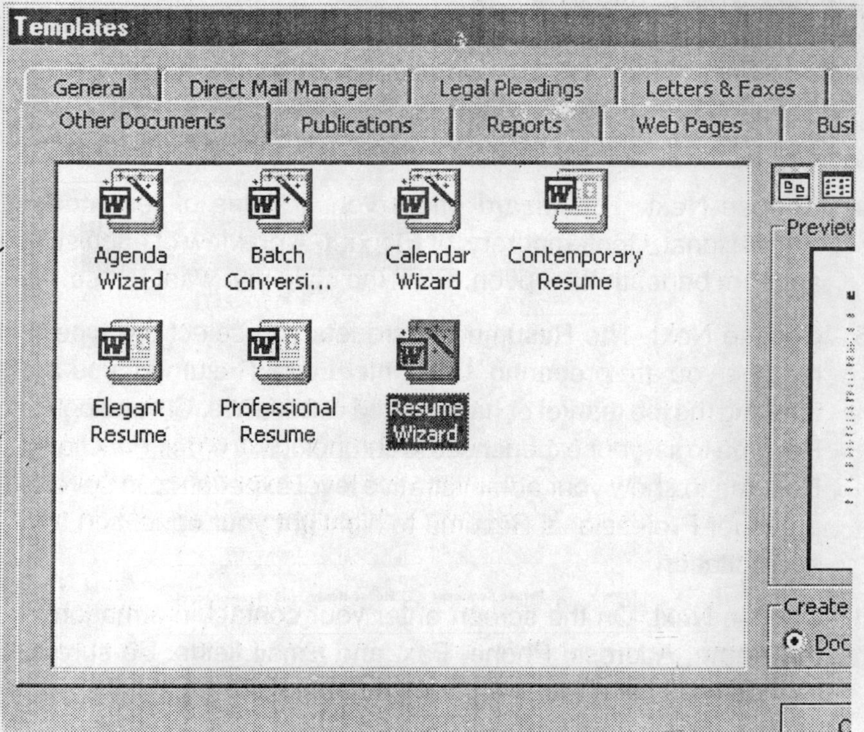

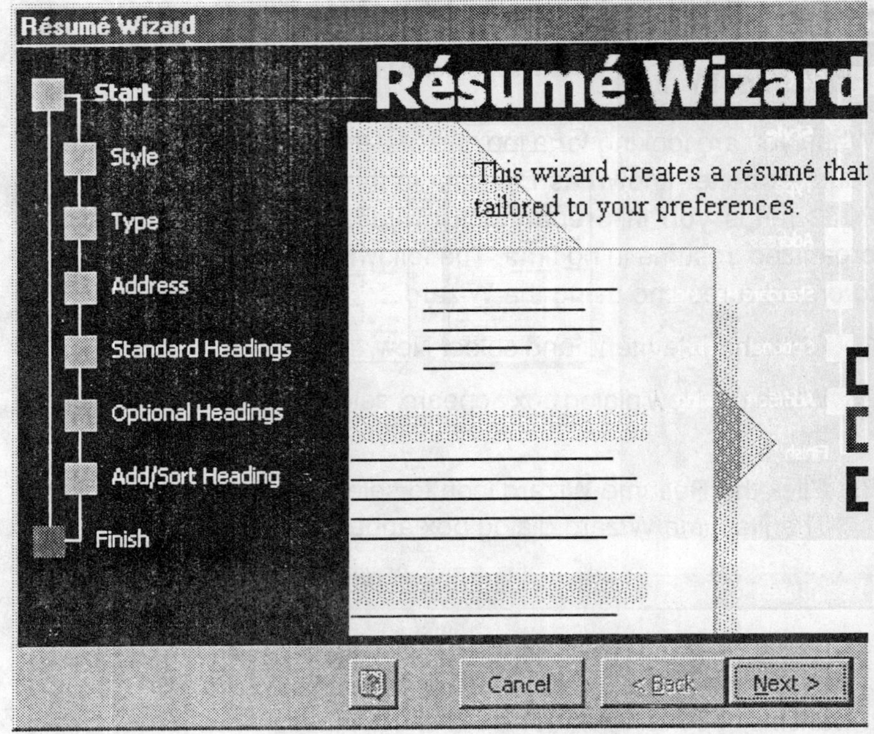

4. Choose Next. The wizard offers you 3 styles of resumes—Professional, Contemporary, or Elegant. A preview of each style appears beneath the option. Click the style you want to use.

5. Choose Next. The Resume Wizard lets you select the type of resume you are preparing. Use Entry-Level Resume if you are entering the job market or have limited experience, Chronological Resume to list your experiences in chronological order, Functional Resume to show your administrative level experience in several areas, or Professional Resume to highlight your education and accreditation.

6. Choose Next. On the screen enter your contact information in the Name, Address, Phone, Fax, and Email fields. Be sure to include are codes with the phone numbers.

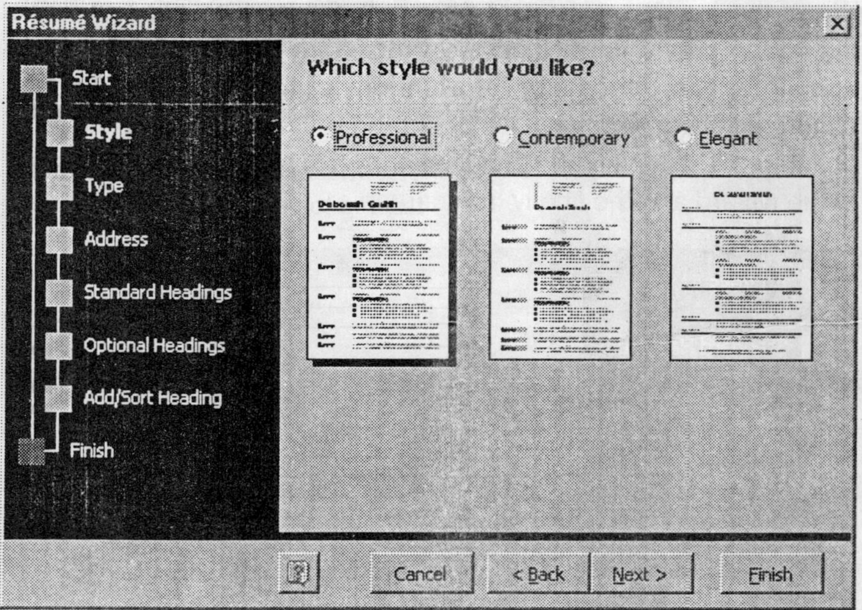

7. Choose Next. The Resume Wizard list a series of headings that can appear on the resume style you choose. Click the ones you want included on your resume to check those boxes and remove the check marks from the headings you don't want to use.

8. Choose Next. Another set of heading choices appears. These can be included, but you probably won't use them unless they are relevant to the objective of the resume. Click to check the headings you want to use.

9. Choose Next. The resume headings you selected are listed on this screen. If you want to add another heading, type the heading in the text box and then choose Add. To set the order of appearance in your resume, select a heading by clicking on it and then choose Move Up or Move Down to move the heading up or down in the list. To remove a heading from the list, select it and then choose Remove.

10. Choose Next. You have filled in all the information needed for the resume, so choose Finish.

When the resume document opens, it displays a series of fields marked in gray and enclosed by brackets ([ ]). Close these fields and enter the necessary information to complete the resume document. Then you save and print the resume as you would any document. On the following pages you would see the various screen of the wizard and the finally the resume.

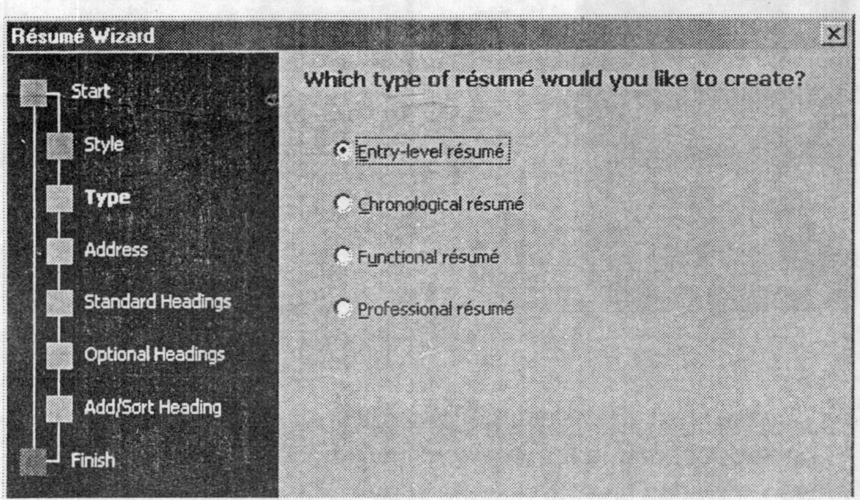

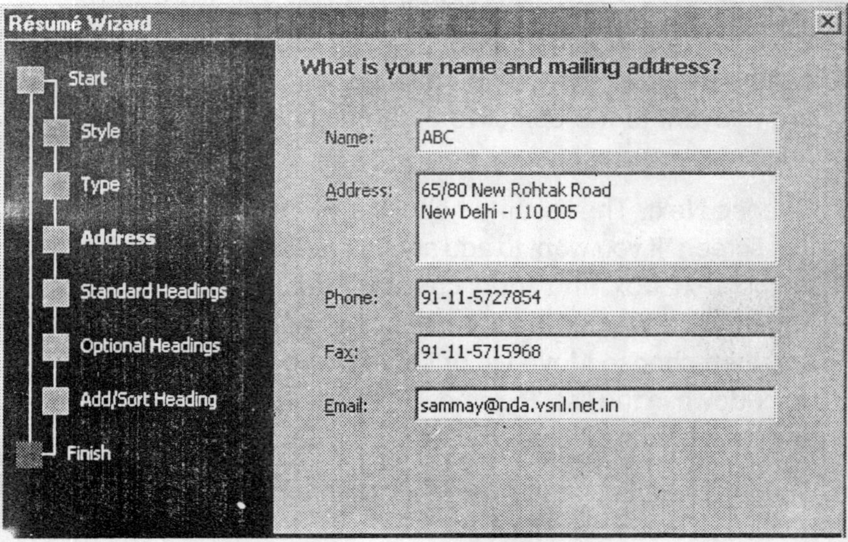

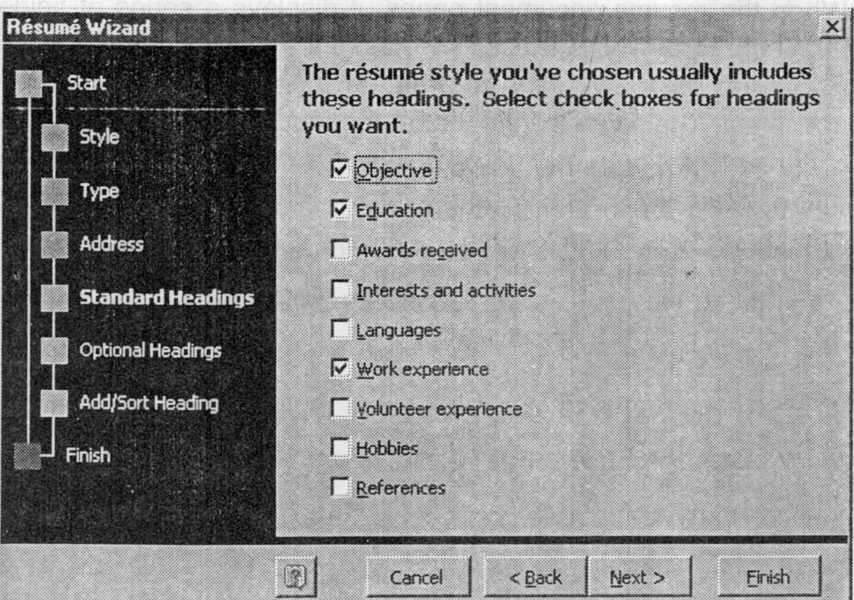
Résumé Wizard
Start
Style
Type
Address
Standard Headings
Optional Headings
Add/Sort Heading
Finish
The résumé style you've chosen usually includes these headings. Select check boxes for headings you want.
Objective
Education
Awards received
Interests and activities
Languages
Work experience
Volunteer experience
Hobbies
References
Cancel
< Back
Next >
Finish

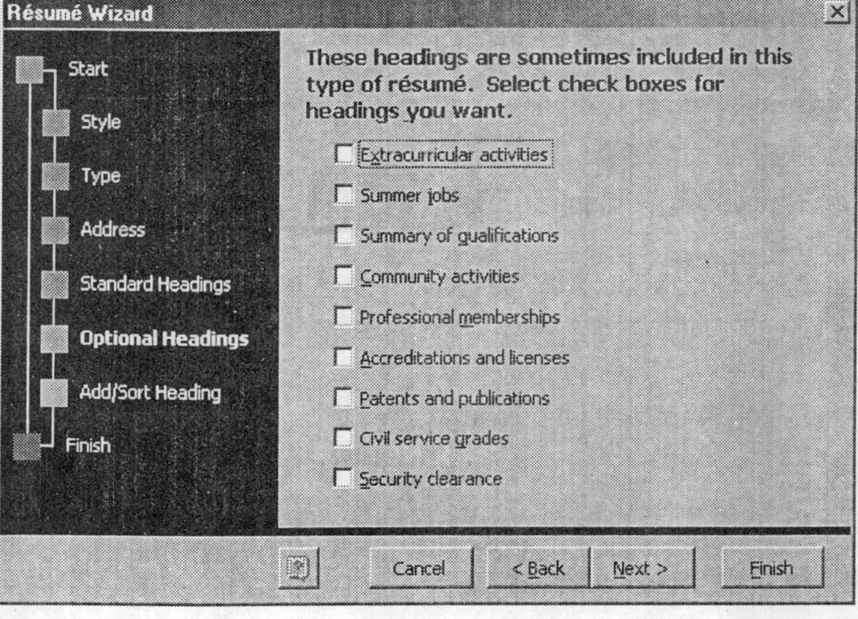
Résumé Wizard
Start
Style
Type
Address
Standard Headings
Optional Headings
Add/Sort Heading
Finish
These headings are sometimes included in this type of résumé. Select check boxes for headings you want.
Extracurricular activities
Summer jobs
Summary of qualifications
Community activities
Professional memberships
Accreditations and licenses
Patents and publications
Civil service grades
Security clearance
Cancel
< Back
Next >
Finish

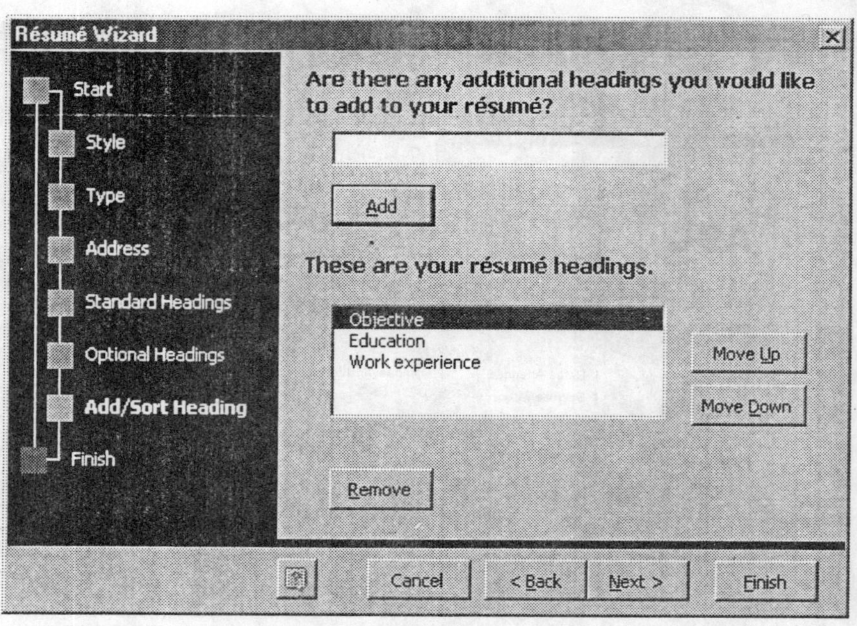
Résumé Wizard
Start
Style
Type
Address
Standard Headings
Optional Headings
Add/Sort Heading
Finish
Are there any additional headings you would like to add to your résumé?
Add
These are your résumé headings.
Objective
Education
Work experience
Move Up
Move Down
Remove
Cancel
< Back
Next >
Finish

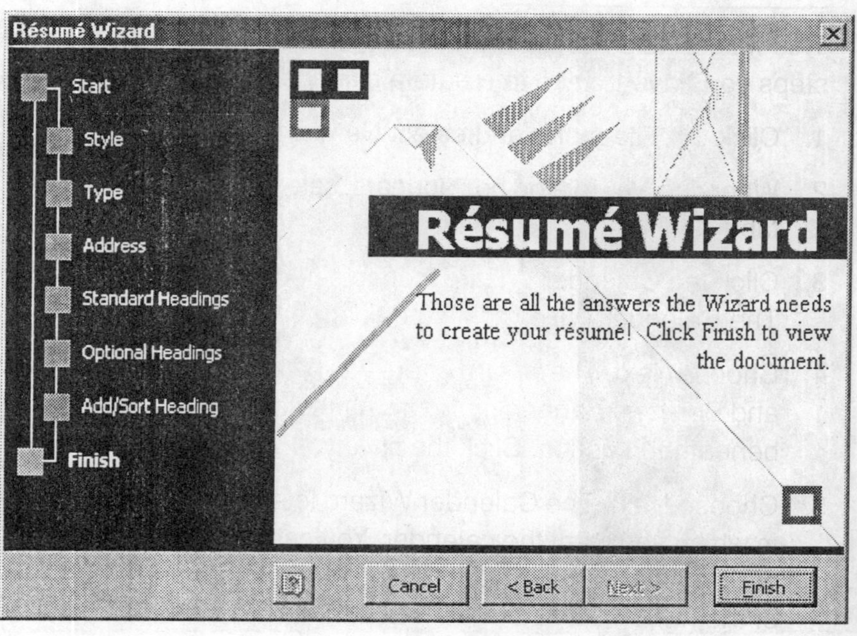
Résumé Wizard
Start
Style
Type
Address
Standard Headings
Optional Headings
Add/Sort Heading
Finish
Résumé Wizard
Those are all the answers the Wizard needs to create your résumé! Click Finish to view the document.
Cancel
< Back
Next >
Finish

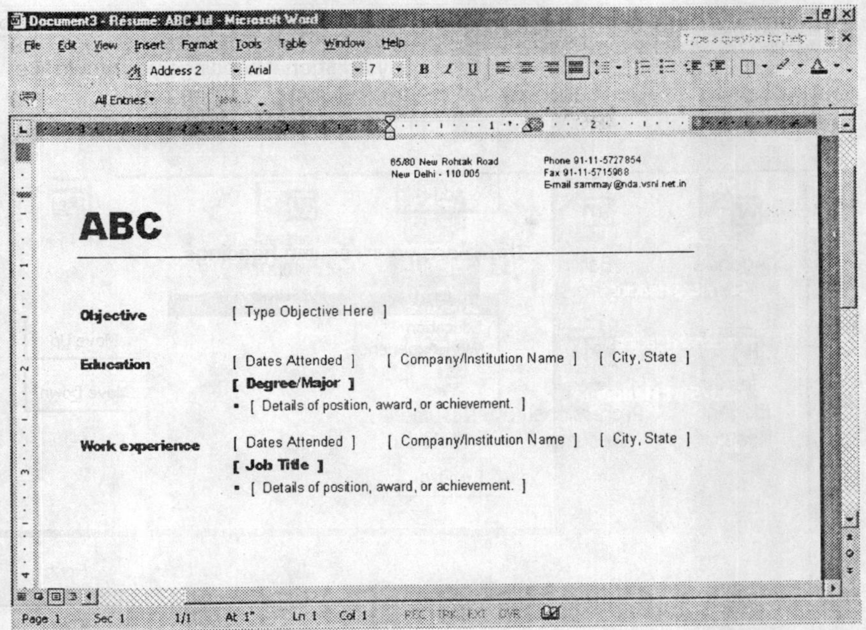

Calender Wizard

This wizard helps you in creating a monthly calender. The following steps you have to take to create a calender using the Wizard.

1. Click the File menu and select New.
2. When the New dialog box appears, select the "Other Documents" tab.
3. Click the Calender Wizard icon to select it and then choose Ok. The Calender Wizard dialog box appears.
4. Choose Next. The wizard offers you 3 styles of resumes—Boxes and Borders, Banner, or Jazzy. A preview of each style appears beneath the option. Click the style you want to use.
5. Choose Next. The Calender Wizard lets you select the direction in which you want the calender. You can select from the options of Portrait (vertical) or Landscape (horizontal). Select at any one of them.

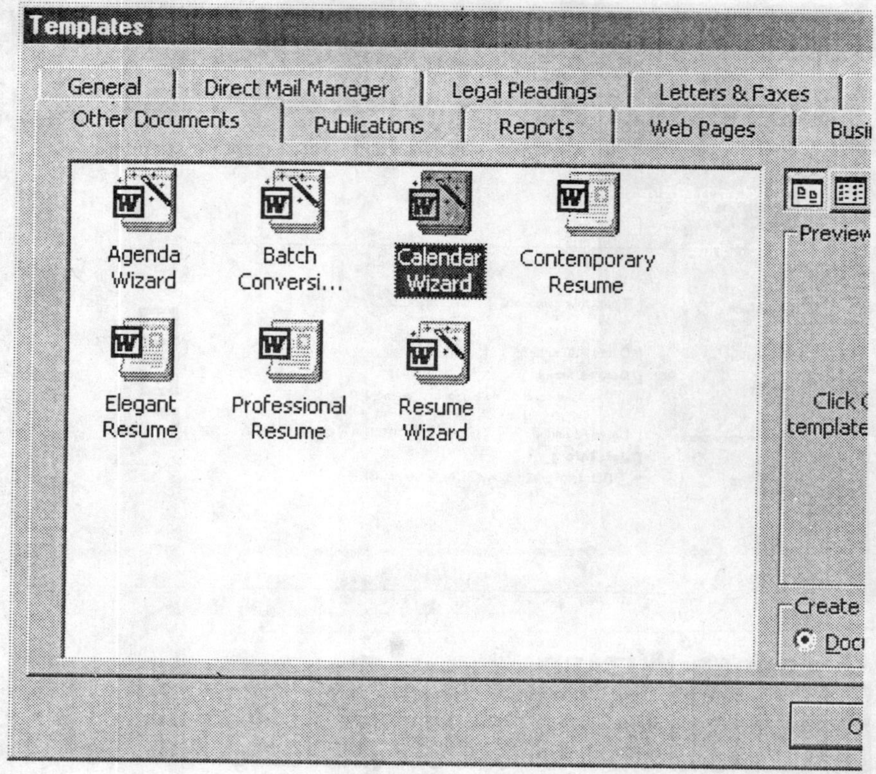

6. Choose Next. On the screen you will see the month and year of the calender. You have to fill in the starting and ending month and year of the calender.
7. Choose Next. You have filled in all the information needed for the calender, so choose Finish.

When the calender appears on the screen with the month and year which you have opted. On the following pages, you will see the various steps involved in creating the calender.

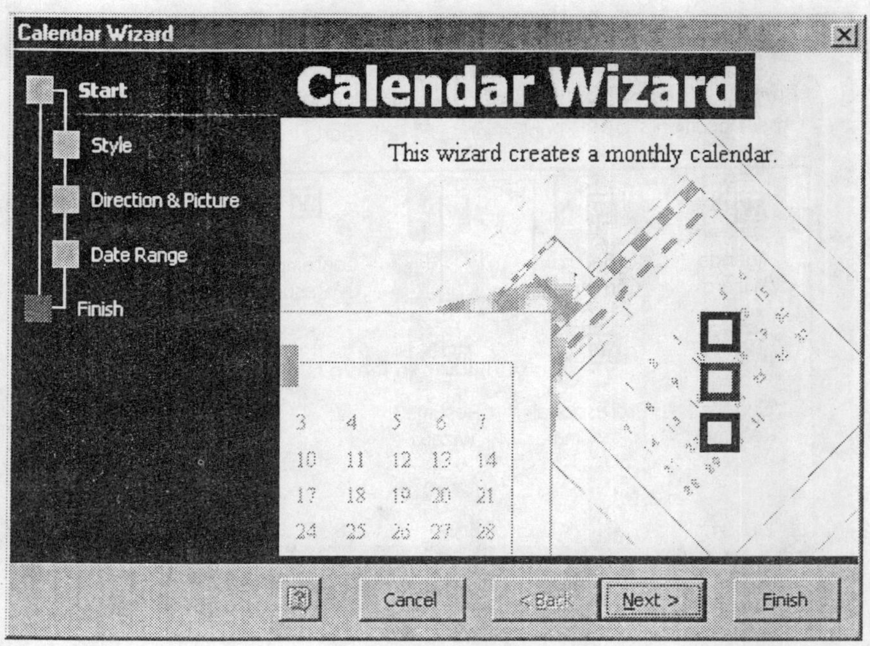
Calendar Wizard
Start
Style
Direction & Picture
Date Range
Finish
Calendar Wizard
This wizard creates a monthly calendar.
Cancel
< Back
Next >
Finish

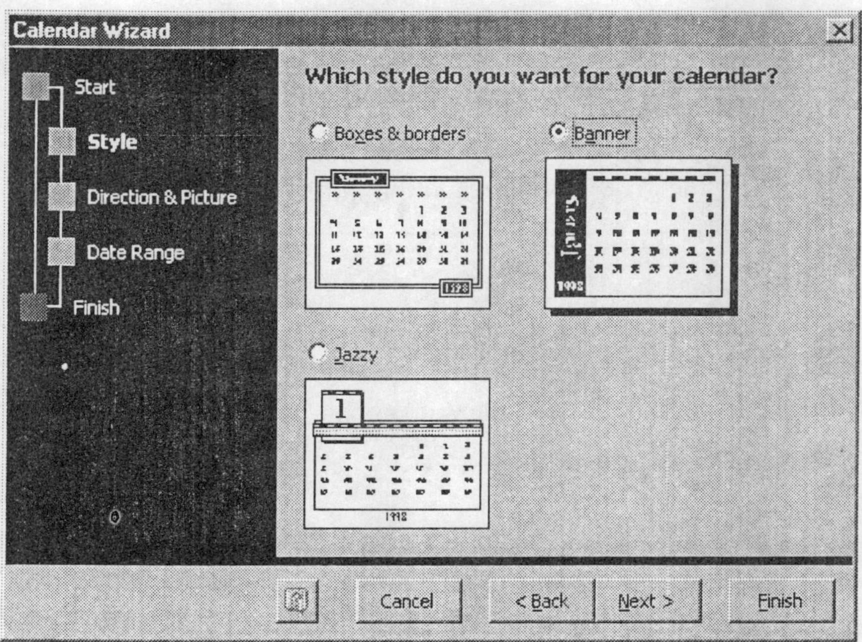
Calendar Wizard
Start
Style
Direction & Picture
Date Range
Finish
Which style do you want for your calendar?
Boxes & borders
Banner
Jazzy
Cancel
< Back
Next >
Finish

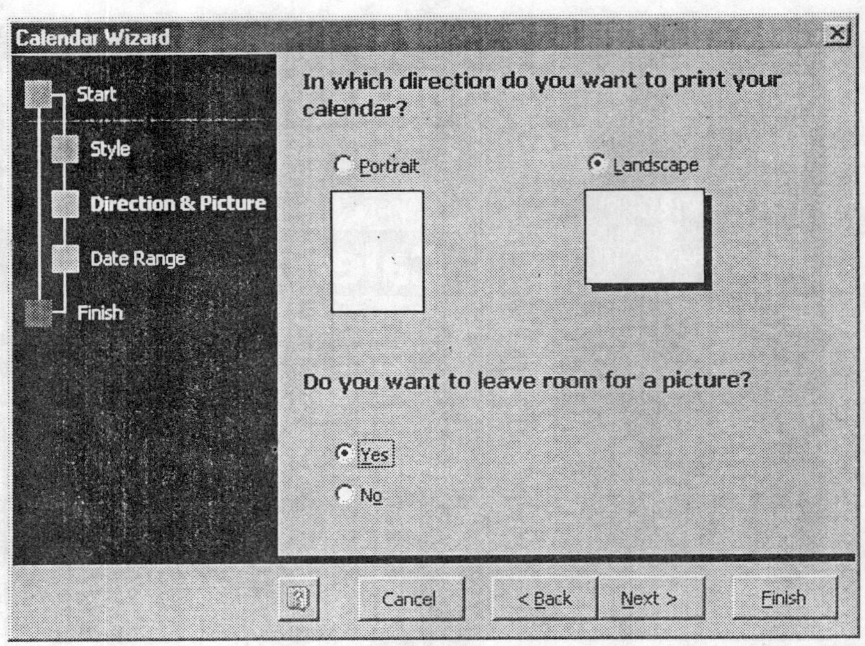
Calendar Wizard
Start
Style
Direction & Picture
Date Range
Finish
In which direction do you want to print your calendar?
Portrait
Landscape
Do you want to leave room for a picture?
Yes
No
Cancel
< Back
Next >
Finish

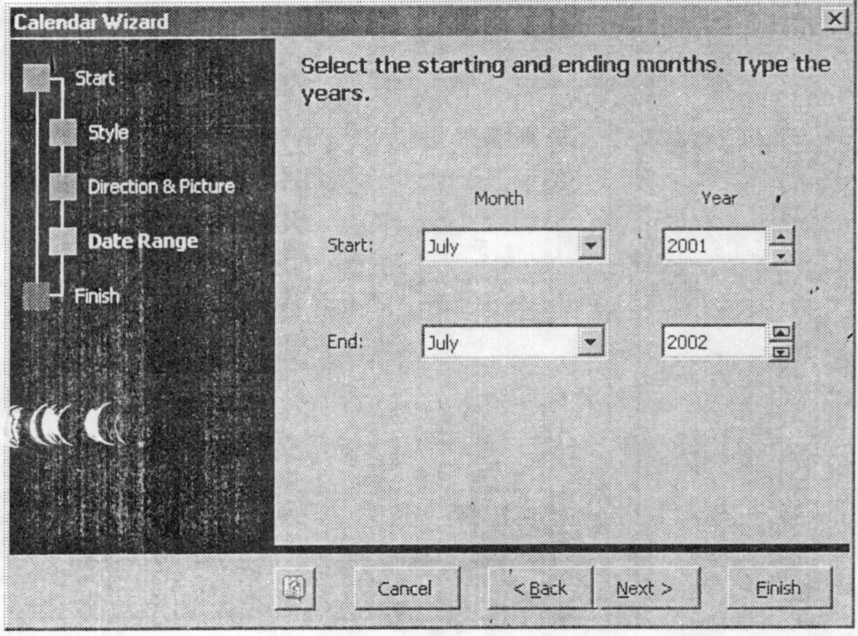
Calendar Wizard
Start
Style
Direction & Picture
Date Range
Finish
Select the starting and ending months. Type the years.
Month
Year
Start:
July
2001
End:
July
2002
Cancel
< Back
Next >
Finish

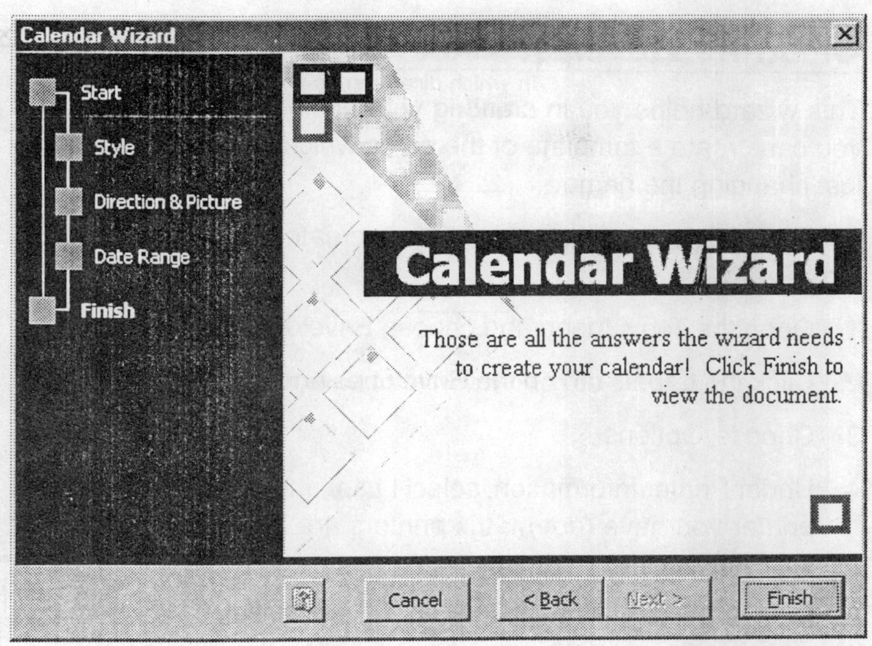
Calendar Wizard
Start
Style
Direction & Picture
Date Range
Finish
Calendar Wizard
Those are all the answers the wizard needs to create your calendar! Click Finish to view the document.
Cancel
< Back
Next >
Finish

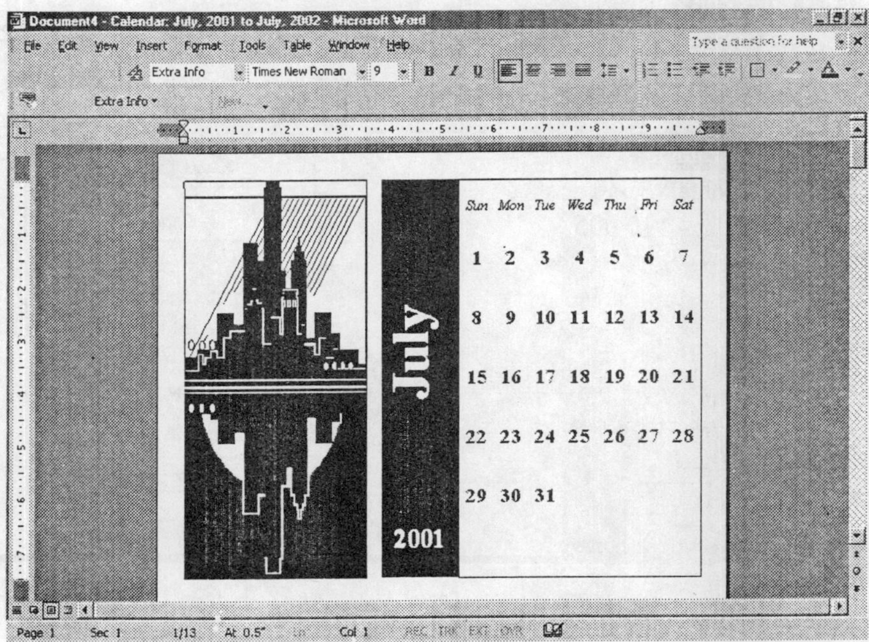
Document4 - Calendar: July, 2001 to July, 2002 - Microsoft Word
File Edit View Insert Format Tools Table Window Help
Type a question for help
Extra Info
Times New Roman
9
Sun Mon Tue Wed Thu Fri Sat
1 2 3 4 5 6 7
8 9 10 11 12 13 14
15 16 17 18 19 20 21
22 23 24 25 26 27 28
29 30 31
July
2001
Page 1 Sec 1 1/13 At 0.5" Col 1 REC TRK EXT OVR

CREATING BUSINESS LABELS

This wizard helps you in creating your business labels. Using this you can create a template of the cards which can be used later by just changing the name.

The following steps you have to take to create business cards using the Wizard.

1. Open the Tools menu and choose Envelopes and Labels.
2. Click the Labels tab on the Envelopes and Labels dialog box.
3. Choose Options.
4. Under Printer Information, select Laser and Ink Jet as the type of printer you have (dot matrix printers are not recommended for creating business cards).
5. From the Label Products drop-down list, select Avery Standard or Avery A4 and A5 sizes.

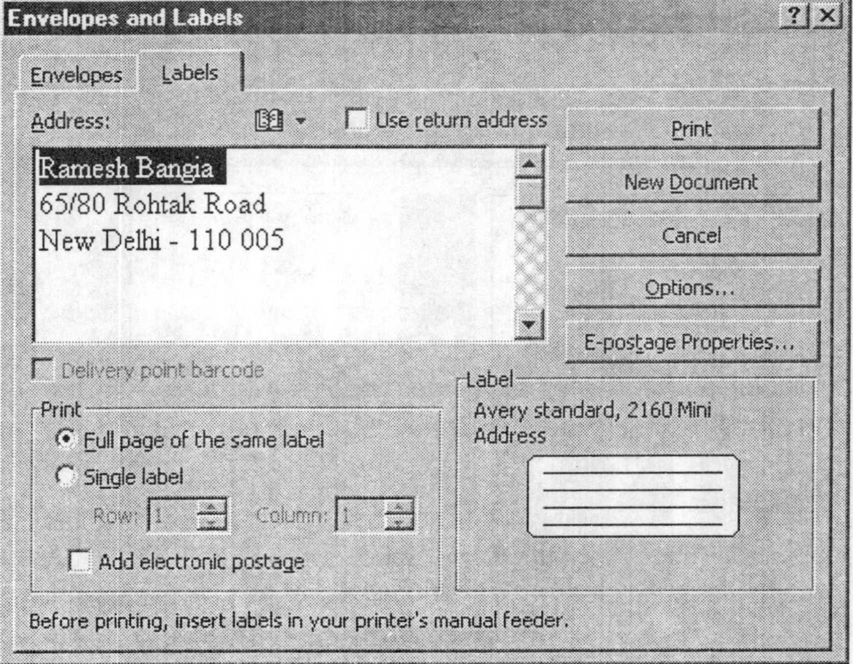

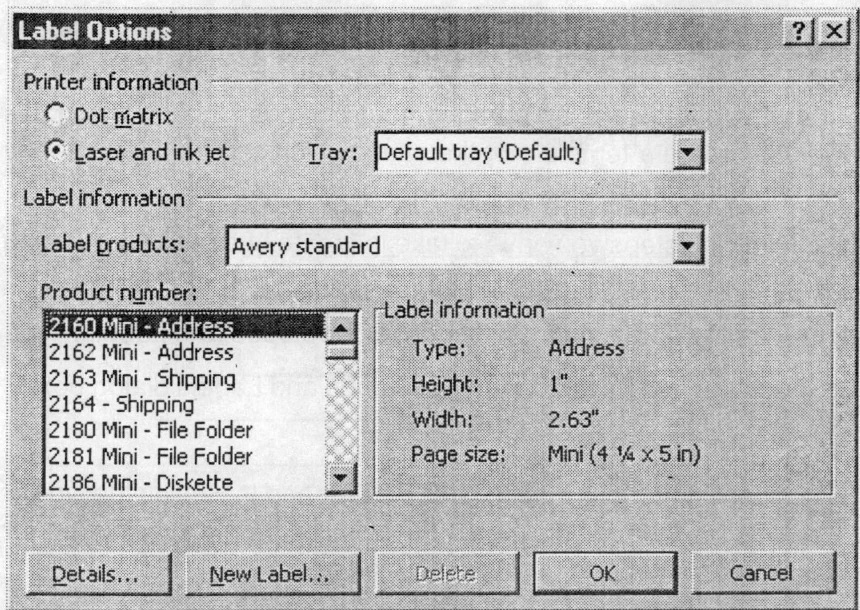

6. From the Product Number list, select one of the business card options. If the business card stock you choose is an Avery product, look for the same number that appears on the box. Otherwise, click each of the business card options and then check the Label information area until you see dimensions that match the size of one card (such as 3.5 inches wide by 2 inches high).
7. Choose Ok.
8. In the Address area, enter the text you want to appear on a single business card. Or, leave this area blank if you want to format the text after you create the business card document. It is often easier, to add the text in the document to make one business card that suits you, and then copy the text to each of the other cards on the page.
9. Select Full Page of the Same Label under Print.
10. Choose New Document.

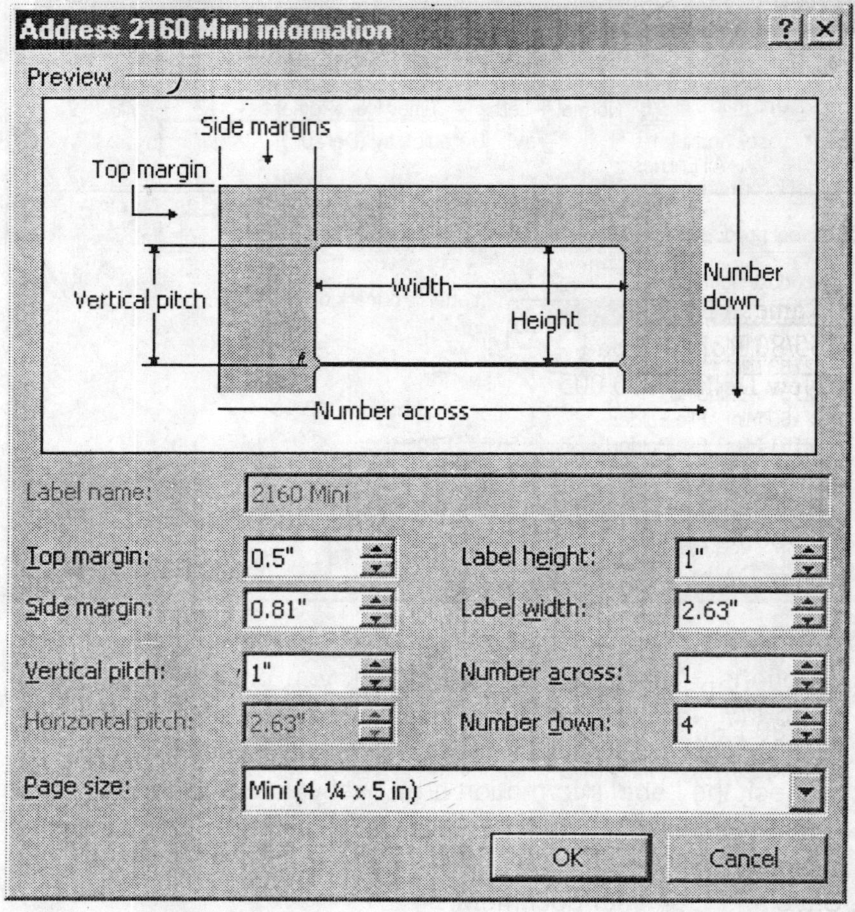

11. From the Table menu, select Show Gridlines to see the outline of each business card.

12. Format and align the text.

13. To add graphics to the business cards, insert the picture or object. Size the graphic to fit on the business card. Copy the graphic to each card on the page.

14. Print a test page and see if your cards fit on the business card template. Adjust any spacing if needed.

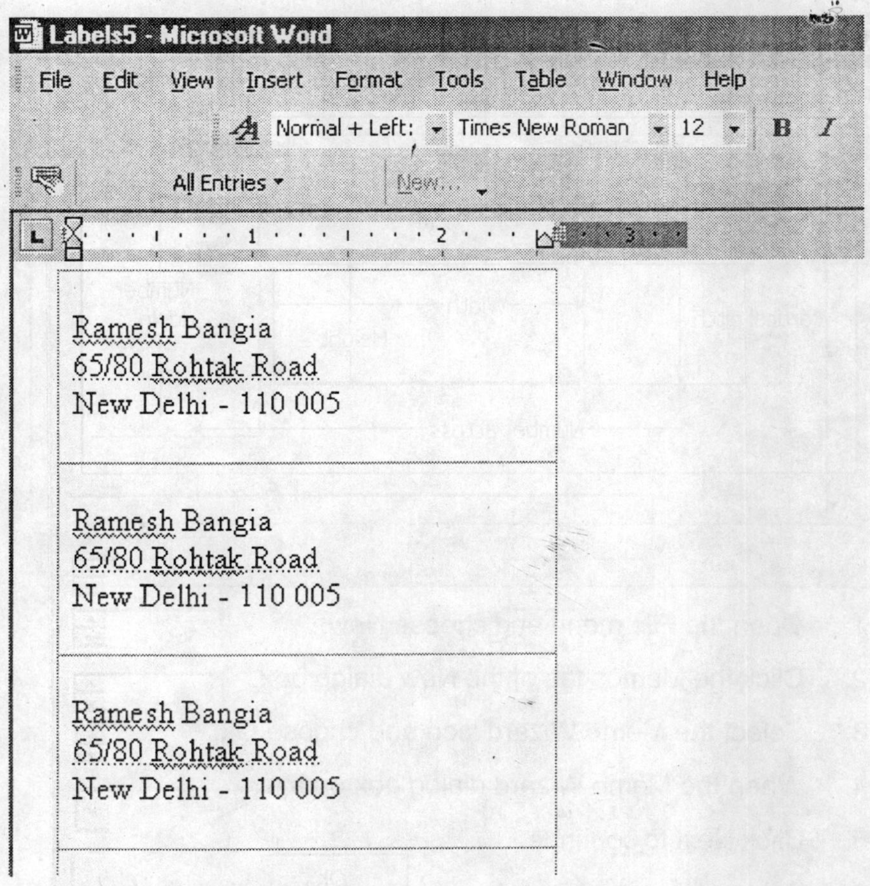

15. Save and print your document.

The above steps as they would appear on your screen are shown here.

Creating Memo from Wizard

Memorandum, or memos are basic business documents. Memos should be easy to read, concise, and meaningful. Word's Memo Wizard helps you set up and format your memo document.

The following steps you have to take to create memo from the Wizard memo.

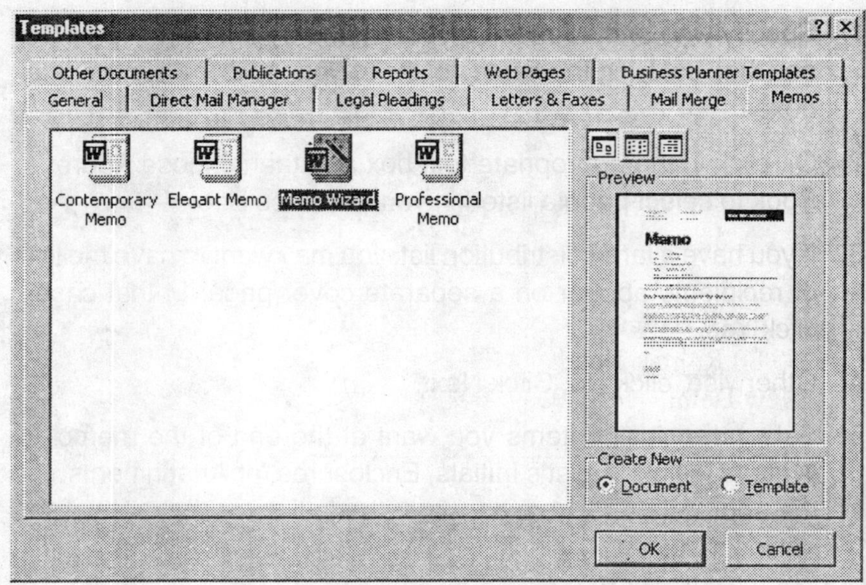

1. Open the File menu and choose New.
2. Click the Memos tab of the New dialog box.
3. Select the Memo Wizard icon and choose Ok.
4. When the Memo Wizard dialog box opens.
5. Click Next to continue.
6. Select the style of memo you want to create—Professional, Contemporary or Elegant—and then click Next.
7. If you want to include a title at the top of your memo document, click Yes and then enter the title text in the text box.
8. If not, click No. Then click Next.
9. Indicate which items you want to include in the header of your memo document: Date, From, Subject or Priority. In the text boxes next to these options, enter the Date, From, and Subject text you want to appear in the header.
10. Click Next.

11. Specify who should receive your memo by checking To or Cc and then entering the names of the recipients in the appropriate boxes.

12. Or, click in the appropriate text box and then choose Address Book to select people listed in your Address Book.

13. If you have a large distribution list, you may want to have the list of recipients appear on a separate cover page. In that case, click Yes.

14. Otherwise, click No. Click Next.

15. Select the closing items you want at the end of the memo—Writer's Initials, typist's Initials, Enclosures, or Attachments. In the appropriate text boxes, enter the initials or the number of enclosures.

16. Click Next.

17. For memos that have more than one page, select the items you want to appear in the header and footer for subsequent pages: Date, Topic, Page Number for the header or Date, Confidential, Page Number for the footer.

18. If you choose to include a topic, enter the text for the topic. Click Next.

19. Click Finish.

20. The Office Assistant appears and offers you the opportunity to change the header or footer, change the memo style, or send the memo to someone else via email or fax (starts the Fax Wizard).

21. Close the Office Assistant if you do not need help, or click the item with which you need assistance.

22. Click the Click Here and Type Your Memo Text field and begin typing the body of your memo. The field is indicated by the square brackets surrounding the click here text.

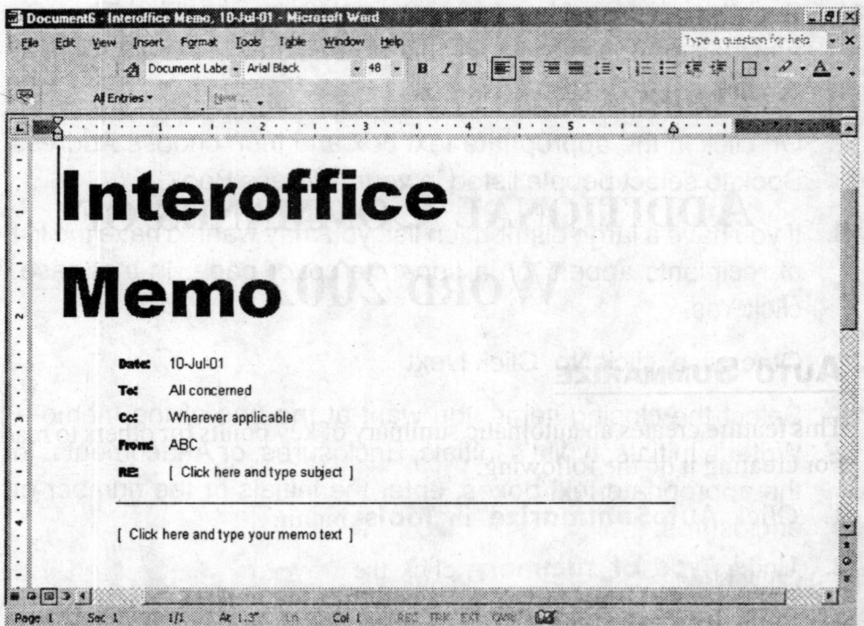

23. Click any other editable fields in your memo, such as Priority, and make the appropriate adjustments.

24. Save your memo and print it.

I have given here the first screen and the final product. In between screens can be seen when operated upon. The end product as shown in a Word document is shown above.

7

Additional Commands of Word 2002

Auto Summarize

This feature creates an automatic summary of key points for others to read. For creating it do the following.

1. Click **AutoSummarize** in **Tools** menu.
2. Under **Type of summary**, click the way you want to display the summary: **Insert an executive summary or abstract at the top of the document** or **Create a new document and put the summary there**.
3. In the **Percent of original** box, type or select the level of detail to include in the summary.

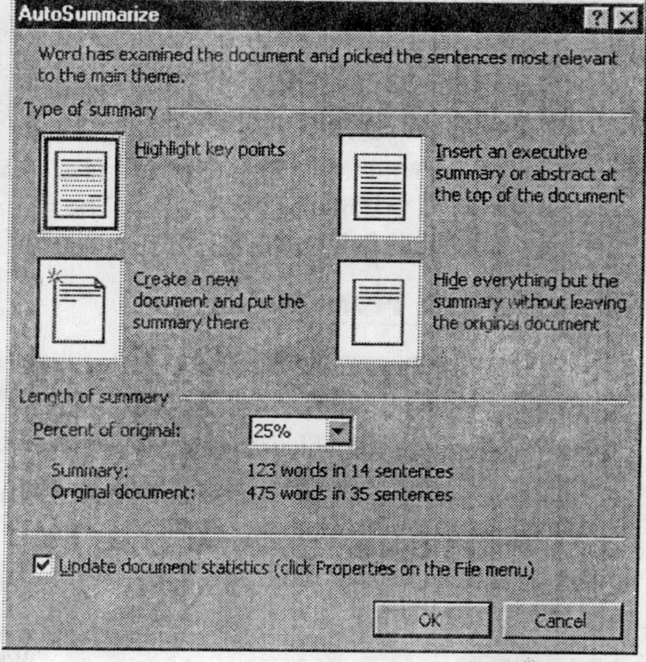

4. If you do not want AutoSummarize to replace your existing keywords and comments on the **Summary** tab in the Properties dialog box (File menu), clear the **Update** document statistics check below.

Once you have created the executive summary or abstract, it is a good idea to review the summary to make sure that it covers your documents key points.

BREAK, INSERT

There are different types of breaks which are possible in Word 2002. Once you access **Break** from the **Insert** menu, you can put in a **Page Break** (to start a new page from here), **Column Break** (to start a new column from here) and **Text wrapping break** (to give a break from the text wrapped).

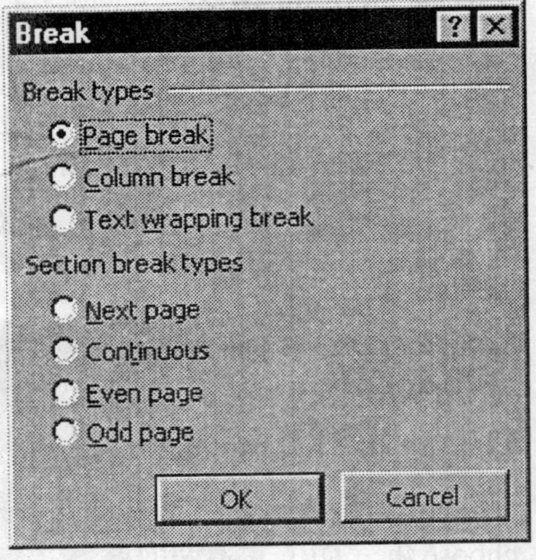

You can also use it for giving breaks in section by jumping to a Next page, Continues page, Even page, Odd page using this command. So whenever the control comes to this point, it would do the needful, i.e., jumping to the next odd page or any other option chosen.

BULLETS AND NUMBERS

It is used to put numbers and bullets in the text. You can choose the bullet of your own and even in numbers you can choose the style.

1. Highlight the text in which you want to put either bullets or numbers.
2. Select **Bullets and Numbering** from the **Insert** menu to get the dialog box.
3. Click bullets or numbers panel, whichever is required.
4. Select the option which you like and the selected text will have the required bullets or numbers.

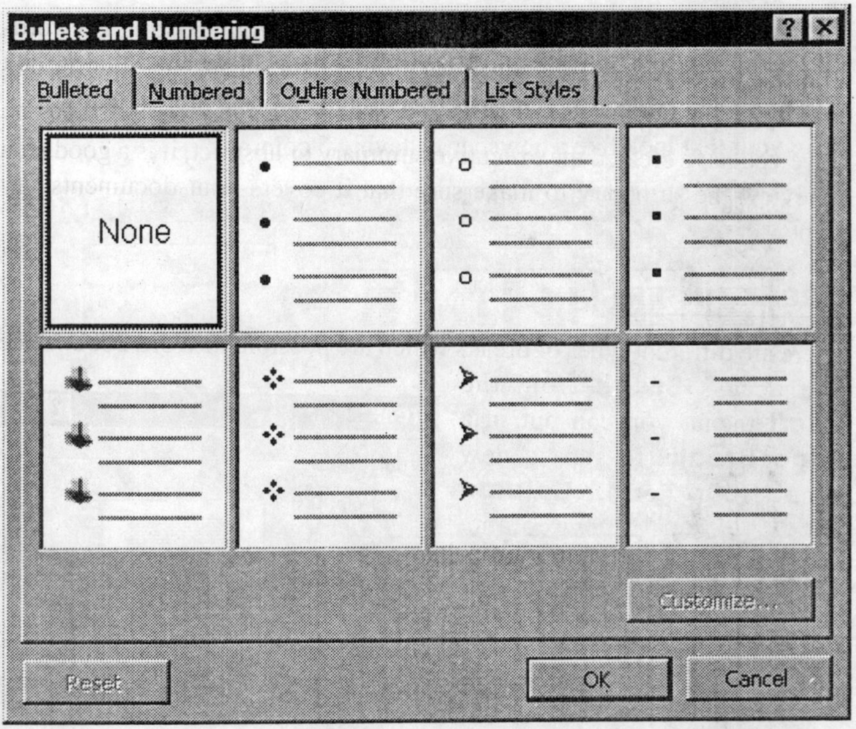

Change Case

Using this option you can change the case of the selected text. You can choose the option of having it all CAPS or in all lowercase. **Sentence case** will make only the first character Caps and the rest of the sentence in lower case. **Title case** will make all the title words start with a capital letter. **Toggle case** will make the Capital letter lower and lower letter as

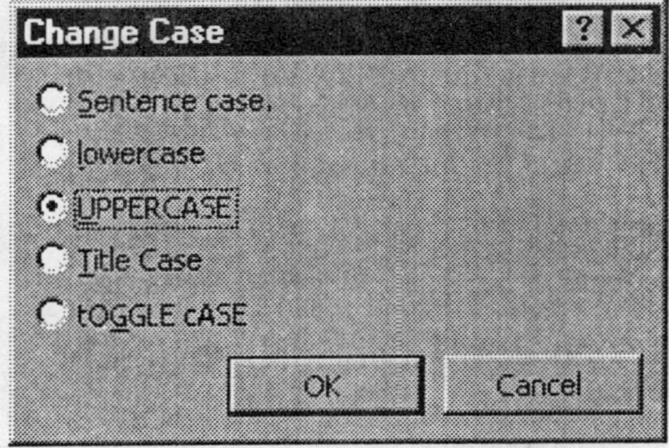

Capital, i.e., reverse the case. So choose the option which you want and click at the proper selection and see the result.

COLUMNS

This command is used to make your text run into different columns. You can choose the number of columns you want to have in your text. You can make your text look like a newspaper having 5 columns.

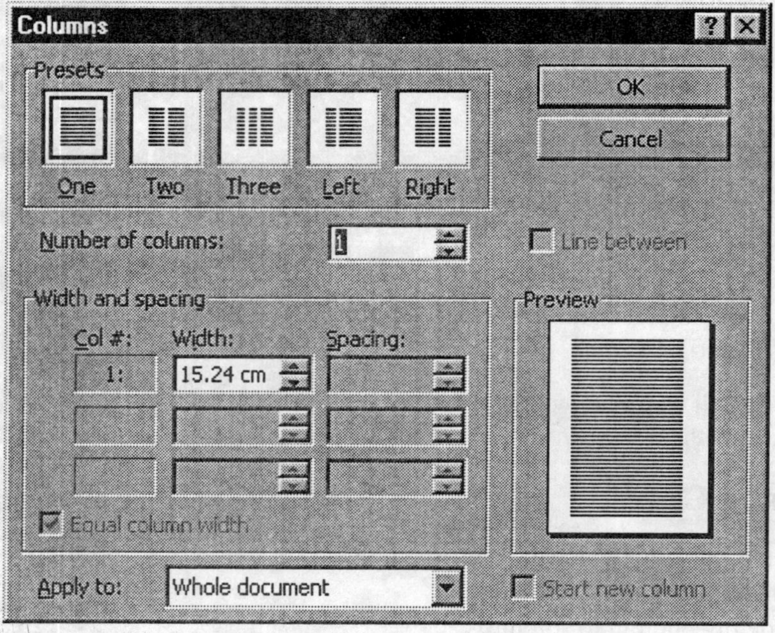

1. Select the text which you want to divide into columns.
2. Select **Columns** from **Format** menu to get **Columns** dialog box as shown above.
3. Choose your options and click Ok.

COMMENT, INSERT

If you want, you can insert a comment into the document, so as to leave a message for the others to read when they go through this document.

1. Place you cursor in the document where you want to put the comment.
2. Select **Comment** from the Insert menu.
3. A new window at the bottom will appear on the screen, as shown above.

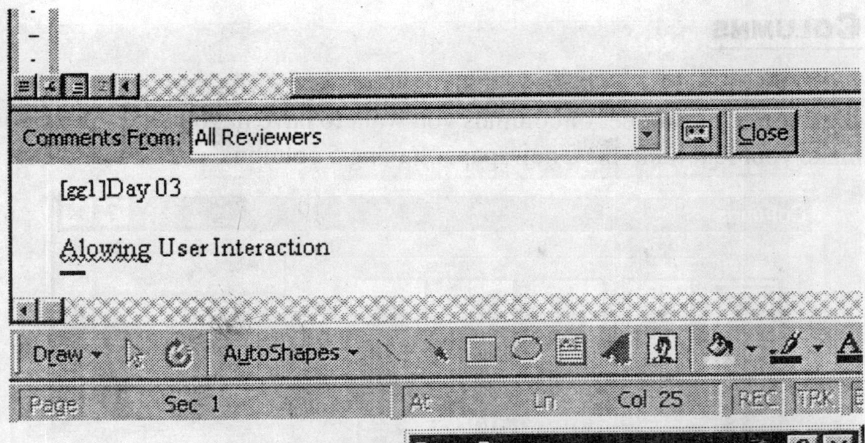

4. Type the comment which you want to place and then click **Close**.
5. It will be placed at this point for others to see.

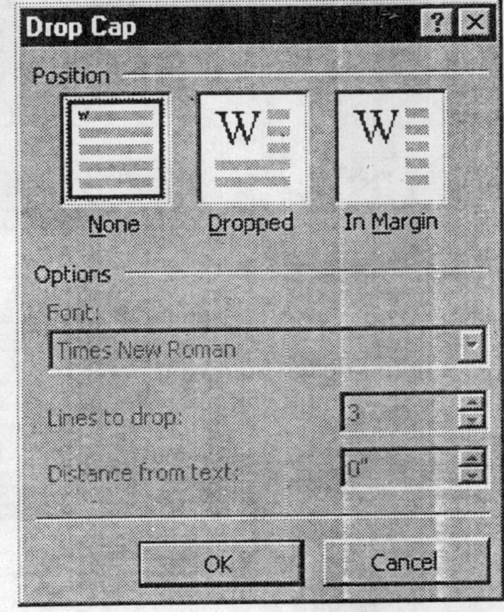

Drop Cap

It is a way of emphasizing the text with the first letter being made big enough to run into 2-3 lines. Word also allows you to do so. This command is available under the **Format** menu with the name **Drop Cap**.

Envelopes and Labels

It is not that Word 2000 has options only for the documents. It also has features for printing envelopes and labels. Access Envelopes and Labels from the Tools menu to get the dialog box as shown on the next page.

Just type the required information in the space provided for and your envelope is ready for printing. Similarly you can type the information for the labels.

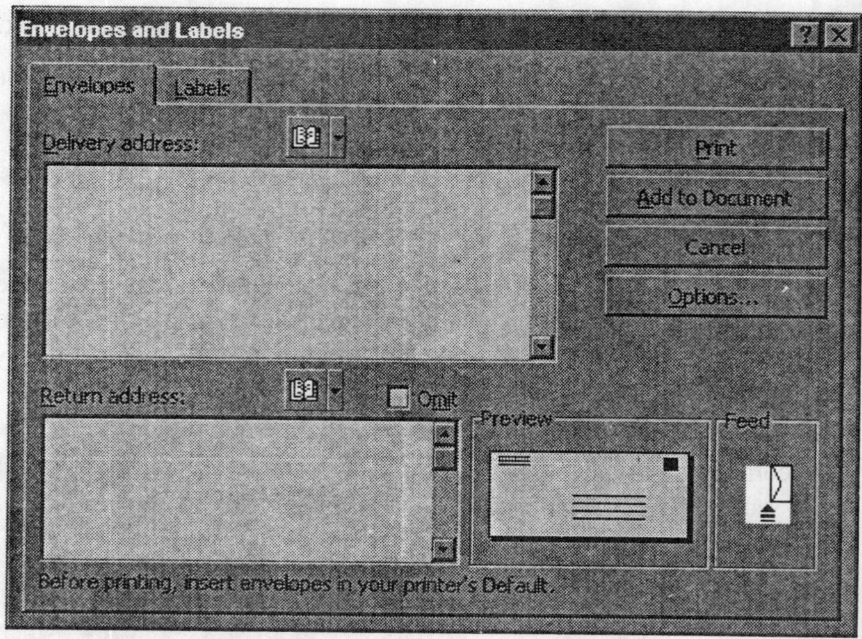

FILE, INSERT

This command is very useful when you are trying to merge more than 1 file. For this do the following:

1. Click **New** for opening a new document.

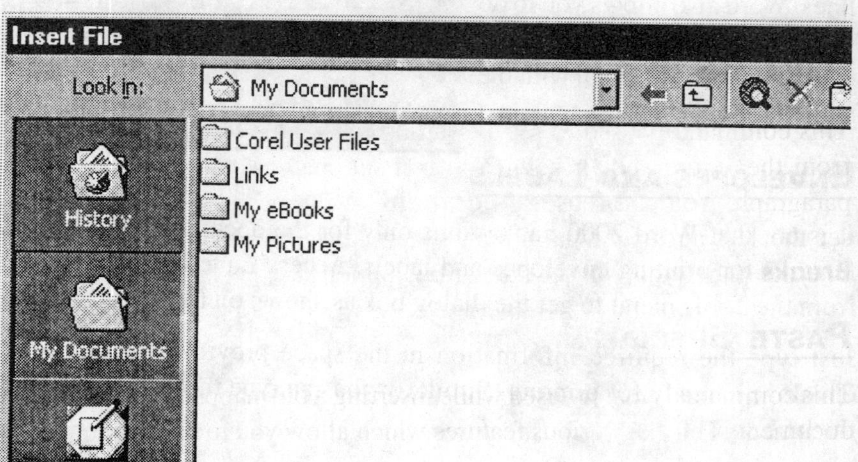

2. Click **Insert** menu and click at **File to open** the file dialog box.
3. Click at the file which you want to insert and the file will be inserted in total.
4. If you want to add more files into it, repeat the steps 2 and 3.

Full Screen

Available under the View menu, this command makes the full screen filled with the document. A small icon on the screen allows you to click back to the original display.

Go To

This command available under **Edit** menu allows you to go to a particular page, section, line, etc.

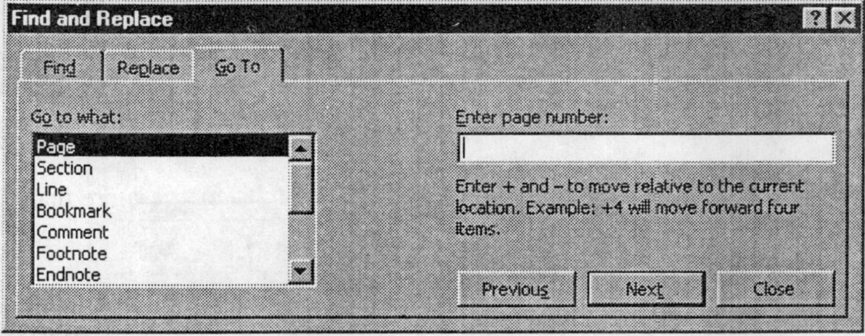

Paragraph

This command is used to set the setting for a paragraph. As you can see from the figure shown here. You can set spacing before and after the paragraph. You can set the **Alignment** of the paragraph. You can also set the left and right paragraph spacing. Using the **Line and Page Breaks** panel you can set the various options of line and page breaks.

Paste Special

This command is mainly used while inserting a bit-mapped picture into the document. This has various features which allow you to paste the picture.

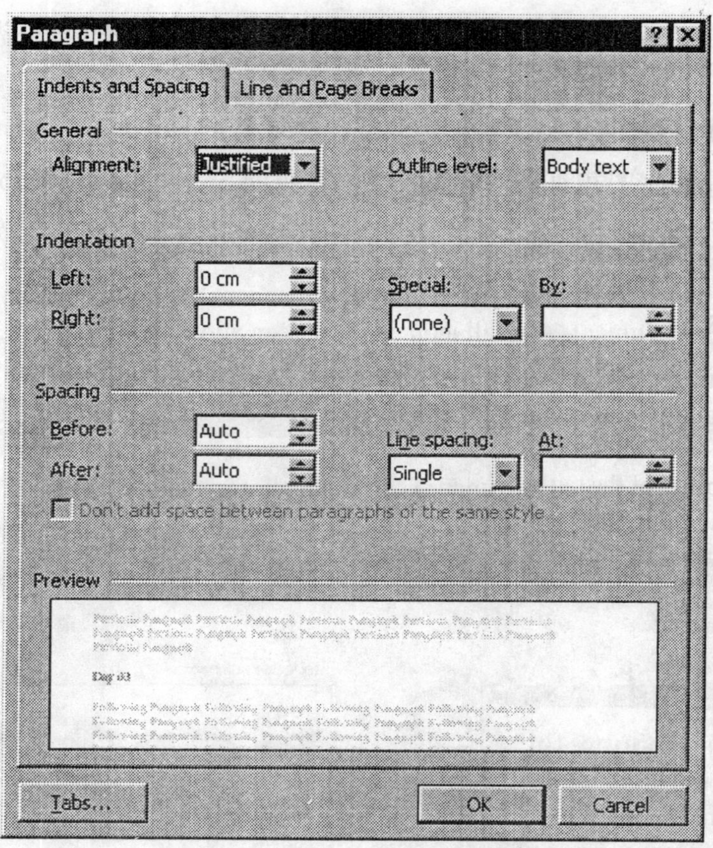

PROTECT DOCUMENT

This is a method by which you can prevent unauthorized persons from changing the document or from removing marked revisions. This method allows you to protect the document by giving it a password. Open the **Tools** menu and **Protect Document**. Select **Tracked Changes** and then type a password in the Password box. Click Ok. Only those users who posses the password can unprotect the document and remove the tracking changes.

Send To

This command which is available under the **File** menu, allows you to send the message across to various options such as fax, mail recipients, mail recipients as an attachment, etc.

Tabs

You can set tabs to set your text in a tabular manner. Unfortunately this command is not much used due to the availability of the table option. Still if you want you can set tabs as you set in good old typewriters.

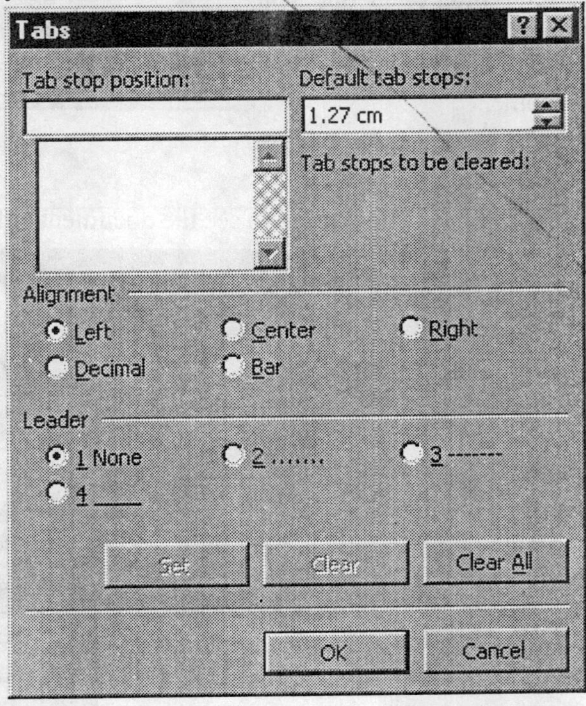

Versions

Another option for working with documents that you want reviewed by several people is to have Word save the current version of the document automatically each time you or another person closes the document after modifying it. All the versions are stored in a single document, but only the most current version displays. The date and time the version was saved is automatically recorded, as is the name of the person making the revisions.

WORD COUNT

Sometimes it is required to know the number of words typed in a particular document. It is usually required when you are given an assignment to write an article of a fixed number of words, maybe 200 or 400. So after typing each line you may like to know of how many words the file has become.

Word Count

Statistics:

Pages	2
Words	463
Characters (no spaces)	2,225
Characters (with spaces)	2,668
Paragraphs	24
Lines	52

Include footnotes and endnotes

Show Toolbar | Close

ZOOM

This command allows you to see the document either in an enlarged form, i.e., 200% or in a smaller form maybe 75%. So with this Word 2002 commands are complete. Now you can go back to your Word 2000 and start using it and

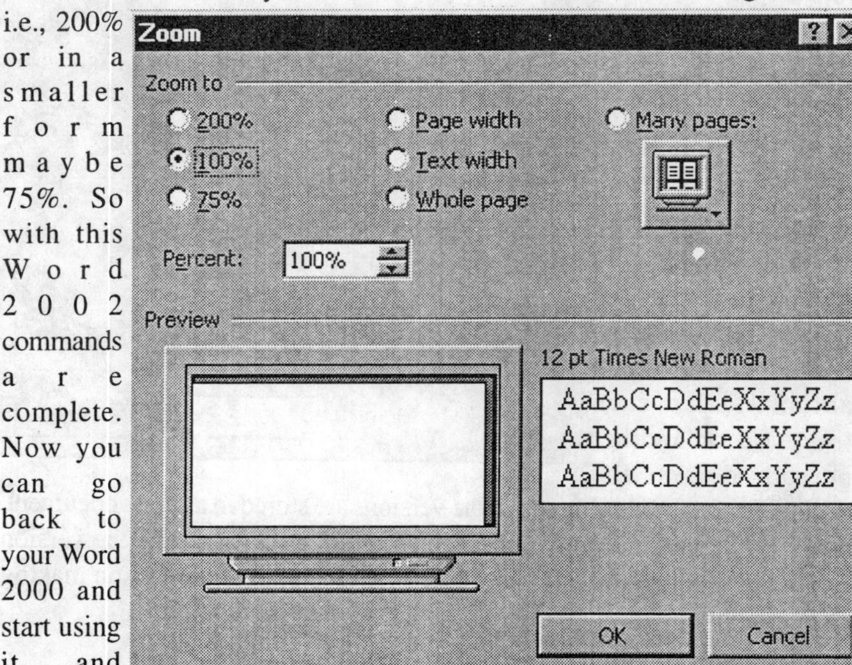

make the best use of the facilities available in the software.

HYPERLINKS

You can assign a hyperlink to a block of text or to a picture in a Word document. The hyperlink connects the text or picture to a target location. The target location can be a Web page, an Office document or other file, or a folder, which can be located on a disk, network drive or Internet site. The target location can also be a specific place within the current document or within another file or, it can be an e-mail address. Clicking the hyperlink displays the target location or sends a message to the target e-mail address.

To create a hyperlink, perform the following steps:

1. Select the text or picture to which you want to assign the hyperlink or simply place the insertion point at the position in your document where you want Word to insert the hyperlink text that you later specify.
2. Open the Insert Hyperlink dialog box by choosing Insert, Hyperlink by clicking the Insert Hyperlink button on the Standard toolbar or by pressing Ctrl + K.
3. Enter or edit the hypertext text in the Text To Display box. Skip this

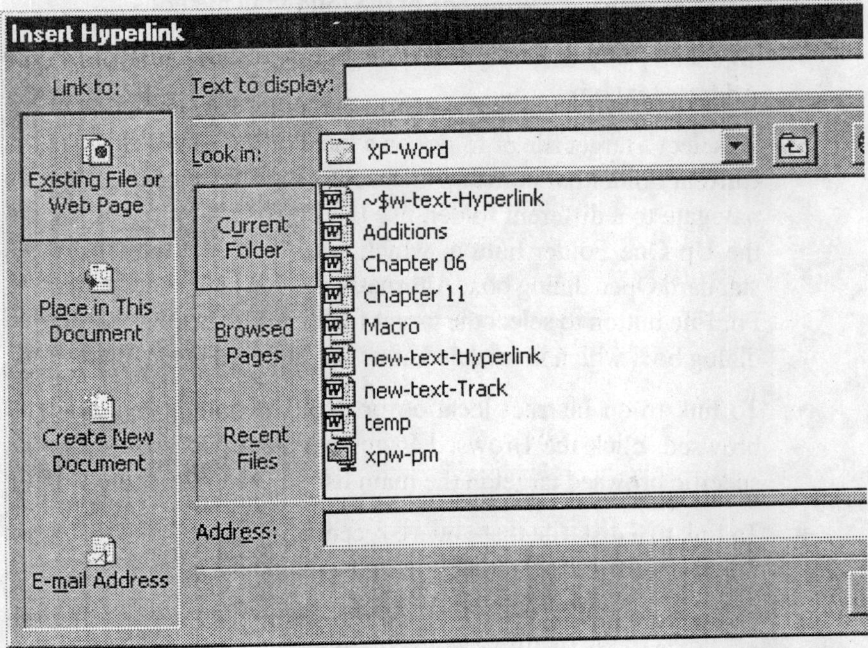

step if you selected the desired text in step 1 or if you are assigning the hyperlink to a picture.

4. In the Link To bar at the left of the Insert Hyperlink dialog box, select the general category of hyperlink you want to create:

   - To link to a different existing document or Web page, select existing File or Web page.
   - To link to a different location within the current document, select Place In This Document.
   - To create a new document or Web page and link to it, select Create New Document.
   - To link to an e-mail address so that clicking the hyperlink sends a message to that address, select E-Mail Address.

   The controls the Word displays in the rest of the dialog box depend on which of these options is selected.

5. If you select Existing File or Web Page in step 4, select the target document or Web page using one of the following methods.

   - To specify any target, type the target's file path or URL into the Address text box.
   - To select a target file or folder on a local or network disk, click the Current Folder bar item and then select the file in the main list. To navigate to a different folder, use the Look In drop-down list and the Up One Folder button, which work just like they do in the standard Open dialog box. Alternatively, you can click the Browse For File button to select the target file or folder in the Link To File dialog box, which is modeled after the standard Open dialog box.
   - To link to an Internet location or disk file that you've recently browsed, click the Browsed Pages bar item and then select the specific browsed target in the main list.
   - To link to a disk file that you've recently opened, click the Recent Files bar iem and select the file in the main list.
   - To run your browser to search for a target on the Internet, click the Browse The Web button.

- To link to a specific location within the target file, click the Bookmark button and indicate the target location by selecting a document heading or bookmark in the Select Place in Document dialog box.

6. If you selected Place in This Document in step 4, specify the target location by selecting a document heading or bookmark in the main list.
7. If you selected Create new Document in step 4, specify the name and location of the new document or Web page as follows:
   - To create a file in the current directory, just type its name into the Name Of new Document text box.
   - To create a file in a different directory, click the Change button to select the directory.
8. If you selected E-Mail Address in step 4, type the target e-mail address into the E-Mail Address text box and, if you want, type a message subject in the Subject text box.
9. To have Word or the browser (Internet Explorer 4.0 or later) display a specific message when you hold the pointer over the hyperlink, click the ScreenTip button and type the message into the Set Hyperlink ScreenTip dialog box.
10. Click the OK button.

To modify a hyperlink you have already defined, select the text or picture again and then use nay of the techniques that were given for opening the Insert Hyperlink dialog box.

Tracking Your Document Changes

You can turn on change tracking whenever you want to start saving a record of all modifications you make to a document so that the modifications can be viewed and later either accepted or rejected. For example, you could turn on change tracking before making tentative document alternations that you might want to reverse later. You could also turn on change tracking in order to communicate to a co-worker the exact ways that you edit a document.

To track your document changes, perform the following steps:

1. To take advantage of Word's new ways of showing changes, switch to

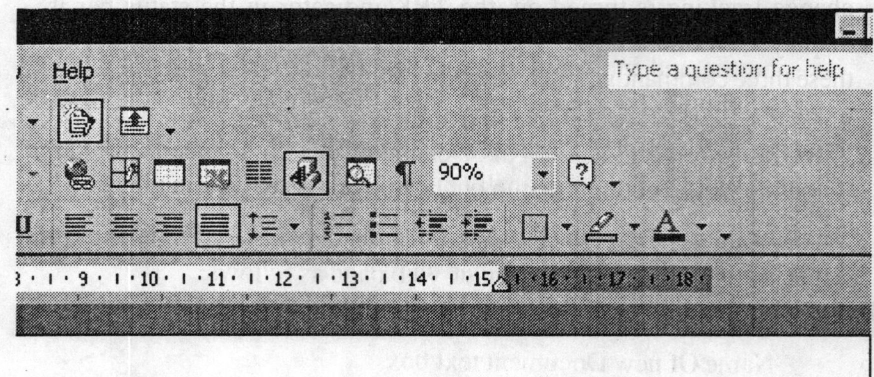

either Web Layout or Print Layout view. In these views – as well as in Print Preview and on the printed document – Word 2002 displays all deletions and indicates all formatting changes within margin "balloons." Displaying deleted text in the margins makes all easier to read your modified paragraphs and avoids throwing off the positions of line and page breaks. You can track and view changes in Normal or Outline view, Word will use its old method for making tracked changes, in which deleted text is left in place, making it more difficult to read the document and visualize the way the final text will actually appear on the page.

2. Turn on change tracking by double-clicking the TRK indicator in the status bar, by choosing Tools, Track changes, or by pressing the Ctrl + Shift + E shortcut key. Word will now start tracking all insertions, deletions and formatting changes you make to the document. When

change tracking is turned on, the TRK indicator in the status bar is displayed in darker type. To turn change tracking off, repeat any of these three commands. When you turn off change tracking, Word retains its record of all changes that have already been tracked, but it doesn't track changes that you subsequently make. When you turn on change tracking, Word will automatically display the Reviewing toolbar.

3. To adjust the change making mode, open the Display For Review drop-down list on the Reviewing toolbar, shown here:

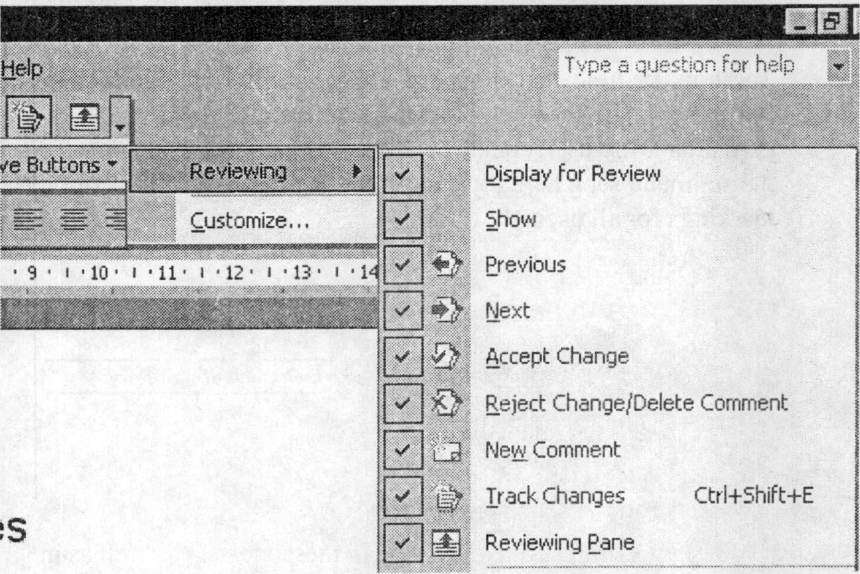

Then, select one of the following two changes marking options from the list.

- To have Word mark all your changes as you edit the document, choose Final Showing Markup. Use this option if you want to monitor your changes as you make them.
- To turn off marking of changes, choose Final. Word will continue to track changes and store the change information internally and you can have Word show the changes later if you want. Use this option if you want to record your changes but don't want the window to be cluttered with markings while you edit. In this mode, Word works almost as it does when change tracking is off.

However, you'll occasionally notice minor quirks; for example, once in a while you might have to press the Backspace key several times before it erases t he preceding character.

4. To filter the particular changes that Word shows, click the Show button on the Reviewing toolbar, then choose an option from the drop-down menu, as follows:

   - To show or hide marking for all insertions and deletions, choose Insertions And Deletions. The markings are shown when the menu item is checked.

   - To show or hide markings for all formatting changes, choose Formatting. To show or hide markings for changes made by a particular Word user, click Reviewers and choose a user name from the submenu seen here (or choose All Reviewers to show or hide markings for all users).

8

Using Drawing Tools in Word 2002

Introduction

It is not that Word is all about text and has no provisions for Graphics. You can either insert drawings into your word document or can create your own drawings using the drawing tools available in Word 2002. You can even use the ready made graphics available with Word 2002. So you either use ready made or make your own drawings.

Creating a Diagram

A diagram is a visual and relational representation of information. A common diagram is an organization chart. You can also create cycle diagrams, radial diagrams, pyramid diagrams, Venn diagrams and target diagrams. When you insert an organization chart into a document, the chart has placeholder that you click and replace with your own. The boxes and the lines of the organization chart are objects that you can move and change.

To place an organizational chart, do the following:

1. Open the document in which you want to place the organization chart.
2. From the Views menu, click at Toolbars, Drawing to have the Drawing toolbar on the screen, if not already there.
3. Click the Diagram Gallery on the Drawing toolbar, to get the dialog box.
4. Double click the OrgChart to have the OrgChart in the document.
5. In the Organization Chart, click the top box to place the insertion point and then type **Indian Cricket Team**.

6. Click the first box in the second row, type **Saurav Ganguly**, click the second box in the second row, type **Rahul Dravid**, click the third box in the second row, and then type **Sachin Tendulkar**. All boxes contain names. The last box is still selected.

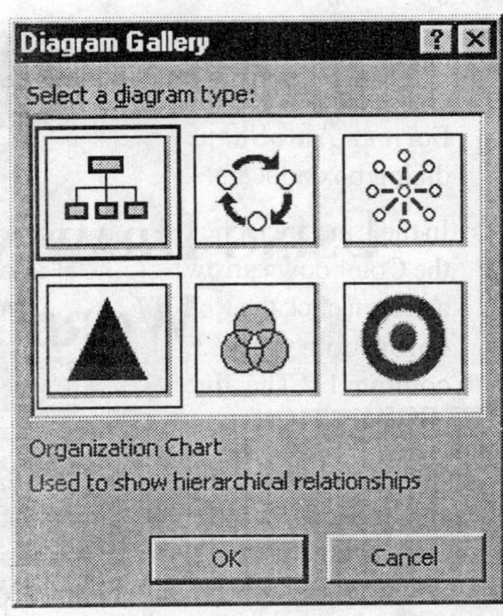

7. On the Organization Chart toolbar, click the Select down arrow and then click All the Connecting Lines. All connecting lines in the organization chart are selected.

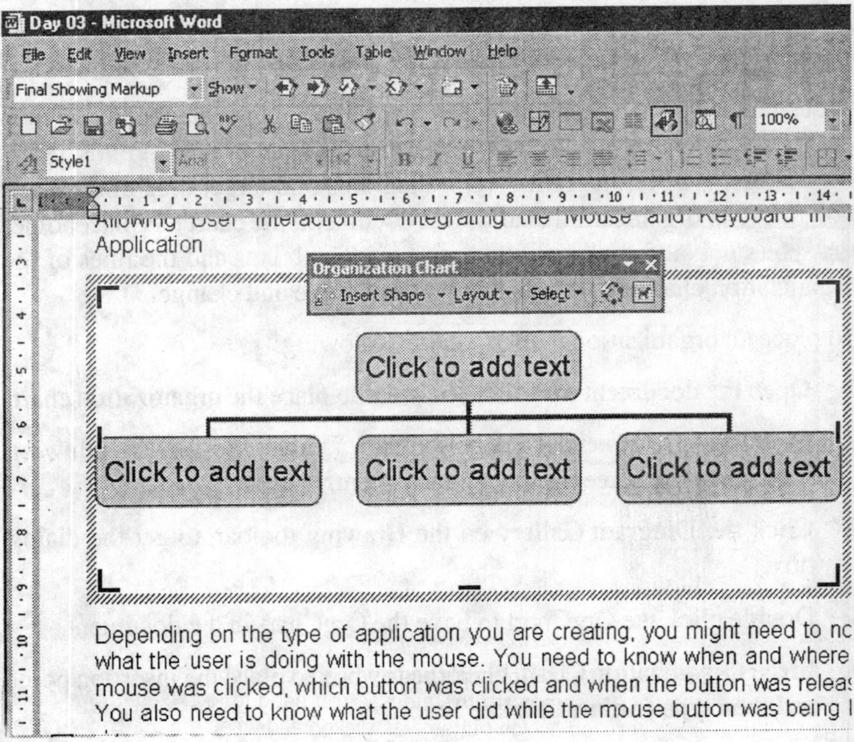

8. On the format menu, click AutoShape. The Format AutoShape dialog box appears.

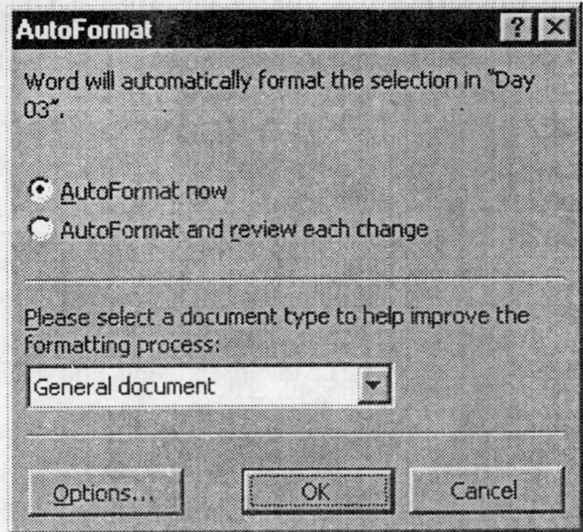

9. In the Line area, click the Color down arrow and then click the Red color box (row 3, column 1). The line color selection is now red.
10. In the Arrows area, click the Begin style down arrow, click the second option in the first row and then click OK. The lines in the organization chart are now red with arrows attached.

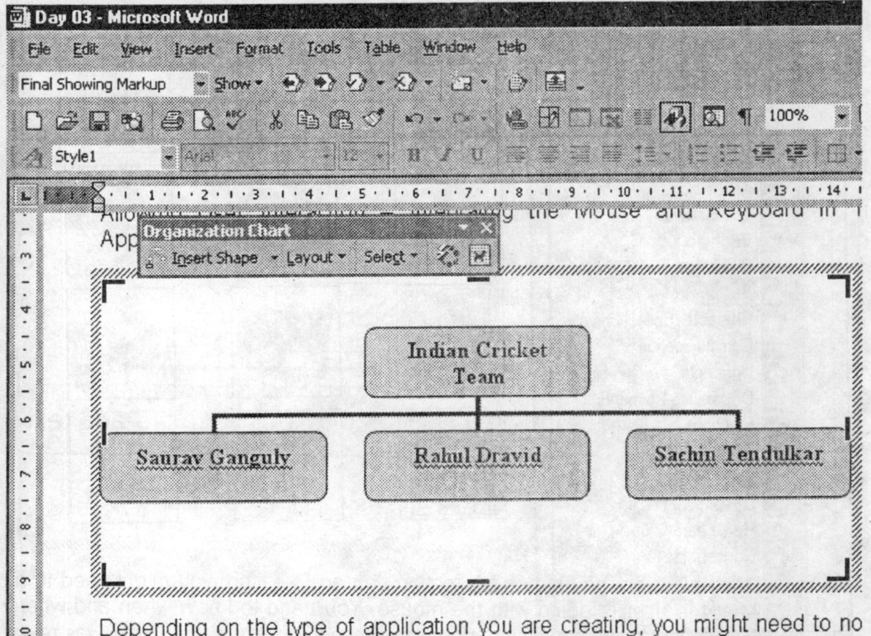

11. Click a blank area of the document of deselect the organization chart.
12. On the Standard toolbar, click the Save button to save the document.
13. Click the Close Window button in the document window.

The OrgChart document closes.

Adding and Modifying Pictures

You can insert nearly any picture, scanned photograph, photo or artwork from a CD-ROM or other program into a document in Word. When you use the Picture submenu on the Insert menu, you specify the source of the picture – a file, Word's clip art collection or a scanner.

To insert a picture from a file on your hard disk you use the From File command on the Picture submenu. To insert from the clip art collection that

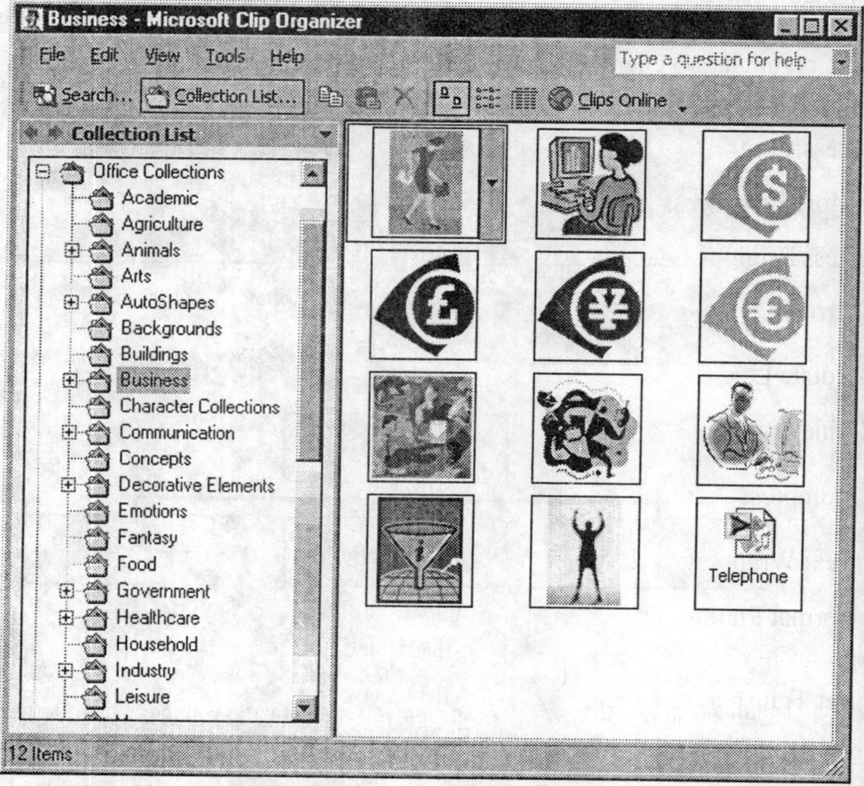

comes with Word, you click the Clip Art command on the Picture submenu or click the

Insert Clip Art button on the Drawing toolbar, which opens the Insert Clip Art task pane. Microsoft Office XP provides hundreds of professionally designed pieces of clip art that you can use in your document. If you have a scanner connected to the computer that you are using, you can scan and insert a picture using the From Scanner command. Once you insert clip art or any picture into your document, you can modify it by using the Picture toolbar.

The following table describes the buttons on the Picture toolbar.

Button Name	***Description***
Insert Picture	Allows you to insert a picture
Color	Allows you to change the coloring of the picture
More Contrast	Applies more contrast
Less Contrast	Reduces contrast
More Brightness	Applies more brightness
Less Brightness	Reduces brightness
Crop	Crops the picture
Rotate Left	Rotates the picture to the left
Line Style	Allows you to change the line style
Compress Pictures	Enables you to reduce the size of pictures
Text Wrapping	Allows you to wrap text around picture
Format Picture	Allows you to change features such as colors, size and lines
Set Transparent Color	Allows you to make selected colors in the picture see-through
Reset Picture	Resets the picture to its original state

WATERMARKS

I am quite sure that you must have seen pages of a book or even pages marked Copy marked across the centre of the page which is very dimmed so that it can be read but not disturb the text written on the paper. These are called watermarks. Word 2002 allows you to create watermarks on the document pages. You can use a picture such as a company logo as a watermark, or you can use words to send a memo that contains a sample organization chart. Here we will use the word Confidential on the page.

1. Open the document in which you want the watermark.
2. Press Enter key and then press the up arrow key to place the insertion point in a blank line at the beginning of the document.
3. On the Insert menu, Point to Picture and then click From File. The Insert Picture dialog box appears.
4. Navigate to the add the picture in the document.
5. Click NIM logo to select it.
6. Drag the lower-right corner sizing handle (which changes to a diagonal double-arrow) up and to the left until you reach the 4-inch mark on the ruler to resize the picture.

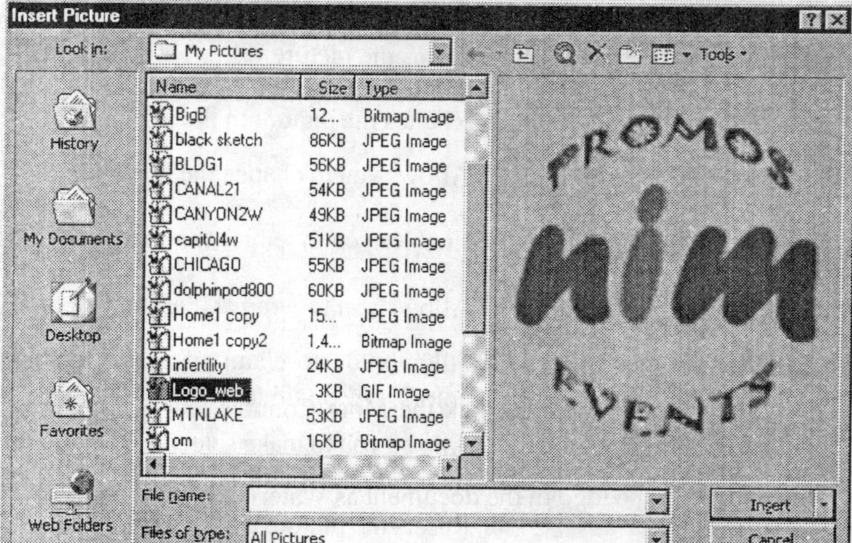

7. On the Picture toolbar, click the Color button and then click Washout. The picture is now washed out.

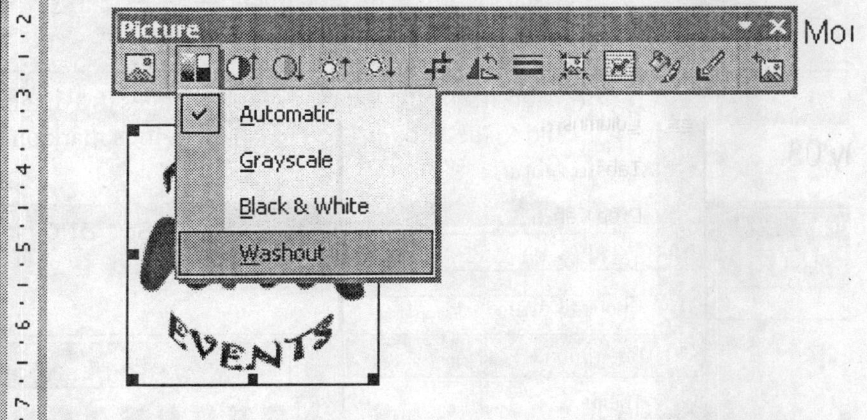

8. On the Picture toolbar, click the Less Brightness button four times to reduce the brightness of the picture.

9. On the Picture toolbar, click the More Contrast button two times to sharpen the picture.

This will place the logo in the document as Watermark.

Text as Watermark

For this we will use the word Confidential as the background for the page. Follow the following steps to do this.

1. Open the file in which you want the watermark.

2. On the Format menu, point to Background and then click Printed Watermark. The Printed Watermark dialog box appears.

20 Click the Text watermark option, click the Text down arrow and then click CONFIDENTIAL to select a watermark style.

21 Click Ok, the word CONFIDENTIAL appears across the page.

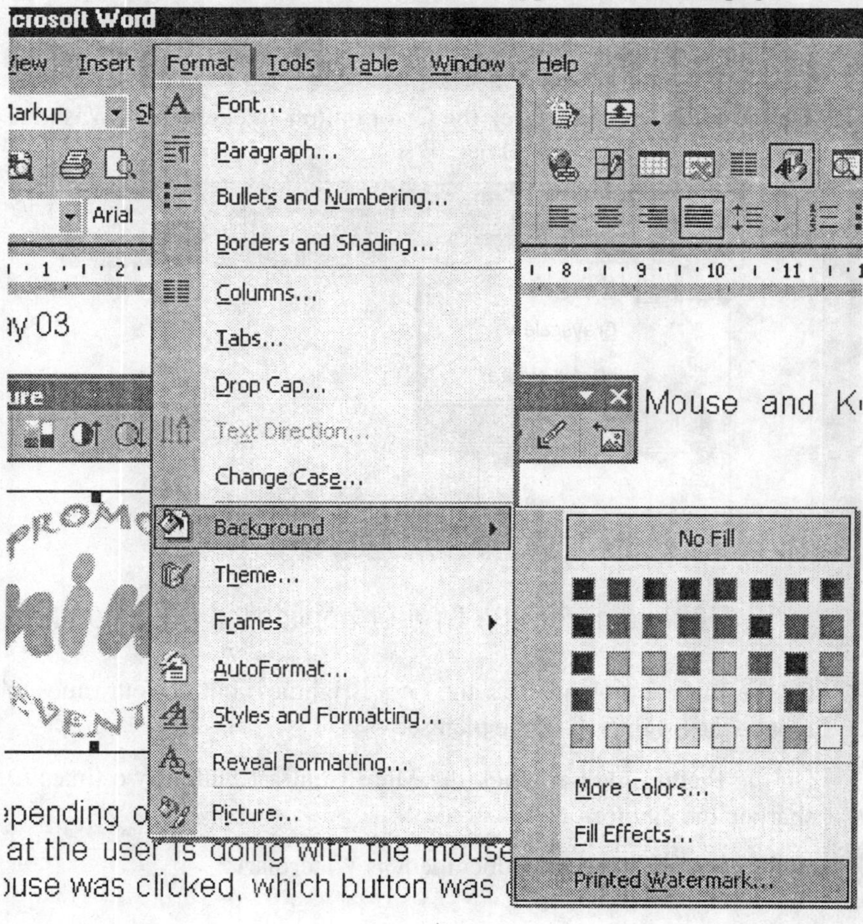

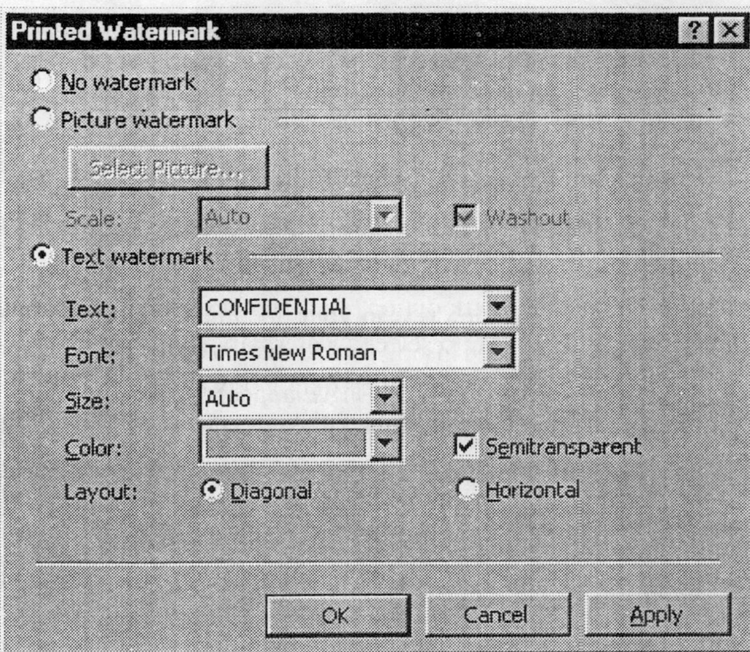

Allowing User Interaction – Integrating the Mouse and Keyboard in Your Application

Depending on the type of application you are creating, you might need to notice what the user is doing with the mouse. You need to know when and where the mouse was clicked, which button was clicked and when the button was released. You also need to know what the user did while the mouse button was being held down.

Another thing that you might need to do is read the keyboard events.. As with the mouse, you might need to know when a key was pressed, how long it was held doing and when it was released.

Today you are going to learn

What mouse events are available for use and how to determine which one is appropriate for your application's needs.

How you can listen to mouse even and how to react to them in your Visual C++ application.

What keyboard events are available for use and what actions will trigger each of these events.

How to capture keyboard events and take action based on what the user pressed.

A CONFIDENTIAL watermark now appears faintly in the background at an angle.

USING WORDART

WordArt allows you to change the shape and appearance of text in your document. Use WordArt to create special effects for your text. You can make WordArt text appear curved, outlined, shadowed or three-dimensional.

To create WordArt of existing text in your document, select the text that you want to enhance, click the Insert WordArt button on the Drawing toolbar, click a selection in the WordArt Galley dialog box and then click Ok. The Edit WordArt Text dialog box appears with your text selection highlighted.

When you work with WordArt, you can use the WordArt toolbar which opens when you insert or select a WordArt object. The following table lists the WordArt toolbar buttons and a brief description of each.

Button Name		***Description***
Insert WordArt		Inserts WordArt
Edit Text	Edit Text...	Edits text within WordArt
WordArt Gallery		Provides graphical options for your WordArt.
Format WordArt		Allows you to change the color, size and layout of the WordArt.
WordArt Shape		Changes the shape of the WordArt.
Text Wrapping		Changes the text wrapping around your WordArt.
WordArt Same Leter Heights		Makes the letters in the WordArt the same height
WordArt Vertical Text		Changes the alignment of the text from horizontal to vertical.
WordArt Alignment		Changes the alignment of the WordArt
WordArt Character Spacing		Changes the spacing between characters in the WordArt

Now we will create a small sentence using WordArt. For this do the following:

1. Click at WordArt icon in a document file.
2. The WordArt Gallery opens.

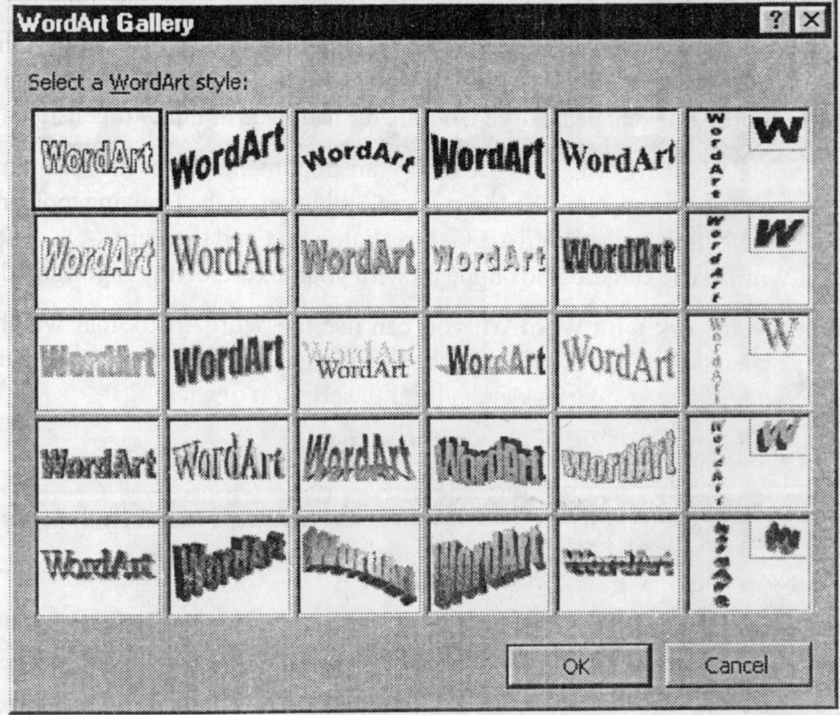

3. Click the option which you want from the list and press Ok. I have chosen here no. 3 on the first row.
4. The Edit WordArt Text dialog box appears, displaying Your Text Here as a placeholder, as shown on the next page.
5. Type your message or text and press Ok. I have typed here Sachin Tendulkar, and the result after pressing Ok is shown on the next page.
6. The text is inserted as an object.
7. Click the WordArt object to select it.

The WordArt toolbar appears and sizing handles surround the object.

Edit WordArt Text
Font:
Arial Black
Size:
36
B
I
Text:
Your Text Here
OK
Day 03 - Microsoft Word
File Edit View Insert Format Tools Table Window Help
Final Showing Markup
Show
Style1
Arial
12
Sachin Tendulkar
Day 03

Besides there are other readymade shapes, arrows, callouts, etc. on the drawing toolbar, which can be used in the document. I have listed them out here.

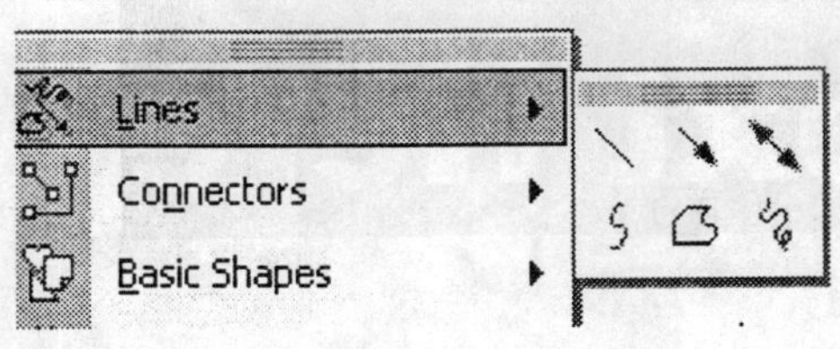

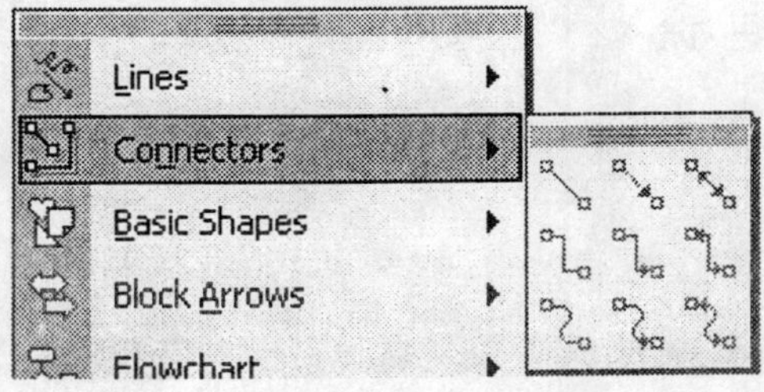

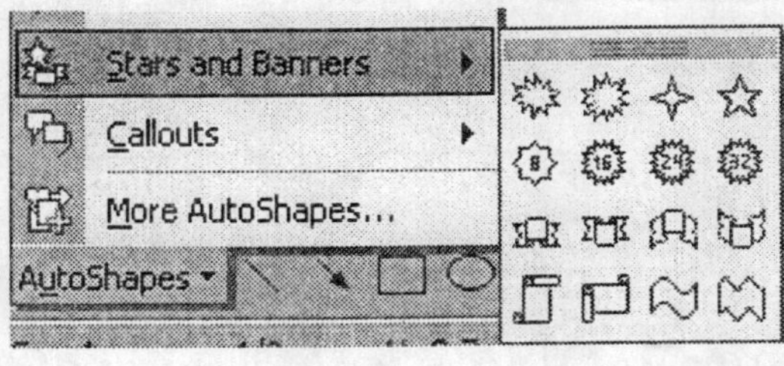

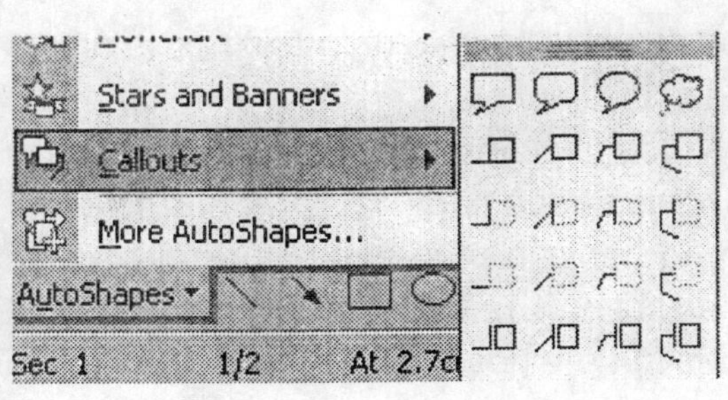

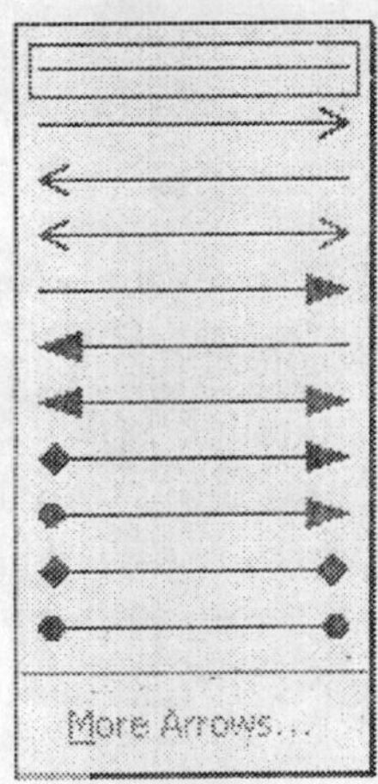

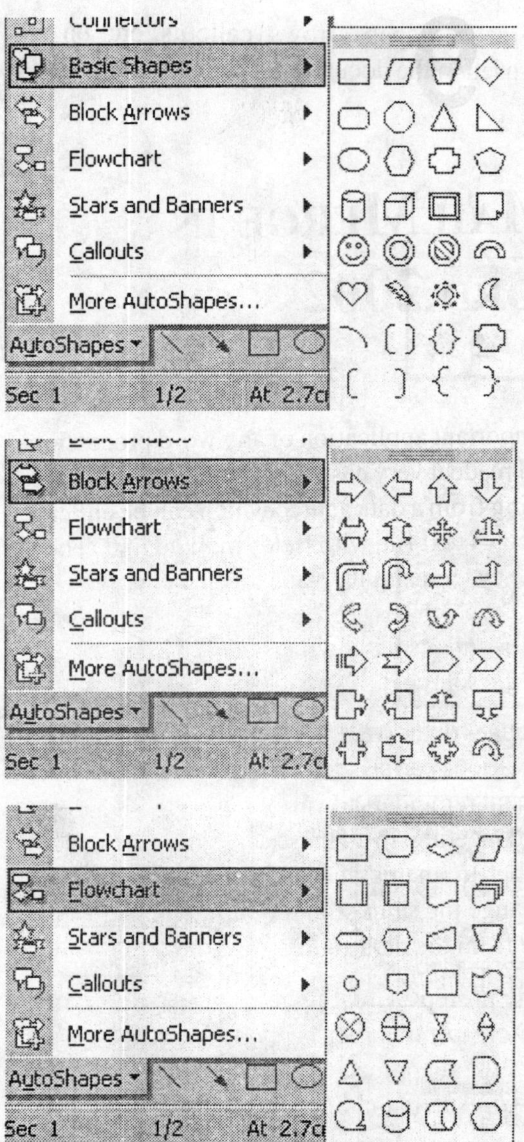
Connectors
Basic Shapes
Block Arrows
Flowchart
Stars and Banners
Callouts
More AutoShapes...
AutoShapes
Sec 1
1/2
At 2.7c
Block Arrows
Flowchart
Stars and Banners
Callouts
More AutoShapes...
AutoShapes
Sec 1
1/2
At 2.7c
Block Arrows
Flowchart
Stars and Banners
Callouts
More AutoShapes...
AutoShapes
Sec 1
1/2
At 2.7c

9

Using MailMerge in Word 2002

Introduction

MailMerge is one of the very important application of any word processing software. Word 2002 has indeed made it very easy to operate. In MailMerge you have the variable data coming from a data source which can be either a database file, spreadsheet, or even a text file with fields marked in it. Then you have the document file whose text remains the same for all the subsequent merged files changing only the data which has been received from the source. So in fact you create multiple documents having the same text but having different fields depending upon the source.

Well, one can think of various useages of the MailMerge. The most important being sending the same letter to various parties. Sending the same invitation to various guests. Sending payment reminders to various creditors. Calling all the directors to the same board meeting. In all these cases, the text would remain more or less the same but the name and address of the receiver would change. You can even change the salutation too, for example, Dear Mr. so and so, picking the name from the data source.

MailMerge in Word 2002 is done in steps. Creating document (text), data source and then merging them before printing. Let us see how it is done. For your information, here I am creating a appreciation letter for the various members of the victories Indian Cricket Team. So, lets start.

1. Start Word 2002.
2. On the Tools menu, point to Letters and Mailing and then click Mail Merge Wizard to open the Mail Merge task pane showing Step 1 to 6 in the wizard.

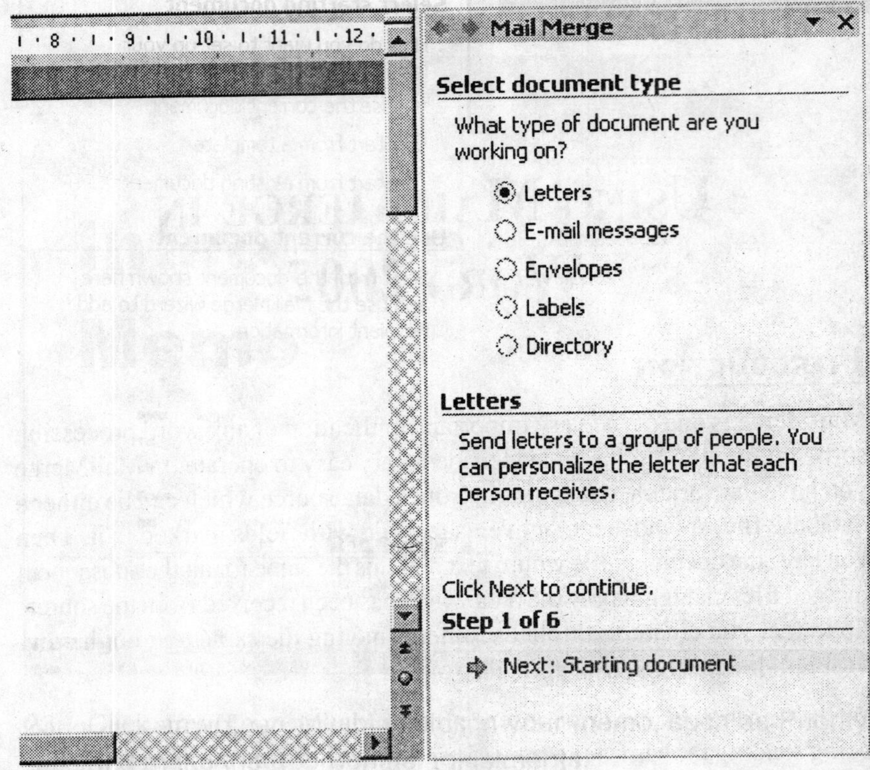

3. In the task pane, click the Letters option, and then click Next: Starting document at the bottom of the pane, to reach the step 2, as shown on the next page.
4. In the task pane, click the Use the current document option, then click Next: Select recipients at the bottom of the pane. Step 3 to 6 in the wizard appears, as shown on next page.
5. In the task pane, click the Type a new list to type a new list of the recipients and click at Create to get a New Address dialog box, shown on next to next page.
6. Here type your first entry with all the details known to you. You can leave the fields blank too, if not required. After entering the first entry, you can click at New Entry to get the next blank form for filling. Once done click at Close to get Save dialog box, to name your data source.

Select starting document

How do you want to set up your letters?

- ◉ Use the current document
- ○ Start from a template
- ○ Start from existing document

Use the current document

Start from the document shown here and use the Mail Merge wizard to add recipient information.

Step 2 of 6

➡ Next: Select recipients

Select recipients

- ○ Use an existing list
- ○ Select from Outlook contacts
- ◉ Type a new list

Type a new list

Type the names and addresses of recipients.

Create...

Step 3 of 6

➡ Next: Write your letter

⬅ Previous: Starting document

New Address List

Enter Address information

Title: Mr
First Name: Sachin
Last Name: Tendulkar
Company Name: Indian Cricket Team
Address Line 1: Prabhadevi Road
Address Line 2: Colaba
City: Bombay
State

New Entry | Delete Entry | Find Entry ... | Filter and Sort... | Custom

View Entries

View Entry Number: First | Previous | 2 | Next | Last

Total entries in list: 2

Close

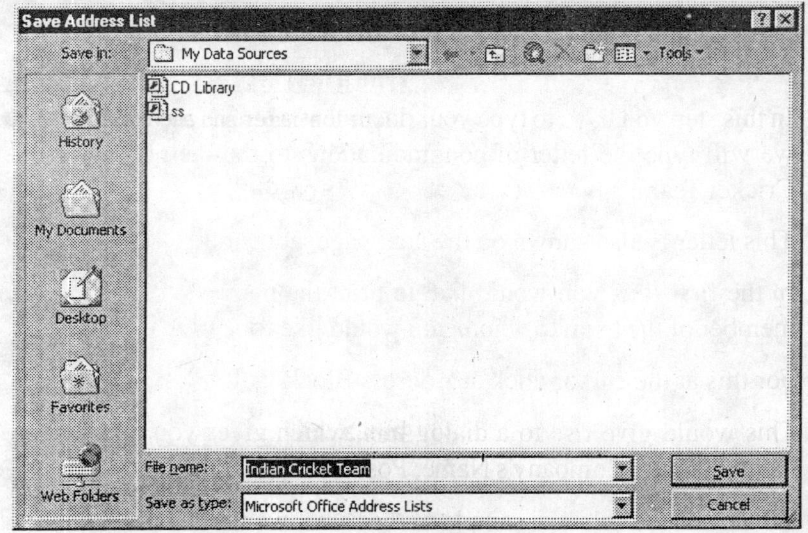

7. Here you are shown the data that you have entered into the Mail Merge Recipients which you can edit, if you want to by clicking at the required field.

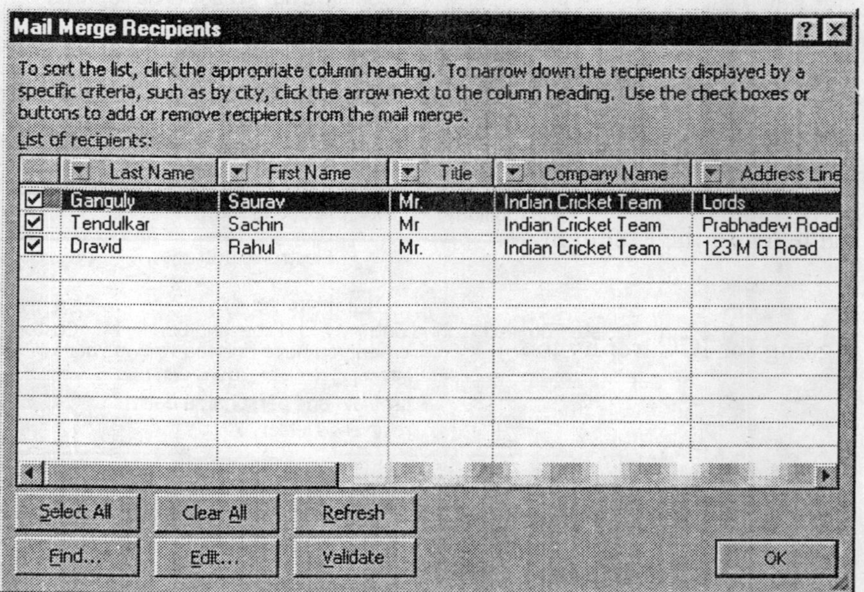

8. When pressed Ok, you are returned to Mail Merge with Step no. 4 displayed by Word 2002, as shown on the next page.
9. In this step you have to type your document. Here as mentioned earlier, we will type the letter of congradulations to the members of Indian Cricket Team.
10. This letter is also shown on the next page, at the bottom.
11. In the first line, you would like to print the name and address of the member of the team to whom you would like to send the letter.
12. For this at the cursor click at Address Block in the Task Pane.
13. This would give rise to a dialog box, which gives you the option of having Name, Company's Name, Postal Address, etc.
14. Whatever you select, a sample of the same, would be shown to you at the bottom of the dialog box.

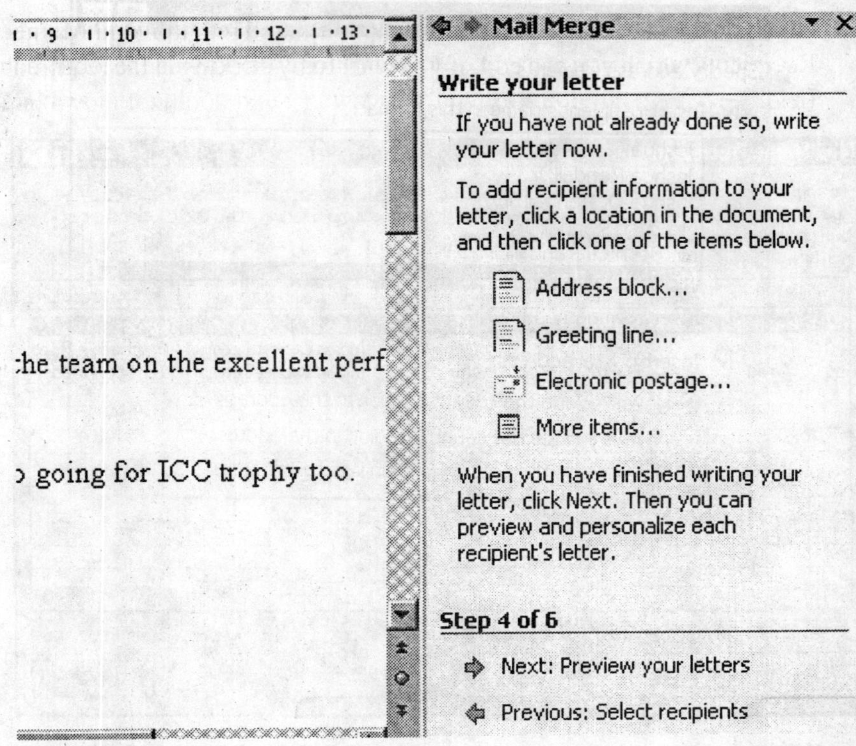

««AddressBlock»»

Dear ««AddressBlock»»

This is to congratulate you and other members of the team on the excellent perf during the team's visit to England.

I sincerely hope that you will keep the same tempo going for ICC trophy too.

Best of Luck

Yours truly,

(Ramesh Bangia)

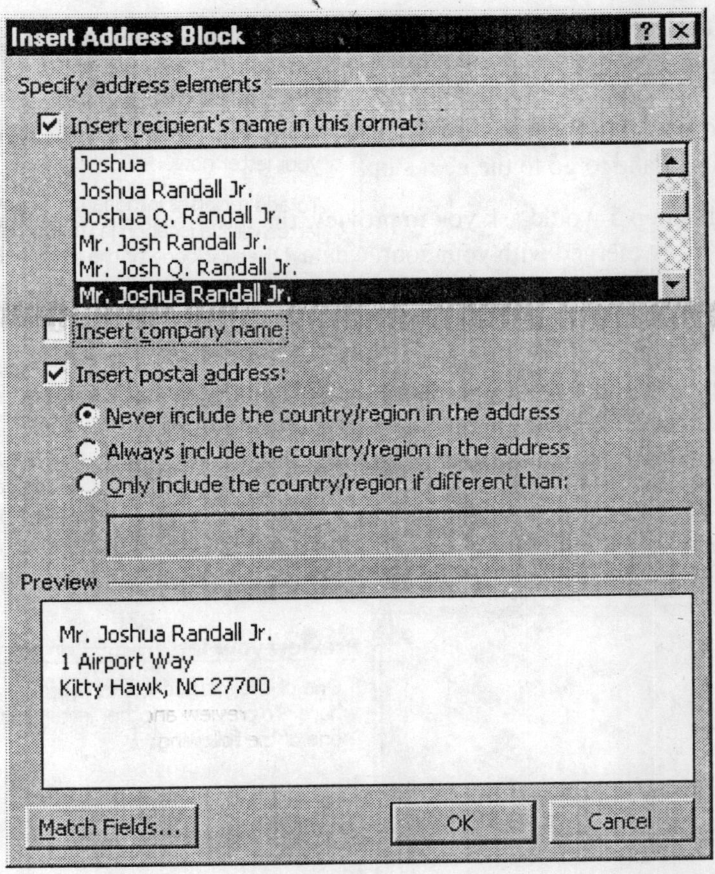

15. Here you can see that I have selected only Name and Postal Address.
16. Once selected you can click Ok.
17. This would give rise to a << <<Address Block>> >> at the position.
18. This line then would be replaced by the Name and Address when the document is merged.
19. In the next line, I have typed Dear and after this I want the name of the member.
20. So I would again click at Address Block in the Task Pane to get the above dialog box, once again.

21. This time I will select the name only and not the address.
22. Once this is done, we would type the complete letter.
23. So now that the matter of Step 4 is complete, we will click at Next in Task Pane to go to the next step.
24. The Step 5 would ask you to preview the letter, which Word 2002 has already merged with your source data.
25. So now your document has number of letters, each belonging to one data source.
26. Since we had made the data for 3 players, i.e., Sachin, Dravid and Ganguly, we have 3 letters in the document, which can be reviewed by moving the cursor up and down.
27. If you feel that there is something wrong, you can go back step by step and make changes.

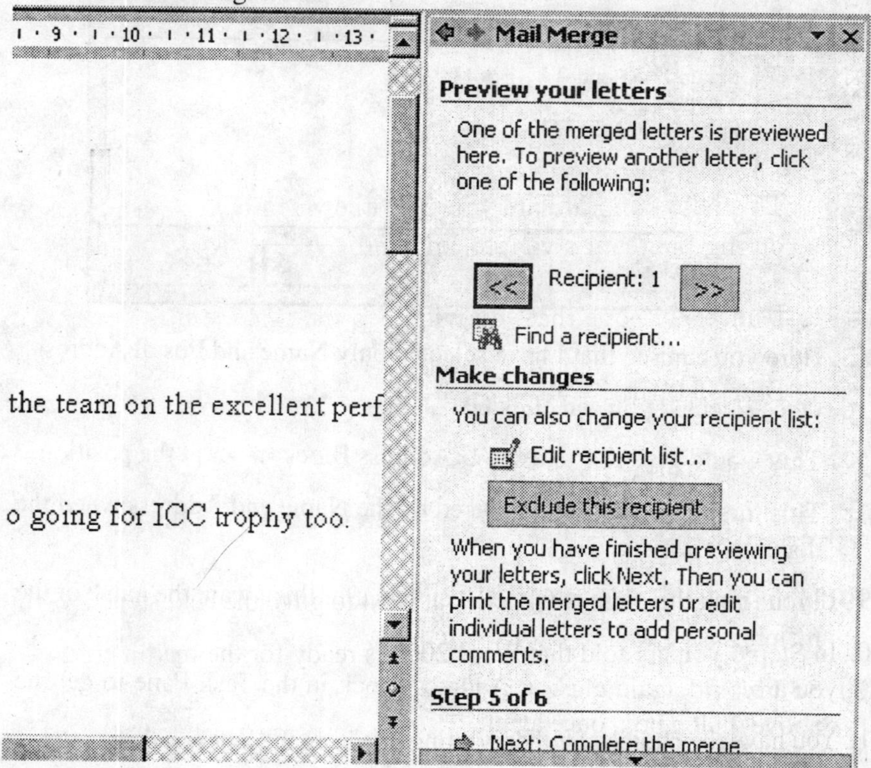

28. The merged letter looks like the one shown below.

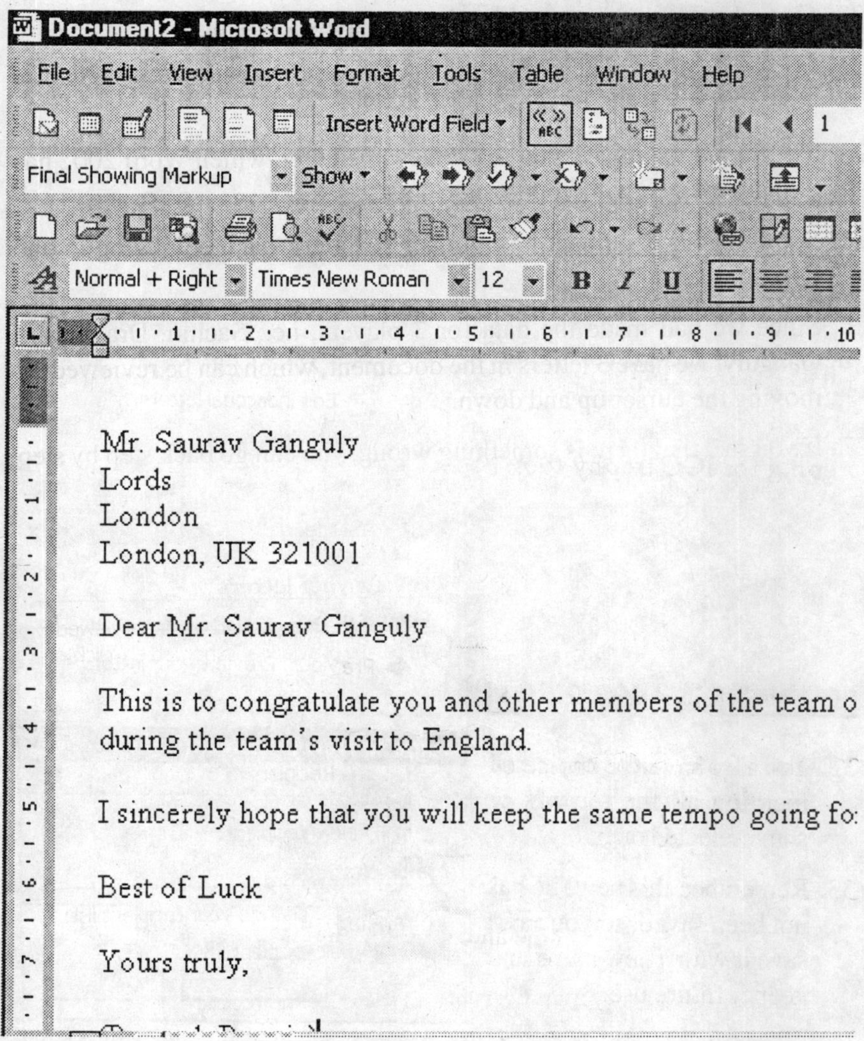

29. If you think the letter is Ok, click at Next to go to the next step.
30. In Step 6 you are told that Word 2002 is ready for the mail merge, if you are.
31. You have the choice of either printing or edting the letters individually.

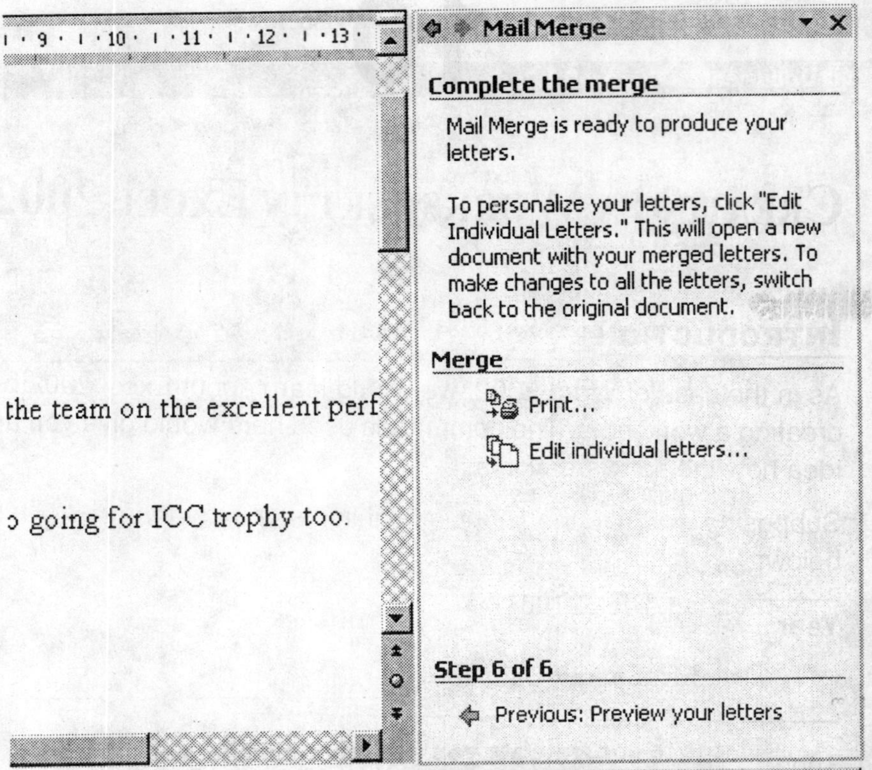

Mail Merge
Complete the merge
Mail Merge is ready to produce your letters.
To personalize your letters, click "Edit Individual Letters." This will open a new document with your merged letters. To make changes to all the letters, switch back to the original document.
Merge
Print...
Edit individual letters...
Step 6 of 6
Previous: Preview your letters
the team on the excellent perf
o going for ICC trophy too.

Merge to New Document
Merge records
All
Current record
From:
To:
OK
Cancel

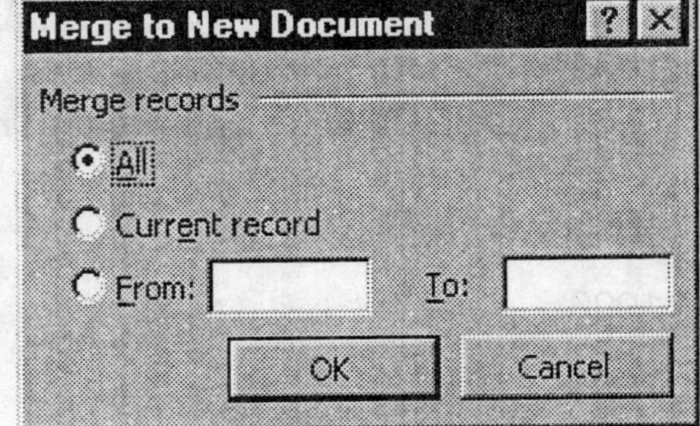

32. You also have the choice of merging all the records or some selected ones.

33. Remember, this new file has not been saved, so you must save it with a new name and keep it future use.

10

CREATING A WORKSHEET IN EXCEL 2002

INTRODUCTION

As in the case of Word 2002, we would learn about Excel 2002 by creating a worksheet. The commands used here would give you an idea how the software works.

Supposing we have the financial highlights of a company as given below:

Year	Total Income (A)	Interest Paid (B)	Profit (C)	Tax (D)	Profit After Tax (E)
1992	4,222	*To be calculated as 20% of the income*	*To be calculated as Income minus Interest (A) - (B)*	*To be calculated as 10% of the Profit*	*To be calculated as Profit minus Tax (C) - (D)*
1993	5,555				
1994	7,331				
1995	8,058				
1996	9,020				
1997	13,740				
1998	15,161				
1999	20,988				

As you can see that there are quite a number of fields which have to be calculated. This will act as a good exercise for you to do.

Let us start from the very beginning, i.e., start the software Microsoft Excel 2002. You will end up with a blank worksheet, ready for you to take action, with the first cell **A1**, totally at your command to do something, as shown in the figure below.

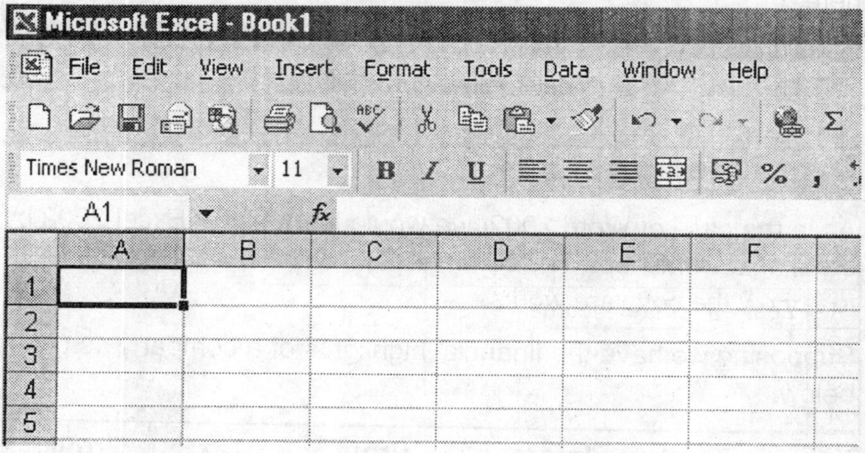

So what we have to do here. We have to type "Year". So just type the word Year and press **Enter**. You will see the word being shown in the formula bar too. This will also take you to the cell **A2**. But, for typing the next heading, you have to go to the cell **B1**. So use the arrow keys right and up to reach **B1**.

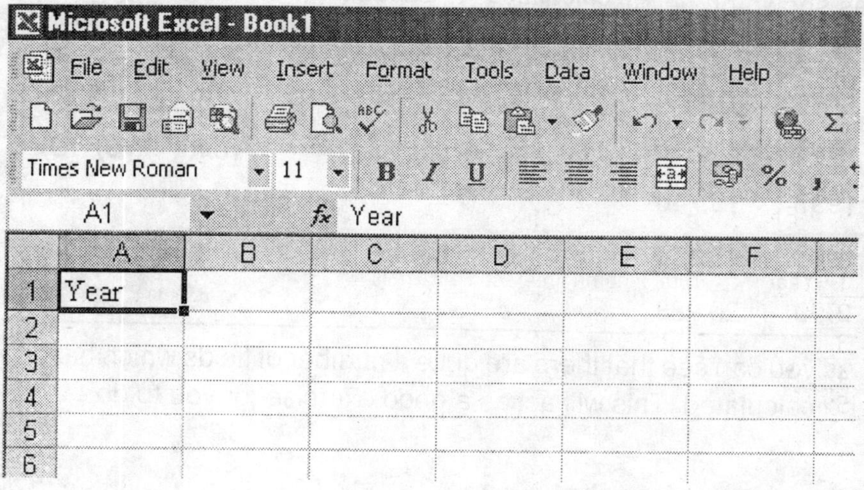

Next we have to type "Total Income". (Please note that for the sake of convenience I had shown this heading in 2 lines, but, if permitted we will type it in one line. Also (A), (B), etc., in the table are just symbolic and are not to be typed).

So for type the next heading, "Total Income" in the cell **B1**, as shown here.

Microsoft Excel - Book1

File Edit View Insert Format Tools Data Window Help

Arial 10 B I U %

B1 Total Income

	A	B	C	D	E	F
1	Year	Total Income				
2						
3						
4						

Do you notice anything wrong here? Well, the cell is not big enough to carry your heading. So what will we do? We will increase the width of the column **B**, by using one of the methods mentioned in earlier chapter.

This way now we will type the complete headings, i.e., all of them, as shown on below.

Microsoft Excel - Book1

File Edit View Insert Format Tools Data Window Help

Arial 10 B I U %

F1 Profit After Tax

	A	B	C	D	E	F
1	Year	Total Income	Interest Paid	Profit	Tax	Profit After Tax
2						
3						
4						
5						

But, since these are headings, and are to be highlighted. We will make them **Bold** and put them in the centre of the cells. This way they will look good.

Highlight all the cells by just clicking at cell **A1** and then while pressing **Shift** key click mouse in the cell **F1**, the whole row gets highlighted.

Now click at **B** in the formatting bar to make the whole text as **Bold**.

With the text in the cells remaining highlighted, click at ≣ in the formatting bar. This will make the text in the cells centralized in all the cells. This is shown in the figure shown below.

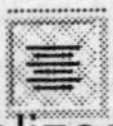

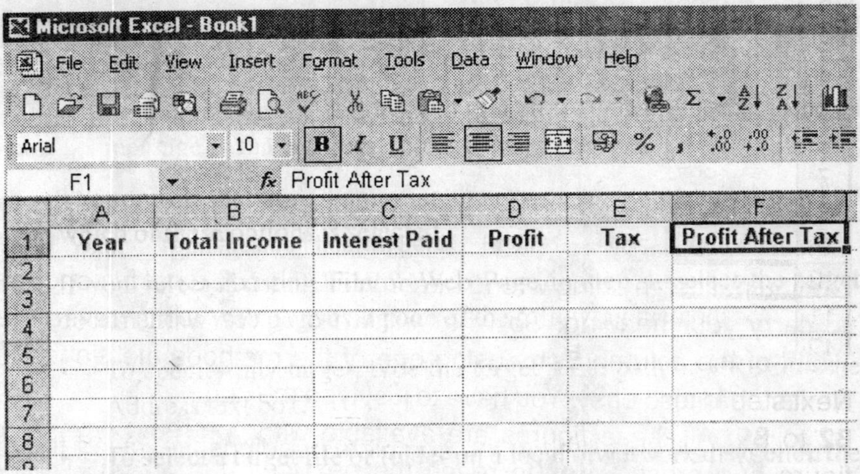

	A	B	C	D	E	F
1	**Year**	**Total Income**	**Interest Paid**	**Profit**	**Tax**	**Profit After Tax**

So now we have the headings ready. It was not very difficult, was it? Now all we have is the numeric data. Let us type them too. First of all we will type the various years.

By using the arrow keys, reach the cell **A2**. This is here that we have to type the first year, i.e., **1992**. Type it and press **Enter** to see the data getting aligned to the right. Remember, Excel aligns the numeric data to the right as a default. By pressing **Enter** you must have reached **A3** and this is where you wanted to be for typing the next year, i.e., **1993**.

So now type one year and press **Enter** to reach the next cell for typing the next year, till you reach the last year, i.e., **1999**. At this stage your worksheet will look like the one shown here.

Microsoft Excel - Book1

File Edit View Insert Format Tools Data Window Help

Arial 10 B I U %

A10 fx

	A	B	C	D	E	
1	Year	Total Income	Interest Paid	Profit	Tax	Pro
2	1992					
3	1993					
4	1994					
5	1995					
6	1996					
7	1997					
8	1998					
9	1999					
10						
11						
12						

Next step is also easy. You have to just type the numbers in the cells **B2** to **B9**. All these figures are available with you. Just type one figure and press **Enter** to reach the next cell and so on till you reach the last cell in the column. After doing this your worksheet will look like the one shown on the next page.

It would not be a bad idea to save this worksheet at this stage. For god forbid, if something happens, like power cut or so. So just press **Ctrl+S** to give the save command, as you would give in any other software. Now all you have to do it to give it a name and decide where you want to save this worksheet. Let us give the name **Finance** to it.

Now we come to the interesting part of this worksheet. So far we have typed whatever was available. Now we have to generate the

Microsoft Excel - Book1

File Edit View Insert Format Tools Data Window Help

Arial 10 B I U % ,

B9 fx 20988

	A	B	C	D	E	
1	Year	Total Income	Interest Paid	Profit	Tax	Pro
2	1992	4,222				
3	1993	5,555				
4	1994	7,331				
5	1995	8,058				
6	1996	9,020				
7	1997	13,740				
8	1998	15,161				
9	1999	20,988				
10						
11						

figures. The column **C** is of Interest Paid which is to be calculated by using the formula.

$$\text{Interest Paid} = \frac{\text{Total Income} \times 20}{100}$$

Transformed to the computer language it will become:

Interest Paid = (Total Income x 20)/100

If we put this in Cell **C2**, it will become:

C2 = SUM(B2*20/100)

Try putting this in the cell **C2** and see the result. It will be shown as below. It has given a figure of 844.40. Calculate the amount manually to see whether the result is Ok or not. It is correct, isn't it? Now we have to apply this formula to all the cells from **C3** to **C9**. Do you

Microsoft Excel - Book1

File Edit View Insert Format Tools Data Window Help

Arial 10

C2 =SUM(B2*20/100)

	A	B	C	D	E	
1	Year	Total Income	Interest Paid	Profit	Tax	Pro
2	1992	4,222	844.4			
3	1993	5,555				
4	1994	7,331				
5	1995	8,058				
6	1996	9,020				
7	1997	13,740				
8	1998	15,161				
9	1999	20,988				

have to put the formula for each cell or there is a method in Excel which allows you to copy the formula in each of the cell.

Well, fortunately there is. So this is how you will do it.

COPYING FORMULA

1. Click at cell **C2** to have the formula displayed in the formula bar.
2. Now with your mouse having clicked at cell **C2**, press the right button of the mouse.
3. You will get a dialog box, as shown below, which has various commands at your disposal.
4. Choose copy, as shown here, to copy the formula.
5. Next step now is to paste the formula in their respective cells.
6. Now click at cell **C3** with the mouse (left button).
7. Click the right button again to get the dialog box.
8. This time click at **Paste** instead.

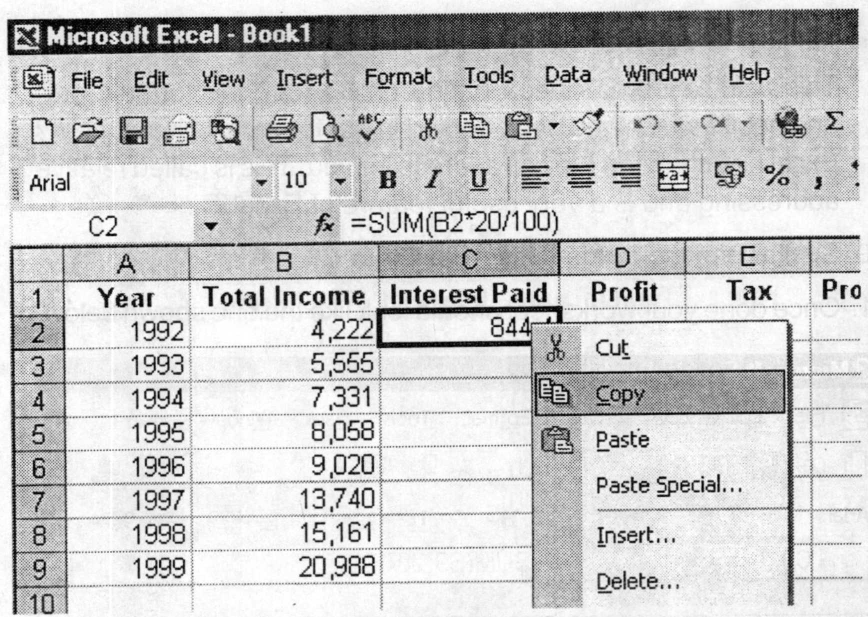

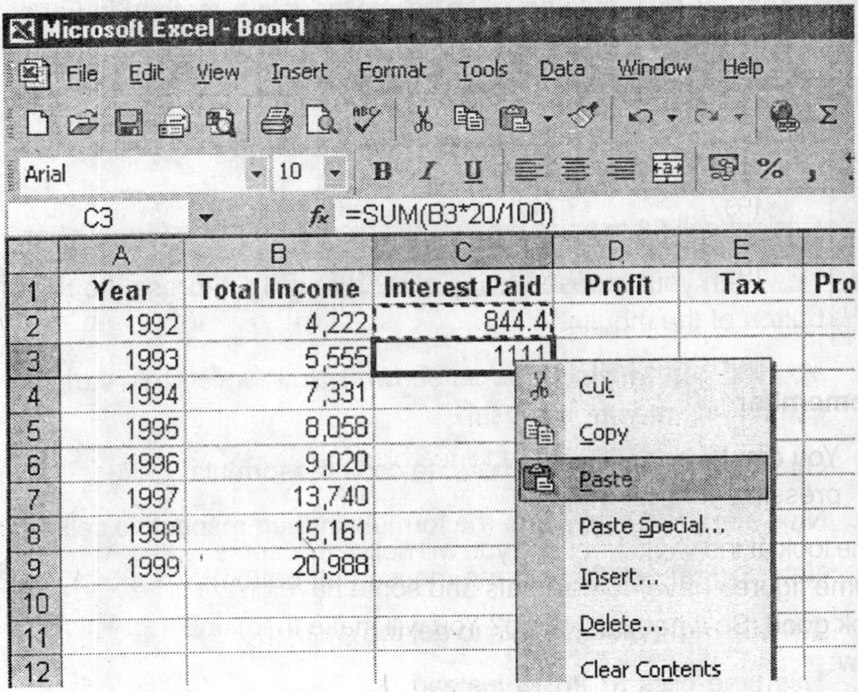

Microsoft Excel - Book1

File Edit View Insert Format Tools Data Window Help

Arial 10

C3 =SUM(B3*20/100)

	A	B	C	D	E	
1	Year	Total Income	Interest Paid	Profit	Tax	Pro
2	1992	4,222	844.4			
3	1993	5,555	1111			
4	1994	7,331				
5	1995	8,058				
6	1996	9,020				
7	1997	13,740				
8	1998	15,161				
9	1999	20,988				
10						
11						
12						

Cut
Copy
Paste
Paste Special...
Insert...
Delete...
Clear Contents

9. Immediately you will get the figure in cell **C3**.

   This calculation has been based on **B3** (see the formula bar) and not **B2** which had been copied in our formula. Is it not great? Excel has changed the cell address for you. This is called relative addressing and is a very useful feature of Excel.

10. Similar pasting in the cells from **C4** to **C9** can also be done.

11. Once done your worksheet should look like the one shown below.

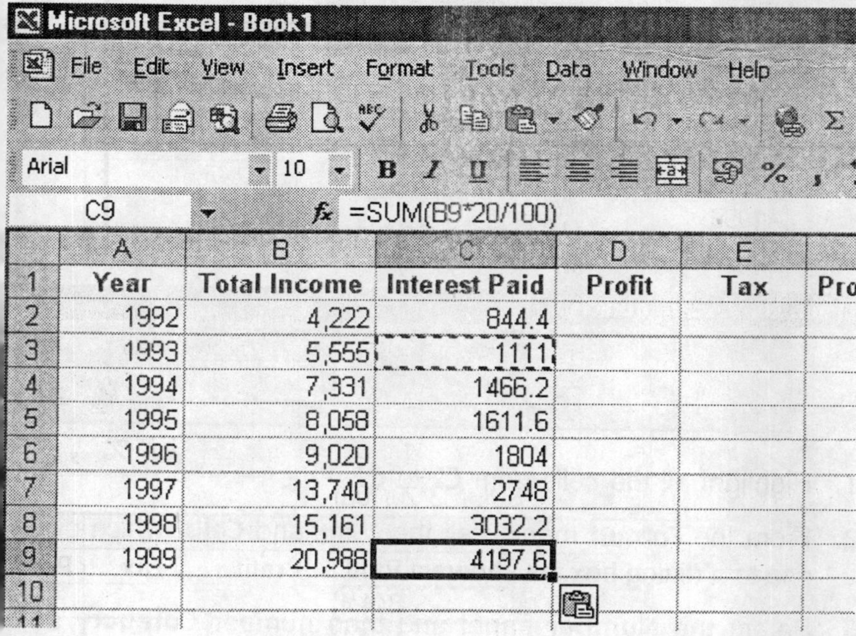

	A	B	C	D	E	
1	Year	Total Income	Interest Paid	Profit	Tax	Pro
2	1992	4,222	844.4			
3	1993	5,555	1111			
4	1994	7,331	1466.2			
5	1995	8,058	1611.6			
6	1996	9,020	1804			
7	1997	13,740	2748			
8	1998	15,161	3032.2			
9	1999	20,988	4197.6			
10						

Remember

1. You can take out the dotted lines blinking around the cell **C2** by pressing the **Esc** key.

One look at the worksheet and you will notice that something is wrong. Some figures have no decimals and some have one. This does not look good. So what will you do? You will make them uniform. This is how:

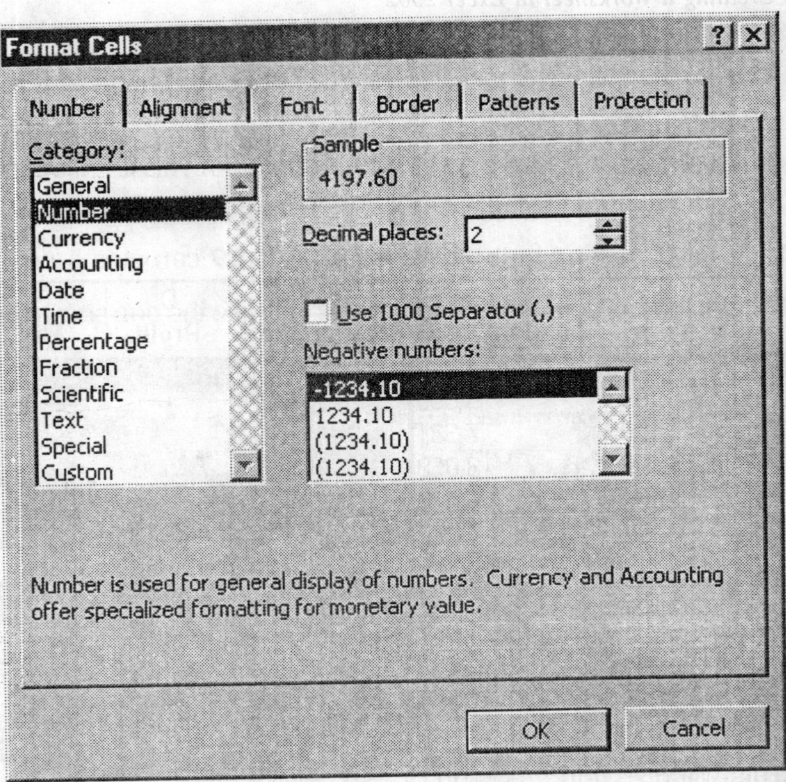

1. Highlight all the cells from **C2** to **C9**.
2. From the **Format** menu, call the command **Cells**, which gives rise to a dialog box, as shown above.
3. Select the **Number** panel and then number **Category** and select the **Decimal** places as 2 and click Ok.
4. All your cells now have 2 places of decimals, as shown on the next page.

Now that we have the figures of Column **C** are ready, we can proceed ahead to the next column, i.e., **D**. This column has "Profit", which is nothing but the difference of "Income" and "Interest". So let us calculate that.

Microsoft Excel - Book1

File Edit View Insert Format Tools Data Window Help

Arial 10 B I U %

C2 =SUM(B2*20/100)

	A	B	C	D	E	
1	Year	Total Income	Interest Paid	Profit	Tax	Pro
2	1992	4,222	844.40			
3	1993	5,555	1111.00			
4	1994	7,331	1466.20			
5	1995	8,058	1611.60			
6	1996	9,020	1804.00			
7	1997	13,740	2748.00			
8	1998	15,161	3032.20			
9	1999	20,988	4197.60			
10						

Click at cell **D2** and put the formula

=SUM(B2 – C2)

This will give you the figure for **D2**. Calculate it manually to make sure that the formula is right.

Microsoft Excel - Book1

File Edit View Insert Format Tools Data Window Help

Arial 10 B I U %

D2 =SUM(B2-C2)

	A	B	C	D	E	
1	Year	Total Income	Interest Paid	Profit	Tax	Pro
2	1992	4,222	844.40	3,377.6		
3	1993	5,555	1111.00			
4	1994	7,331	1466.20			
5	1995	8,058	1611.60			
6	1996	9,020	1804.00			
7	1997	13,740	2748.00			

Now, as we had done in the earlier case of Interest Paid, we will copy the formula and paste it in other cell, as shown below.

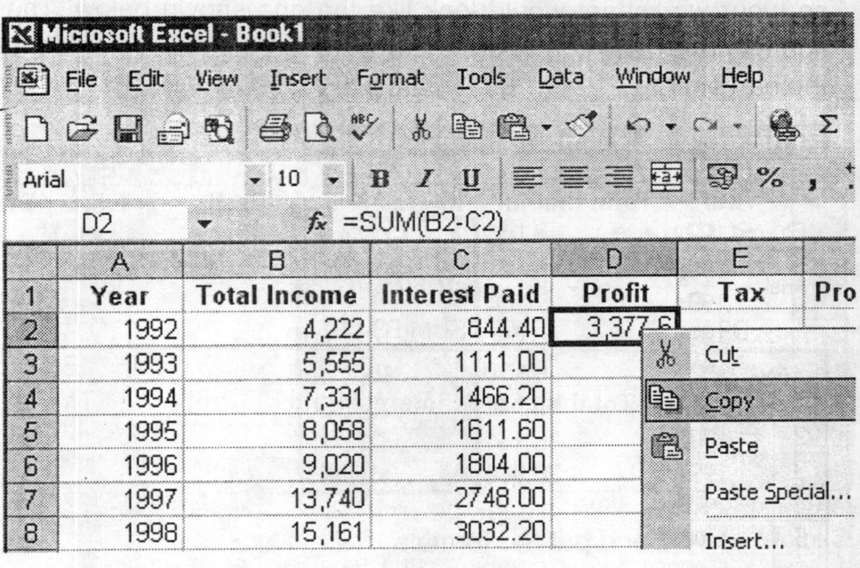

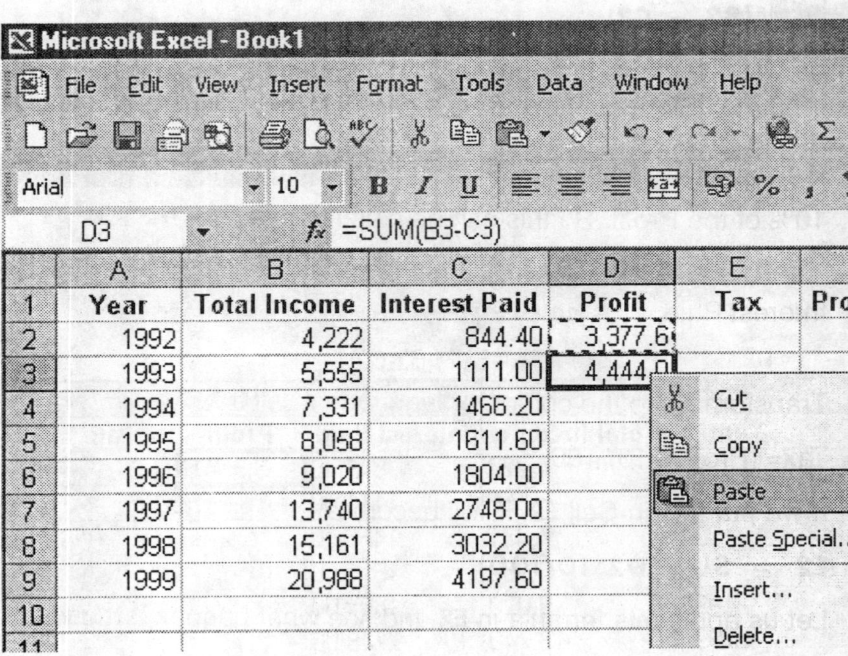

One by one you would be able to calculate all the figures of Profit and would be able to fill up the whole column **D**. After you have done so, your worksheet would look like the one shown below. These figures have been corrected to 2 places of decimals as was done in the earlier case.

Microsoft Excel - Book1

File Edit View Insert Format Tools Data Window Help

Arial 10

D9 =SUM(B9-C9)

	A	B	C	D	E	
1	**Year**	**Total Income**	**Interest Paid**	**Profit**	**Tax**	**Pr**
2	1992	4,222	844.40	3,377.60		
3	1993	5,555	1111.00	4,444.00		
4	1994	7,331	1466.20	5,864.80		
5	1995	8,058	1611.60	6,446.40		
6	1996	9,020	1804.00	7,216.00		
7	1997	13,740	2748.00	10,992.00		
8	1998	15,161	3032.20	12,128.80		
9	1999	20,988	4197.60	16,790.40		
10						

Next in line is the column called Tax. This is as said on Page 73, 10% of the Profit. So this can be calculated as below:

$$\text{Interest Paid} = \frac{\text{Profit} \times 10}{100}$$

Transformed to the computer language it will become:

Tax= (Profit x 10)/100

If we put this in Cell **E2**, it will become:

E2 = SUM(D2*10/100)

Let us apply this formula in **E2** and see what happens. It gives you

Microsoft Excel - Book1

File Edit View Insert Format Tools Data Window Help

Arial 10

E2 fx =SUM(D2*10/100)

	A	B	C	D	E	Pr
1	Year	Total Income	Interest Paid	Profit	Tax	Pr
2	1992	4,222	844.40	3,377.60	337.76	
3	1993	5,555	1111.00	4,444.00		
4	1994	7,331	1466.20	5,864.80		
5	1995	8,058	1611.60	6,446.40		
6	1996	9,020	1804.00	7,216.00		
7	1997	13,740	2748.00	10,992.00		
8	1998	15,161	3032.20	12,128.80		
9	1999	20,988	4197.60	16,790.40		

the result as 337.76. Copying this formula to the other cells, i.e., from **E3** to **E9**, you can fill up the whole column and make the worksheet look like the one shown below.

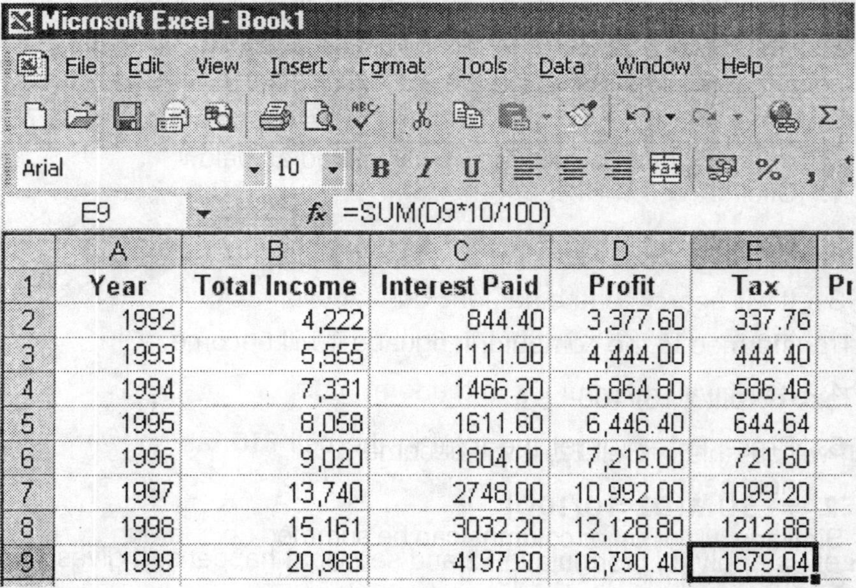

Microsoft Excel - Book1

File Edit View Insert Format Tools Data Window Help

Arial 10

E9 fx =SUM(D9*10/100)

	A	B	C	D	E	Pr
1	Year	Total Income	Interest Paid	Profit	Tax	Pr
2	1992	4,222	844.40	3,377.60	337.76	
3	1993	5,555	1111.00	4,444.00	444.40	
4	1994	7,331	1466.20	5,864.80	586.48	
5	1995	8,058	1611.60	6,446.40	644.64	
6	1996	9,020	1804.00	7,216.00	721.60	
7	1997	13,740	2748.00	10,992.00	1099.20	
8	1998	15,161	3032.20	12,128.80	1212.88	
9	1999	20,988	4197.60	16,790.40	1679.04	

The last column in this case is the "Profit After Tax", which can be calculated after subtracting "Tax" from the "Profit". This calculation I am not showing here, since I assume that you should be able to do this easily. However, your resultant worksheet should look like the one shown here.

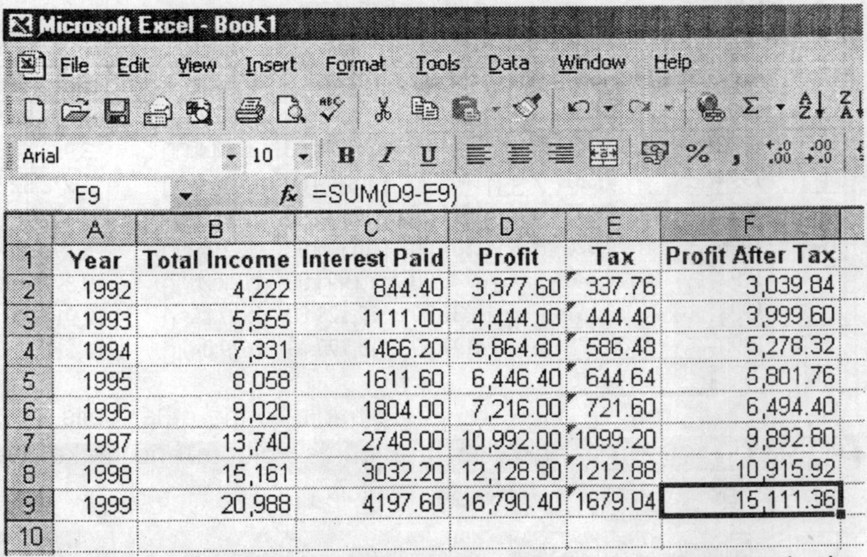

Microsoft Excel - Book1

File Edit View Insert Format Tools Data Window Help

Arial 10

F9 =SUM(D9-E9)

	A	B	C	D	E	F
1	Year	Total Income	Interest Paid	Profit	Tax	Profit After Tax
2	1992	4,222	844.40	3,377.60	337.76	3,039.84
3	1993	5,555	1111.00	4,444.00	444.40	3,999.60
4	1994	7,331	1466.20	5,864.80	586.48	5,278.32
5	1995	8,058	1611.60	6,446.40	644.64	5,801.76
6	1996	9,020	1804.00	7,216.00	721.60	6,494.40
7	1997	13,740	2748.00	10,992.00	1099.20	9,892.80
8	1998	15,161	3032.20	12,128.80	1212.88	10,915.92
9	1999	20,988	4197.60	16,790.40	1679.04	15,111.36
10						

You think the worksheet is complete. No. You still have to do the column totals without which the whole worksheet looks incomplete.

For this follow the following steps.

1. Click at cell **B10** to get the total of figures from **B2** to **B9**.
2. Now click at Σ symbol in the Standard toolbar.
3. It will search for the numeric cells above and put the formula for the same and highlight the cells it has selected.
4. It will wait for your Ok in the form of **Enter** to put the result.
5. Press **Enter** to get the total in the cell **B10**, as shown on the next page.

Similarly all the other columns can be summed up showing the result as shown on the next page.

Microsoft Excel - Book1

File Edit View Insert Format Tools Data Window Help

Arial 10

B10 fx =SUM(B2:B9)

	A	B	C	D	E	F
1	Year	Total Income	Interest Paid	Profit	Tax	Profit After Tax
2	1992	4,222	844.40	3,377.60	337.76	3,039.84
3	1993	5,555	1111.00	4,444.00	444.40	3,999.60
4	1994	7,331	1466.20	5,864.80	586.48	5,278.32
5	1995	8,058	1611.60	6,446.40	644.64	5,801.76
6	1996	9,020	1804.00	7,216.00	721.60	6,494.40
7	1997	13,740	2748.00	10,992.00	1099.20	9,892.80
8	1998	15,161	3032.20	12,128.80	1212.88	10,915.92
9	1999	20,988	4197.60	16,790.40	1679.04	15,111.36
10		84,075				
11						

Microsoft Excel - Book1

File Edit View Insert Format Tools Data Window Help

Times New Roman 10

F10 fx =SUM(F2:F9)

	A	B	C	D	E	F
1	Year	Total Income	Interest Paid	Profit	Tax	Profit After Tax
2	1992	4,222	844.40	3,377.60	337.76	3,039.84
3	1993	5,555	1111.00	4,444.00	444.40	3,999.60
4	1994	7,331	1466.20	5,864.80	586.48	5,278.32
5	1995	8,058	1611.60	6,446.40	644.64	5,801.76
6	1996	9,020	1804.00	7,216.00	721.60	6,494.40
7	1997	13,740	2748.00	10,992.00	1099.20	9,892.80
8	1998	15,161	3032.20	12,128.80	1212.88	10,915.92
9	1999	20,988	4197.60	16,790.40	1679.04	15,111.36
10		84,075.00	16,815.00	67,260.00	6,726.00	60,534.00
11						
12						

Now you can say that your worksheet is complete. But, supposing we want to make any change. This is done deliberately to show you the main advantage of Excel software.

Supposing, we change the figure of the year 1996 from 9,020 to 9,200, which we can assume that it was wrongly given to us or was a typing mistake. Try changing this figure in the cell **B6** and see the resultant effect.

Microsoft Excel - Book1

File Edit View Insert Format Tools Data Window Help

Times New Roman 10 B I U %

B6 fx 9200

	A	B	C	D	E	F
1	Year	Total Income	Interest Paid	Profit	Tax	Profit After Tax
2	1992	4,222	844.40	3,377.60	337.76	3,039.84
3	1993	5,555	1111.00	4,444.00	444.40	3,999.60
4	1994	7,331	1466.20	5,864.80	586.48	5,278.32
5	1995	8,058	1611.60	6,446.40	644.64	5,801.76
6	1996	9,200	1840.00	7,360.00	736.00	6,624.00
7	1997	13,740	2748.00	10,992.00	1099.20	9,892.80
8	1998	15,161	3032.20	12,128.80	1212.88	10,915.92
9	1999	20,988	4197.60	16,790.40	1679.04	15,111.36
10		84,255.00	16,851.00	67,404.00	6,740.40	60,663.60
11						

What have you noticed? Well since all the figures are mostly inter-linked, if you change one figure all the relative figures change automatically. This is the main advantage of Excel or for that an electronic spreadsheet.

Now if you apply this to the accounting department and assume that these figures relate to actual working of the finance department. Try changing the figures of one voucher and the poor accountant would have to sit probably the whole night to recalculate all the totals in the Balance Sheet. But, now with this kind of spreadsheet, this can be done in a flash.

Coming back to our worksheet. There are 3 things more to be done. Firstly, we will decorate it using the options available under the **AutoFormat** command. Then we will see a preview of our worksheet and then print it on our printer.

For decorating with the AutoFormat. Call the command from the Format menu, after highlighting the cells which you want to include in this AutoFormat and you will see the dialog box, as shown here.

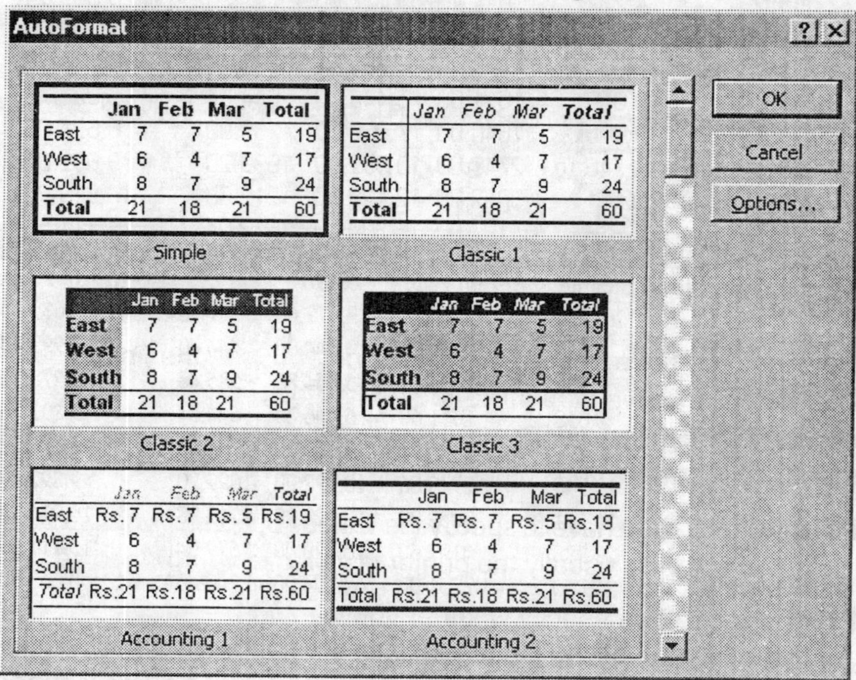

As you can see, there are various options available under this. Ranging from Simple, Classic, Accounting to 3-D ones. For our worksheet we are going to choose the one called Classic 2.

Just click at this and it would be applied. I am quite sure you would be interested to know the result of this. Turn over to the next page and see the result. I am quite sure that you are impressed with your work. You can make it look more impressive using the features of Borders, Patterns, etc. But, due to constrain of colour (this book is in black and white) I am not using the colours here.

Microsoft Excel - Book1

File Edit View Insert Format Tools Data Window Help

Arial 10 B I U % ,

B6 fx 9200

	A	B	C	D	E	F
1	**Year**	Total Income	Interest Paid	Profit	Tax	Profit After Tax
2	**1992**	4,222	844.40	3,377.60	337.76	3,039.84
3	**1993**	5,555	1111.00	4,444.00	444.40	3,999.60
4	**1994**	7,331	1466.20	5,864.80	586.48	5,278.32
5	**1995**	8,058	1611.60	6,446.40	644.64	5,801.76
6	**1996**	9,200	1840.00	7,360.00	736.00	6,624.00
7	**1997**	13,740	2748.00	10,992.00	1099.20	9,892.80
8	**1998**	15,161	3032.20	12,128.80	1212.88	10,915.92
9	**1999**	20,988	4197.60	16,790.40	1679.04	15,111.36
10		84,255.00	16,851.00	67,404.00	6,740.40	60,663.60
11						

Now that you have to print it on your printer to see the final result. But, before that we would like to see its **Preview**. This command is part of the **Print** command which is available under the **File** menu. There are various other options in the print dialog box.

Printer You have to specify the various options of your printer. It is usually the printer installed in your Windows.

Print range You specify whether you want to print the whole file or few selected pages.

Print what You can choose to print a selected portion of the worksheet, or a full worksheet or even few selected worksheet.

Preview As said earlier, this gives you the preview of the worksheet which you can see before printing.

Copies You can print number of copies of the worksheet and even collate the various pages of the worksheet.

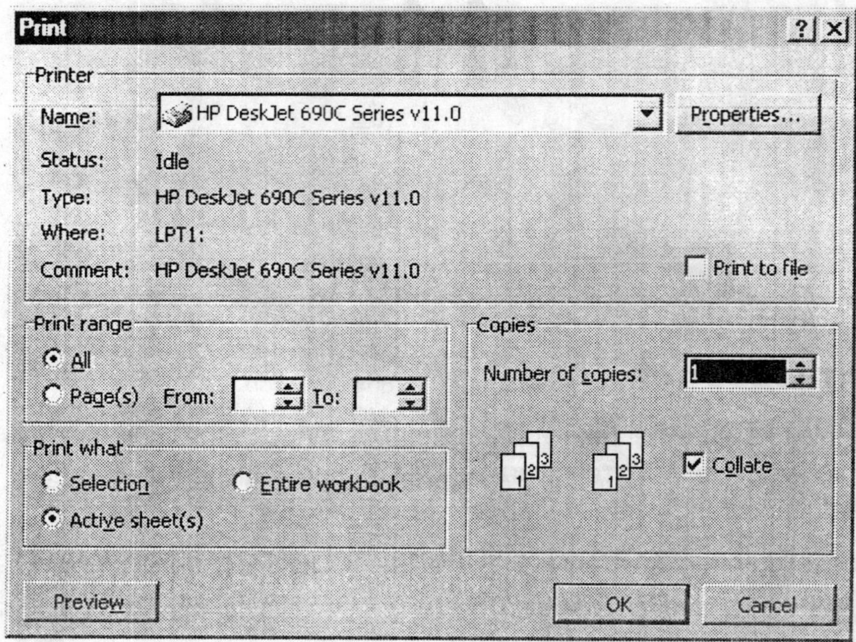

I am quite sure that now you have the confidence of creating a similar worksheet on your own. Why, similar, in fact, any worksheet for that matter. Do it yourself and improve your knowledge of the software.

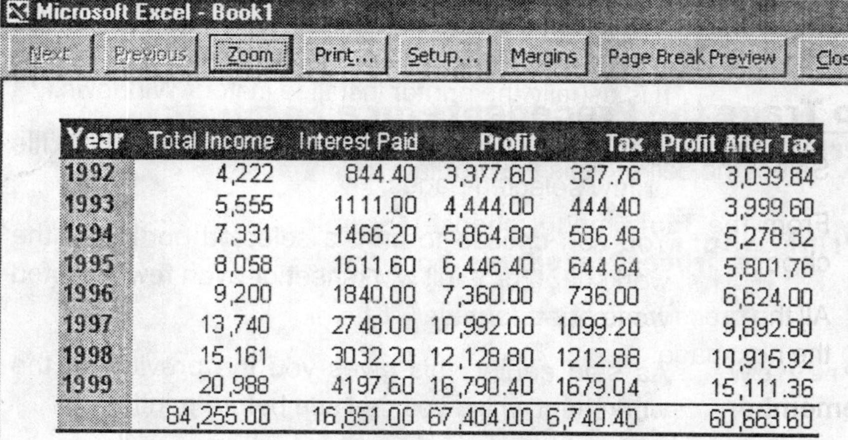

Year	Total Income	Interest Paid	Profit	Tax	Profit After Tax
1992	4,222	844.40	3,377.60	337.76	3,039.84
1993	5,555	1111.00	4,444.00	444.40	3,999.60
1994	7,331	1466.20	5,864.80	586.48	5,278.32
1995	8,058	1611.60	6,446.40	644.64	5,801.76
1996	9,200	1840.00	7,360.00	736.00	6,624.00
1997	13,740	2748.00	10,992.00	1099.20	9,892.80
1998	15,161	3032.20	12,128.80	1212.88	10,915.92
1999	20,988	4197.60	16,790.40	1679.04	15,111.36
	84,255.00	16,851.00	67,404.00	6,740.40	60,663.60

11

Advanced Techniques of Excel 2002

Introduction

In this chapter I will take you through the various other commands which you may not use in your regular routine working but are quite useful and can be used whenever required.

These commands are not new to Excel but are important while making the best use of the software.

Auditing a Workbook

To avoid bogus results from incorrect formulas, you can have Excel identify the cells that have supplied data for a formula. That way, you can easily see whether all the cells you wanted have been included in the calculation.

To Trace the Precedents for a Formula:

1. Select the cell or cells that contain the formulas.
2. From the **Tools** menu, choose **Formula Auditing**, and then choose **Trace Precedents** from the submenu.
3. All the precedents of the formula will be highlighted as shown on the next page.

Remember

1. To clear the arrows that have appeared to show the cells that

Microsoft Excel - finance

File Edit View Insert Format Tools Data Window Help

Arial 10 B I U % ,

E6 fx =SUM(D6*10/100)

	A	B	C	D	E	F
1	Year	Total Income	Interest Paid	Profit	Tax	Profit After Tax
2	1992	4,222	844.40	3,377.60	337.76	3,039.84
3	1993	5,555	1111.00	4,444.00	444.40	3,999.60
4	1994	7,331	1466.20	5,864.80	586.48	5,278.32
5	1995	8,058	1611.60	6,446.40	644.64	5,801.76
6	1996	9,200	1840.00	7,360.00	736.00	6,624.00
7	1997	13,740	2748.00	10,992.00	1099.20	9,892.80
8	1998	15,161	3032.20	12,128.80	1212.88	10,915.92
9	1999	20,988	4197.60	16,790.40	1679.04	15,111.36
10		84,255.00	16,851.00	67,404.00	6,740.40	60,663.60
11						

are included in the formula, choose **Remove All Arrows** from the **Auditing** submenu menu.

2. The Auditing toolbar contains Trace Precedents and Remove All Arrows buttons. To view the Auditing toolbar, choose **Show Auditing Toolbar** from the Auditing submenu.

COMMENTS INSERTING

A comment is an annotation that you attach to a cell to provide information about the cell's contents. This capability enables several people to review the same worksheet and attach their comments.

To insert a comment:

1. Select the cell to which you want to attach a comment.
2. From the **Insert** menu, choose **Comment**.
3. In the yellow text box that opens and displays your name, type the text for the comment.

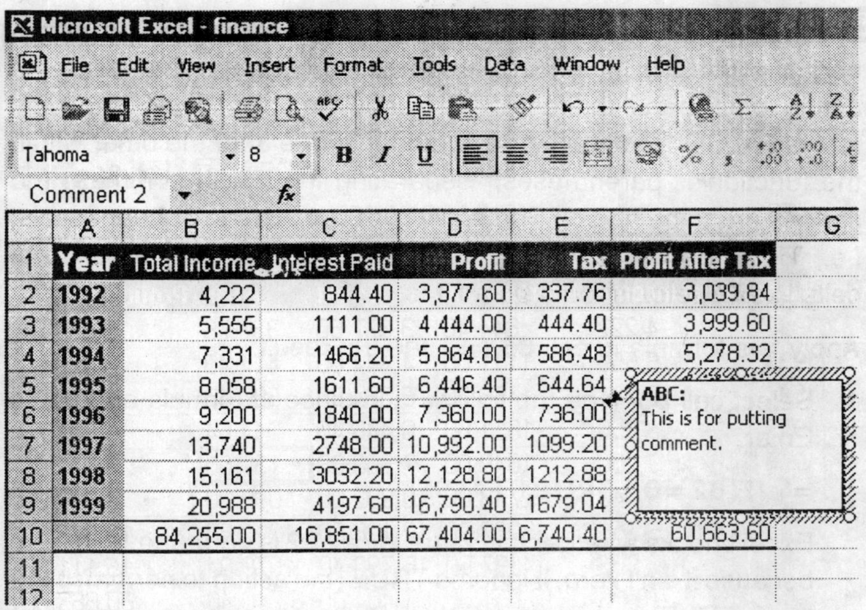

	A	B	C	D	E	F
1	Year	Total Income	Interest Paid	Profit	Tax	Profit After Tax
2	1992	4,222	844.40	3,377.60	337.76	3,039.84
3	1993	5,555	1111.00	4,444.00	444.40	3,999.60
4	1994	7,331	1466.20	5,864.80	586.48	5,278.32
5	1995	8,058	1611.60	6,446.40	644.64	
6	1996	9,200	1840.00	7,360.00	736.00	
7	1997	13,740	2748.00	10,992.00	1099.20	
8	1998	15,161	3032.20	12,128.80	1212.88	
9	1999	20,988	4197.60	16,790.40	1679.04	
10		84,255.00	16,851.00	67,404.00	6,740.40	60,663.60

4. Click in another cell to close the text box.

Remember

1. A comment is indicated by a comment marker (a small red triangle) at the upper right corner of the cell. To view the comment, pass the cursor over the cell.
2. To remove a comment, right-click in the cell, and choose Delete Comment from the shortcut menu.

Formulas That Make Decisions

There will be a time when you want Excel to carry out one task under certain circumstances and another task if those circumstances don't apply. If you are familiar with any programming language, it is the case of IF, WHEN or IF, THEN. You have a similar IF function in Excel.

How the IF function works

In its simplest form, the IF function tests the value of a cell and does one thing if the test is positive (**TRUE**) and another if the test is negative (**FALSE**). It requires three arguments: the test data, the action to perform if the test is TRUE and the action to perform if the test is FALSE. You supply the arguments one after the other within the function's parentheses, separating them with commas (no spaces are to be given). The text which you want to appear as it is, i.e., TRUE or FALSE should be given under quotes, reference of cells like **C5**, etc., should be as it is.

Apply this formula in cell **B6** and see the result:

1. Select cell **B6**, type the following in place of formula and press Enter:

   = IF(B2=0, TRUE, FALSE)

   Excel checks whether the value in cell **B2** is zero (the test), and because it isn't zero, it ignores TRUE (the action to perform if the test is TRUE) and displays FALSE (the action to perform if the test is FALSE) in cell **B6**.

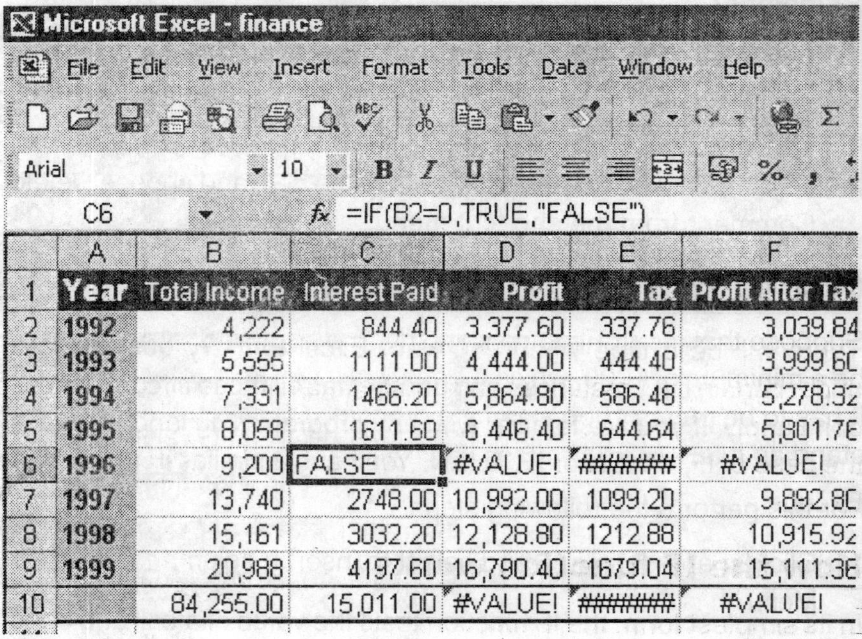

Microsoft Excel - finance

File Edit View Insert Format Tools Data Window Help

Arial 10 B I U % ,

C6 fx =IF(B2=0,TRUE,"FALSE")

	A	B	C	D	E	F
1	Year	Total Income	Interest Paid	Profit	Tax	Profit After Tax
2	1992	4,222	844.40	3,377.60	337.76	3,039.84
3	1993	5,555	1111.00	4,444.00	444.40	3,999.60
4	1994	7,331	1466.20	5,864.80	586.48	5,278.32
5	1995	8,058	1611.60	6,446.40	644.64	5,801.76
6	1996	9,200	FALSE	#VALUE!	#######	#VALUE!
7	1997	13,740	2748.00	10,992.00	1099.20	9,892.80
8	1998	15,161	3032.20	12,128.80	1212.88	10,915.92
9	1999	20,988	4197.60	16,790.40	1679.04	15,111.36
10		84,255.00	15,011.00	#VALUE!	#######	#VALUE!

2. Double-click cell **B6**, change formula to

   = IF(B2>1000, TRUE, FALSE")

   and press Enter. The entry in cell **B6** instantly changes from FALSE to TRUE because the value in cell **B2** is greater than one thousand; that is, the test is TRUE.

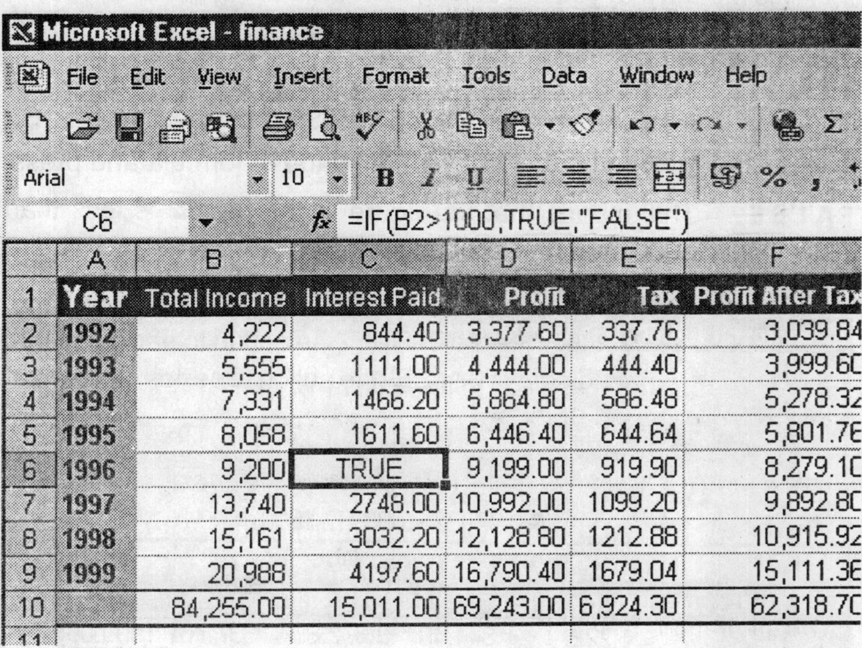

Microsoft Excel - finance

File Edit View Insert Format Tools Data Window Help

C6 =IF(B2>1000,TRUE,"FALSE")

	A	B	C	D	E	F
1	Year	Total Income	Interest Paid	Profit	Tax	Profit After Tax
2	1992	4,222	844.40	3,377.60	337.76	3,039.84
3	1993	5,555	1111.00	4,444.00	444.40	3,999.60
4	1994	7,331	1466.20	5,864.80	586.48	5,278.32
5	1995	8,058	1611.60	6,446.40	644.64	5,801.76
6	1996	9,200	TRUE	9,199.00	919.90	8,279.10
7	1997	13,740	2748.00	10,992.00	1099.20	9,892.80
8	1998	15,161	3032.20	12,128.80	1212.88	10,915.92
9	1999	20,988	4197.60	16,790.40	1679.04	15,111.36
10		84,255.00	15,011.00	69,243.00	6,924.30	62,318.70

Now this was very simple. Isn't it. However, you can also build tests that involve other functions.

Suppose that in our Finance worksheet, we say that the Tax has to be a minimum of 1000, which means that if the Tax is less than 1000 it has to be put as 1000 and if it more that 1000, then the figure will stand as it is.

For this perform the following steps.

1. Click at any entry in **E** and select to insert a column from **Insert** Menu.

2. Use the Cut, Paste and Format buttons to restore the entries now in **E2:E9** to **F2:F9**.

3. Click at **F2** and apply the formula

   =IF(E2>1000, E2, 1000)

   This means that you are asking the system to check if it is above 1000, One of the two possibilities will arise:

TRUE This means that the figure in cell is more than 1000, then the column will be replaced by the figure in **E2**, which means that it is not changed.

FALSE This means that the figure in the cell **E2** is less than 1000, then the second condition will be met, i.e., figure in cell **F2** will be replaced with the figure of 1000.

Microsoft Excel - finance

File Edit View Insert Format Tools Data Window Help

Arial 10 B I U % ,

F2 =IF(E2>1000,E2,1000)

	A	B	C	D	E	F	
1	Year	Total Income	Interest Paid	Profit	Tax	Tax	Profi
2	1992	4,222	844.40	3,377.60	337.76	1000.00	
3	1993	5,555	1111.00	4,444.00	444.40	444.40	
4	1994	7,331	1466.20	5,864.80	586.48	586.48	
5	1995	8,058	1611.60	6,446.40	644.64	644.64	
6	1996	9,200	1840.00	7,360.00	736.00	736.00	
7	1997	13,740	2748.00	10,992.00	1099.20	1099.20	
8	1998	15,161	3032.20	12,128.80	1212.88	1212.88	
9	1999	20,988	4197.60	16,790.40	1679.04	1679.04	
10		84,255.00	16,851.00	67,404.00	6,740.40	7,402.64	
11							
12							
13							
14							

Repeat this for all the other cells of column **F**. The easiest way out to repeat the formula in each column.

Headers and Footers

Excel lets you add headers and footers to print information at the top and bottom of every page of the printout. The information can include any text, as well as page numbers, the current date and time, the workbook file name, and the worksheet tab name.

You can choose the headers and footers suggested by Excel, or you can include any text plus special commands to control the appearance of the header or footer. For example, you can apply, bold, italic, or underline to the header or footer text. You can also left-align, center, or right-align your text in a header or footer.

To add headers and footers, follow these steps:

1. Open the **View** menu and choose **Header and Footer**. The Page Setup dialog box appears.
2. To select a header, click the **Header** drop-down arrow, Excel displays a list of suggested header information. Scroll through the list and click the header you want. The sample header appears at the top of the **Header/Footer** tab.
3. To select a footer, click the **Footer** drop-down arrow, Excel displays a list of suggested footer information. Scroll through the list and click on a footer you want. The sample footer appears at the bottom of the **Header/Footer** tab.
4. Click Ok to close the Page Setup dialog box and return to your worksheet. Or click the **Print** button to display the Print dialog box, and click Ok to print your worksheet.

Merging Workbooks

Sharing work is to maintain multiple copies of a shared workbook and track the changes in each for the same period of time. At the end of that time, you can merge the copies.

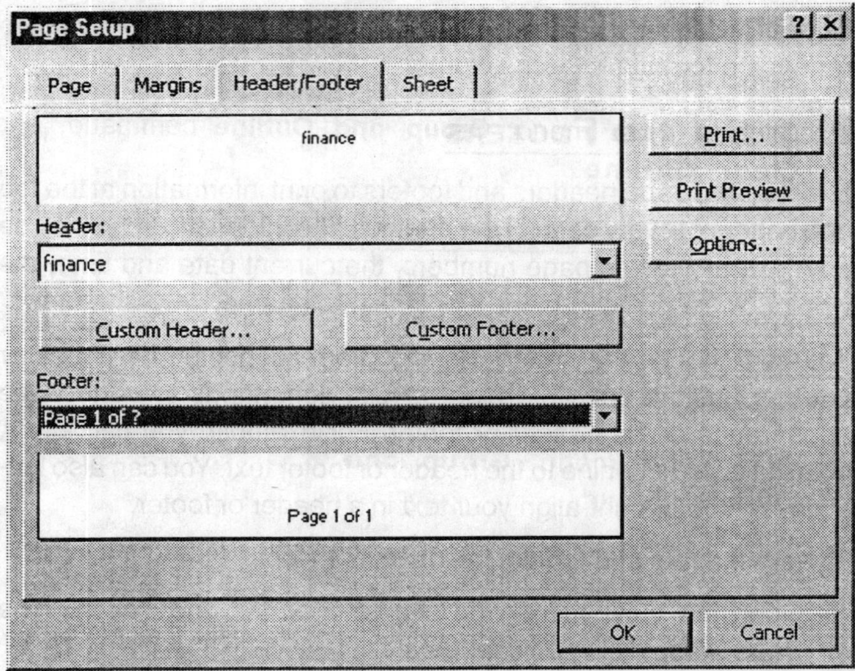

To merge workbooks:

1. From the **Tools** menu, choose **Merge Workbooks**.
2. Select the workbooks to merge into the current one.
3. Click Ok.

OUTLINES

Outline a Worksheet Automatically

1. Select a single cell to outline or the entire worksheet
2. Select a range of cells to outline
3. Click **Data** menu, **Group and Outline** command, and click at **Auto Outline**.

An outline created with outline symbols to the left of the row heading and/or above column headings.

Clear Entire Outline

1. Select any cell in outline
2. Click at **Data** menu, **Group and Outline** command, and **Clear Outline**.

Show or Hide Outline Symbols

1. Click at **Tools** menu, Hide Details command

Group Rows or Columns in an Outline

1. Select rows or columns to group
2. Click **Data** menu, **Group and Outline**, Group...

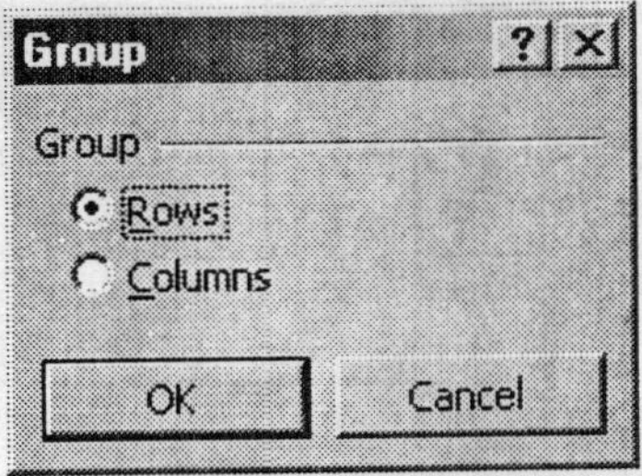

If Group dialog box appears

1. Select Rows or Columns
2. Click Ok

Ungroup Rows or Columns in an Outline

1. Select group in outline to ungroup
2. Click **Data** menu, **Group and Outline** command, Ungroup...

If Ungrouped dialog box appears

1. Select **Rows** or **Columns**
2. Click Ok

Remove Group from Outline

1. Select group in outline to remove
2. Click **Data** menu, **Group and Outline**, Clear **Outline**

Set Outline Options

1. Click **Data** menu, **Group and Outline**, Settings...

Microsoft Excel - finance

File Edit View Insert Format Tools Data Window Help

Arial 10 B I U % ,

B4 fx 7331

	A	B	C	D	E	F
1	Year	Total Income	Interest Paid	Profit	Tax	Profit Afte
2	1992	4,222	844.40	3,377.60	337.76	3,0
3	1993	5,555	1111.00	4,444.00	444.40	3,9
4	1994	7,331	1466.20	5,864.80	586.48	5,2
5	1995	8,058	1611.60	6,446.40	644.64	5,8
6	1996	9,200	1840.00	7,360.00	736.00	6,6
7	1997	13,740	2748.00	10,992.00	1099.20	9,8
8	1998	15,161	3032.20	12,128.80	1212.88	10,9
9	1999	20,988	4197.60	16,790.40	1679.04	15,1
10		84,255.00	16,851.00	67,404.00	6,740.40	60,6
11						
12						
13						

2. Select or deselect Direction options.

Printing Column and Row Labels on Every Page

Excel provides a way for you to select labels and titles that are located on the top edge and left side of a large worksheet, and print them on every page of the printout. This option is useful when a worksheet is too wide to print on a single page. If you don't use this option, the extra columns or rows will be printed on subsequent pages without any descriptive labels.

Do the following for this:

1. Open the **File** menu and choose **Page Setup**. The Page Setup dialog box appears.

2. Click the **Sheet** tab to display the Sheet options.
3. To repeat column labels and a worksheet title, click the **Collapse Dialog button** to the right of the Rows to repeat at top text box.
4. Drag over the rows you want to print on every page. A dashed line border surrounds the selected area, and absolute cell references with dollar signs appear in the Rows to repeat at top text box.
5. Click the **Collapse Dialog** button to return to the Page Setup dialog box.
6. To repeat row labels that appear on the left of the worksheet, click the Collapse Dialog button to the right of the Columns to repeat at left text box. Excel reduces the Page Setup dialog box. Then click Ok.

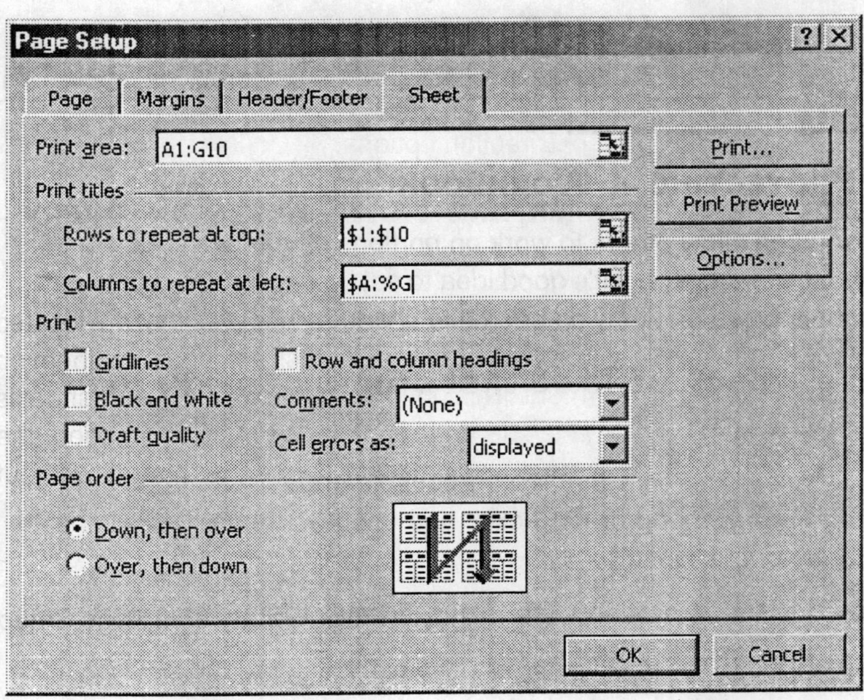

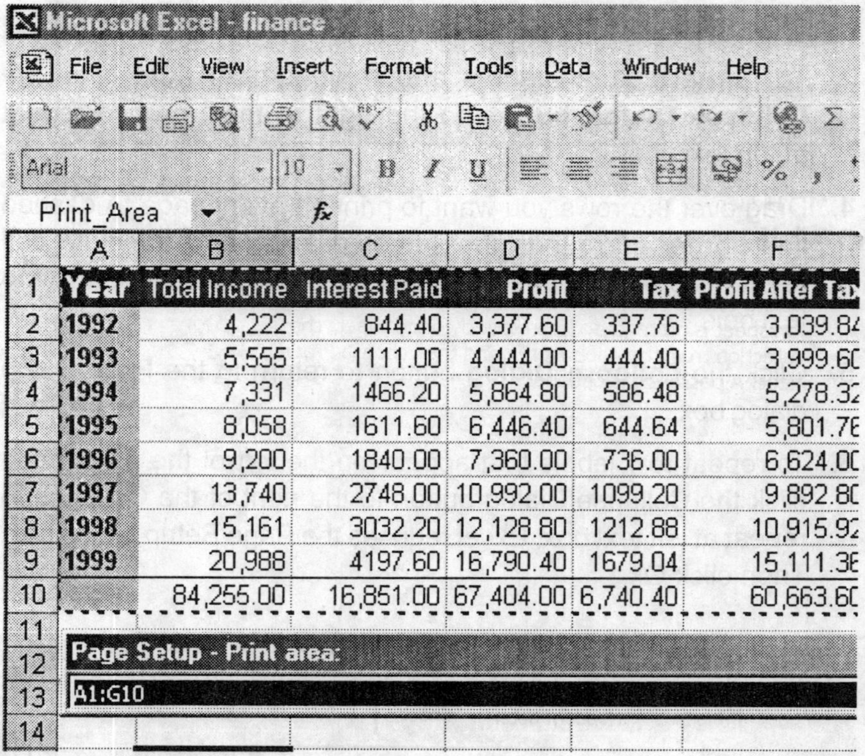

Microsoft Excel - finance

File Edit View Insert Format Tools Data Window Help

Print_Area

	A	B	C	D	E	F
1	Year	Total Income	Interest Paid	Profit	Tax	Profit After Ta
2	1992	4,222	844.40	3,377.60	337.76	3,039.8
3	1993	5,555	1111.00	4,444.00	444.40	3,999.6
4	1994	7,331	1466.20	5,864.80	586.48	5,278.3
5	1995	8,058	1611.60	6,446.40	644.64	5,801.7
6	1996	9,200	1840.00	7,360.00	736.00	6,624.0
7	1997	13,740	2748.00	10,992.00	1099.20	9,892.8
8	1998	15,161	3032.20	12,128.80	1212.88	10,915.9
9	1999	20,988	4197.60	16,790.40	1679.04	15,111.3
10		84,255.00	16,851.00	67,404.00	6,740.40	60,663.6

Page Setup - Print area:

A1:G10

Protecting a Workbook

You can allow others to work on portions of your workbook or all of your workbook, but it's good idea to set up cell formatting options in advance so that they do not make changes inadvertently..

To unlock cells so that others can edit the cell contents:

1. Select the cells that will be editable and choose **Cells** from the **Format** menu or right-click and choose Format Cells from the shortcut menu.
2. On the **Protection** tab in the Format Cells dialog box, clear the **Locked** check box.

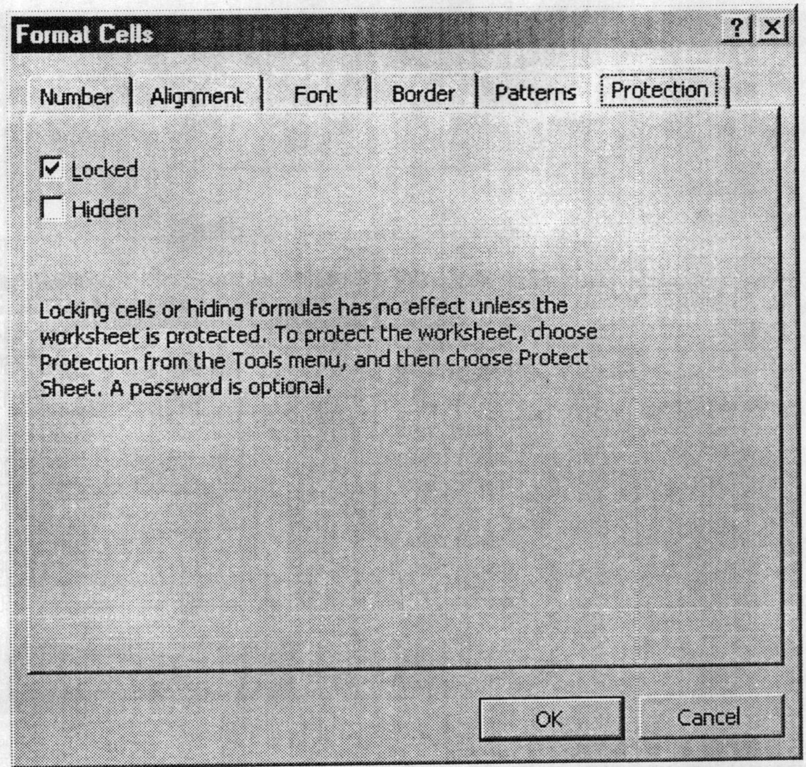

3. Click Ok.

Remember

1. To hide formulas, check Hidden on the Protection tab in the Format Cells dialog box.

To protect a workbook:

1. From the **Tools** menu, choose **Protection**, and choose **Protect Sheet** from the submenu.
2. In the Protect Sheet dialog box, you can assign a password so that you are the only one who can remove the protection.
3. Click Ok.

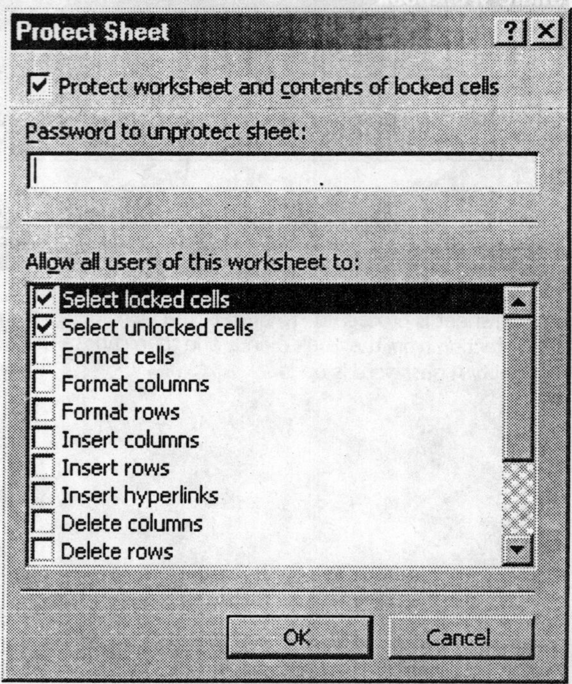

To share a workbook:

1. From the **Tools** menu, choose **Share Workbook**.
2. On the Editing tab in the Chart Workbook dialog box, enable changes by more than one user.
3. On the **Advanced** tab, specify when you want the changes updated and how you want conflicts handled.
4. Click Ok.

Remember

1. To return the workbook to its unshared state, choose Share Workbook from the Tools menus and clear the Allow Changes check box.
2. You can protect and share in one step by choosing Protect and Share Workbook from the Protection submenu.

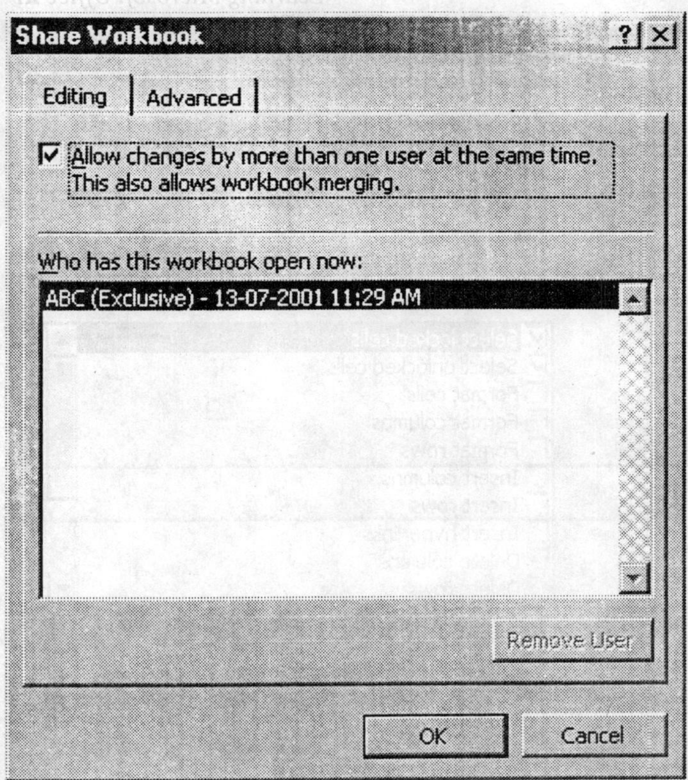

Ranges, Naming

When you assign a name to a range, you can use the range name in formulas rather than the range address. Range names make it easier to refer to data and easier to understand formulas.

To name a range:

1. Select the range that you want to name.
2. From the **Insert** menu, choose **Name**, and then choose **Define from the Name** submenu.
3. Enter the name in the Define Name dialog box.
4. Click Ok.

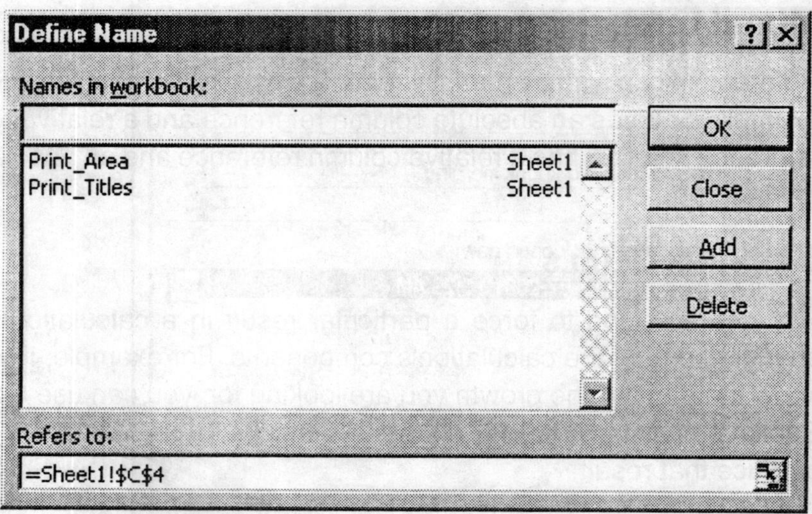

Remember

1. To use the name in a formula, choose **Paste** from the **Name** submenu.
2. You can assign a name to an individual cell or to a range of cells.

REFERENCES

By default, Excel uses relative references in its formulae. Relative references refer to cells by their position in relation to the cell containing the formula. So when you copy the formula in cell **F5** to cell **F6**, Excel changes the reference from **E5** to **E6**.

Absolute references

When you don't want a reference to be copied as a relative reference, you need to use an absolute reference. Absolute references refer to cells by their fixed position in the worksheet. To make a reference absolute, you add dollar signs before its column letter and now number. For example, you would enter it as **$C$4:$C$9**. You could then copy formula that contained this reference anywhere on the worksheet and it would always refer to the range **C4:C9**.

Mixed references

References can also be partially relative and partially absolute. For example, **$C3** has an absolute column reference and a relative row reference and **C$3** has a relative column reference and an absolute row reference.

SEEKING GOALS

Use goal seeking to force a particular result in a calculation by changing one of the calculation's components. For example, if you know the percentage growth you are looking for, you can use Goal Seeking to determine the changes that would be necessary to produce that result.

To seek a goal:

1. From the **Tools** menu, choose **Goal Seek**.
2. In the Goal Seek dialog box, specify the cell whose value you want to set (this should be a cell whose value is usually calculated through a formula), the value you want that cell to have, and the cell whose value can vary to make the result come out to the value you want.

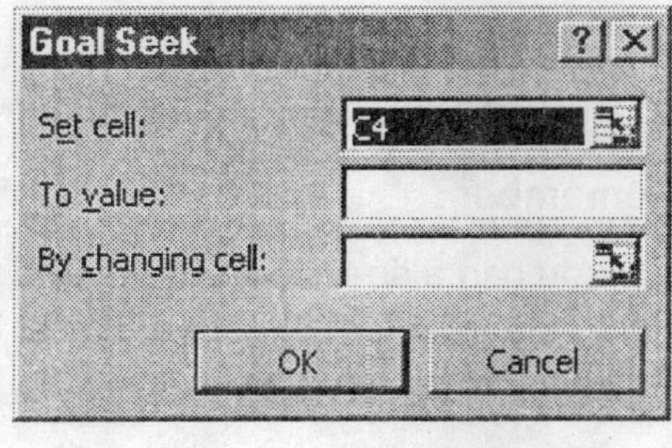

3. Click Ok.
4. If a solution is possible, the Goal Seek Status dialog will tell you, and the variable cell you specified will change.
5. Click Ok to accept the change or click Cancel to reject it.

SHEETS NAMING

You can replace the default sheet names (Sheet1, Sheet2, and so

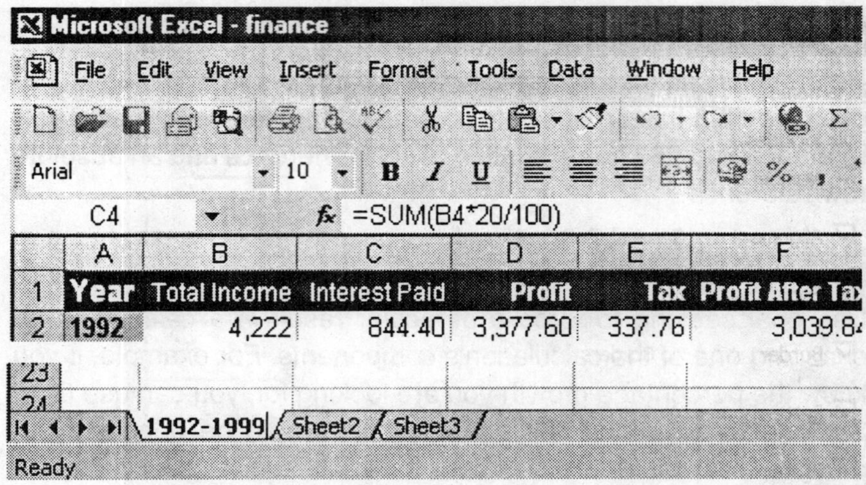

on) with useful informative names (for example, Finance, Personnel, Manufacturing, Secretarial, etc).

To Name a Sheet:

1. Double click the tab of the sheet you want to rename.
2. Type the new name over the current name in the sheet tab.

Remember

1. You can also choose Sheet and then Rename from the Format menu to select the sheet name in the tab of the current sheet, ready to be typed over.
2. Sheet names can be up to 31 characters long and can include spaces.

STYLES

Create a Style by Example

1. Select cell containing desired formats
2. Click **Format** menu, Style...

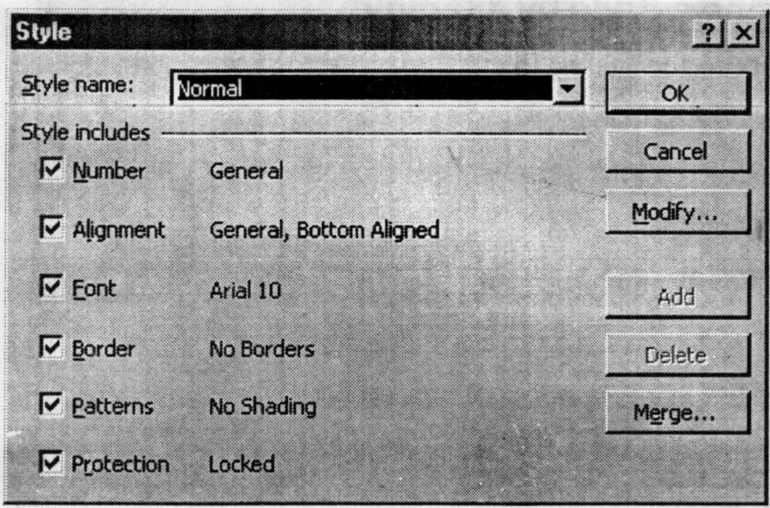

3. Type a name for style in Style Name: The style's formats in Style includes box.

Exclude formats of selected cell from style:

1. Deselect Style Includes (by example) options: Number, Font, Alignment, Border, Patterns, Protection
2. Click Ok.

Create a Style by Defining It

1. Click **Format** menu, Style...
2. Type a name for style in Style Name.

Exclude formats of selected cell from style:

1. Deselect Style Includes options:
2. Click Modify...
3. Click tab of format category to include
4. Select options for selected tab

Redefine a Style by example

1. Select cell containing formats to assign to style
2. Click Format menu, Style...
3. Type (do not select) name of style to redefine in Style name.
4. Click Add...

If Redefine prompt appears

1. Click Yes
2. Click Ok

Redefine a Style by Defining It

1. Click **Format** menu, Style...
2. Select name of style to redefine in Style Name

Exclude format categories from style:

1. Deselect Style Includes options:

Change formats:

1. Click Modify...
2. Click tab of format category to change
3. Select options for selected tab.
4. Repeat steps for each format category to change
5. Click Ok

Apply a Style

Add the Style box to the Formatting toolbar if you use styles often. Then select or define styles quickly without opening menus.

1. Select cell(s) to which to apply style
2. Click Format menu, Style...

3. Select style name in Style Name
4. Click Ok

Copy Styles from Another Workbook

1. Open source and destination workbooks
2. Select destination workbook
3. Click Format menu, Style...
4. Click Merge...
5. Select name of source workbook in Merge Styles From: list
6. Click Ok

If merge styles message appears

1. Click **Yes** to replace styles in destination workbook that have the same name.

   Or

2. Click **No** to retain styles that have the same names in destination workbook.
3. Click Ok

Delete a Style

1. Click **Format** menu, Style...
2. Select name of style to delete in Style Name

   Normal style cannot be deleted.

3. Click Delete
4. Click Ok

Working with Workbooks

You can transfer data between two workbooks or compare the information in one workbook with that in another.

To compare the two workbooks, lets name them **Book1** and **Book2**.

1. Open Book1 and click at New Workbook button. Excel displays a new workbook called Book2.
2. To see both the workbooks at the same time, choose **Arrange** from the Windows menu to display a dialog box.
3. Click Ok to accept the default Tiled option. Excel arranges Book2 and Book1 side by side on your screen.

Copying Entries Between Workbooks

The procedure for copying information between workbooks is the same as for copying between sheets in one workbook.

Do the following:

1. Activate Book1 by clicking its title bar.
2. Select a range and click the **Copy** button.
3. Click **A1** cell of **Book2** and click the **Paste** button. The data will be pasted in Book2.
4. Press **Ctrl + Home** to move to cell **A1** and see the full result.

Moving Sheets Between Workbooks

A sheet can be easily moved within a workbook or from one workbook to another. For example, you can move a worksheet from Book1 to Book2.

Do the following:

1. Activate the Book1 window.
2. Activate the Books2 Window.
3. Point to the Sheet1 tab and hold down the left mouse button. The pointer is now an arrow with a sheet attached to it.
4. Drag the sheet pointer until it sits between Sheet2 of the Book1

workbook. Excel indicates with an arrowhead where it will place the selected sheet.

5. Release the mouse button.

Deleting Sheets

Before deleting a sheet from a workbook, you should always display it. Excel permanently deletes the sheet, so it is wise to do a quick visual confirmation before sending a sheet into other world.

Do the following:

1. With the Book1 sheet active, choose the **Delete Sheet** command from the **Edit** menu. Excel warns you that the sheet will be permanently deleted.
2. Click OK. Excel removes the sheet from the workbook.

Worksheet Fitting on a Page

If your worksheet is too large to print on one page even after you change the orientation and margins, you might consider using the Fit to option. This option shrinks the worksheet to make it fit on the specified number of pages. You can specify the document's width and height.

Follow these steps to scale a worksheet to fit on a page:

1. Open the **File** menu and choose **Page Setup**. The Page Setup dialog box appears.
2. Click the **Page** tab to display the Page options.
3. In the Fit to XX page wide by XX tall text boxes, enter the number of pages in which you want Excel to fit your data.
4. Click Ok to close the Page Setup dialog box and return to your worksheet. Or click the Print button in the Page Setup dialog box to display the Print dialog box, and then click Ok to print your worksheet.

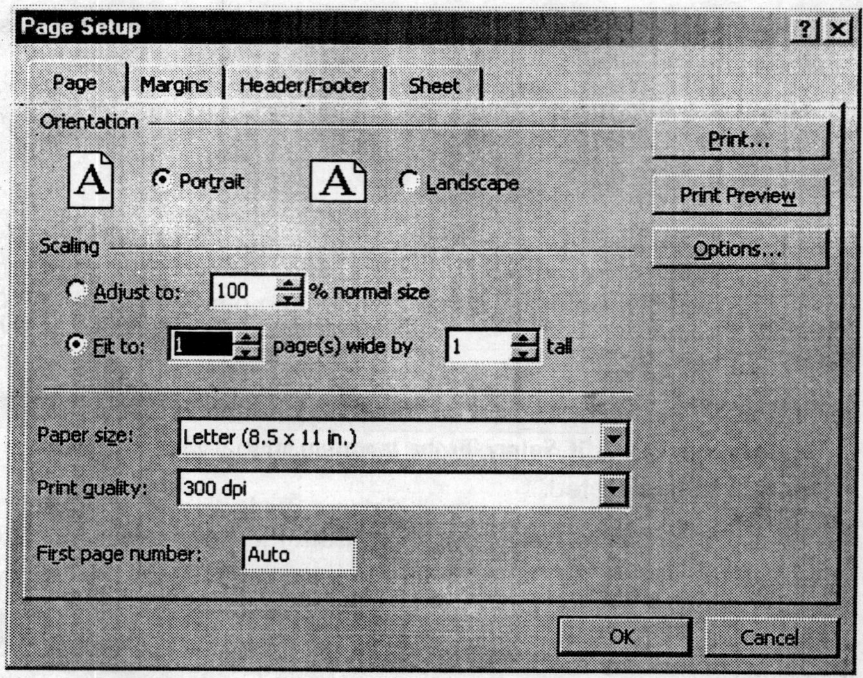

Consolidation of Worksheets

This command as the name sounds is used to consolidate the data of more than one worksheet in a single worksheet. The common data of various worksheets can be combined to create the worksheet to reflect the result of the consolidation.

This consolidation can be effected with the help of various statistical functions like Sum, Count, Average, Max, Min and StdDev. This is vary useful when you have the data availble in the monthly format and you would like to combine the data in a single worksheet to create a total consolidate data for the year.

In a similar example, I have taken the salaries and deductions of 3 moths i.e., April, 2002; May 2002 and June 2002. I have tried to consolidate the data in a new worksheet.

Let us see how this is done.

The following data has been taken for consolidation. This data is various sheets of the same file.

	A	B	C	D	E
1	Salary for the month of April, 2002				
2					
3	**No.**	**Name**	**Salary**	**Deduction**	**Nett. Payable**
4	1	Sachin Tendulkar	10,000	2,000	8,000
5	2	Saurav Ganguly	12,000	1,000	11,000
6	3	Rahul Dravid	11,000	1,500	9,500
7		**Total**	**33,000**	**4,500**	**28,500**
8					

	A	B	C	D	E
1	Salary for the month of May, 2002				
2					
3	**No.**	**Name**	**Salary**	**Deduction**	**Nett. Payable**
4	1	Sachin Tendulkar	10,000	1,000	9,000
5	2	Saurav Ganguly	12,000	2,000	10,000
6	3	Rahul Dravid	11,000	1,500	9,500
7		**Total**	**33,000**	**4,500**	**28,500**

	A	B	C	D	E
1	Salary for the month of June, 2002				
2					
3	**No.**	**Name**	**Salary**	**Deduction**	**Nett. Payable**
4	1	Sachin Tendulkar	10,000	500	9,500
5	2	Saurav Ganguly	12,000	700	11,300
6	3	Rahul Dravid	11,000	0	11,000
7		**Total**	**33,000**	**1,200**	**31,800**
8					

1. Open a blank sheet and type the heading for consolidation, for example, the consolidation results for the month of April, May and June, 2002.
2. Make cell A4 the active cell.
3. From from the Data menu choose the Consolidate command.
4. This gives rise to Consolidate dialog box, as shown on next page.
5. Here the Sum function is there by default. You can choose to have another function like Average, if you want to have average

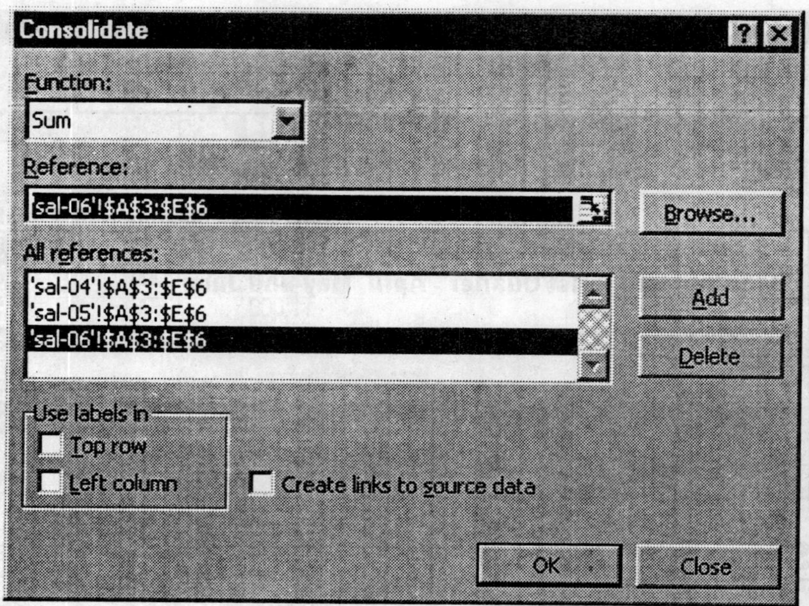

of the fields. In all cases the corresponding cells of each of the ranges that you specify in the next step would take effect.

6. Click the Reference box and then indicate the first reference by choosing the sal-04 tab and selecting the range of cells to be consolidated. In this case they are from A3 to E6. See how it is reflected in the Reference.
7. After choosing the range, click at Add to register it in the All references box.
8. Similarly do it for all the months and their ranges and have them stored in the All Reference column.
9. If you are using labels, make sure to point them out. In our case they are at the top of all the columns, so we will select the option Top row.
10. Click Ok to have the data consolidated in the worksheet.
11. The consolidated data is shown on the next page.

Microsoft Excel - Book4

File Edit View Insert Format Tools Data Window Help

Arial 10

A3 No.

	A	B	C	D	E
1	Salary for the 1st Quarter - April, May and June				
2					
3	No.	Name	Salary	Deduction	Nett. Payable
4	3		30,000	3,500	26,500
5	6		36,000	3,700	32,300
6	9		33,000	3,000	30,000
7			99,000	10,200	88,800

Scenarios Manager

Human mind is made of What-if situations. The same what-if can be applied to your worksheet to see if the results of the selection displays the good or bad results.

Each time you change the data, the previous solution is lost. To address this limitation, the Scenario Manager helps you keep track of multiple what-if models. Using the Scenarios manager, you can create new forecasting scenarios, view existing scenario, run scenario management commands and display consolidated scenario reports. Let us start with creating a worksheet and then apply the scenario to it.

On the next page a worksheet is shown which has been taken as an example for creating a scenario. Here the figures are very simple and calculated. If you want you can use the constant figures too. Next we perform the following steps to create and view the scenario.

1. Click at Scenarios in the Tools menu.

2 A Scenario manager dialog box would appear on the screen, as shown on the next page.

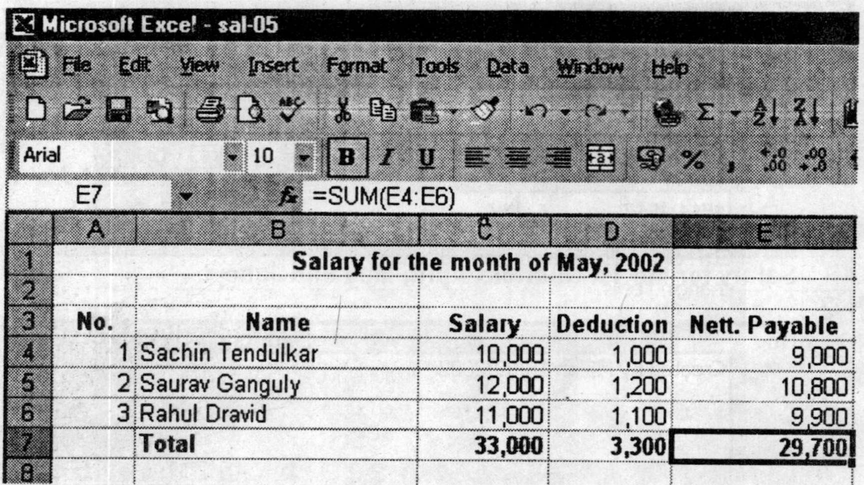

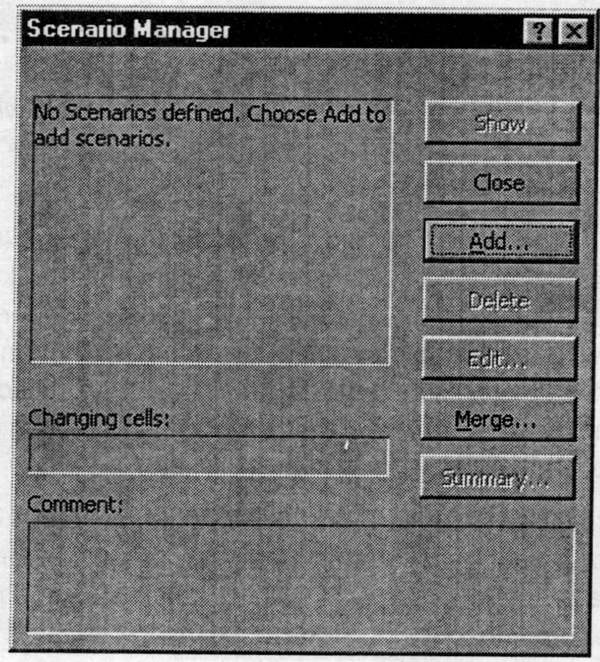

3. As the dialog box says, click at Add to add a scenario.
4. This gives rise to another dialog box, which is called Add scenario.
5. In this dialog box, you have to firstly name the screnario.

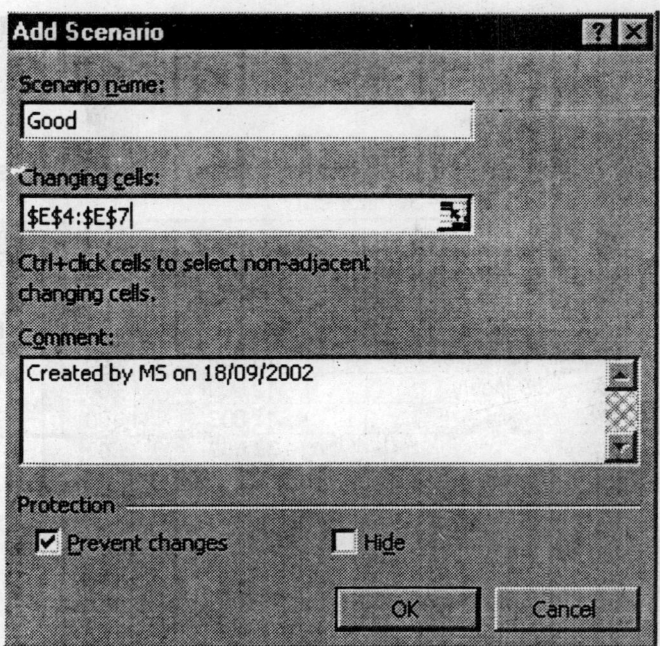

6. I have named it as Good.

7. You can type the cell names or choose them by clicking at those cells. I have chosen cells from E4 to E7.

8. Click OK to add your scenario to the Scenario Manager. You'll see the Scenario Values dialog box, which asks you for your model's variables. The default values are the numbers that were already in the cells.

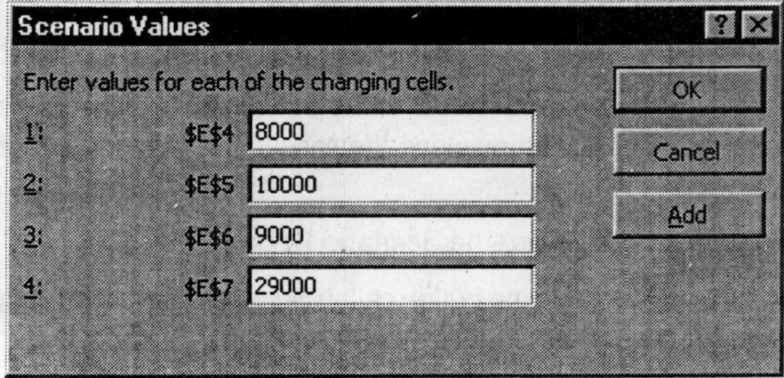

9. Type the various values which you want to see in the scenario.
10. Click Add to create a second scenario. If you do not want another set, just click at Ok.
11. This will return you to the scenario manager with your scenario added to it.

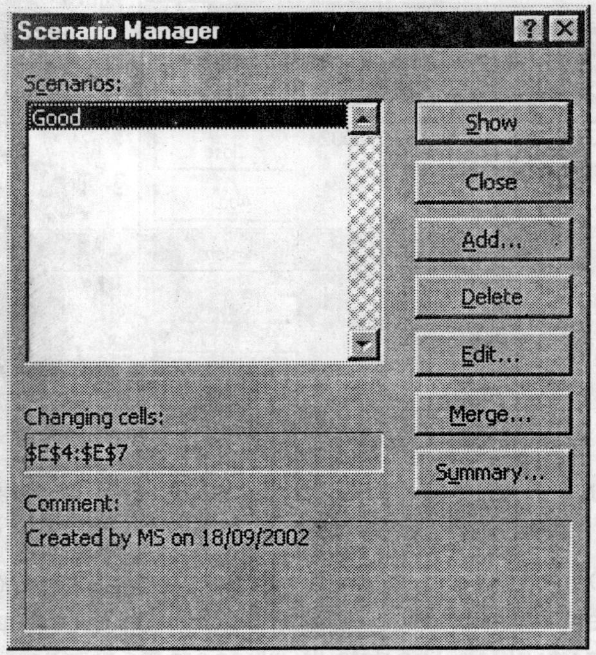

12. As mentioned you can add another scenario to it.
13. Now we will see how this scenario works. For this click at Show.
14. Excel substitutes the values in the scenario for the variables in your worksheet and displays the results in your worksheet, as shown on the next page.
15. Next step is of having the Scenario Reports.
16. For this you choose the button called Summary from the Scenario Manager dialog box.

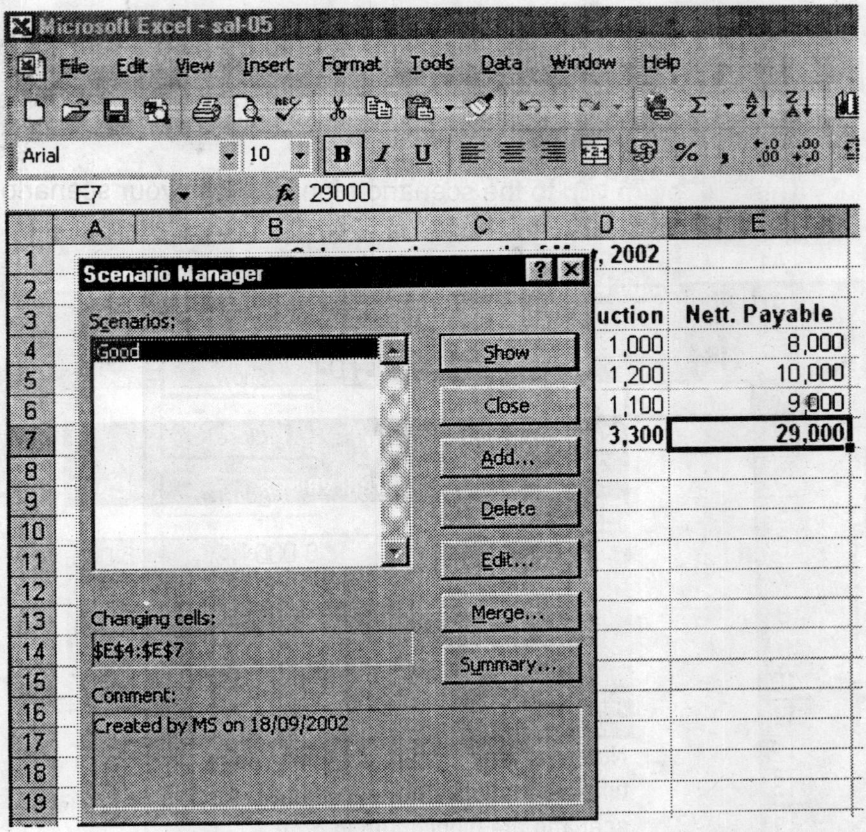

17. For this you will have to click at a cell where the summary would be placed.

18. You also have to define whether you want the summary or the PivtoTable report. Click any one of the two.

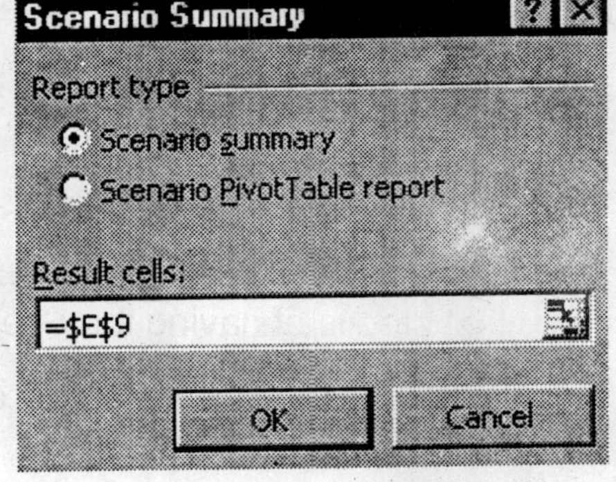

19. I have taken here Scenario summary and have given E9 as the cell for showing the results.

20. The net results will be shown as below.

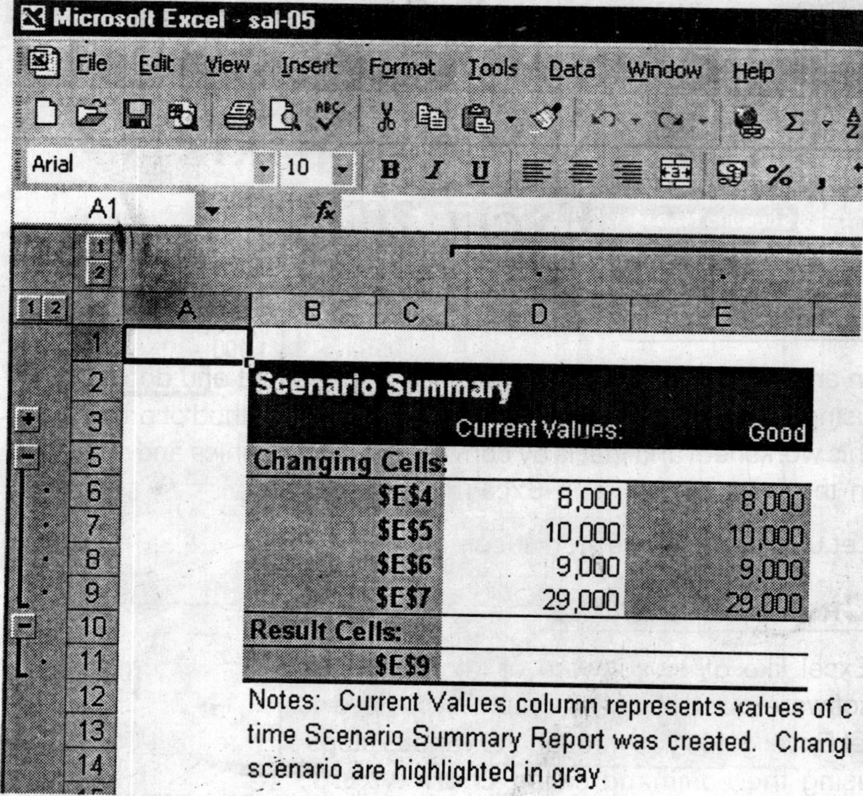

12

WORKING WITH CHARTS IN EXCEL 2002

INTRODUCTION

In an earlier chapter we had created a worksheet and decorated it using the AutoFormat mode. There is another method of presenting this worksheet and that is by converting it into graphics and specially in the form of **Charts** in Excel.

Let us use the same worksheet to make charts of the same.

CREATING GRAPHS

Excel like other software of Microsoft Office, makes use of the software called Microsoft Graph. If you have no idea about the Charts, let Excel guide you through the various steps are creating Charts by using the command called **Chart Wizard**.

For this you do the following:

1. Select the entire worksheet area which you want to include in your chart.

   In our case we would select the whole worksheet from **A1** to **F10**, which includes the totals.
2. Select **Chart** from the **Insert** menu.
3. The **Wizard Chart Step 1 of 4** menu will be given to you to select the type of chart you want for your worksheet.

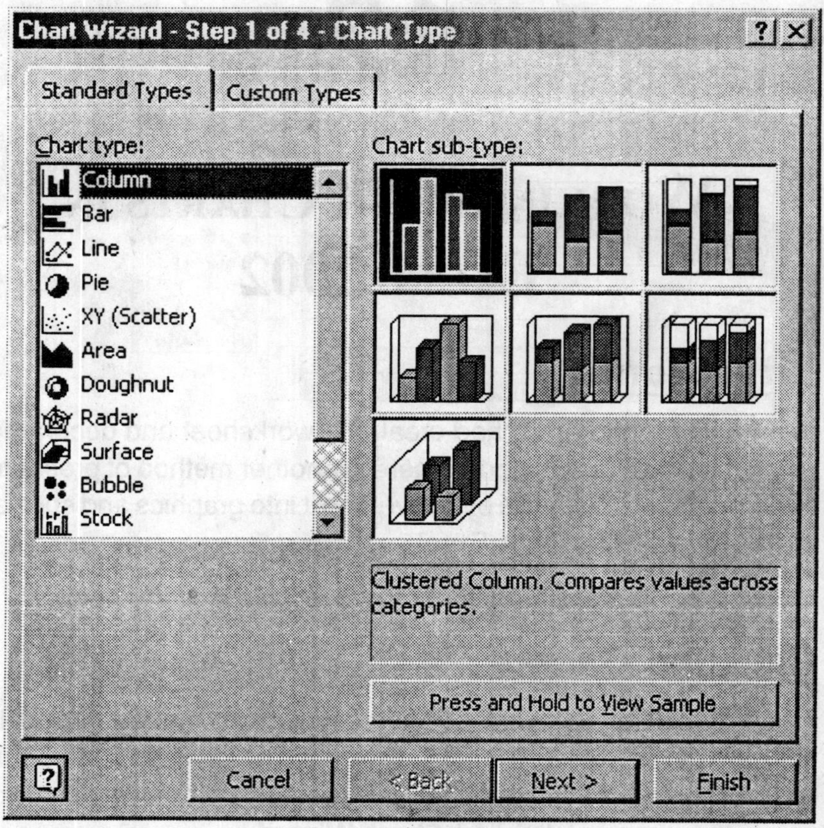

For our worksheet we have selected **Column Chart** type, as can be seen in the first of the four Chart Wizard dialog box.

Press **Next** to reach **Wizard Chart Step 2 of 4**.

4. In this chart you can opt for different ways of representing your chart, i.e., row wise or column wise.

   For our worksheet we have selected columns.

5. Press **Next** to reach the next step.

6. **Chart Wizard Step 3 of 4** gives you the option of naming the chart and the Y and X-axis.

   In our case we have named the worksheet as **Finance**.

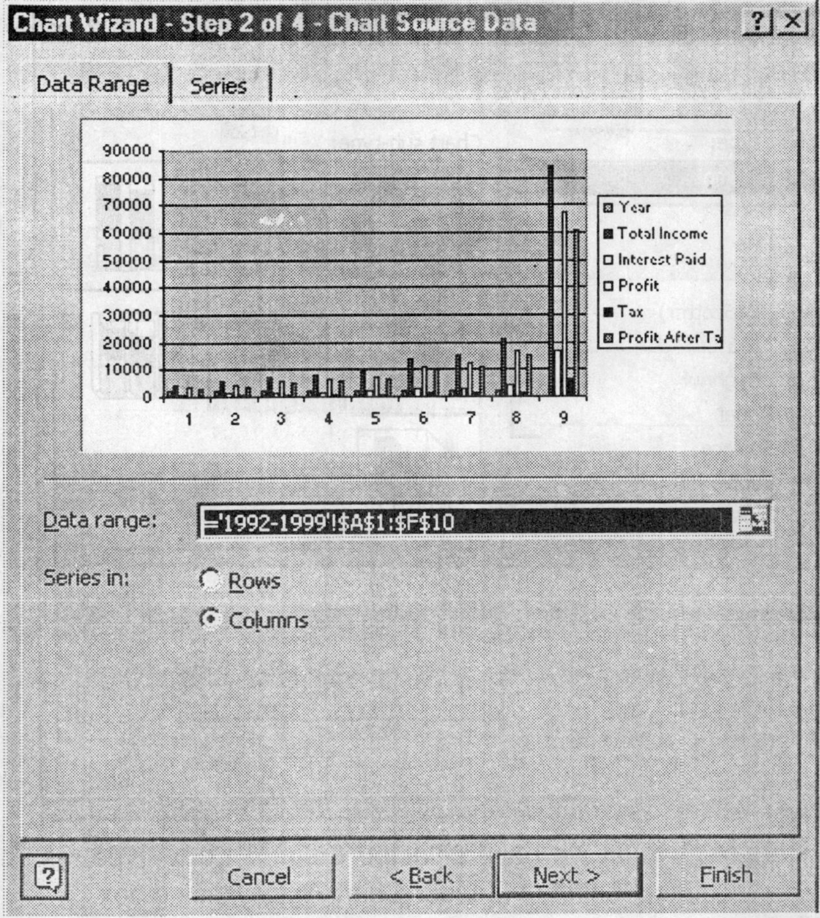

Press **Next** to reach the next step.

7. **Chart Wizard Step 4 of 4** gives you the option of placing this chart in the worksheet as an object or in the form of a new cell.
8. Once this is over, you can press **Finish** to end the Chart Wizard routine.
9. A new chart will be placed in your worksheet with the Chart toolbar present for making the changes which you may require to do to your chart.

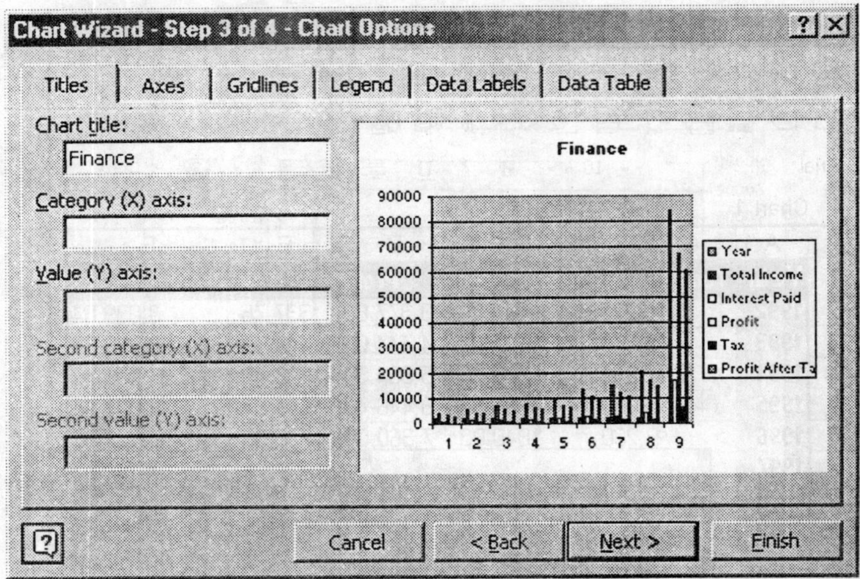

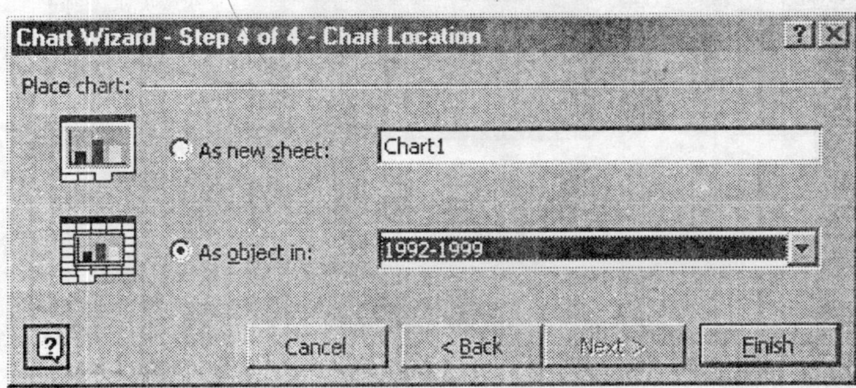

10. The Step 4, Step 5, and the final Chart are shown on the next two pages.

Modifying Chart

If you move the pointer slowly over areas of a chart, you can see ToolTips identifying the items that make up the chart. Each item can be formatted separately.

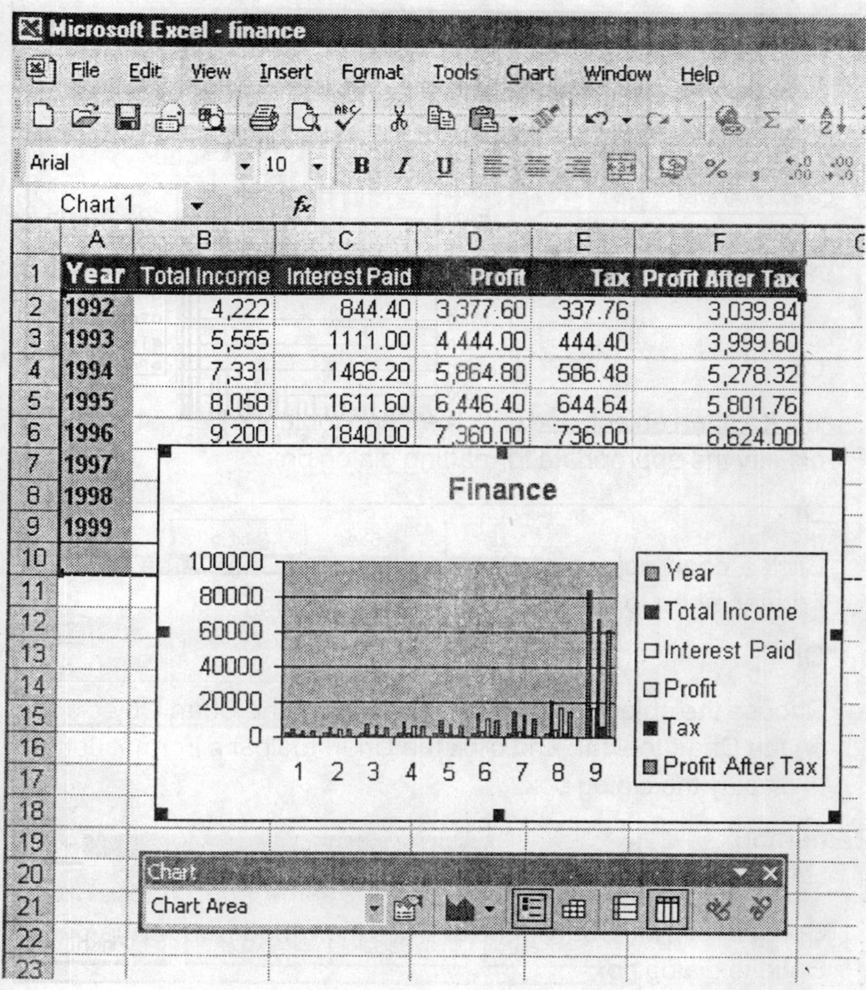

To modify a chart

1. Double click a chart object to display the formatting dialog box appropriate for that object.

   Or

   Right-click a chart object, and choose the appropriate formatting dialog box from the shortcut menu.

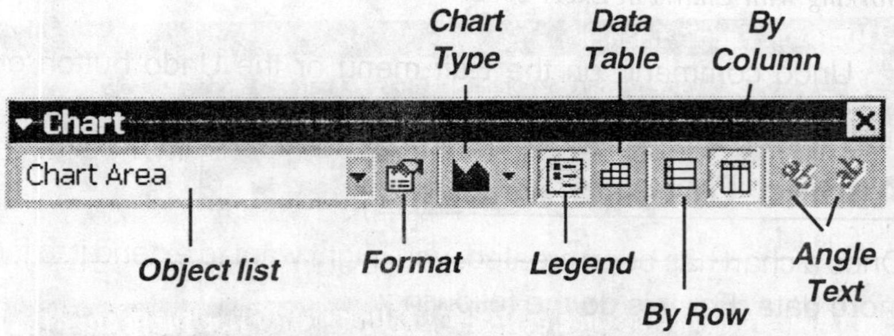

Or

Click a chart object, and click the Chart toolbar's Format button to display the appropriate formatting dialog box

Or

Click a chart object, and choose Selected Chart Area from the Format menu to display the appropriate dialog box.

Or

Choose the object you want to modify from the Chart Objects list on the Chart toolbar, and click the Chart toolbar's Format button to display the dialog box.

Remember

1. To modify several chart elements at the same time, choose Chart Options from the Chart menu and use the various tabs in the Chart Options dialog box.
2. Drag the chart to move it on the sheet, or drag the handles of the chart window to resize the chart.
3. Format the most general elements of the chart first (such as the chart area), and then format individual elements within that area (such as axis labels).
4. Don't be afraid to experiment with options you don't completely understand; you can easily undo almost any change by using the

Undo command on the Edit menu or the Undo button on the Standard toolbar.

Adding Data to a Chart

Once a chart has been created, you might want to extend it to include more data. For this do the following:

1. Select the chart.
2. From the **Chart** menu, choose **Source Data**.
3. In the Source Data dialog box, add more rows using the **Series** tab or extend the data range to include more columns using the **Data Range** tab.
4. Click Ok. The new row or column is added to the Chart.

Add a Data Table to a Chart

You can add a table of the data that is represented by the chart and add a trendline that shows the general trend, such as growth or decline, that emerges in the data.

1. Click the **Data Table** button on the Chart toolbar. The Data Table appears below the chart.

Add a Trendline

1. Click a data series for which you want to add a trendline.
2. From the **Chart** menu, choose **Add Trendline**.
3. In the Add Trendline dialog box, define the kind of trendline you want and set the options.
4. Click Ok.
5. The trendline is added, as seen in the figure on the next page.

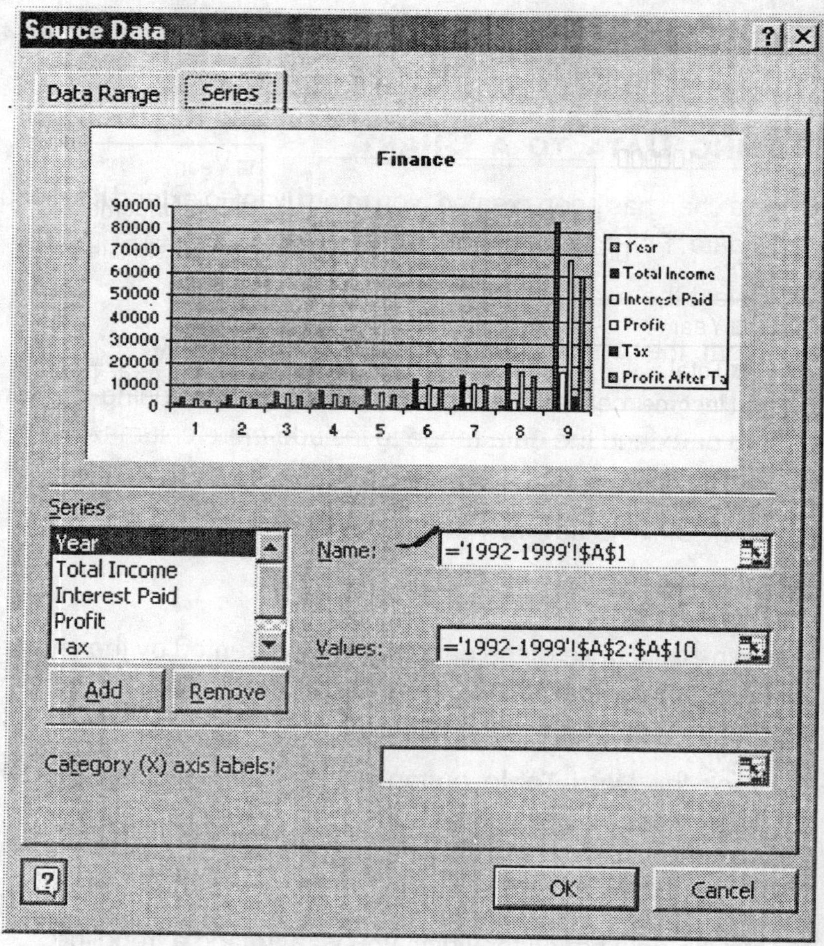

Creating a PivotTable Report

PivotTable reports can help you look at data in different ways. Once the reports are created, you can swap rows with columns for different views.

1. Click in the selected data area.
2. From the Data menu, choose PivotTable to start the PivotTable Wizard.

Finance
100000
0
1
2
3
4
5
6
7
8
9
Year
Total Income
Year
Total Income
Interest Paid
Profit
Tax
Profit After Tax
Legend

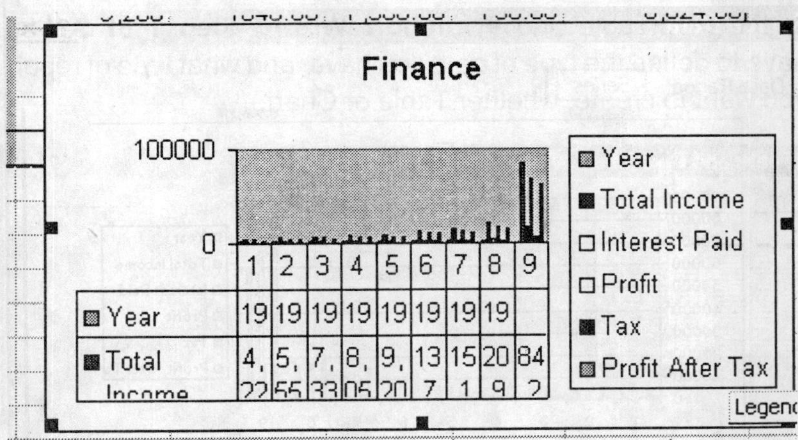

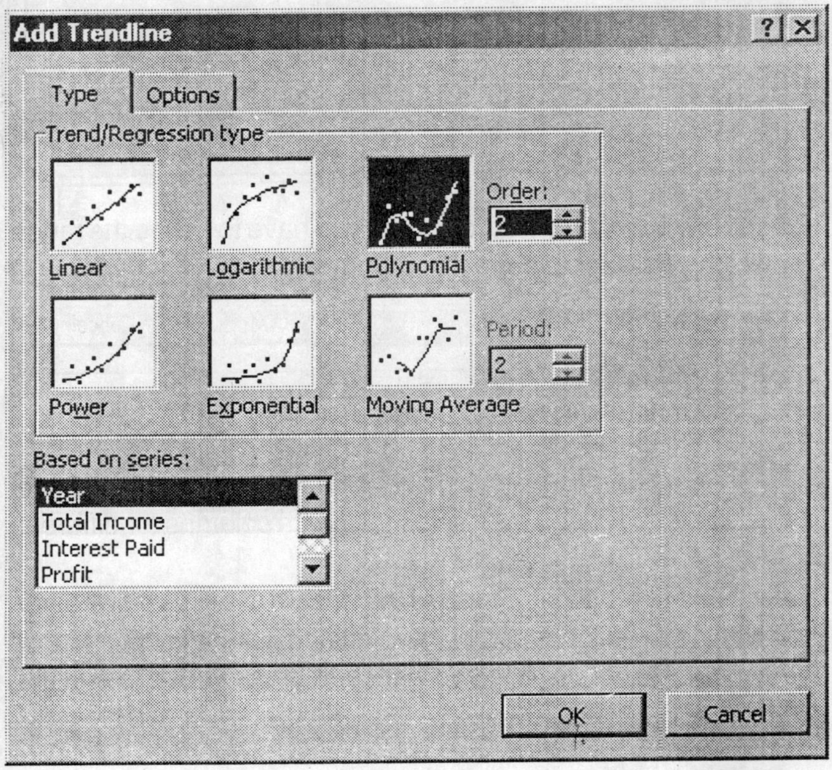

Add Trendline
Type
Options
Trend/Regression type
Linear
Logarithmic
Polynomial
Order:
2
Power
Exponential
Moving Average
Period:
2
Based on series:
Year
Total Income
Interest Paid
Profit
OK
Cancel

3. In the PivotTable and **PivotChart Wizard Step 1 of 3**, you have to define the type of data you have, and what type of report you want to create, whether Table or Chart.

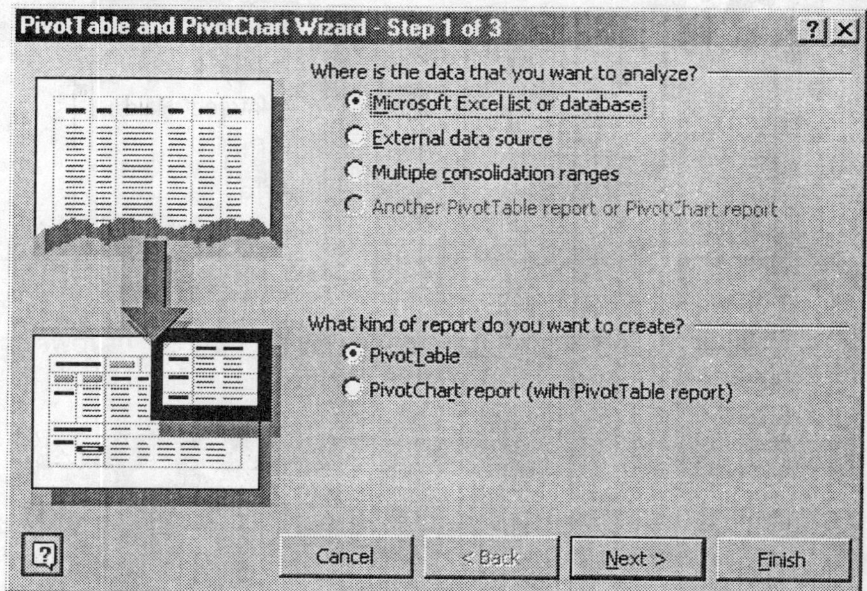

2. Press **Next** to reach the step 2. Here you have to define the range for which you want to have this report.

3. Press **Next** to reach the Step 3 of the Wizard. It asks you whether you want to have the report in the existing worksheet or on a new worksheet. Select the one you want and press **Finish** to end the Wizard.

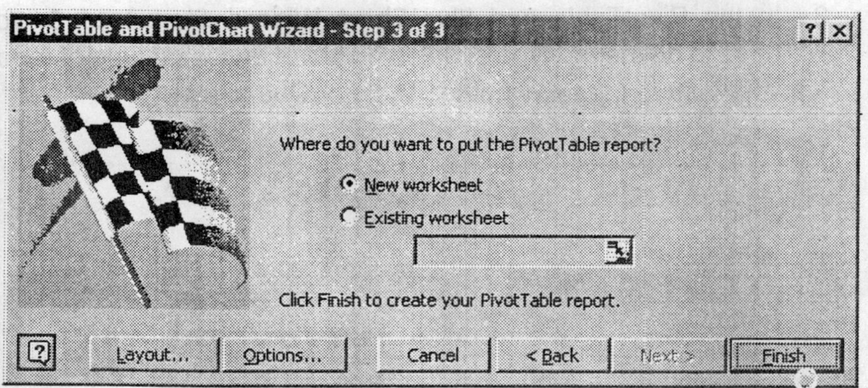

4. You will be given a worksheet view as shown on the next page. Position the table items to create the view you want. The rows and columns items are listed below the button area on the PivotTable toolbar.
5. Click the **Format Report** button on the PivotTable toolbar.
6. Choose a format from the AutoFormat dialog box.
7. Click Ok.

MODIFYING THE CHART TYPE

Excel provides many chart types to help you display data in a way that will best communicate its meaning.

To modify the Chart Type

1. Click the chart.
2. From the **Chart** menu choose **Chart Type**.
3. Select a type in the Chart Type dialog box.
4. Click Ok.

   Or

1. Click the chart.

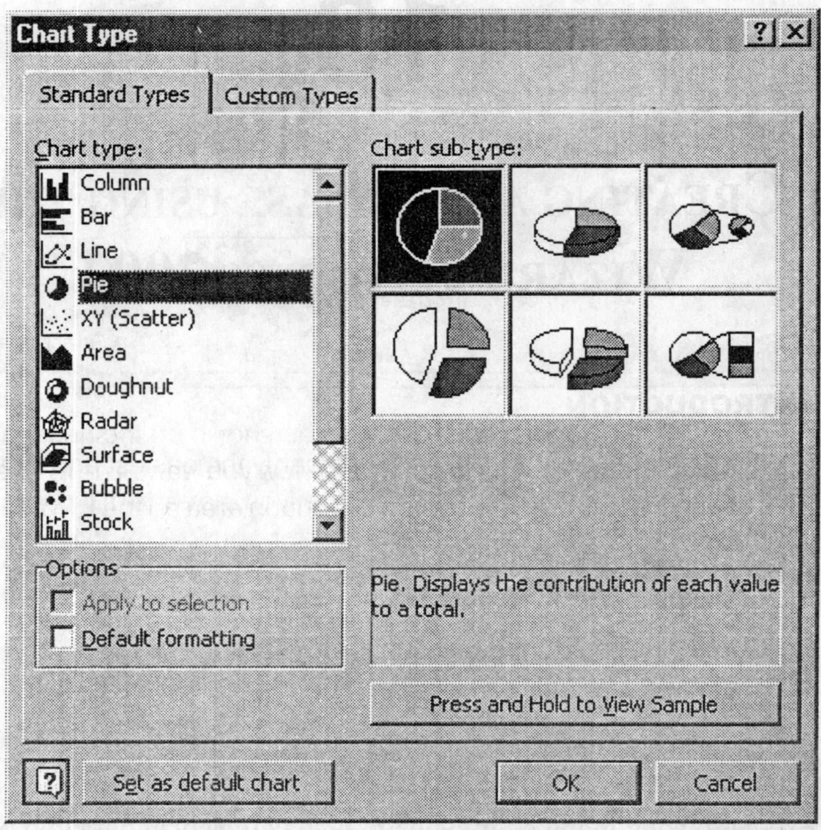

2. Select a type from the Chart Type list on the Chart toolbar.

The Chart type changes.

13

Creating a Database using the Wizard in Access 2002

Introduction

Creating database with a Wizard is probably the easiest and fastest method of creating a database where you have to fill up some information and the database is ready for you. It not only creates **Tables** for you but all the Forms, Reports, etc., connected with it are done too.

Creating Database using the Wizard

As done in the earlier chapter, start Access 2002. Now, click at Templates in the task panel to get the following dialog box.

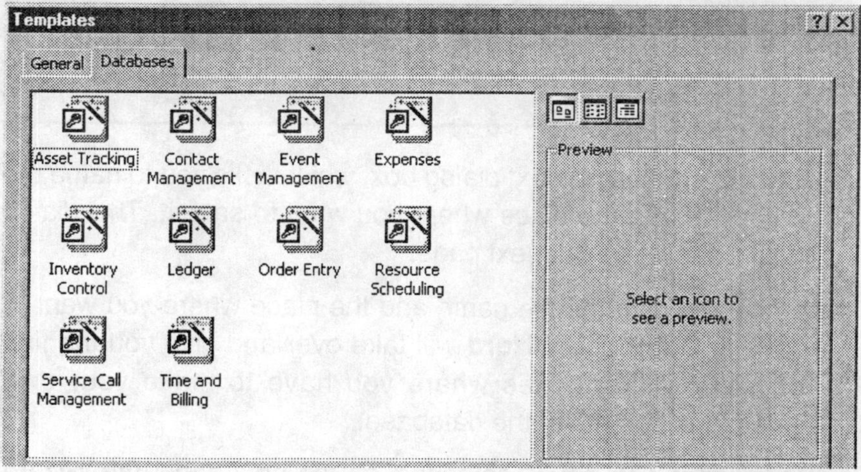

Then do the following:

1. Click at the option **Databases**.
2. Choose here the type of database you want. I have chosen here the Inventory control.

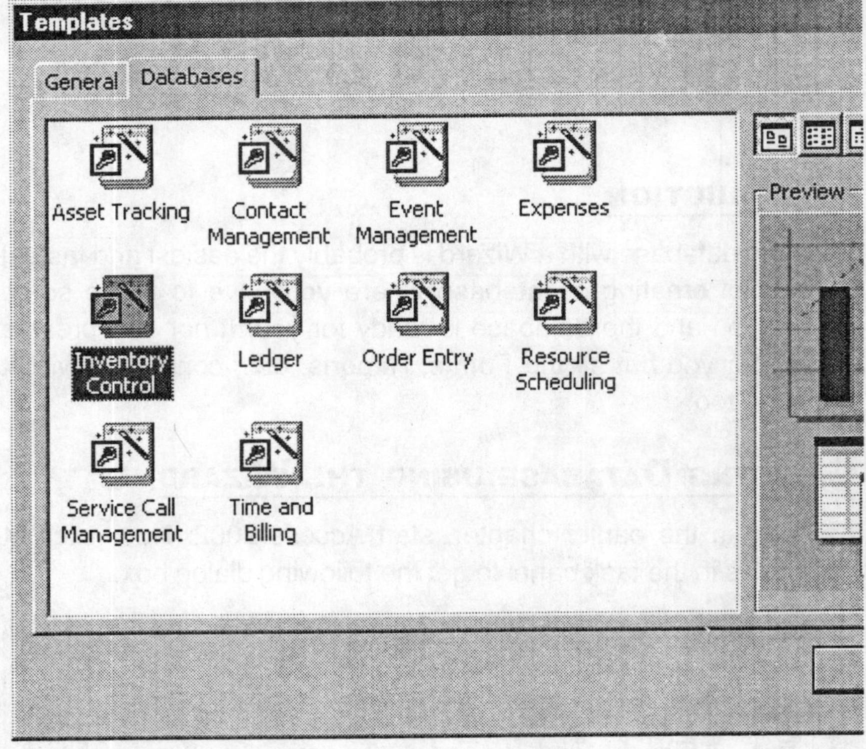

3. Click Ok to get the next dialog box, which asks you to name the database and the place where you want to save it. This dialog box is shown on the next page.
4. Once you give the file name and the place where you want to save it, **Database Wizard** will take over and give you the first of many dialog boxes where you have to make your own selections and make the database.
5. In the first dialog box, as shown on the next page, the Wizard

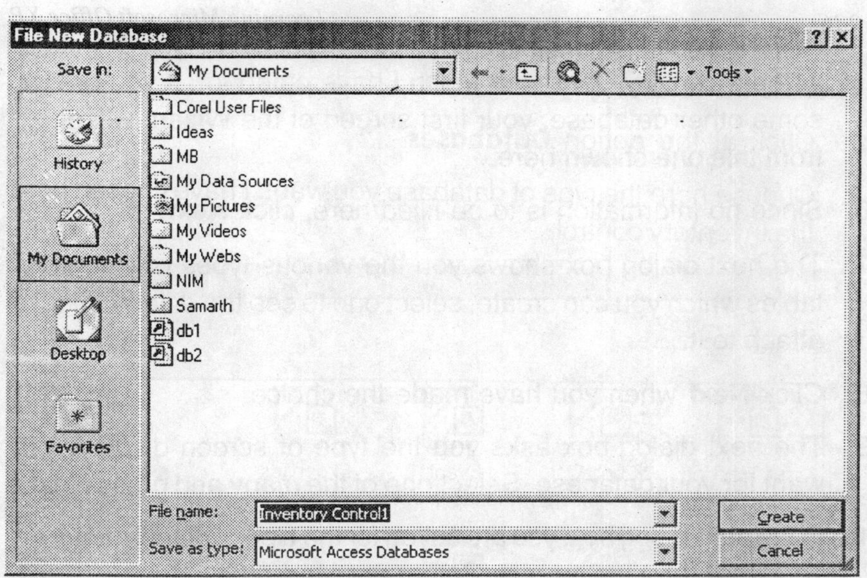

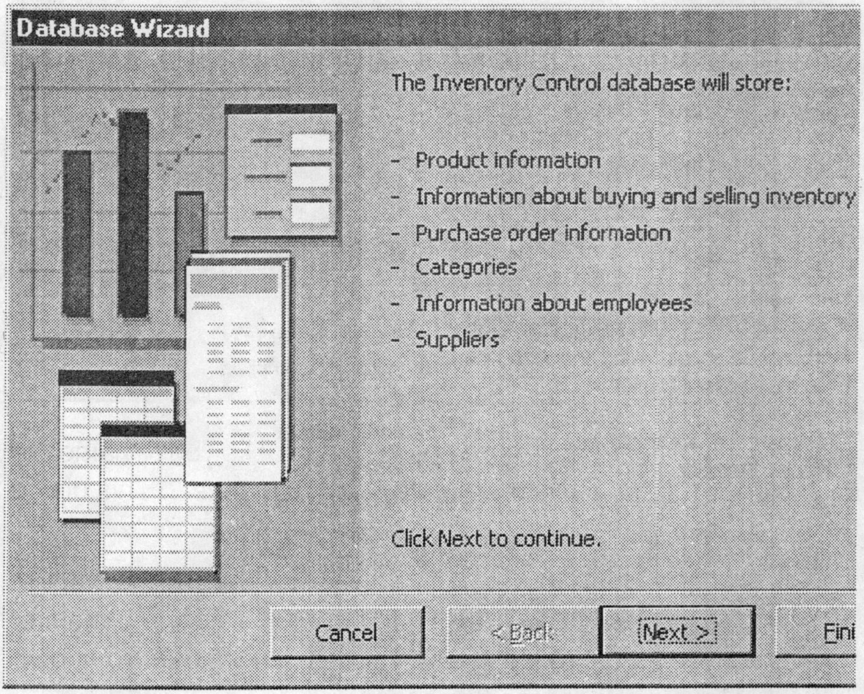

Database Wizard

The Inventory Control database will store:

- Product information
- Information about buying and selling inventory
- Purchase order information
- Categories
- Information about employees
- Suppliers

Click Next to continue.

Cancel | < Back | Next > | Fini

has shown the various information the database is going to store in the Inventory Database which I have opted for. If you opt for some other database, your first screen of the Wizard will differ from this one shown here.

6. Since no information is to be filled here, click **Next**.
7. The next dialog box shows you the various types of inventory tables which you can create, select one to see the different fields attach to it.
8. Click **Next** when you have made the choice.
9. The next dialog box asks you the type of screen display you want for your database. Select one of the many and press **Next**.
10. In the next dialog box, you are asked for the type of output printouts you want for your reports. Select one and press **Next**.

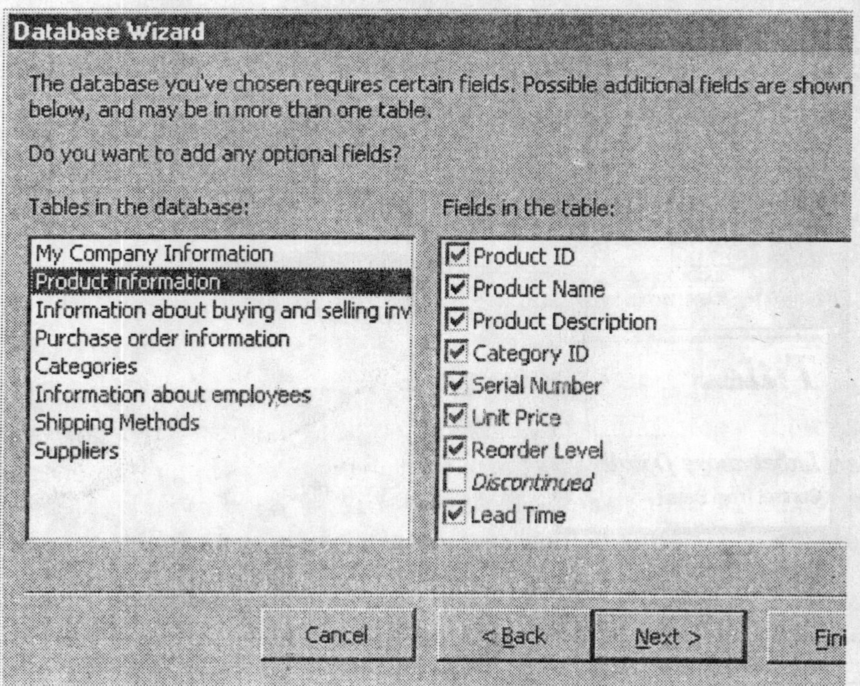

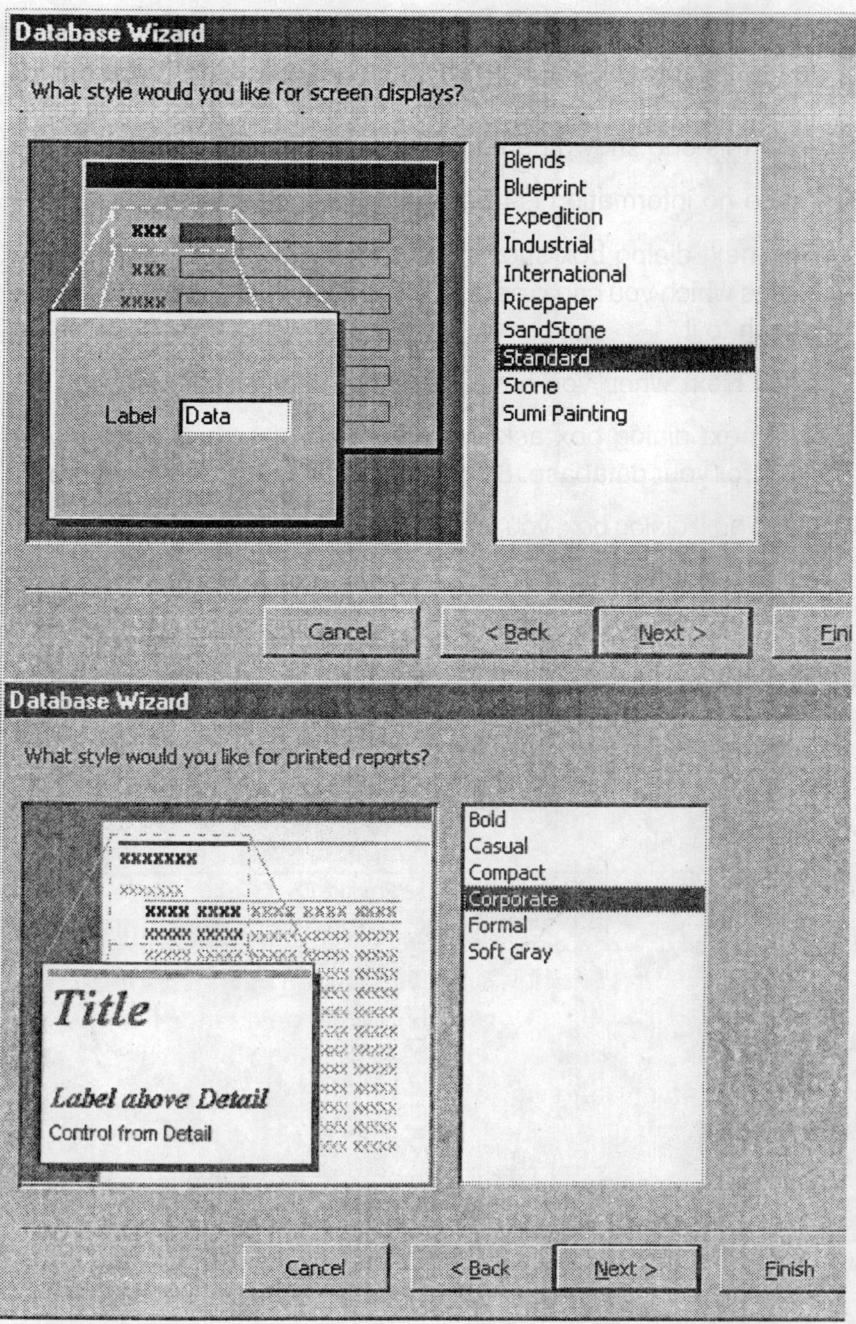
Database Wizard
What style would you like for screen displays?
XXX
XXX
XXXX
Label
Data
Blends
Blueprint
Expedition
Industrial
International
Ricepaper
SandStone
Standard
Stone
Sumi Painting
Cancel
< Back
Next >
Fini
Database Wizard
What style would you like for printed reports?
XXXXXXX
XXXXXXX
XXXX XXXX
XXXXX XXXXX
Title
Label above Detail
Control from Detail
Bold
Casual
Compact
Corporate
Formal
Soft Gray
Cancel
< Back
Next >
Finish

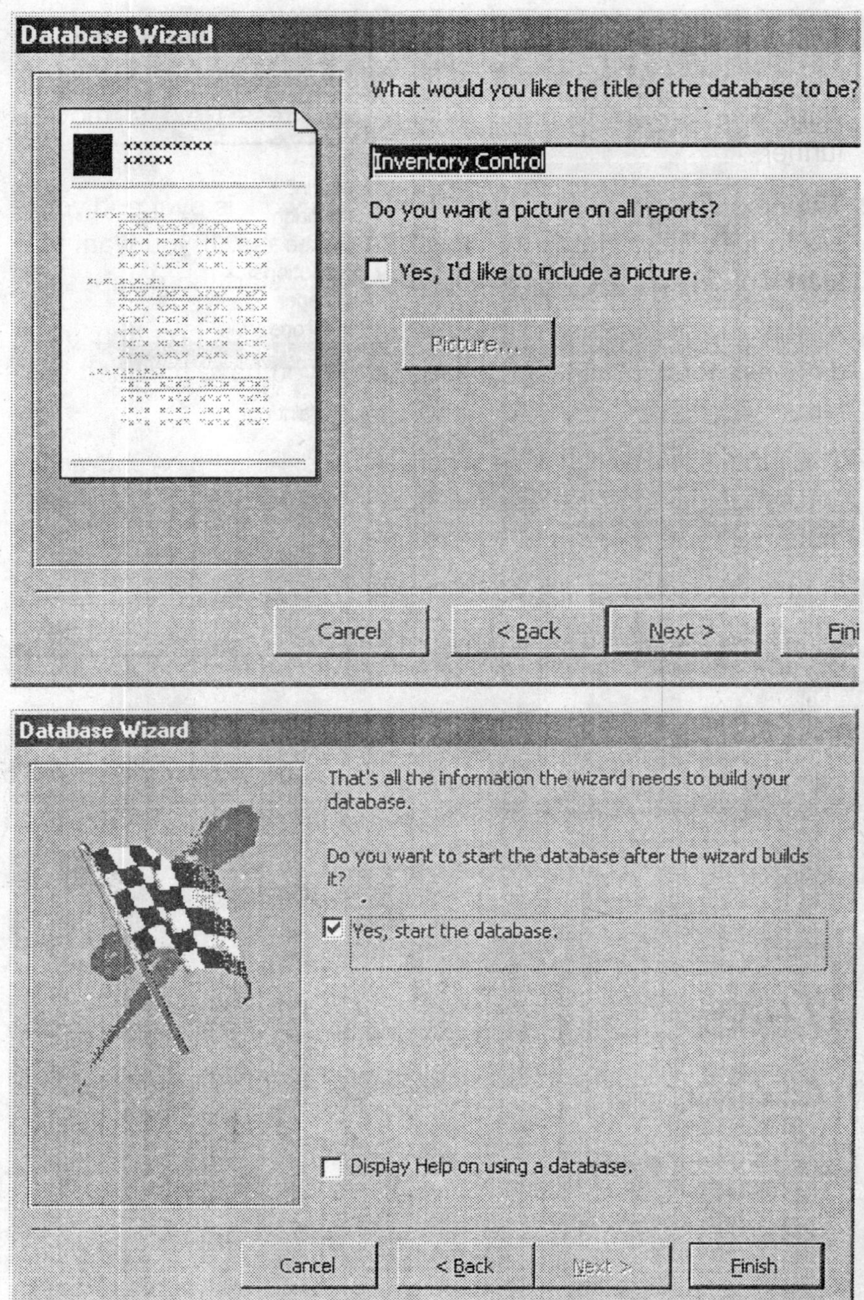
Database Wizard
What would you like the title of the database to be?
Inventory Control
Do you want a picture on all reports?
Yes, I'd like to include a picture.
Picture...
Cancel
< Back
Next >
Database Wizard
That's all the information the wizard needs to build your database.
Do you want to start the database after the wizard builds it?
Yes, start the database.
Display Help on using a database.
Cancel
< Back
Next >
Finish

11. The next dialog box asks you to fill the name of the database which you would like to put on the top of your database. If you want you can opt to put a picture too. Press **Next** to move further.
12. The next dialog box says that the wizard's work is over and you are to just press **Finish** to create the database. If you want to start working on it straightaway, say **Yes** to start the database.
14. At this stage Access will start the process of creating the database for you with all the information you have provided so far.
15. This process takes little time, where Access will keep on showing you the various processes it is going through but none of that matters to you and you are not supposed to interrupt it too.
16. In between Access will ask you for the information, as shown below to fill up the details of the company for which this Inventory Control database is being created.

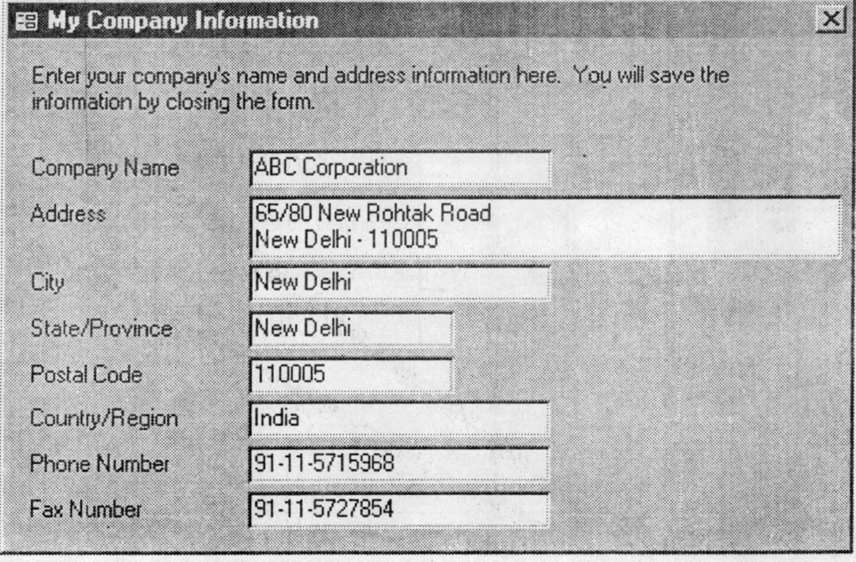

17. Fill up the information according to the information that you want to fill and close the dialog box.
18. Next you would be given a dialog box which is the main box of your database. Access calls it **Main Switchboard**. It is called so because it is from here you will switch to various information mentioned here.
19. We will now go through the various options one by one.
20. The first option **Enter/View Products** will give you the dialog box, which allows you to see the product information and allows you add and change the same.
21. Next in line is **Enter/View Other Information**.
22. This gives rise to another set of options. Select one of them to

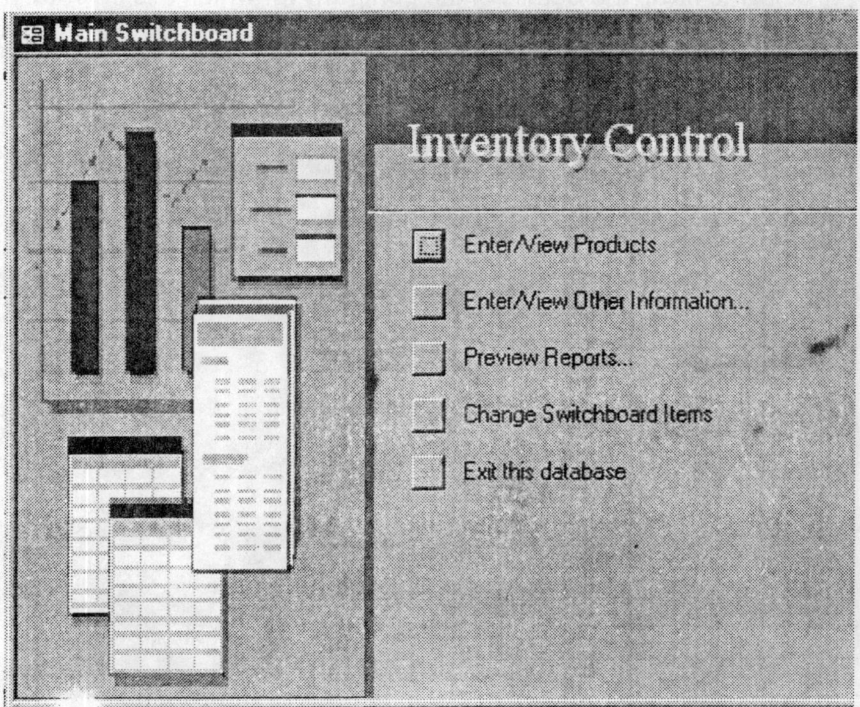

Products
Product ID
(AutoNumber)
Product Name
Description
Category
Lead Time
Reorder Level
Units on Hand
Units on Order
Inventory Transactions:
Date
PO ID
Description
Ordered
Purchase Orders...
Record:
1
of 1

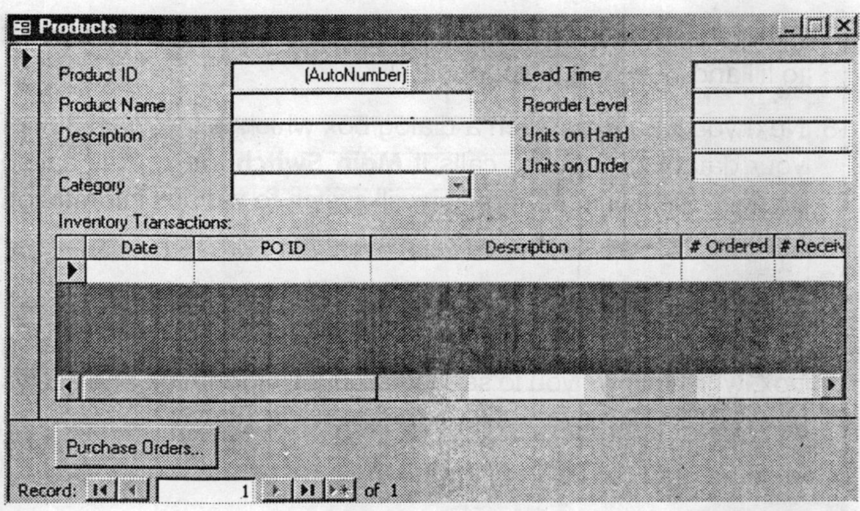

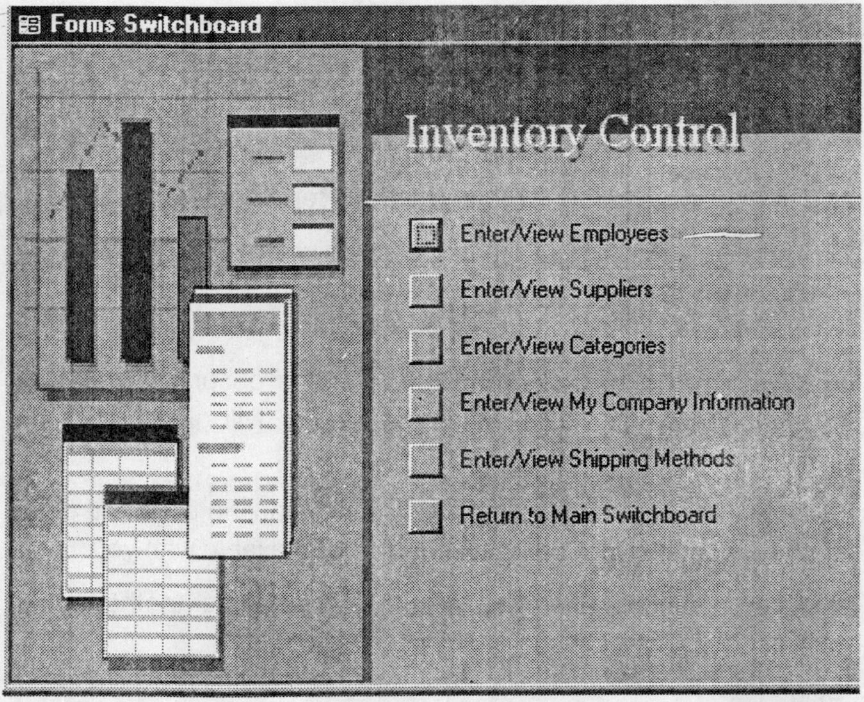

Forms Switchboard
Inventory Control
Enter/View Employees
Enter/View Suppliers
Enter/View Categories
Enter/View My Company Information
Enter/View Shipping Methods
Return to Main Switchboard

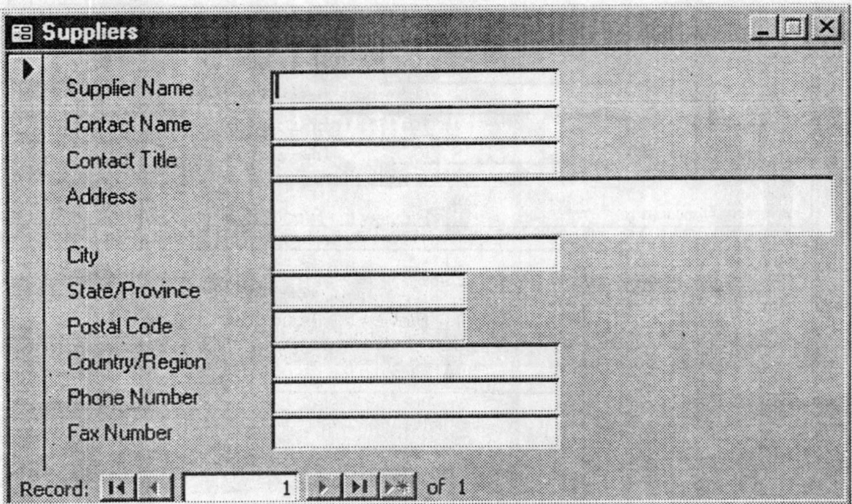

see the information regarding that. Selection of **Suppliers information** will lead to the following dialog box to fill up.

23. You can come back to the Main Switchboard by pressing the said switch.
24. Next is the option of **Previewing Reports**.
25. This also has various options. Selecting one of them, for example, **Preview the Product Summary**, gives a view of the product summary report, as shown below.
26. If you want you can change the various options of the Main Switchboard by opting to change them, will give rise to the following dialog box.
27. Now that your database is ready, start working on it and enjoy the process of filling it up with the data available with you.
28. As an additional exercise, I suggest you choose another option and see the process of creation of a database.

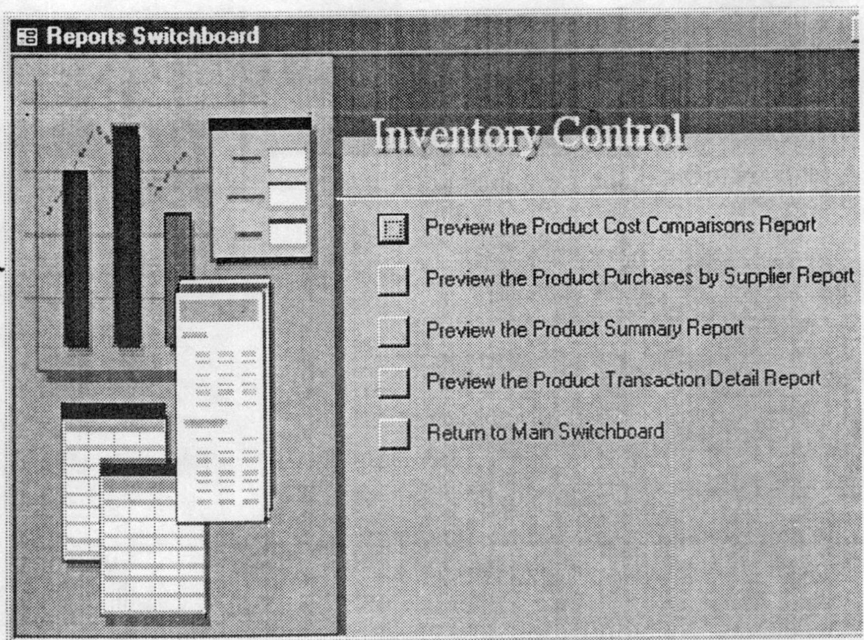

Product Summary

Product Summary

Product Name	*Reorder Level*	*Lead Time*

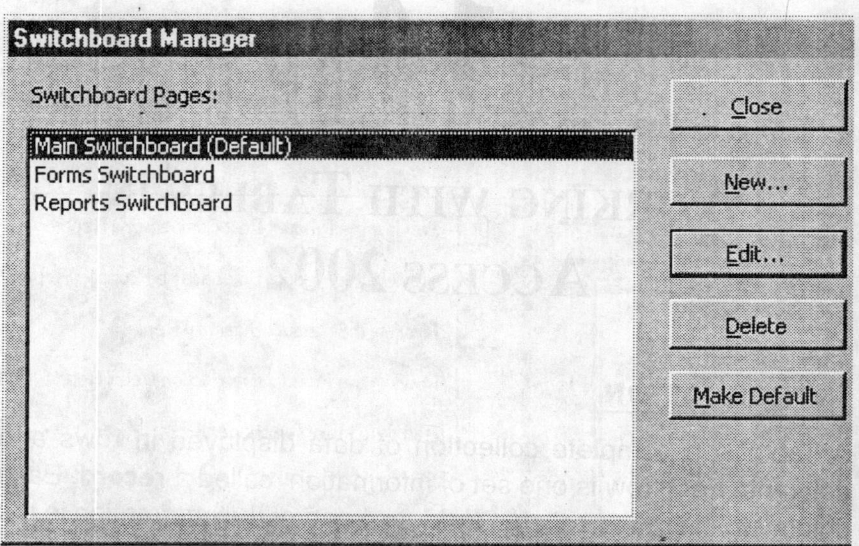
Switchboard Manager
Switchboard Pages:
Main Switchboard (Default)
Forms Switchboard
Reports Switchboard
Close
New...
Edit...
Delete
Make Default

14

WORKING WITH TABLES IN ACCESS 2002

INTRODUCTION

A Table is a complete collection of data displayed in rows and columns. Each row is one set of information, called a **record**. Each column in the row is called a **field**, one part of the information in the record.

CREATING A TABLE USING THE TABLE WIZARD

The **Table Wizard** helps you start a new table and set up its fields. The wizard provides various sample fields that you might use to create a database for both business and personal usage.

To create a table using the Table Wizard:

1. In the Database window, click the **Tables** tab.
2. Click the **New** button on the Database window toolbar.
3. In the **New Table** dialog box, choose **Table Wizard** from the list.
4. Click Ok.
5. In the first page of the Table Wizard, click **Business** or **Personal** to choose a database type. I have chosen Business here.
6. Click a table in the list of **Sample Tables**, and then double-

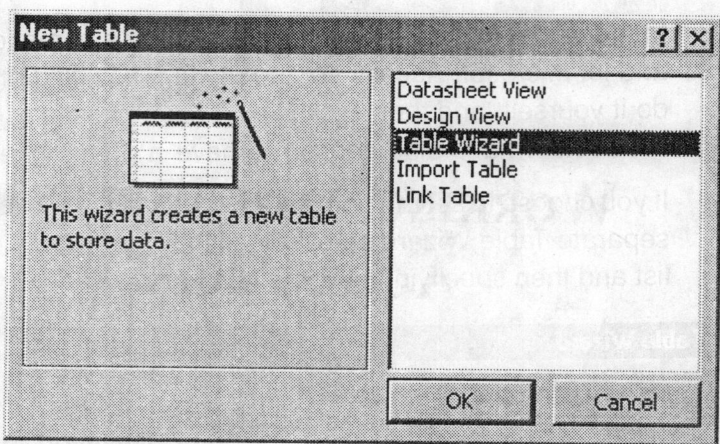

click a field in the list of sample fields to add the field to your table. I have chosen Products here.

7. Continue adding other fields from the same sample table or other sample tables until you have all the fields you need, and then click **Next**.

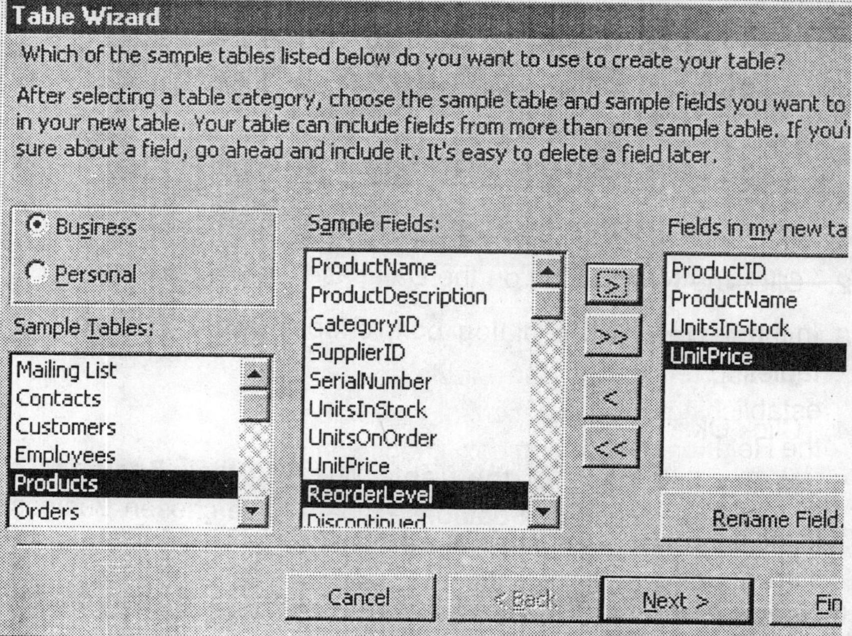

8. In the next page of the Table Wizard, enter a name for the table and let Microsoft Access set the primary key field or choose to do it yourself, and then click Next. I have chosen to name it as **Products**. I have also chosen to have a primary key.

   If you choose to set the primary keys, you make the decision in a separate Table Wizard step, selecting a field from a drop-down list and then specifying how the numbers are added.

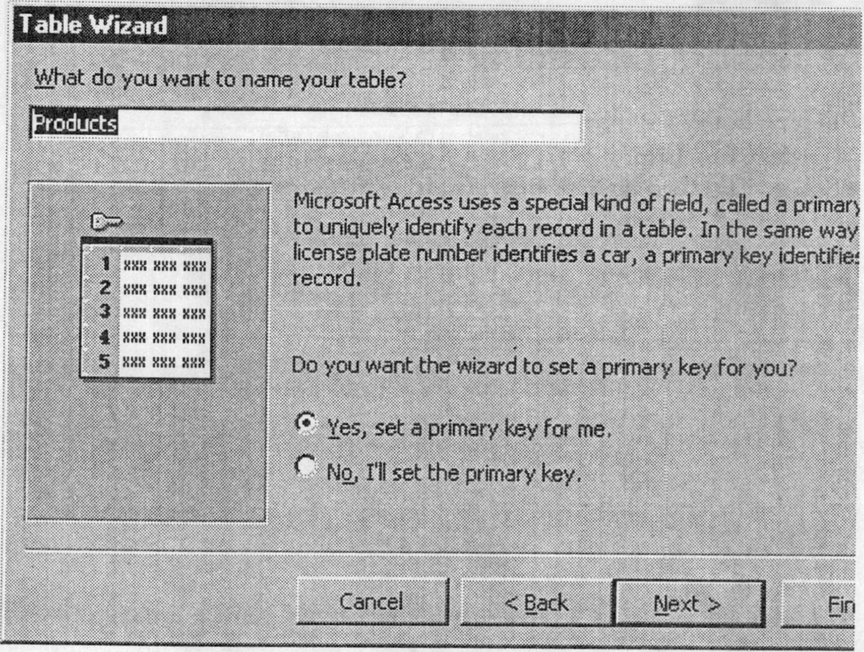

9. In the next page of the Table Wizard, choose one of the existing tables to relate to the new table, and then click **Next**. If you are establishing a new relationship or changing an existing one, in the Relationships dialog box, choose one of the three options to define a relationship between the two tables, and then click Ok.

10. In the final page of the Table Wizard, choose to modify the design, start entering data, or enter data using a form that the wizard creates, and then click **Finish**.

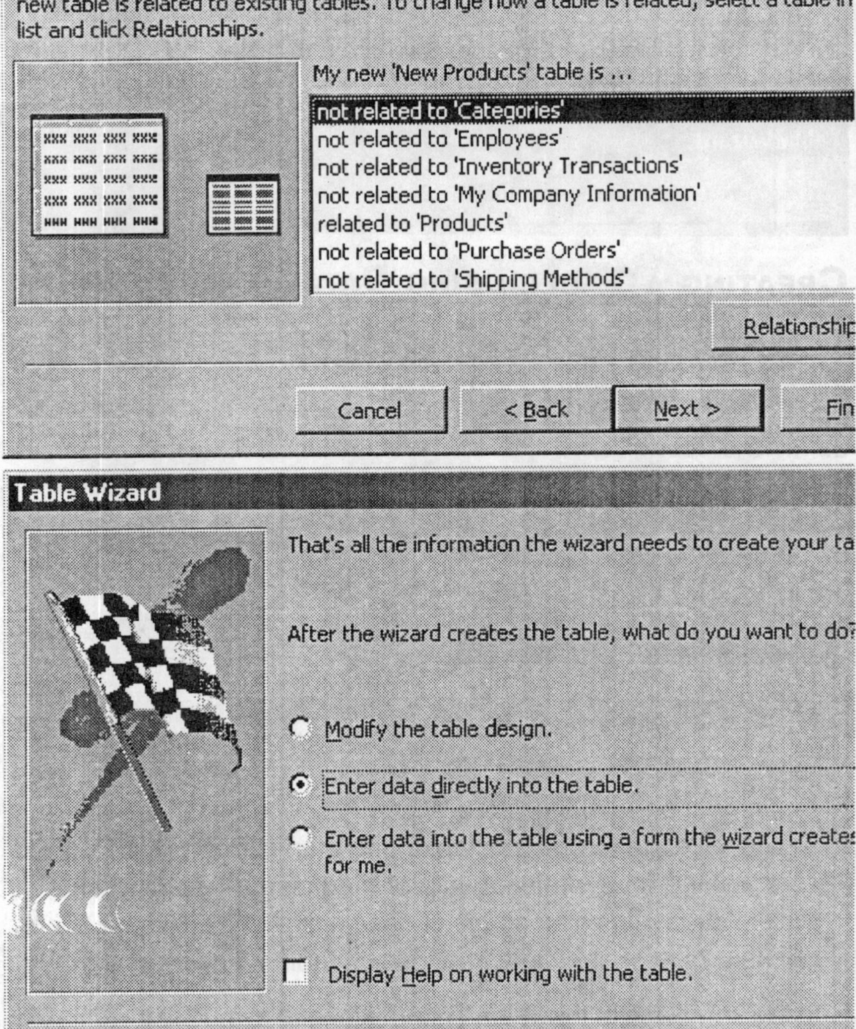

Table Wizard
Is your new table related to any other tables in your database? Related tables have mat
records. Usually, your new table is related to at least one other table in the current data
In some cases, the wizard will create table relationships for you. The list below shows ho
new table is related to existing tables. To change how a table is related, select a table in
list and click Relationships.
My new 'New Products' table is ...
not related to 'Categories'
not related to 'Employees'
not related to 'Inventory Transactions'
not related to 'My Company Information'
related to 'Products'
not related to 'Purchase Orders'
not related to 'Shipping Methods'
Relationship
Cancel
< Back
Next >
Fin
Table Wizard
That's all the information the wizard needs to create your ta
After the wizard creates the table, what do you want to do?
Modify the table design.
Enter data directly into the table.
Enter data into the table using a form the wizard creates for me.
Display Help on working with the table.
Cancel
< Back
Next >
Fin

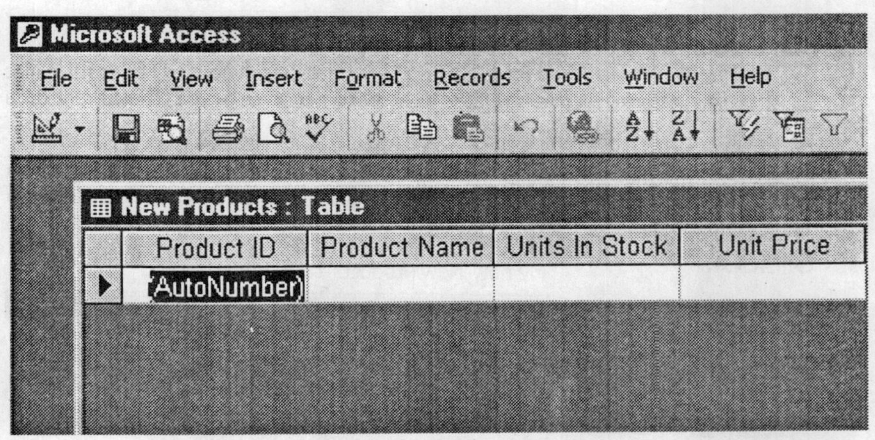

Creating a Table using Datasheet View

1. In the Database window, click the **Tables** tab.
2. Click the **New** button on the Database window toolbar.
3. In the **New Table** dialog box, select **Datasheet View**.
4. Click Ok.
5. In the new table window, double-click a field name and rename it.

Table1 : Table

Field1	Field2	Field3	Field4

Creating a Table using Design View

1. In the Database window, click the **Tables** tab.
2. Click the **New** button on the Database window toolbar.
3. In the **New Table** dialog box, select **Design View**.
4. Click Ok.
5. Enter the field name and select a data type for each.
6. Add a description if you want.

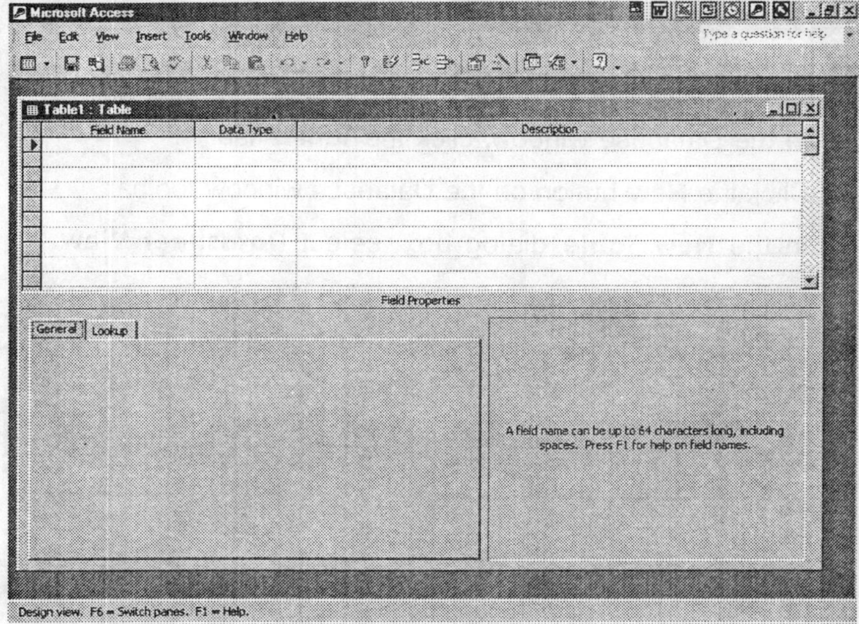

Adding a Field to the Table in Design View

1. On the Tables tab of the Database window, choose a table and click the Design button.
2. In the Table window, click a blank row in the **Field Name** column.

3. Enter a field name press the Tab key to move to the next column.
4. Choose a data type from the drop-down list in the **Data Type** column, as shown below.
5. Press the Tab key to move to the next column and enter a description for the field in the Description column.
6. Save the changes to the table design.

Table1 : Table

Field Name | Data Type

Text
Memo
Number
Date/Time
Currency
AutoNumber
Yes/No
OLE Object
Hyperlink
Lookup Wizard...

Field Properties

FIELD SIZE AND FORMAT

If the field data type is text, you can set the number of characters allowed and specify formatting rules. If the field data type is a numeric value, you can choose the range of numbers to be accepted and the number of decimal places to be stored.

1. On the **Tables** tab of the Database window, choose a table and click the Design button.
2. In the Table window, click the name of the field to format.
3. Click the **Field Size** text box and then enter a number if the field is text, or choose from the drop-down list of options if the field is numeric or some other data type.
4. Click the **Format** box and then, if the field is a text field, enter one of the symbols as mentioned below:

Symbol	Result
@	A text character is required in the field (either a character or a space).
&	A text character is not required.
<	All characters entered will become lowercase.
>	All characters entered will become uppercase.

5. Save the changes to the table design.
6. For a text field, you can enter any field size between 0 and 255. The default is 50.
7. When you are setting the field size for a Number field, choose the option that requires the fewest number of bytes but that is still suitable for your data.

Entering Data in a Table

To fill a table with data, you enter the data record by record. To complete each record, you enter information into the fields of the record.

You probably will want to use a form to enter data into a table, but you can also enter the data directly into the rows and columns of the table.

1. Click the **Tables** tab in the Database window.
2. Double-click a table name.

   Or

   Select the table to add to and click **Open**.
3. Click the **New Record** button on the Access toolbar to add a new record.
4. Enter data in the first field and then press Tab to move to the next field.

New Products : Table

		Product ID	Product Name	Units In Stock	Unit Price
	+	1	Powder	3	Rs.36.00
	+	2	Toothpaste	2	Rs.45.00
	+	3	Shaving Cream	4	Rs.22.00
	+	4	Blades	10	Rs.2.00
	+	5	Cream	1	Rs.60.00
▶		(AutoNumber)			

5. If the field shows an arrow button, you can click the button to display the list and then select an entry in the list.
6. Press **Tab** after the last field in the record to move to the start of a new record. The record you have completed is saved automatically.
7. You do not need to do anything special to save each new record. When you move to the next record, the previous record is saved automatically.

EDITING DATA IN A TABLE

You can easily change the information in any field of any record.

1. Click any field in the table to position an insertion point in the field.

   Or

   Double-click any word or number in a field to select it.
2. Edit the entry as you would edit text in Word.
3. Click a different record to save the changes.
4. To select an entire field, click anywhere in the field and press **F2**.
5. To move to the previous field for corrections, press **Shift + Tab**.

6. To replace the entry in a field with the entry in the same field of the previous record, click in the field and press **Ctrl** + ' (apostrophe).
7. While you edit a field, the pencil symbol appears to the left of the record to indicate that your changes have not yet been saved.

Saving a Table

After you create a table, you must save it.

1. From the File menu, choose **Save**.

   Or

   Press **Ctrl** + **S**

   Or

   Click the **Save** button on the Access toolbar.
2. In the **Save As** dialog box, enter a name for the new table.
3. Click Ok. The new table is added to the list of tables in the Database window.
4. To save a table as a form that you can use for data entry or a report that you can print, or to save it with a new name, select the table on the Tables tab in the Database window and then choose **Save As** from the **File** menu.

Indexing a Field

A required field must have an entry before the record can be saved. An indexed field is specially prepared so that its information can be searched through more quickly when you later search the database.

1. On the **Tables** tab of the Database window, choose a table and click Design.

   Or

   If the table is already open, click the **Design View** button.

New Products : Table

	Field Name	Data Type
🔑	ProductID	AutoNumber
▶	ProductName	Text
	UnitsInStock	Number
	UnitPrice	Currency

Field Properties

General | Lookup

Field Size	50
Format	
Input Mask	
Caption	Product Name
Default Value	
Validation Rule	
Validation Text	
Required	No
Allow Zero Length	No
Indexed	Yes (Duplicates OK)
Unicode Compression	No
IME Mode	No Control
IME Sentence Mode	None

2. In the Table window, click the name of the field to format.
3. Click the Required box and choose **Yes** or **No** from the drop-down list.
4. Click the Indexed box and choose an option from the drop-down list. Various index options are:

Option	***Result***
No	This field is not indexed
Yes (Duplicates Ok)	This field is indexed and duplicates **ar** allowed.

Yes (No Duplicates) This field is indexed and each entry is unique.

5. To save changes to the table design, click the **Save** button on the Access toolbar, or press **Ctrl + S**, or choose **Save** from the **File** menu.
6. Primary key fields are automatically indexed.
7. To view a list of fields that are indexed, click the **Indexes** button on the Access toolbar while the table is shown in Design view.

DATA TYPE OPTIONS

Text	A string of characters used to store alphanumeric data. The maximum number of characters you can store in a single text field is 255.
Memo	Stores long text field. No maximum is specified by the user, but Access imposes a limit of 64,000 characters. The Notes field is a memo field.
Number	Stores numeric data.
Date/Time	Stores dates and times.
Currency	A special numeric data type used for monetary values because it prevents round-off errors during calculations.
AutoNumber	A special numeric data type that can be used for primary key fields. Fields of this data type always are read-only, because Access automatically inserts the next number in the sequence or a random number when a data record is created.
Yes/No	Stores Boolean data, which can contain only one or two values, such as **On/Off** or **Yes/No** or **True/False**.

OLE Object A special type of object or component provided by a Windows OLE server.

Hyperlink Stores the text for a hyperlink address. Access enables you to store addresses to Web documents, network files, and local files.

List of Activities on the Table Menu

Print and Print Preview Enables you to print the data in the table. The printout will have the same look as if you had printed with the Datasheet View window.

Cut and Copy Enables you to use the Windows clipboard to cut and paste or copy and paste an entire table, data and all. You can paste a copied or cut table into the currently open database, or into a completely different database.

Save As Allows you to save the table's data and definition to a new table, or to a form, report, or data access page.

Export Allows you to export the table's definition and data to an external Access file. You can also export to a different type of file, such as an HTML file or a Microsoft Excel spreadsheet file.

Send To A flyout menu which provides a mechanism for e-mailing the table to someone else.

Add to Group A flyout menu which enables you to organize the objects in the database into groups, providing a more logical way to locate the objects.

Create Shortcut	Enables you to create a Windows shortcut to the selected table. You can place the shortcut on your desktop or in any location you specify.
Delete	Enables you to delete the table as well as any data it contains. Access warns you if the table is involved in any relationship with other tables. You then can instruct Access to remove these relationships and delete the table.
Rename	Enables you to rename the table. You can also rename a table by clicking it name after selecting it.
Properties	Displays the properties of the current table. You can also view the table properties by clicking the Details button on the Database window or choosing View, Details from the main menu.

15

Working with Reports

Introduction

A Report will print your database in a format which looks best on the paper using the printer attached to your computer. You can even have the report displayed on the monitor too. These reports are generated by the queries using the information available in the tables. As usual Access provides you a easy way out in the form of a Wizard called **Report Wizard**.

Creating a Report using the ReportWizard

You can choose to have a report by using ReportWizard and then change it if required.

1. On the **Reports** tab of the Database window, click the **New** button.
2. In the **New Report** dialog box, select **Report Wizard**.
3. Click Ok.
4. On the first page of the Report Wizard, select the table or query on which the report will be based, select the fields to display, and click **Next** to get the next dialog box.
5. Select here the fields which you want to put in the report and press **Next** to get the next page.
6. Select here the grouping levels and press **Next** to go to the next page.

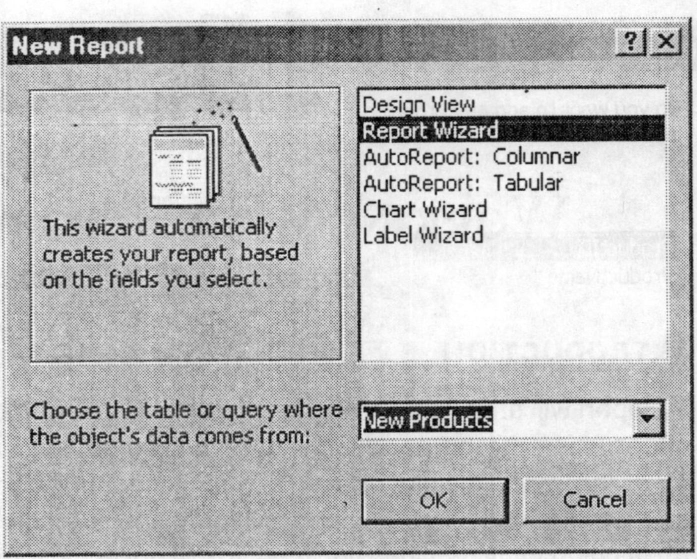

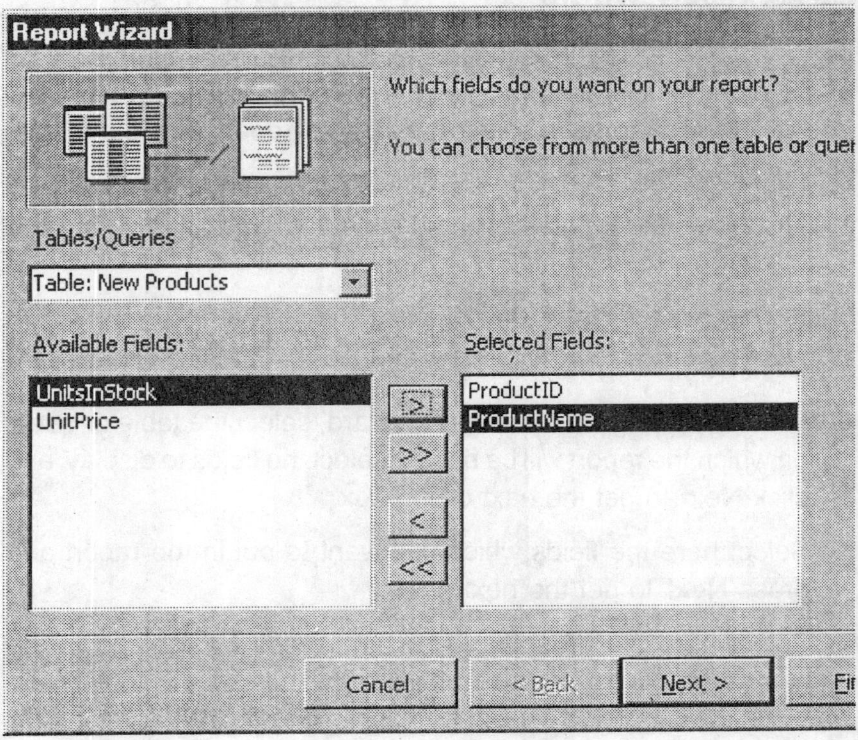

Report Wizard

Which fields do you want on your report?

You can choose from more than one table or quer

Tables/Queries

Table: New Products

Available Fields:

UnitsInStock
UnitPrice

>
>>
<
<<

Selected Fields:

ProductID
ProductName

Cancel
< Back
Next >
Fi

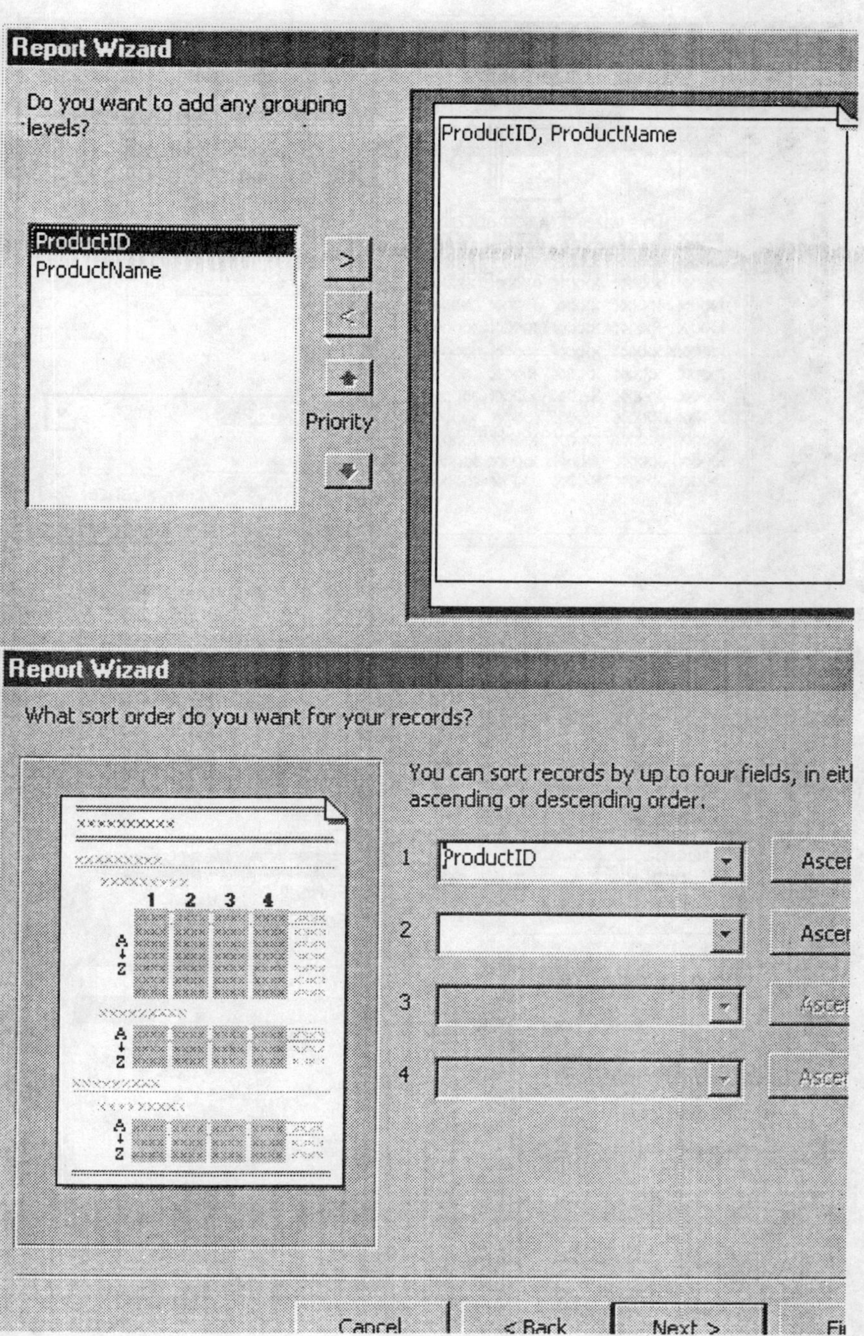
Report Wizard
Do you want to add any grouping levels?
ProductID
ProductName
>
<
Priority
ProductID, ProductName
Report Wizard
What sort order do you want for your records?
You can sort records by up to four fields, in eit
ascending or descending order.
1
ProductID
Ascer
2
Ascer
3
Ascer
4
Ascer
1 2 3 4
A
Z
Cancel
< Back
Next >
Fi

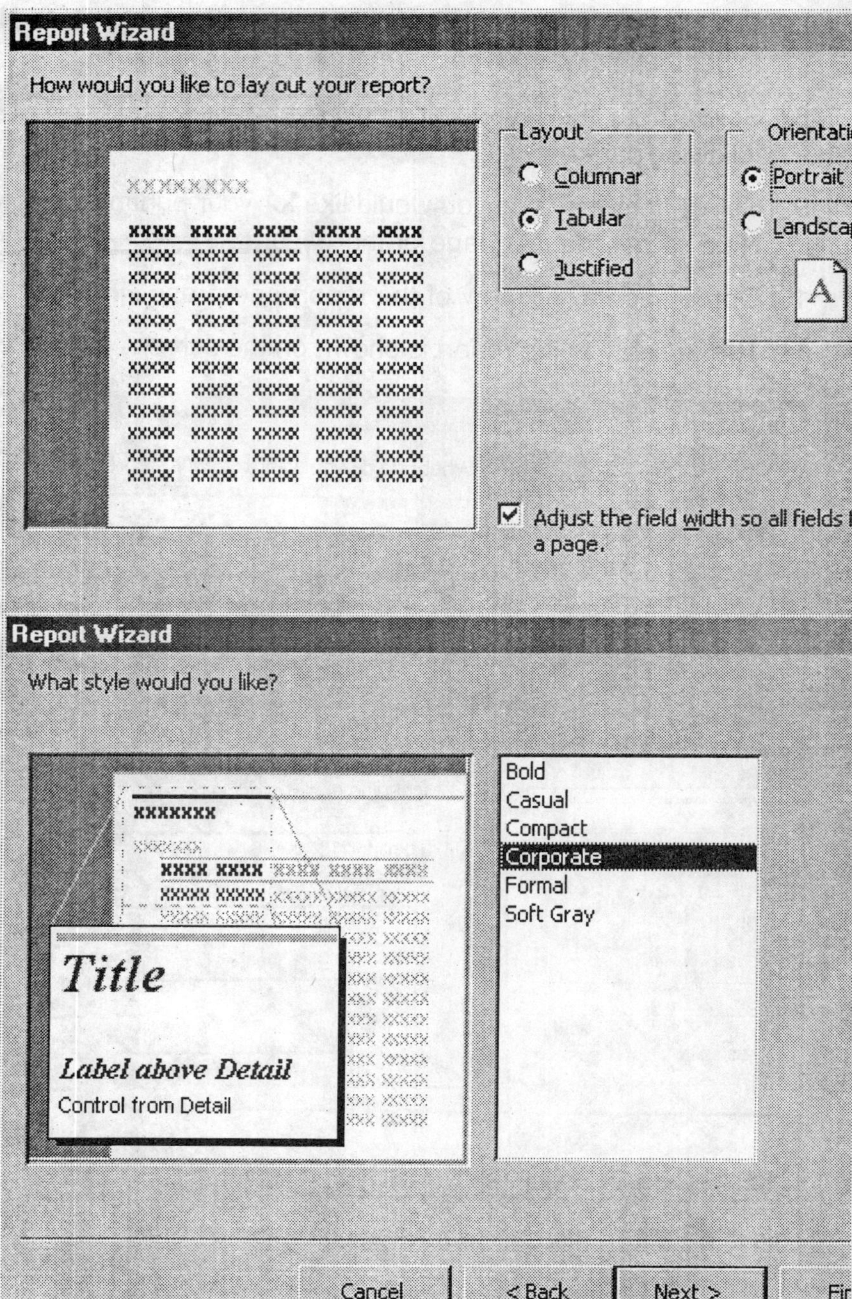
Report Wizard
How would you like to lay out your report?
Layout
Columnar
Tabular
Justified
Orientatic
Portrait
Landscap
Adjust the field width so all fields f
a page.
Report Wizard
What style would you like?
Title
Label above Detail
Control from Detail
Bold
Casual
Compact
Corporate
Formal
Soft Gray
Cancel
< Back
Next >

7. Select here the grouping and summary options and press **Next** to get the following page.
8. Select here the layout for printing and click **Next** to get the following page.
9. Select here the style you would like for your printing and press **Next** to get the last page of the Wizard.
10. Opt to see the preview of the report and press **Finish**.
11. The preview of the report is shown on the screen.

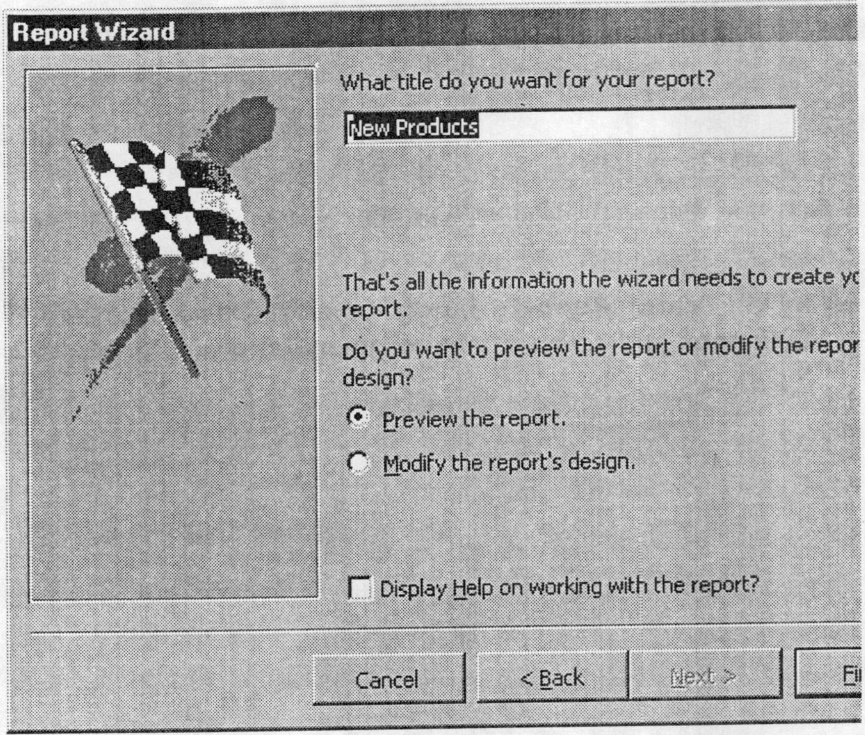

CREATING A REPORT USING AN AUTOREPORT

This is no doubt the quickest way of creating a report.

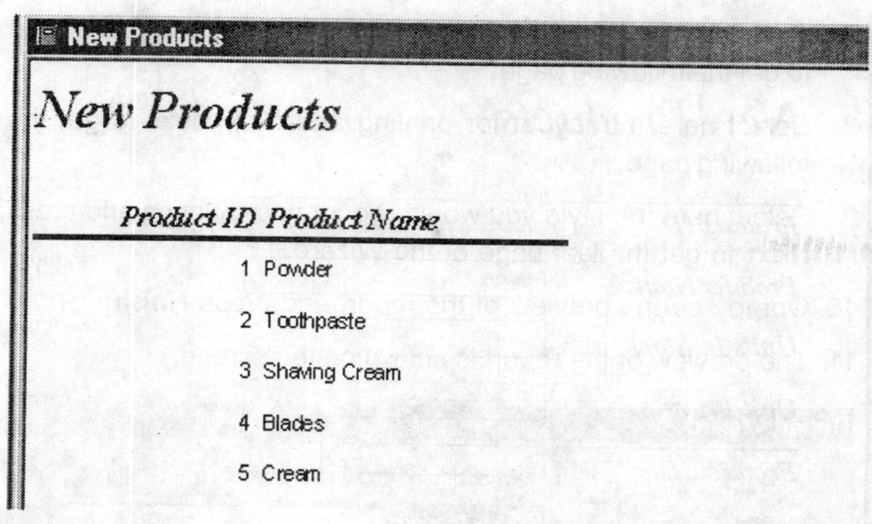

Columnar Report

1. On the **Report** tab of the Database window, click the **New** button.
2. In the **New Report** dialog box, select **AutoReport: Columnar** and select a table or query on which to base the report.

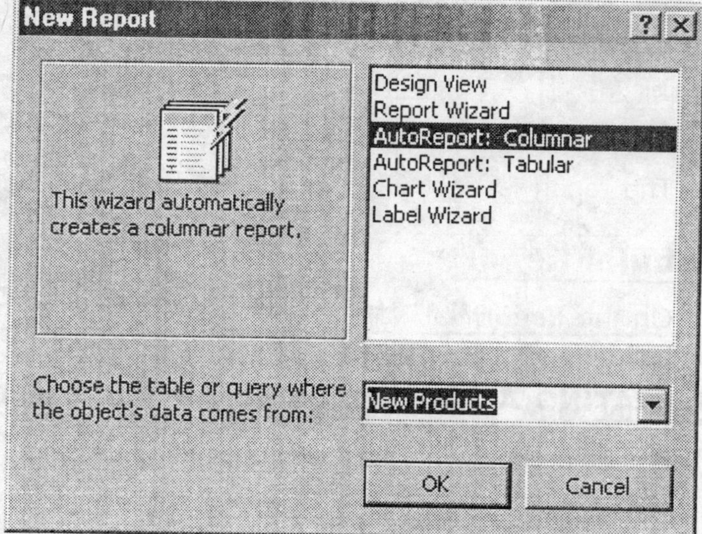

New Products

New Products

Product ID	1
Product Name	Powder
Units In Stock	3
Unit Price	Rs.36.00
Product ID	2
Product Name	Toothpaste
Units In Stock	2
Unit Price	Rs.45.00
Product ID	3
Product Name	Shaving Cream
Units In Stock	4

Page: 1

3. Click Ok.
4. The report is displayed in the **Print Preview**.

Tabular Report

1. On the **Report** tab of the Database window, click the **New** button.
2. In the **New Report** dialog box, select **AutoReport: Tabular** and select a table or query on which to base the report.
3. Click Ok.

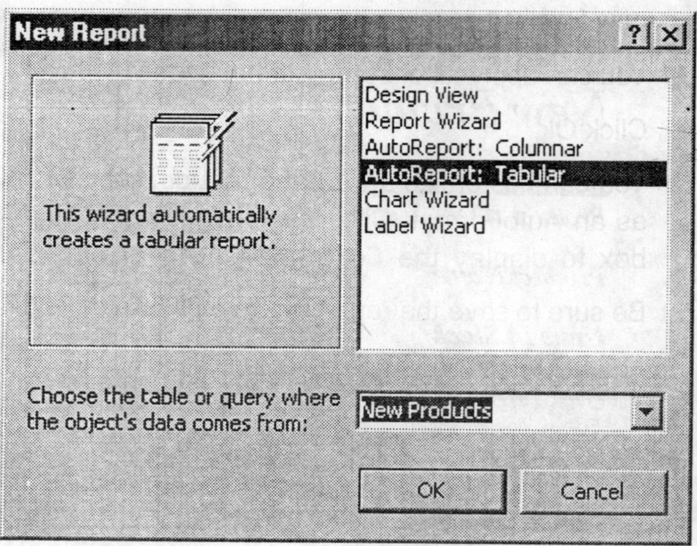

4. The report is displayed in the **Print Preview** as shown below.

New Products

New Products

Product ID	*Product Name*	*Units In Stock*	*Unit Price*
1	Powder	3	Rs.36.00
2	Toothpaste	2	Rs.45.00
3	Shaving Cream	4	Rs.22.00
4	Blades	10	Rs.2.00
5	Cream	1	Rs.60.00

AutoFormat for the Report

You can choose AutoFormat for a formatting your report. This way you can get a good looking report without much of an effort.

1. With the report open in Design view, click the **AutoFormat** button on the Access toolbar, as shown on the next page.

2. In the AutoFormat dialog box, shown on the next page, select a new format.
3. You can apply all or some attributes only.
4. Click Ok.
5. You can customize an AutoFormat or add your own formatting as an AutoFormat. Click **Customize** in the AutoFormat dialog box to display the **Customize AutoFormat** dialog box.
6. Be sure to save the report after you have revised it.

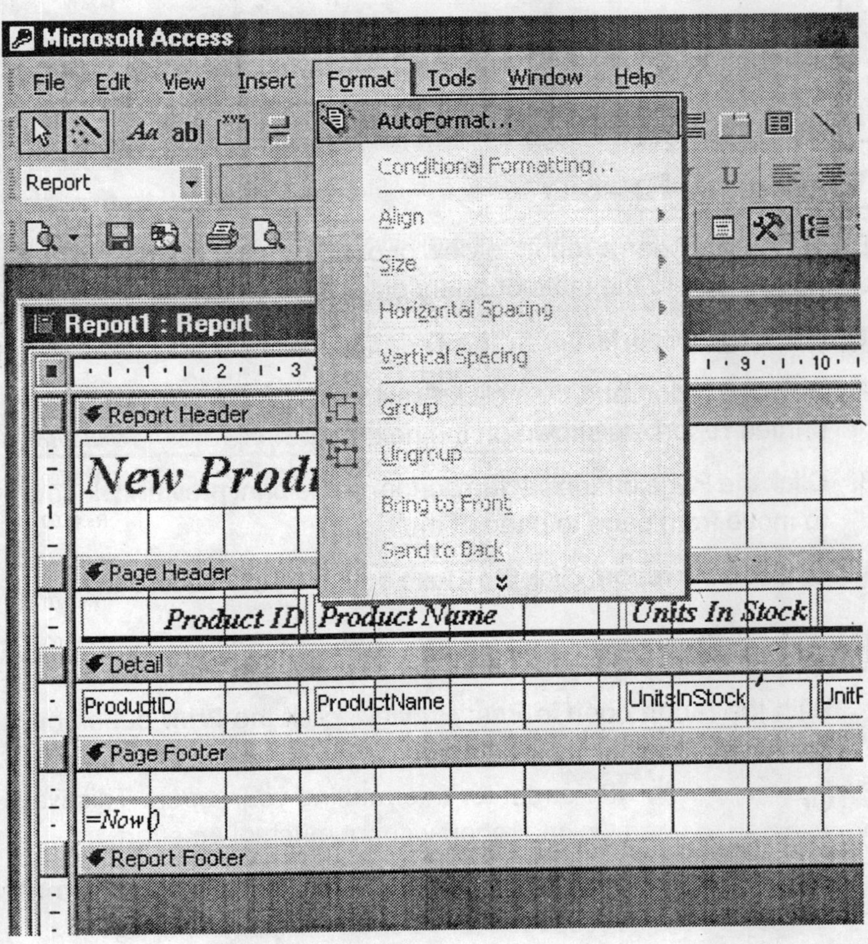

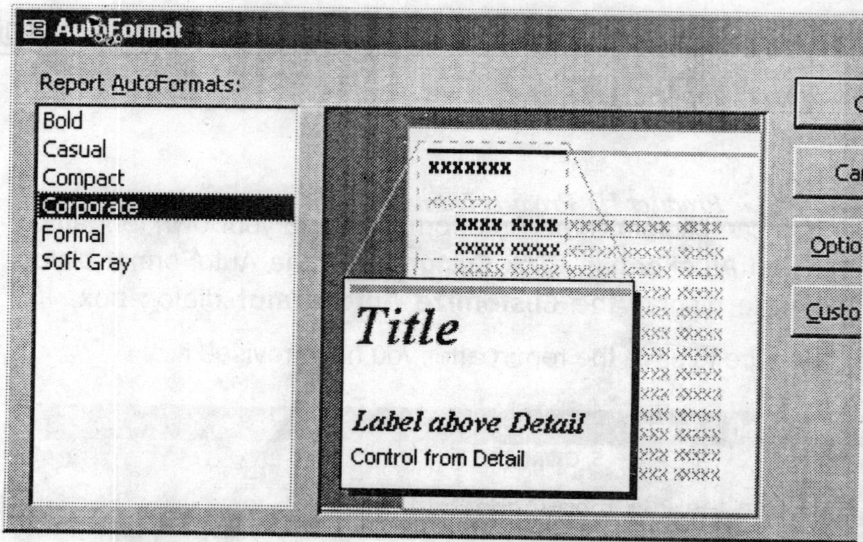

Viewing a Report

Each time you open a report to view or print it, the report reflects any changes made to the table or query on which it is based.

1. Click the **Reports** tab in the Database window.
2. Select a report and then click **Preview** to view a preview of the printed report, as shown on the next page.
3. Click the Page buttons at the bottom of the print preview window to move from page to page of the report.
4. To close the report, click the **Close** button on the Access toolbar.

Print a Report

1. With the report open in Print Preview, click the **Print** button on the Access toolbar.

   Or

   Press **Ctrl + P**

   Or

New Products

New Products

Product ID	Product Name
1	Powder
2	Toothpaste
3	Shaving Cream
4	Blades
5	Cream

From the **File** menu, choose Print.

2. You can also print a report be selecting the report on the Reports tab and clicking the Print button or choosing Print from the File menu.
3. Make sure that your **printer** is turned **ON** to print the report.

Sorting and Grouping Records in a Report

A report can group together similar records and it can also sort the entries within groups.

1. With the report open in Design view, click the **Sorting and Grouping** button on the Access toolbar.
2. In the Sorting and Grouping dialog box, use the drop-down menu to select the field you want to group on.

   Or

   Drag a field from the field list.
3. Select the sorting method for the grouping.
4. If you want, select a second field to group on, within the first grouping.

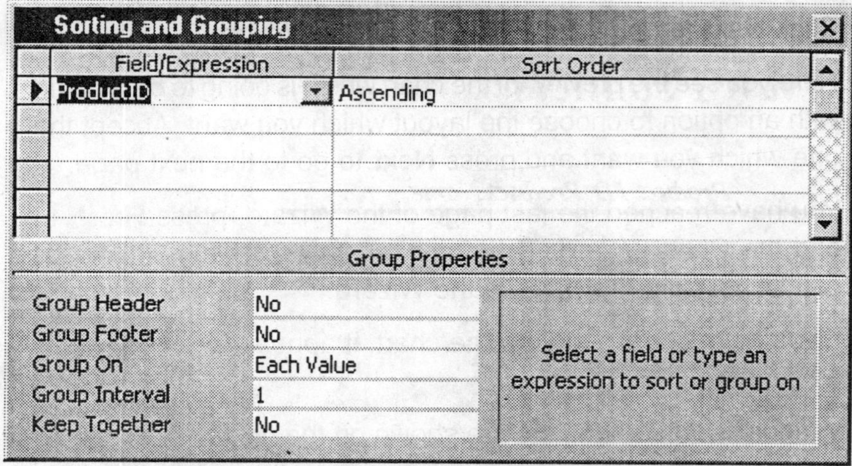

5. Click a new row to save your changes.

6. Close the dialog box.

CREATING CHARTS

You can create a report in chart format, which represents numeric information graphically.

1. On the **Reports** tab of the Database window, click the New button.

2. In the New Report dialog box, select **Chart Wizard** and select a table or query on which to base the report.

3. Click Ok.

4. In the first step of the Chart Wizard, select the fields which you want to include in your chart, as shown on the next page, I have selected the fields as shown.

6. Clicking **Next** to get the next page of the Chart Wizard.

7. Here you have to select the type of the chart which you want to use for your presentation. Here I have chosen the **3D Area Chart**.

8. Click **Next** to go to the next page of the Wizard.

9. Here you see the preview of the chart which is going to be created with an option to choose the layout which you want. Accept the one which you want and press **Next** to go to the next page.

10. You have reached the last page of the Wizard, press **Finish** to end the Chart Wizard. There are other options too which you can select from this page of the Wizard.

11. If you have chosen to view the chart, it appears on the screen, as shown.

12. Various other screens too are shown on the next pages.

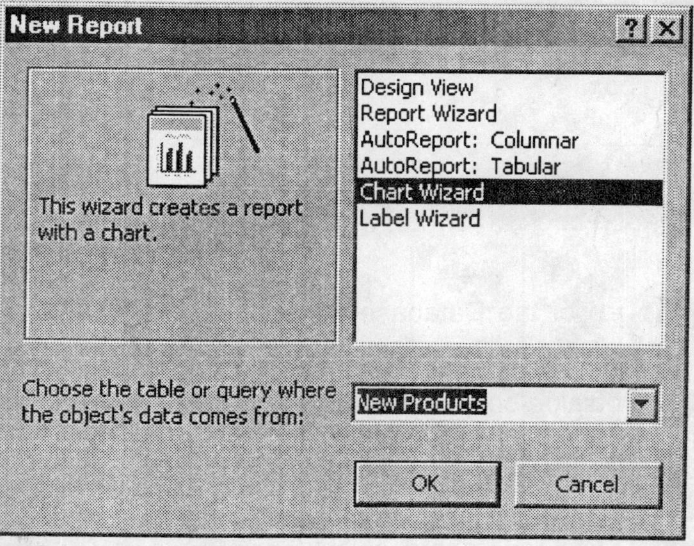

Creating Labels

You can create labels that can be used for sending a mailing to a mailing list.

1. On the **Reports** tab of the Database window, click the New button.

2. In the New Report dialog box, select **Label Wizard** and select a table or query on which to base the labels.

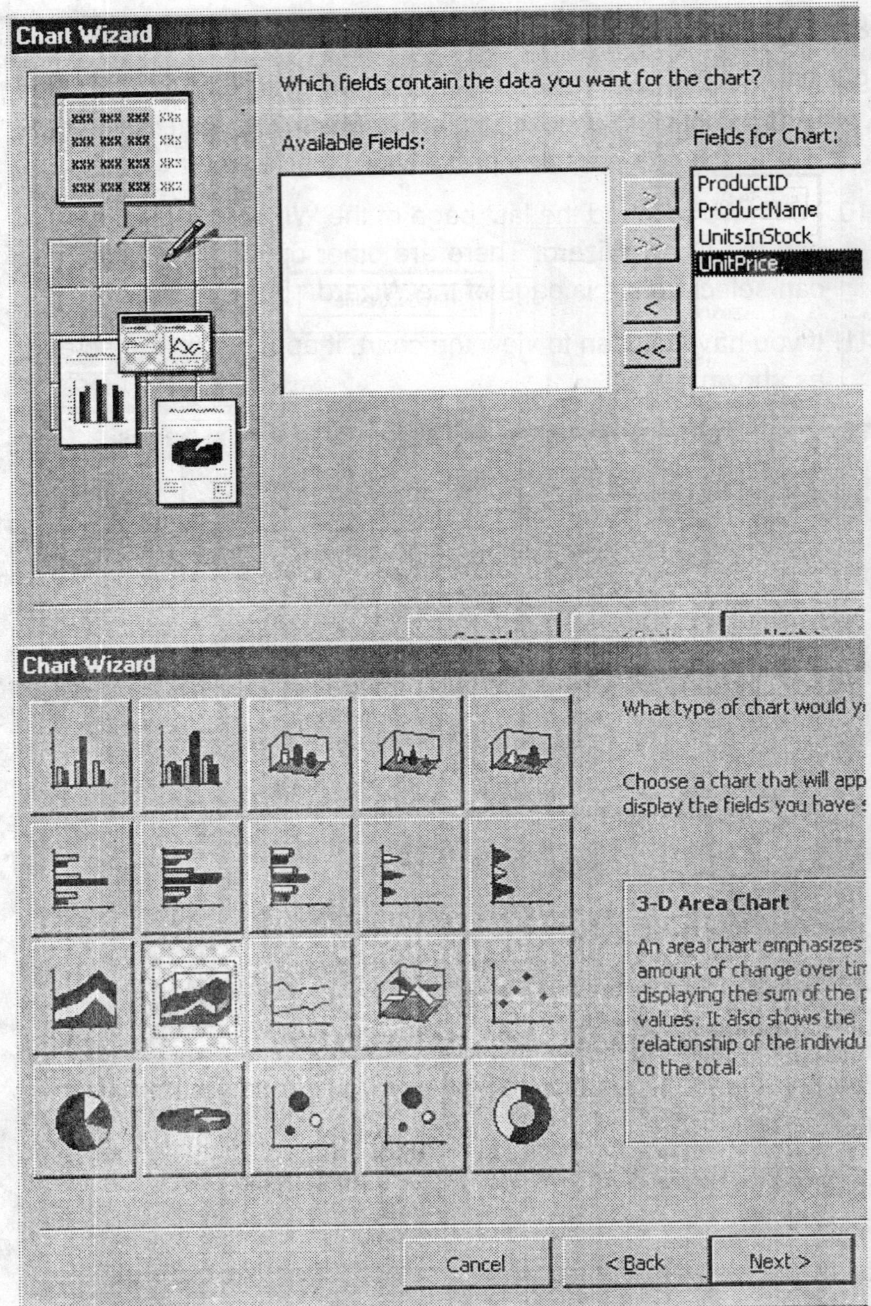
Chart Wizard
Which fields contain the data you want for the chart?
Available Fields:
Fields for Chart:
ProductID
ProductName
UnitsInStock
UnitPrice
Chart Wizard
What type of chart would y
Choose a chart that will app
display the fields you have
3-D Area Chart
An area chart emphasizes
amount of change over tir
displaying the sum of the
values. It also shows the
relationship of the individu
to the total.
Cancel
< Back
Next >

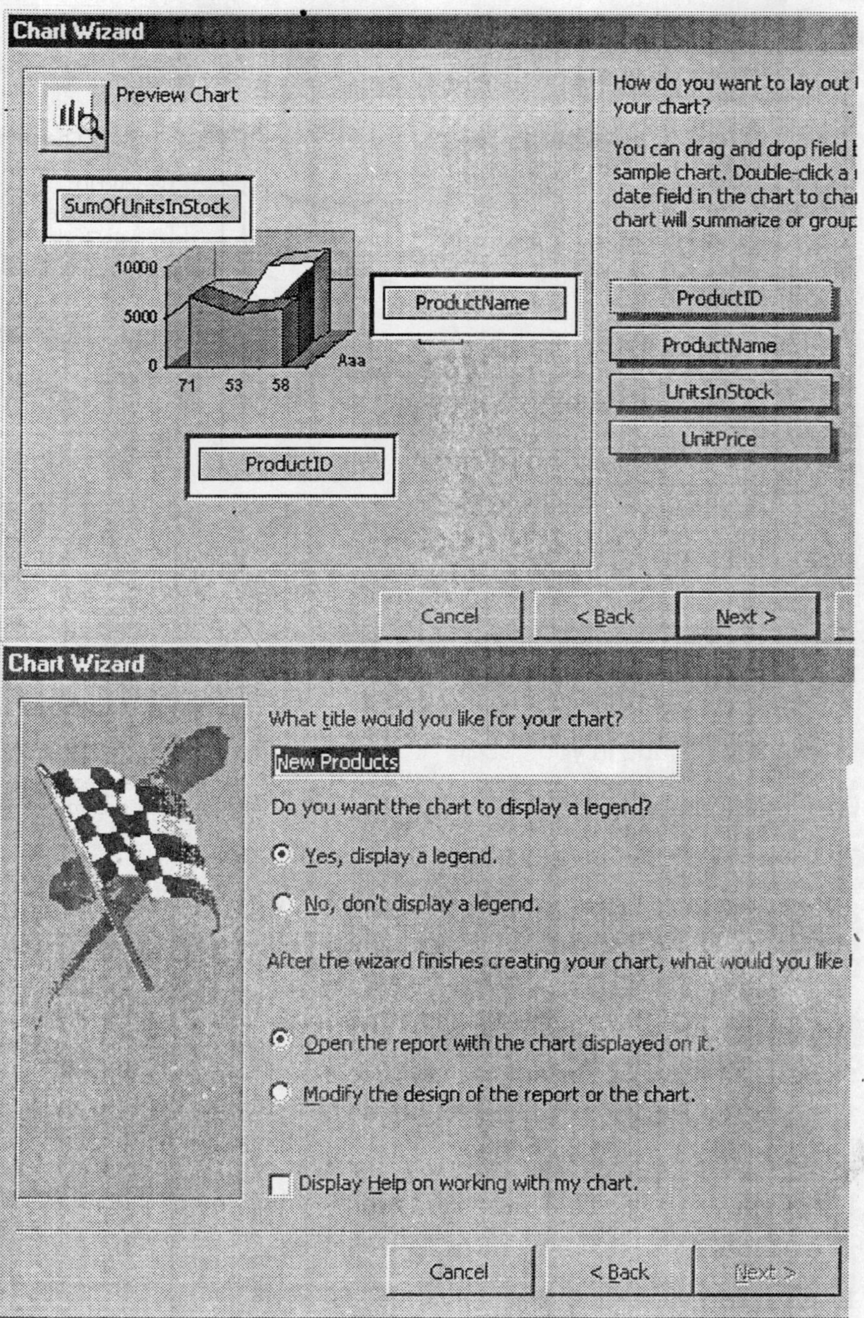
Chart Wizard
Preview Chart
SumOfUnitsInStock
10000
5000
0
71 53 58
Aaa
ProductName
ProductID
How do you want to lay out
your chart?
You can drag and drop field
sample chart. Double-click a
date field in the chart to cha
chart will summarize or group
ProductID
ProductName
UnitsInStock
UnitPrice
Cancel
< Back
Next >
Chart Wizard
What title would you like for your chart?
New Products
Do you want the chart to display a legend?
Yes, display a legend.
No, don't display a legend.
After the wizard finishes creating your chart, what would you like
Open the report with the chart displayed on it.
Modify the design of the report or the chart.
Display Help on working with my chart.
Cancel
< Back
Next >

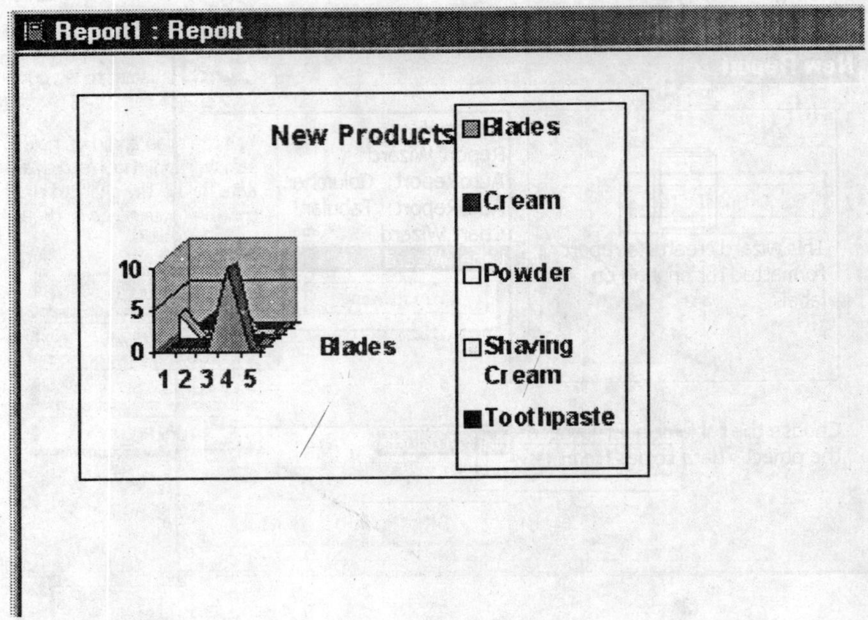

3. Click Ok.
4. In the first step of the Label Wizard, select the fields which you want to include in your label.
6. Clicking **Next** to get the next page of the Label Wizard.
7. Here you have to select the type of labels you want.
8. Click **Next** to go to the next page of the Wizard.
9. Here you select the various options of the label, like font, etc.
10. In the next screen, select how the various fields would appear on the screen.
11. In the next screen, you select the field on which you would like your labels would be sorted.
12. When you click **Finish**, you would see the result of the label wizard.
13. On the next pages, see the various screens.

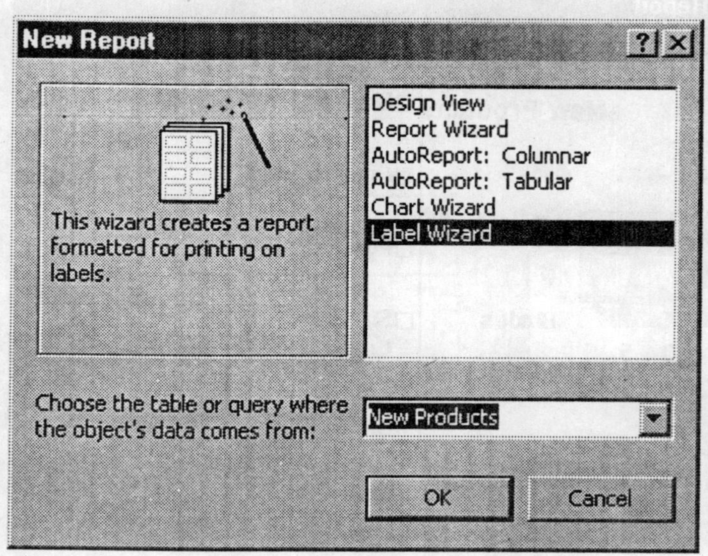
New Report
This wizard creates a report formatted for printing on labels.
Design View
Report Wizard
AutoReport: Columnar
AutoReport: Tabular
Chart Wizard
Label Wizard
Choose the table or query where the object's data comes from:
New Products
OK
Cancel

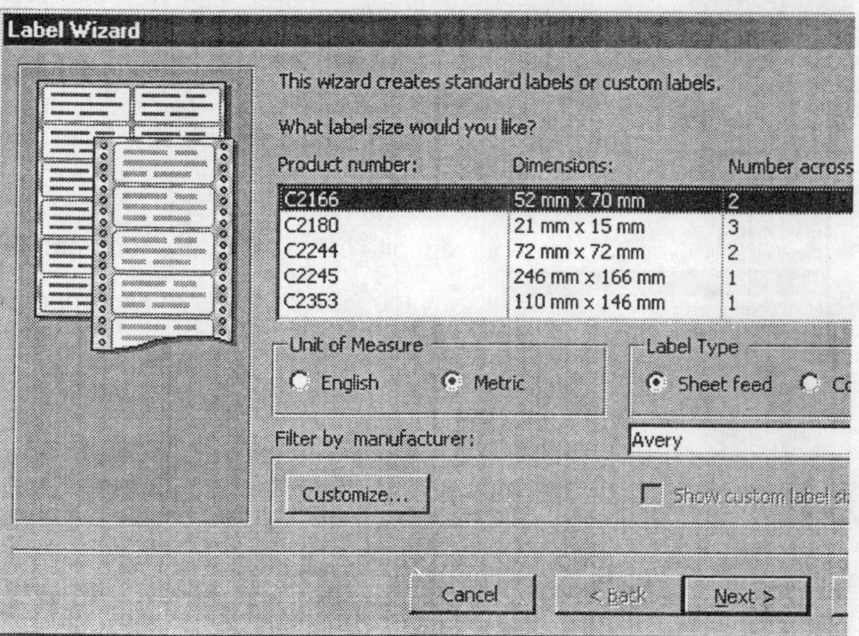
Label Wizard
This wizard creates standard labels or custom labels.
What label size would you like?
Product number:
Dimensions:
Number across
C2166
52 mm x 70 mm
2
C2180
21 mm x 15 mm
3
C2244
72 mm x 72 mm
2
C2245
246 mm x 166 mm
1
C2353
110 mm x 146 mm
1
Unit of Measure
English
Metric
Label Type
Sheet feed
Filter by manufacturer:
Avery
Customize...
Cancel
< Back
Next >

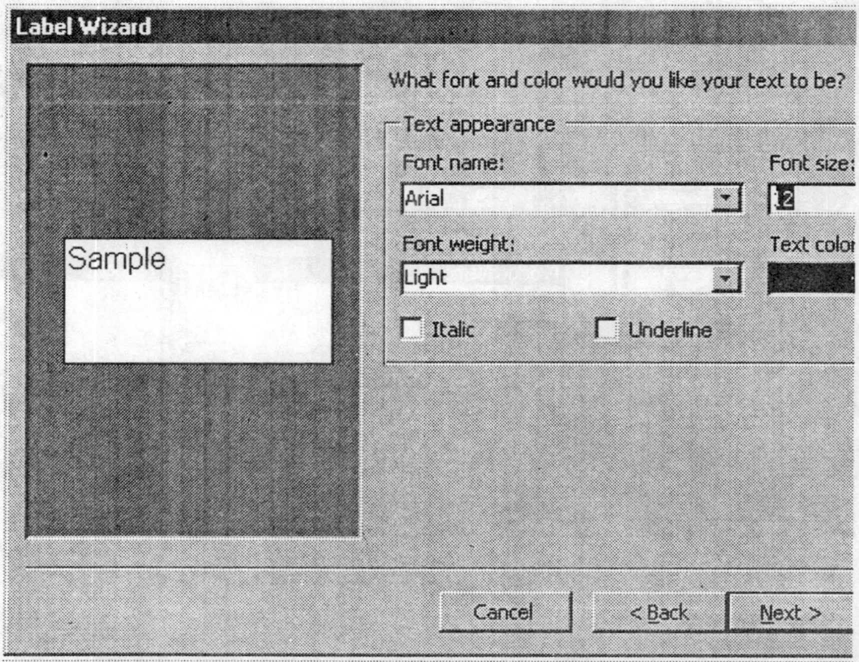

Label Wizard

Sample

What font and color would you like your text to be?

Text appearance

Font name: Arial

Font size: 12

Font weight: Light

Text color

Italic

Underline

Cancel | < Back | Next >

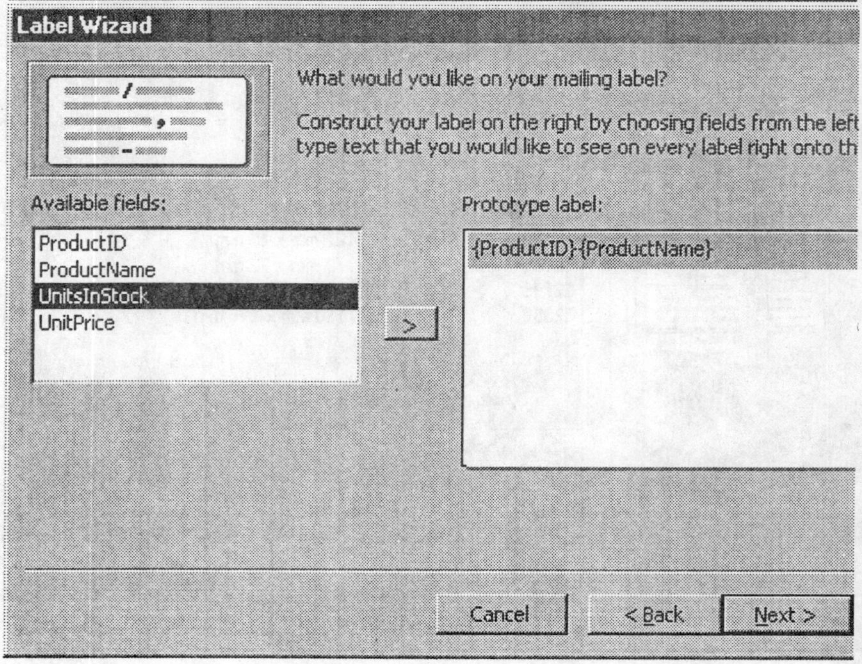

Label Wizard

What would you like on your mailing label?

Construct your label on the right by choosing fields from the left
type text that you would like to see on every label right onto th

Available fields:

ProductID
ProductName
UnitsInStock
UnitPrice

>

Prototype label:

{ProductID}{ProductName}

Cancel | < Back | Next >

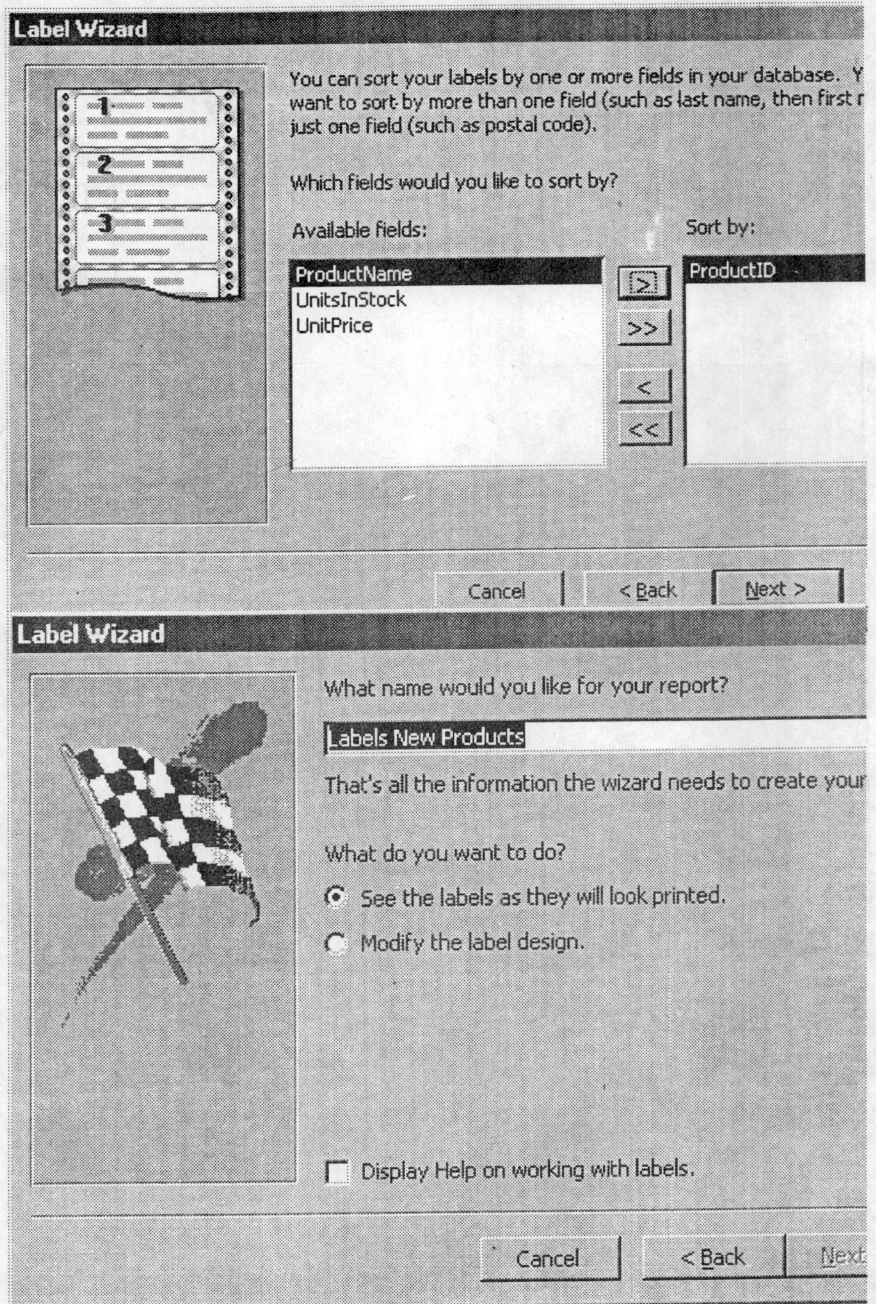
Label Wizard
You can sort your labels by one or more fields in your database. Y
want to sort by more than one field (such as last name, then first r
just one field (such as postal code).
Which fields would you like to sort by?
Available fields:
Sort by:
ProductName
UnitsInStock
UnitPrice
ProductID
Cancel
< Back
Next >
Label Wizard
What name would you like for your report?
Labels New Products
That's all the information the wizard needs to create your
What do you want to do?
See the labels as they will look printed.
Modify the label design.
Display Help on working with labels.
Cancel
< Back

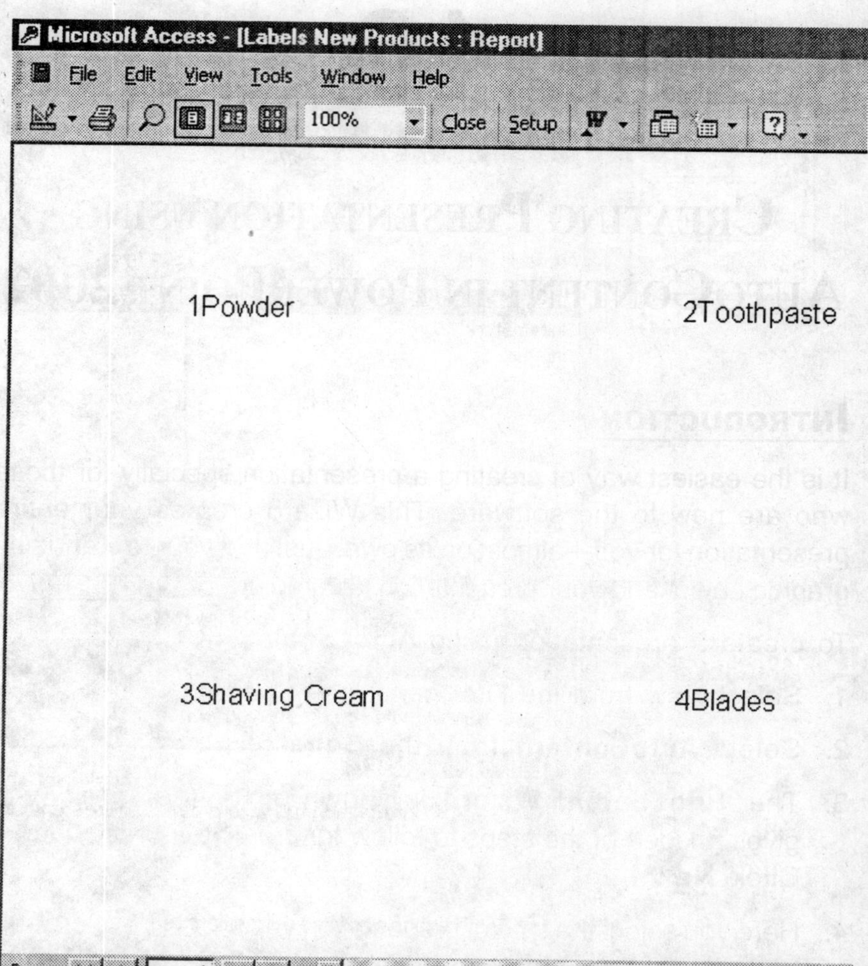
Microsoft Access - [Labels New Products : Report]
File Edit View Tools Window Help
100%
Close Setup
1Powder
2Toothpaste
3Shaving Cream
4Blades
Page: 1

16

Creating Presentation using AutoContent in PowerPoint 2002

Introduction

It is the easiest way of creating a presentation specially for those who are new to the software. This Wizard creates your entire presentation for you—almost on its own. Just add your text and any graphic object and your presentation is complete.

To create a presentation using **AutoContent**

1. Select **New** from the **File** menu.
2. Select **AutoContent** from the **General Panel**.
3. The **AutoContent Wizard** is shown on the screen, which gives an idea of the steps to follow for creating a presentation. Click **Next**
4. Here you select the type of presentation you want, I have chosen here **Marketing Plan**. You can choose different ones from the different categories. Click **Next**.
5. Define here the type of output you want. I have chosen here, On-screen presentation.

   Different options here are:

   On-screen presentation It allows you to run the presentation on a computer monitor or on a projector that is connected to the computer.

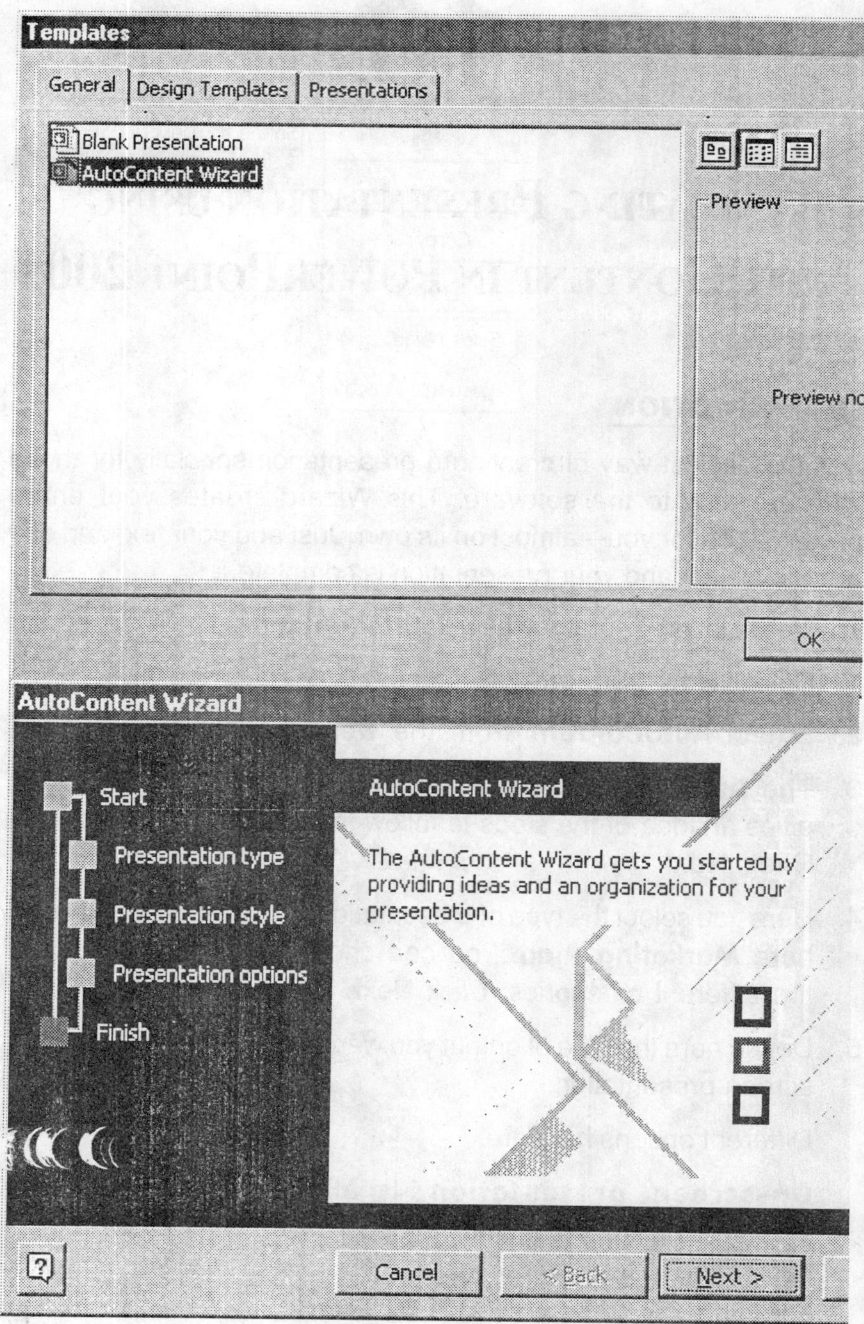

Templates
General
Design Templates
Presentations
Blank Presentation
AutoContent Wizard
Preview
Preview no
OK
AutoContent Wizard
Start
Presentation type
Presentation style
Presentation options
Finish
AutoContent Wizard
The AutoContent Wizard gets you started by providing ideas and an organization for your presentation.
Cancel
< Back
Next >

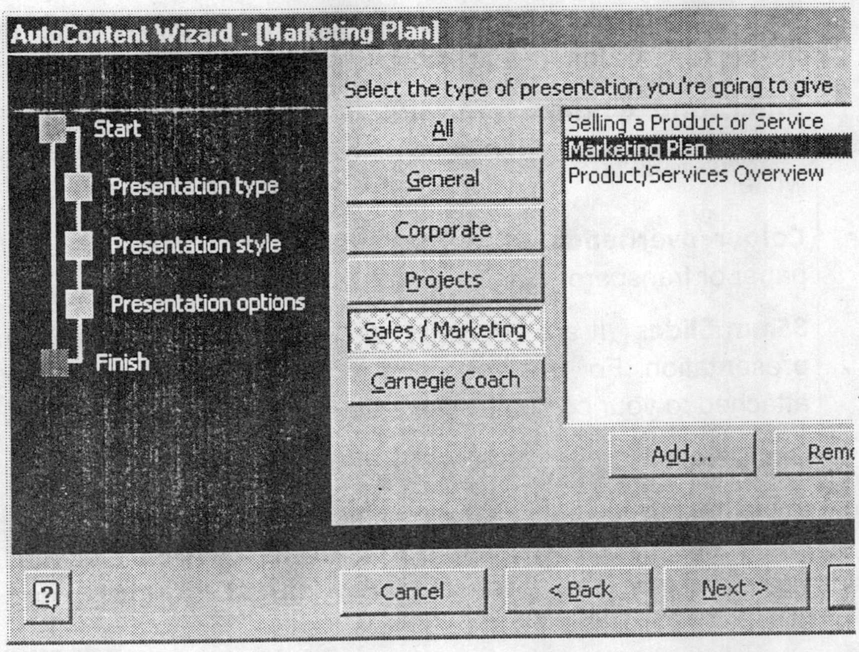
AutoContent Wizard - [Marketing Plan]
Start
Presentation type
Presentation style
Presentation options
Finish
Select the type of presentation you're going to give
All
General
Corporate
Projects
Sales / Marketing
Carnegie Coach
Selling a Product or Service
Marketing Plan
Product/Services Overview
Add...
Cancel
< Back
Next >

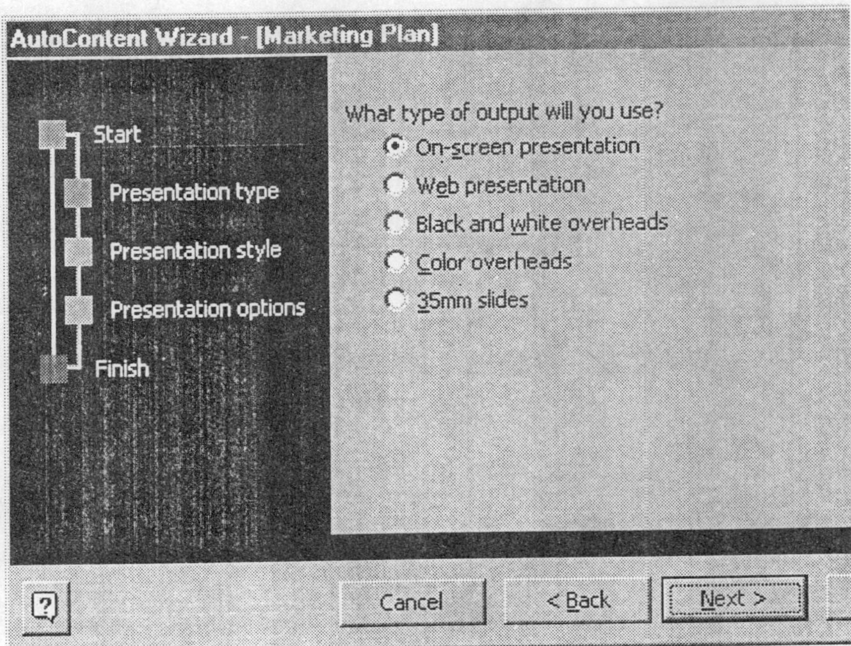
AutoContent Wizard - [Marketing Plan]
Start
Presentation type
Presentation style
Presentation options
Finish
What type of output will you use?
On-screen presentation
Web presentation
Black and white overheads
Color overheads
35mm slides
Cancel
< Back
Next >

Web presentation It allows you to create a presentation in the appropriate format that can be viewed easily over the Intenet.

Black and white overheads It creates a presentation that will be printed either on paper or transparency in black and white.

Colour overheads It creates presentation in the form of paper or transparency in colour

35mm Slides It allows you to use a slide projector to give a presentation. For this you need to have the slide converter attached to your computer to create slides.

Click **Next**.

6. In the next dialog box, give title of the presentation and the text you want to appear on the footer page. I have put them as **ABC Consultancy Co. Ltd.** and **For the financial year 2000-2001**. Click **Next**.

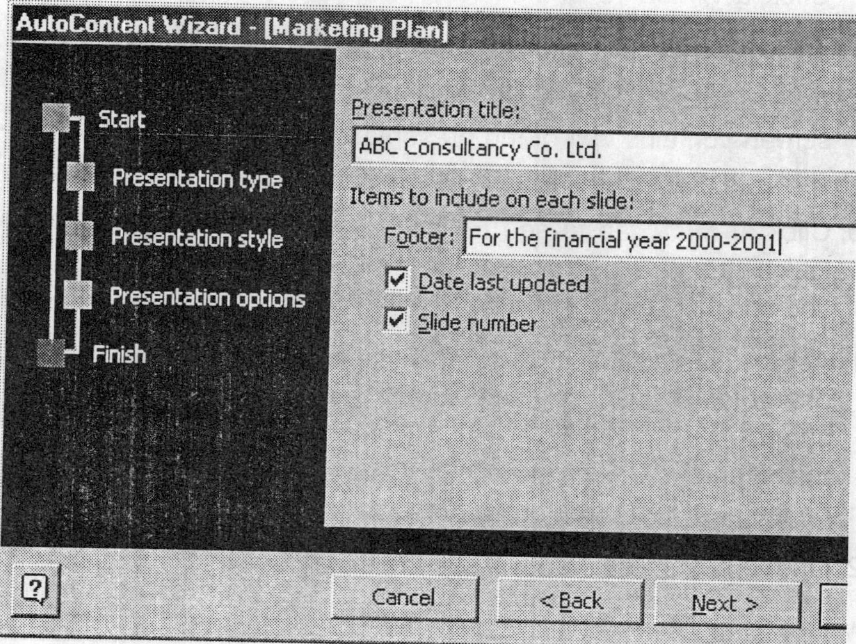

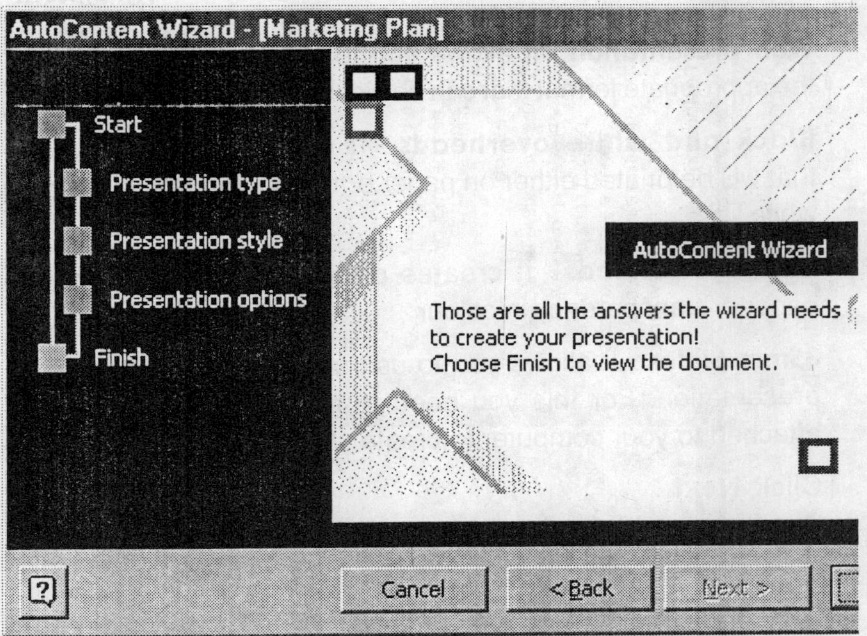

7. Click a **Finish** to end the **AutoContent Wizard** session.
8. The presentation you have chosen can be seen on the screen.
9. As you can see from the presentation, the left hand side of the screen contains text of the presentation and on the right hand side you can see the presentation.
10. Click at **Slide** tap to see full screen presentation as it would look on the screen. It is shown on the next to next page. Of course you can come back to outline view by clicking the outline tab.
11. As you can see that there are as many as 17 slides in this presentation, each representing different head, like marketing summary, completion, production definition, etc. You can see the different slides on the screen when you move the vertical bar on the right hand side of the presentation.
12. On the next page, you will see the slide number **2** and **17**.

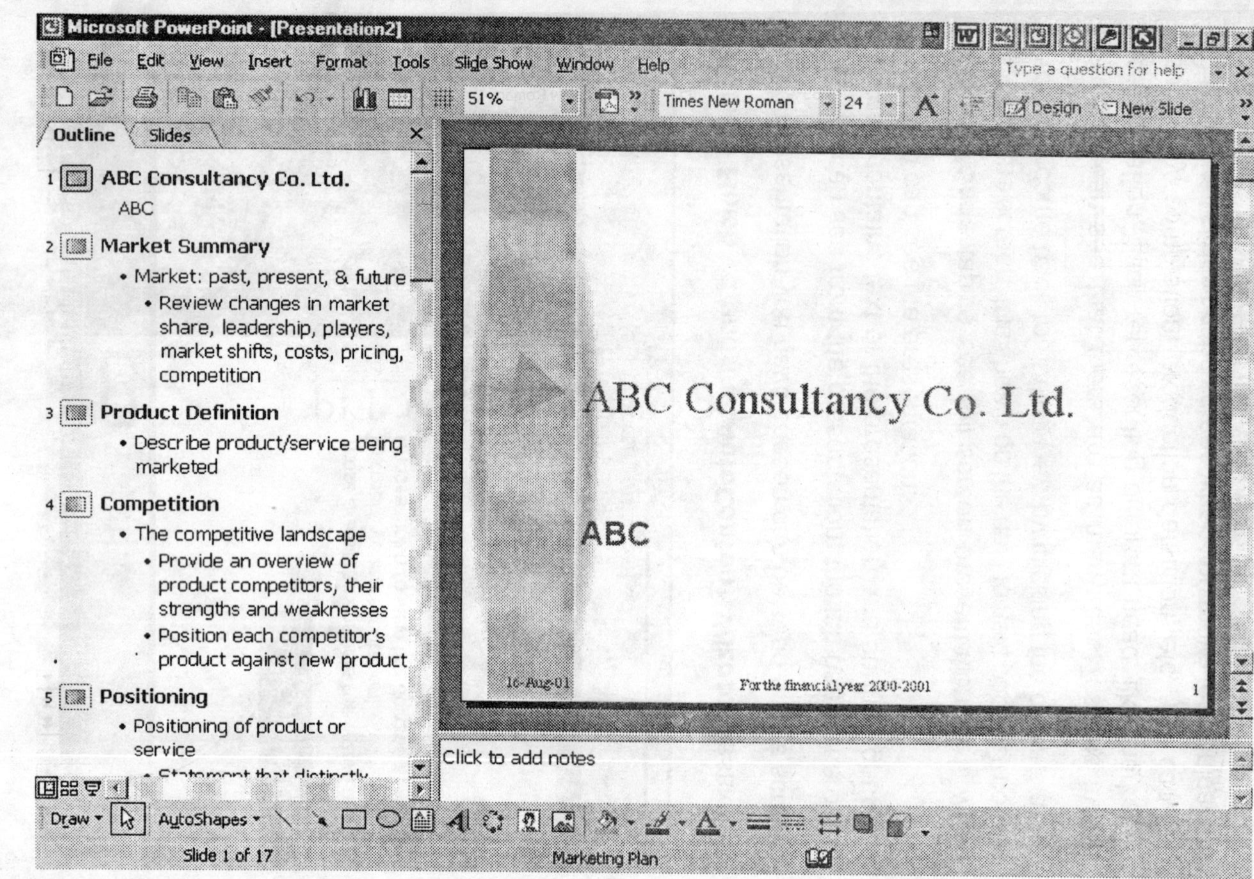

Microsoft PowerPoint - [Presentation2]
File Edit View Insert Format Tools Slide Show Window Help
Type a question for help
51%
Times New Roman
24
Design
New Slide
Outline
Slides
1 ABC Consultancy Co. Ltd.
ABC
2 Market Summary
• Market: past, present, & future
• Review changes in market share, leadership, players, market shifts, costs, pricing, competition
3 Product Definition
• Describe product/service being marketed
4 Competition
• The competitive landscape
• Provide an overview of product competitors, their strengths and weaknesses
• Position each competitor's product against new product
5 Positioning
• Positioning of product or service
ABC Consultancy Co. Ltd.
ABC
16-Aug-01
For the financial year 2000-2001
1
Click to add notes
Draw
AutoShapes
Slide 1 of 17
Marketing Plan

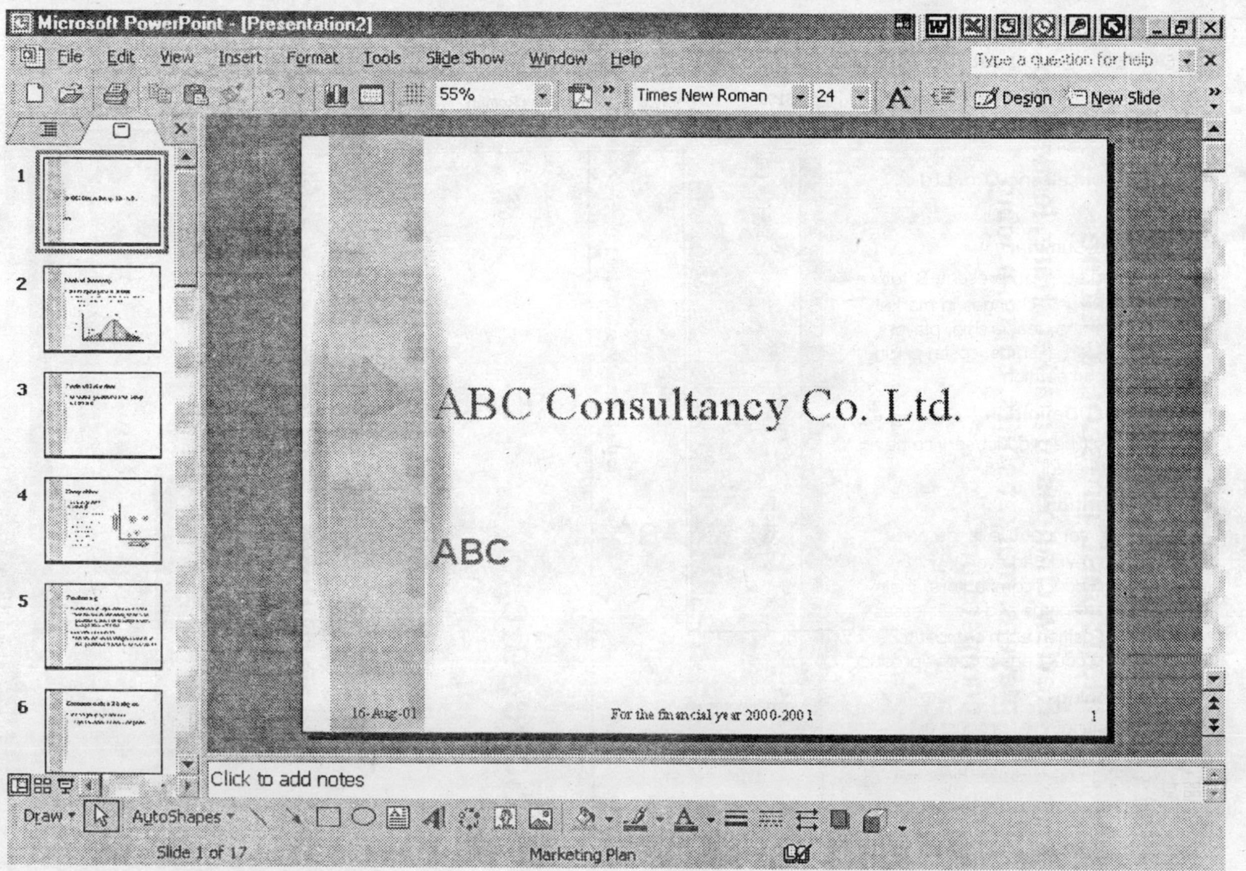
Microsoft PowerPoint - [Presentation2]
File Edit View Insert Format Tools Slide Show Window Help
Type a question for help
55%
Times New Roman
24
Design
New Slide
1
2
3
4
5
6
ABC Consultancy Co. Ltd.
ABC
16-Aug-01
For the financial year 2000-2001
1
Click to add notes
Draw
AutoShapes
Slide 1 of 17
Marketing Plan

Market Summary

- **Market: past, present, & future**
  - **Review changes in market share, leadership, players, market shifts, costs, pricing, competition**

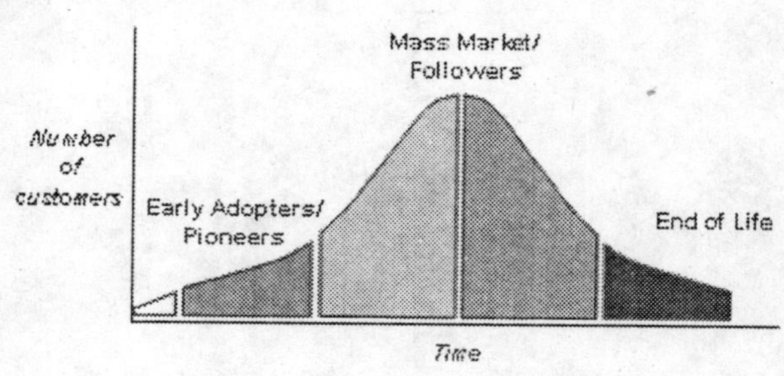

5-Aug-01 For the financial year 2000-2001 2

Schedule

- 18-month schedule highlights
- Timing
  - Isolate timing dependencies critical to success

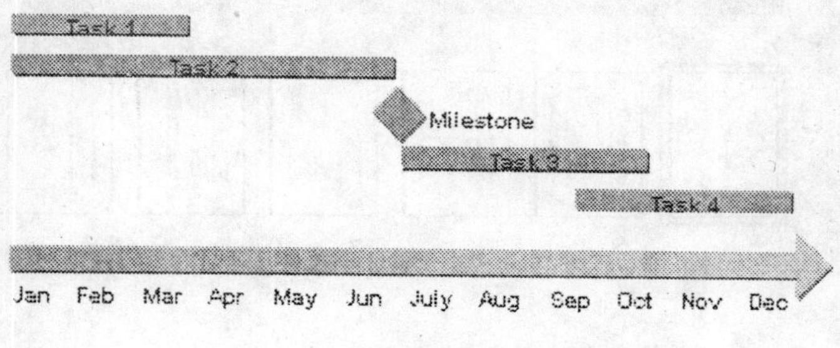

Aug-01 For the financial year 2000-2001 17

13. By choosing the **Slide Sorter view** you can see all the slides on the screen but in very small form and **12** at a time. Slide sorter view of our presentation is shown on the next page.

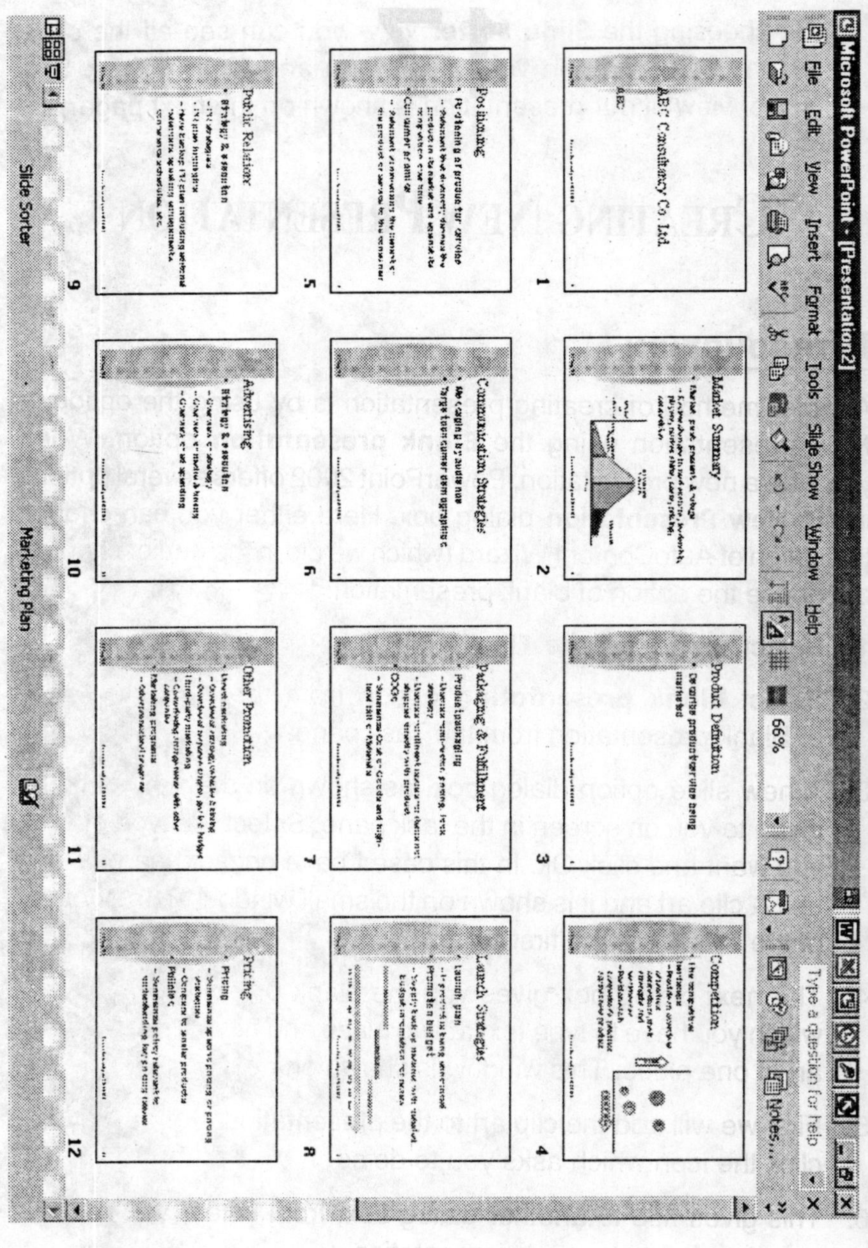
Microsoft PowerPoint - [Presentation2]
File Edit View Insert Format Tools Slide Show Window Help
66%
Notes...
Type a question for help
ABC Consultancy Co. Ltd.
Market Summary
Product Definition
Competition
Positioning
Communication Strategies
Packaging & Fulfillment
Launch Strategies
Public Relations
Advertising
Other Promotion
Pricing
1
2
3
4
5
6
7
8
9
10
11
12
Slide Sorter
Marketing Plan

17

Creating New Presentation

Introduction

Another method of creating presentation is by using the option of **New** presentation using the **Blank presentation** option. When you start a new presentation, PowerPoint 2002 offers several options in the **New Presentation** dialog box. Here either you can choose the option of AutoContent Wizard (which we did in the earlier chapter) or choose the option of blank presentation.

1. Select **New** from the **File** menu.
2. Select **Blank presentation** option from the **General** Panel or Blank presentation from the Task pane.
3. A new slide option dialog box, as shown on the next page, is given to you on screen in the task pane. Select the type of slide you want and click Ok. In this case I have chosen the one with text & clip art and it is shown on the small window on the bottom of the screen as the first option.
4. The next dialog box gives you the blank presentation slate in which you have to type text at two place and have to add the clip art at one place. This window is shown on next to next page.
5. First we will add the clip art to the presentation. For this double click the icon which asks you to do so.
6. This gives rise to another dialog box, from where you have to select a clip art for your presentation.

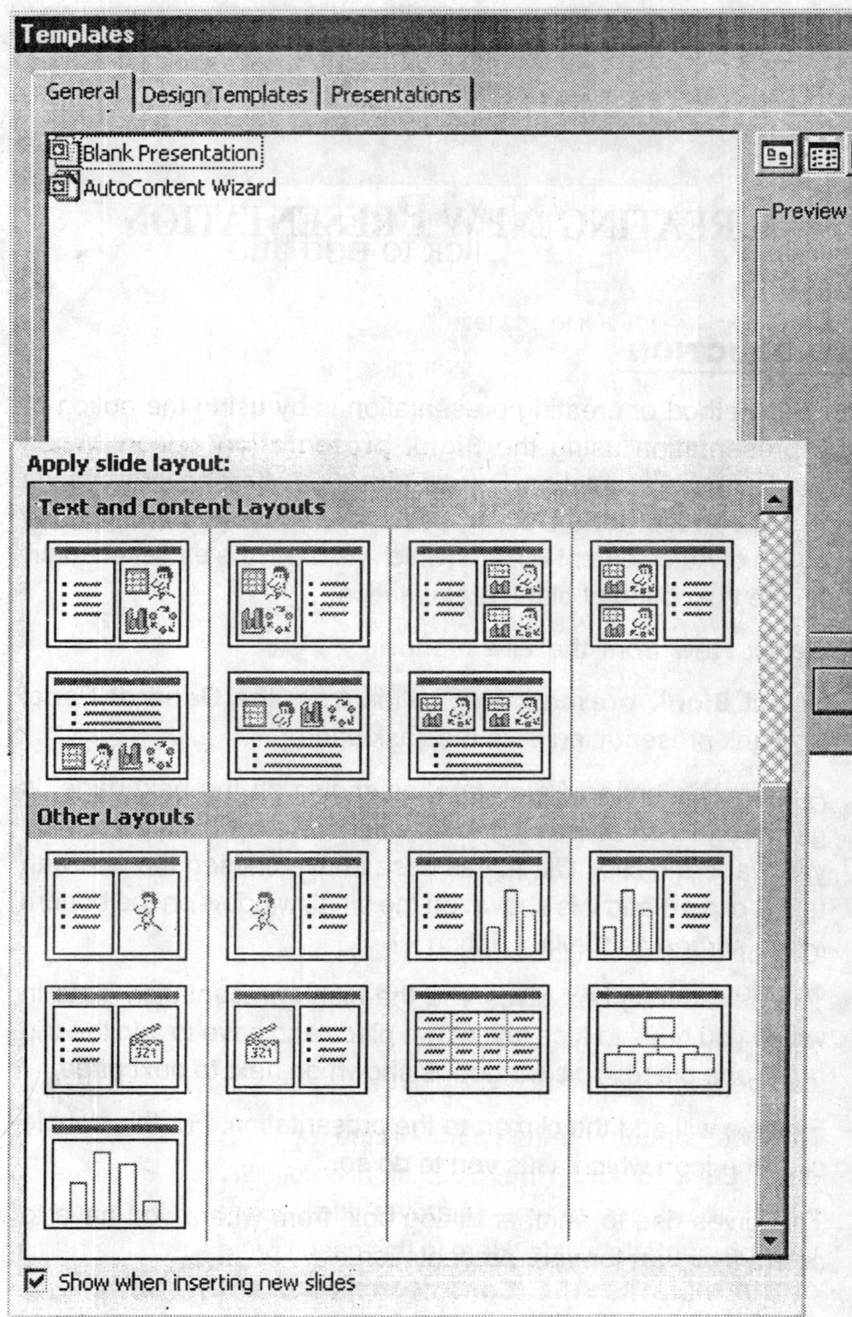
Templates
General
Design Templates
Presentations
Blank Presentation
AutoContent Wizard
Preview
Apply slide layout:
Text and Content Layouts
Other Layouts
Show when inserting new slides

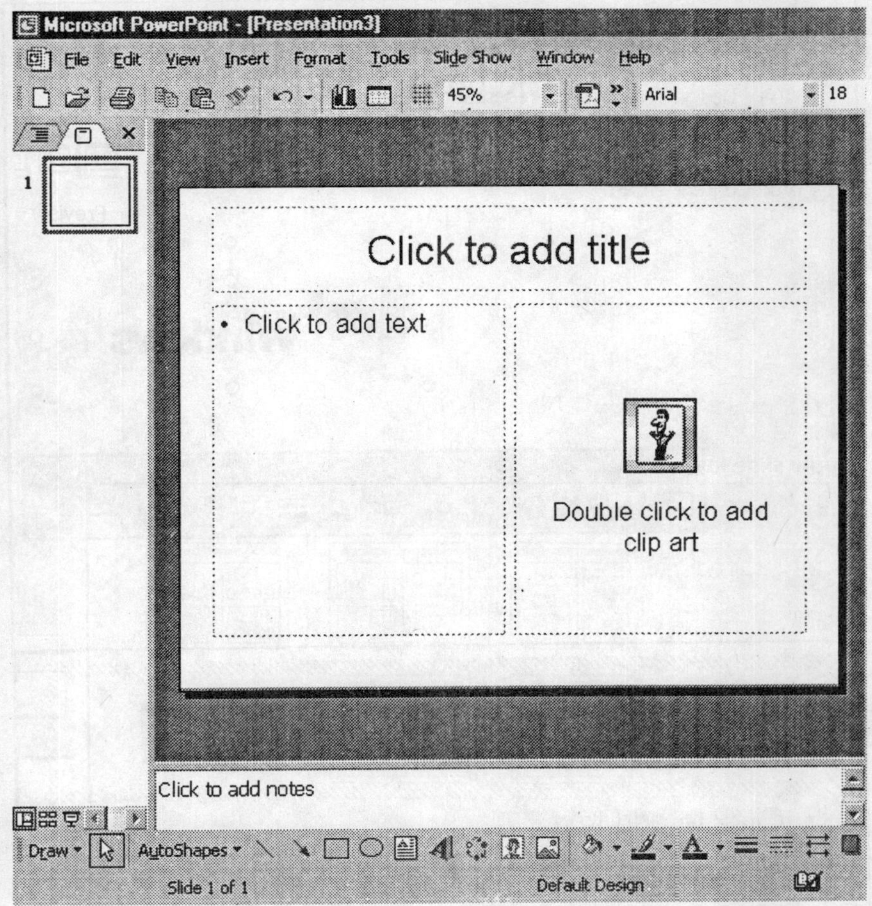

7. Clik on the one which you want. Here I have selected the logo of Windows Me, as shown on the next page.

8. Alongwith the picture, you would notice the picture slider, which can be used to enhance the picture inserted.

9. Now we come to the text part. On the top of the presentation it says, **Click to Add Title**. So click at it to give rise to a cursor which allows you to type whatever title you may like to give to your presentation slide. Here in this case I have typed the name of the slide as **ABC Consultancy Co. Ltd.**

Click to add title

- Click to add text

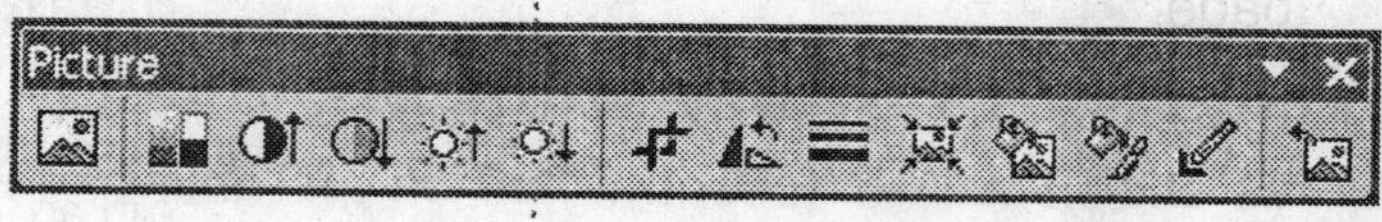

ABC Consultancy Co. Ltd.

- Click to add text

10. See the heading appearing in the text column on the left hand side of the page under the slide number 1.
11. Next in line is the place, Click to add text. Similar to above, click it to obtain cursor and start typing. Here I have typed the matter as **Marketing Plan**.
12. See on the left hand side this text has also appeared on the text window but under the slide number 1 and with different tab and style.
13. Press **Enter** to add another line to this text. This time it is called **Financial Plan**. This can be seen in the figure on the next page.
14. If we now look at it in the slide show view, we will see the figure as shown as the second figure on the next page. Remember you can come back to normal view by pressing **Esc**.

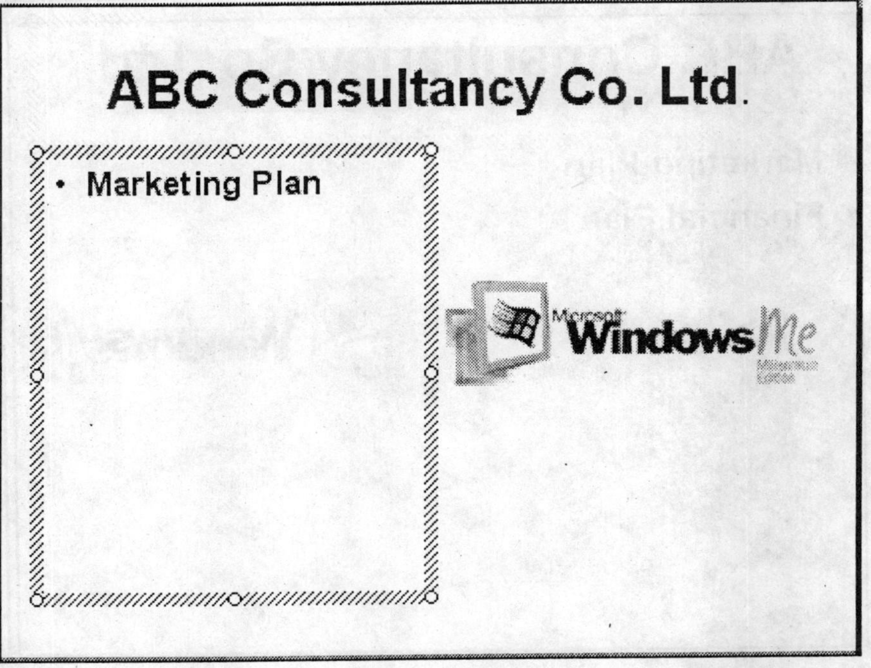

ABC Consultancy Co. Ltd.

- Marketing Plan
- Financial Plan

ABC Consultancy Co. Ltd.

- Marketing Plan
- Financial Plan

18

Creating Presentation from Template

Introduction

This method of creating presentation is by using the templates been made available to you with the software. Templates can provide either the graphic design and color scheme of a presentation (design template) or suggest content and structure, using a set of slides whose text you can edit.

1. Select **New** from the **File** menu.
2. Select **Design Templates** option from the Task pane or from the **New Presentation** dialog box.
3. I have chosen here the option of **Blends** from the various options available under Design Templates.
4. This will give rise to blank presentation as shown next.
6. Now all you have to do here to add the text.
7. In the first line which says, **Click to add Title**, I have chosen to type **Microsoft Office XP Constituents**.
8. On the second option which says, **Click to add text**, type the name of Microsoft Word 2002. Microsoft Excel 2002, Microsoft Access 2002, Microsoft PowerPoint, 2002 and see the presentation, as it looks like on the next page.

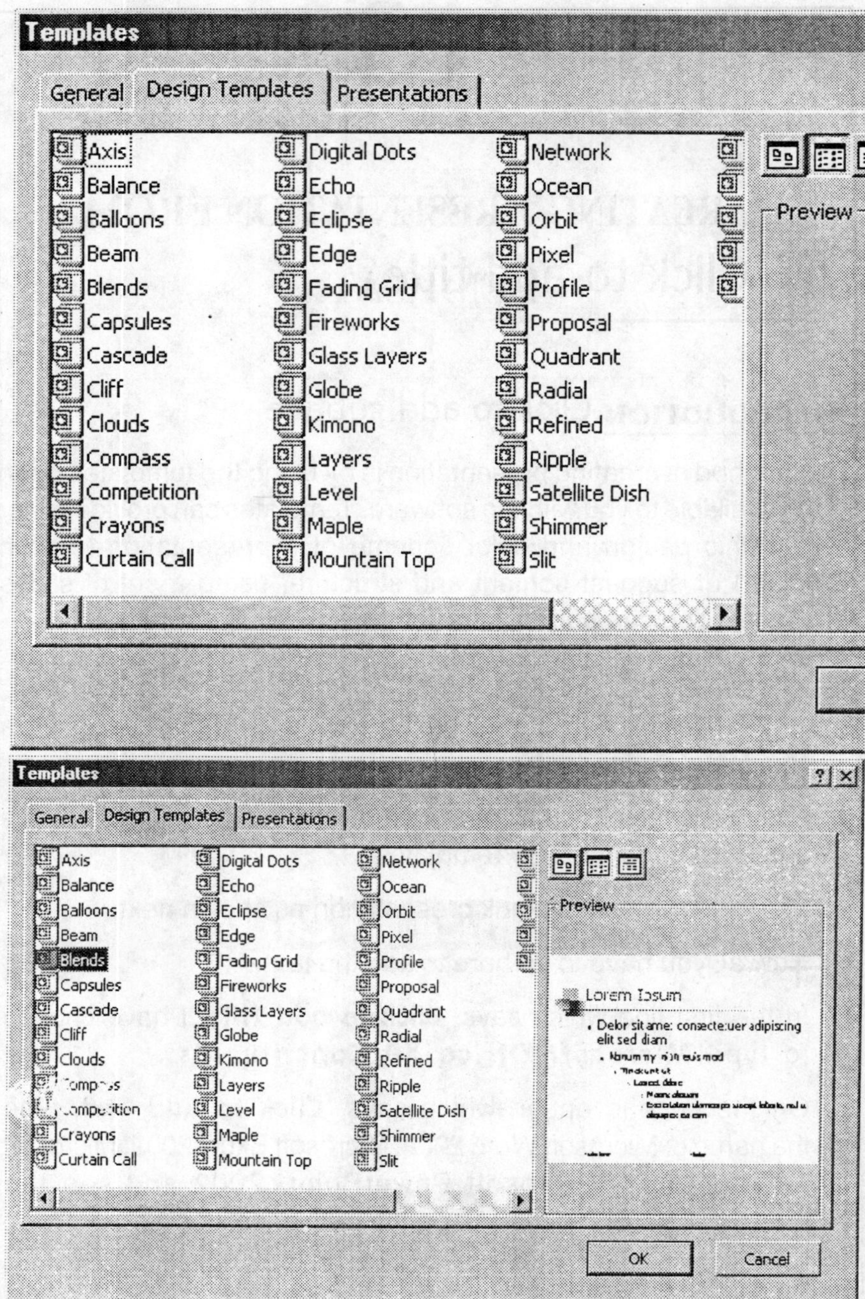
Templates
General
Design Templates
Presentations
Axis
Balance
Balloons
Beam
Blends
Capsules
Cascade
Cliff
Clouds
Compass
Competition
Crayons
Curtain Call
Digital Dots
Echo
Eclipse
Edge
Fading Grid
Fireworks
Glass Layers
Globe
Kimono
Layers
Level
Maple
Mountain Top
Network
Ocean
Orbit
Pixel
Profile
Proposal
Quadrant
Radial
Refined
Ripple
Satellite Dish
Shimmer
Slit
Preview
Templates
General
Design Templates
Presentations
Axis
Balance
Balloons
Beam
Blends
Capsules
Cascade
Cliff
Clouds
Crayons
Curtain Call
Digital Dots
Echo
Eclipse
Edge
Fading Grid
Fireworks
Glass Layers
Globe
Kimono
Layers
Level
Maple
Mountain Top
Network
Ocean
Orbit
Pixel
Profile
Proposal
Quadrant
Radial
Refined
Ripple
Satellite Dish
Shimmer
Slit
Preview
Lorem Ipsum
Delor sit ame: consecte:uer adipiscing elit sed diam
OK
Cancel

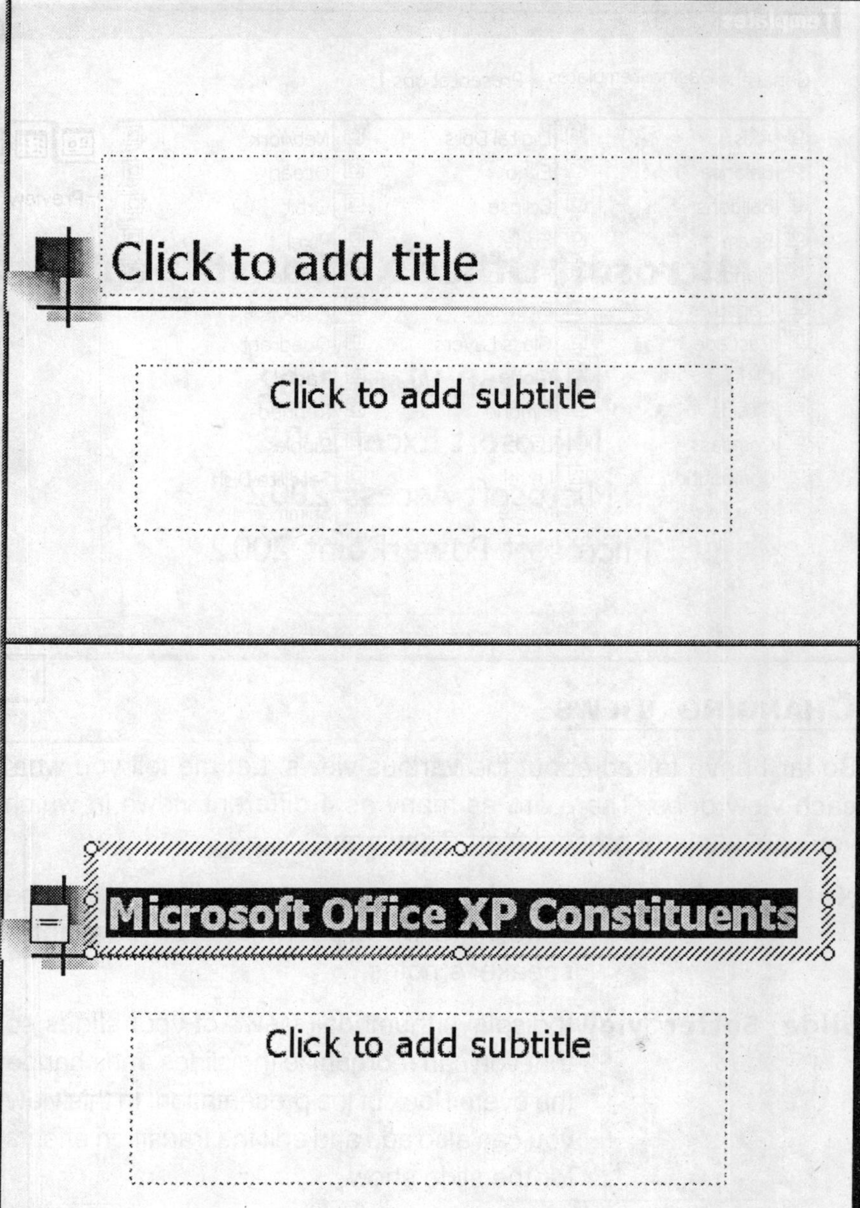
Click to add title
Click to add subtitle
Microsoft Office XP Constituents
Click to add subtitle

Changing Views

So far I have talked about the various views. Let me tell you what each view does. There are as many as 4 different views in which you can see your presentation. They are:

Normal view It displays 3 panes that show the outline, the slide, and an area which you can enter speaker's notes.

Slide Sorter view It displays thumbnail views of your slides so that you can reorganize the slides and change the overall look of the presentation. In this view you can also add and edit the transition effects for the slide show.

Slide Show view It displays the presentation one slide at a time in sequence as an automatic slide show.

Notes Page view It is available only from the view menu, lets you enter and edit speaker's notes for the presenter.

On the next few pages you will see all the 4 views. It would be a good exercise for you to find out which one is which.

Remember

1. Each view shows a different aspect of the same presentation.
2. You can switch from one view to another at any time.
3. Right-click in **Slide Sorter view** or click the button at lower left corner of the current slide to display the **Slide Show shortcut** menu.

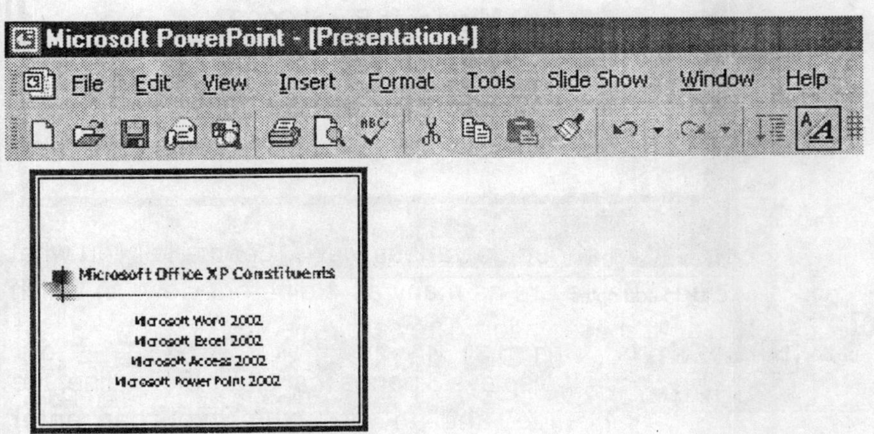

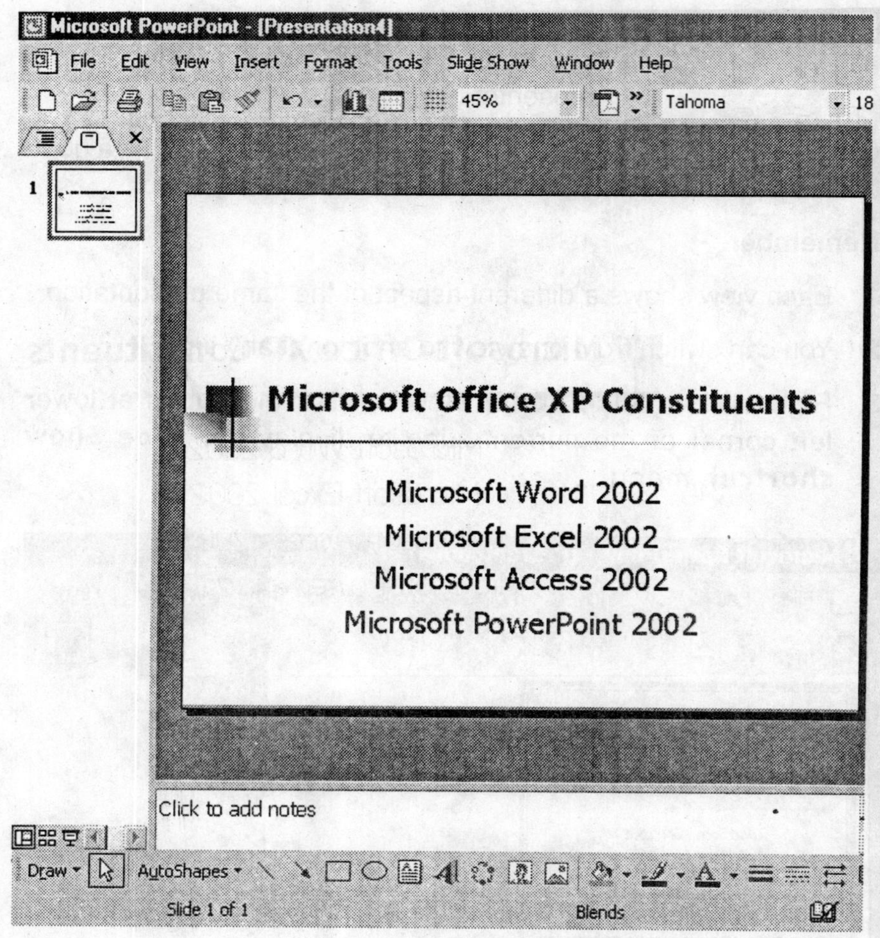
Microsoft PowerPoint - [Presentation4]
File Edit View Insert Format Tools Slide Show Window Help
45%
Tahoma
18
1
Microsoft Office XP Constituents
Microsoft Word 2002
Microsoft Excel 2002
Microsoft Access 2002
Microsoft PowerPoint 2002
Click to add notes
Draw
AutoShapes
Slide 1 of 1
Blends

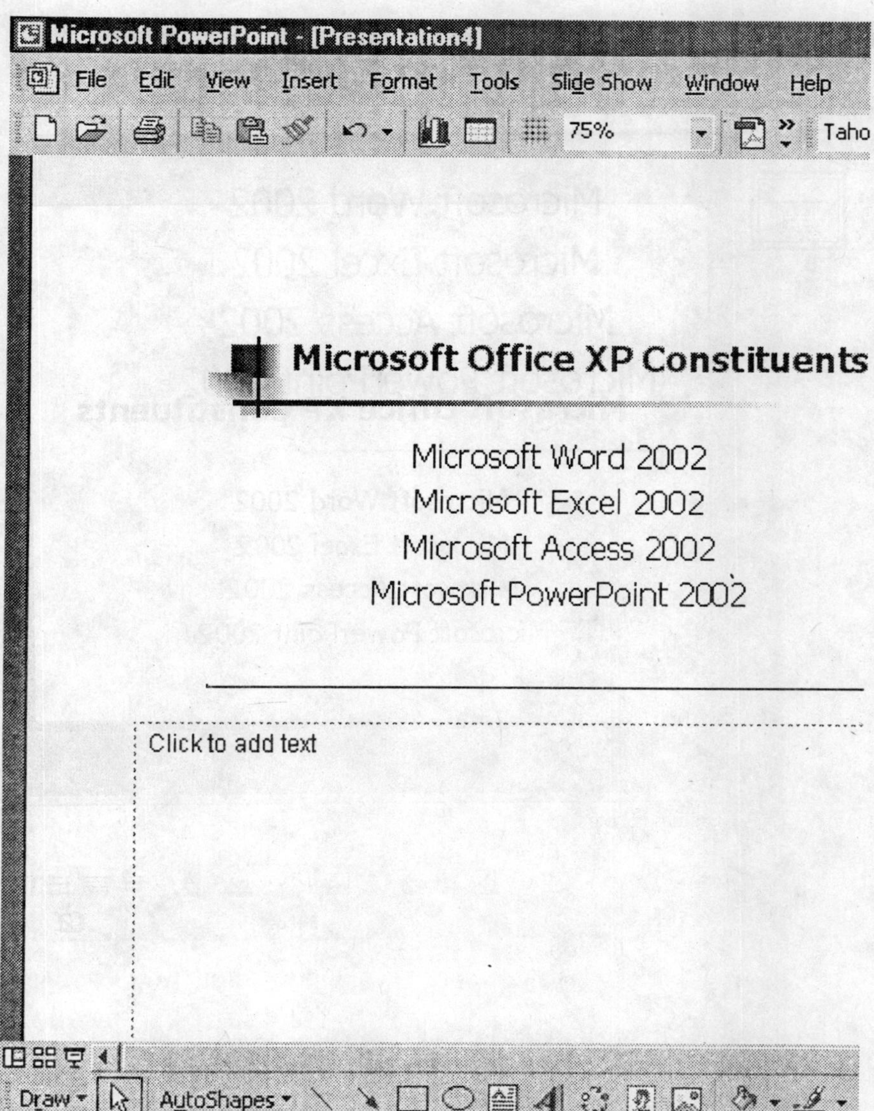
Microsoft PowerPoint - [Presentation4]
File Edit View Insert Format Tools Slide Show Window Help
75%
Taho
Microsoft Office XP Constituents
Microsoft Word 2002
Microsoft Excel 2002
Microsoft Access 2002
Microsoft PowerPoint 2002
Click to add text
Draw
AutoShapes
Notes 1 of 1
Blends

Microsoft Office XP Constituents

Microsoft Word 2002
Microsoft Excel 2002
Microsoft Access 2002
Microsoft PowerPoint 2002

19

Working on Presentations

Introduction

In a presentation, you can make changes according to your needs, specially in those cases where the presentation has been created using the templates provides with the software. Here in this chapter, I will tell you how to make the presentations look better and more meaningful.

Changing the Background Colour & Shading

You can change the background colour of all the slides or a single one depending upon your requirements.

To Change the Background Colours & Shading

1. Select **Background** from the **Format** menu.

   Or

   Right click outside the placeholder areas in Slide, Normal, or a Master view and choose Background from the shortcut menu.

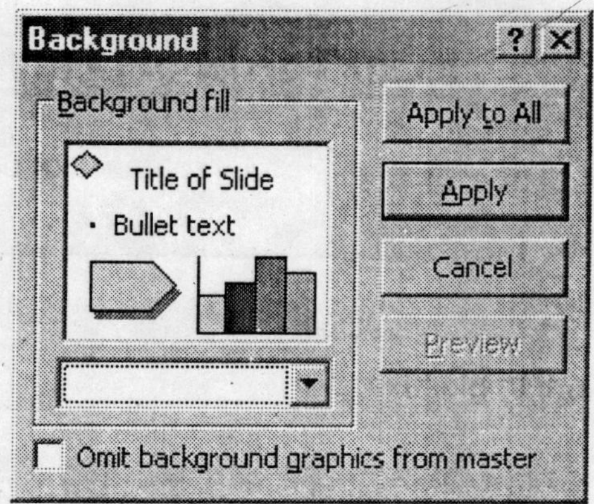

2. In the background dialog

box, pull down the Background fill menu and choose a solid colour or **Fill Effects**.

3. Select the Fill Effects you want from the dialog box.
4. Among the other options of Fill Effect are: **Texture**, **Pattern** and **Picture**.

Changing Header and Footer Information

You can change the Header and Footer information at any time in your presentation. For this do the following:

1. Select **Header and Footer** from the **View** menu.
2. In the dialog box thus obtained, click at the Notes and Handout panel.

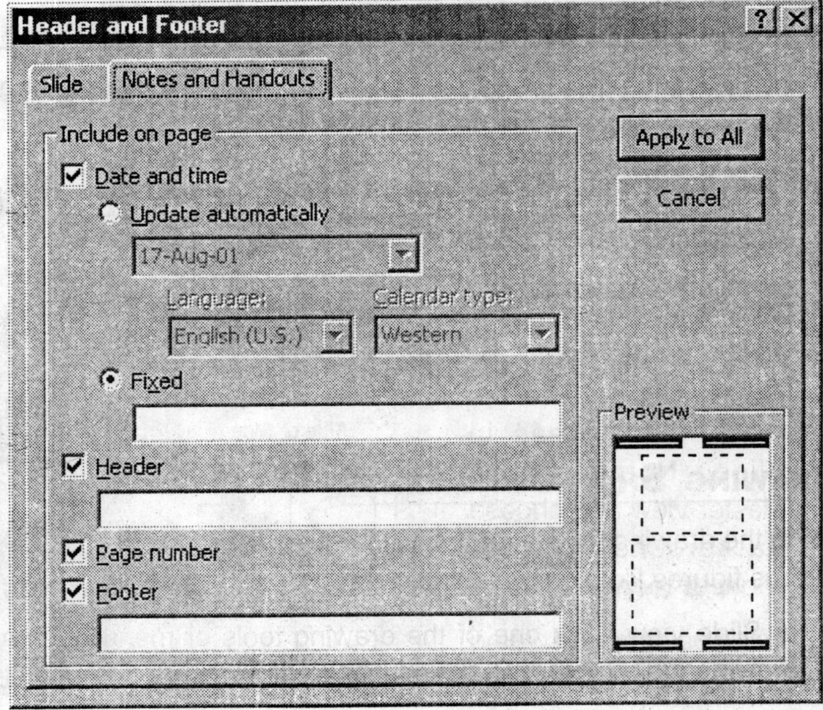

3. Type the fixed text, which is usually the name of the book or the name which is common to all the slides.
4. Type the matter for the Header which is put to be put for the header in all the pages of the presentation.
5. For the Footer too, type the matter which you want to put at the footer of the presentations.

Adding a Logo to the Background

A **Logo** of a company is the unique identification of the company. This small icon of the company is unique and can represent the company at most places. You can create a logo of your own or can use a graphic for this purpose.

1. Select **Slide Master** from **Master** command in the **View** menu.
2. You will get the dialog box as shown on the next page.
3. From the **Insert** menu, select to insert **Picture** and **Clip Art** or any other picture which you may want to use.
4. From the clip art menu, select the clip art.
5. The picture will be placed in the centre of the slide. You can increase or decrease its size and place it anywhere on the slide to be reflected at the slides in the presentation.
6. You can copy and paste a graphic from another program onto the slide master.

Drawing Shapes and Lines

Using the drawing tools available with PowerPoint you can draw the various figures like squares, circles, etc.

1. In Slide view, click one of the drawing tools or menus on the drawing toolbar. Here I have chosen to draw a box.

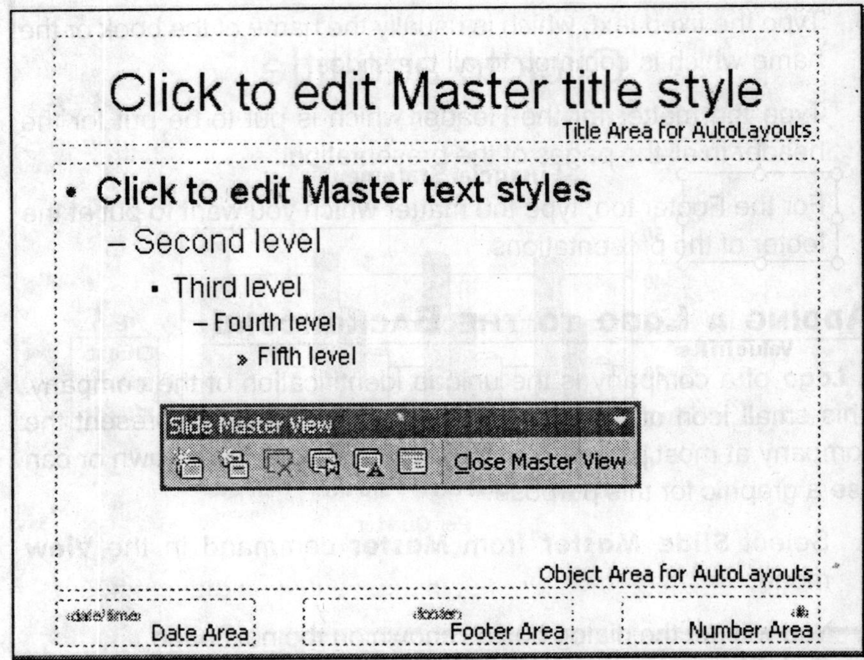

2. Drag with the mouse pointer to create the shape or line. In this case the box.
3. To type text inside the shape, click the shape and then begin typing.
4. To delete a line or shape, click it so that the handles appear, and press **Del**.
5. To keep a shape regular, i.e., drawing a square instead of a rectangle and drawing a circle instead of an oval, etc., hold down the **Shift** key while dragging through the area to create the shape.

Adding Predefined Shapes

Autoshapes are the shapes given to you by the software are much more better looking than the usual ones drawn by you. Make the best use of them to highlight the text or that matter anything in your presentation.

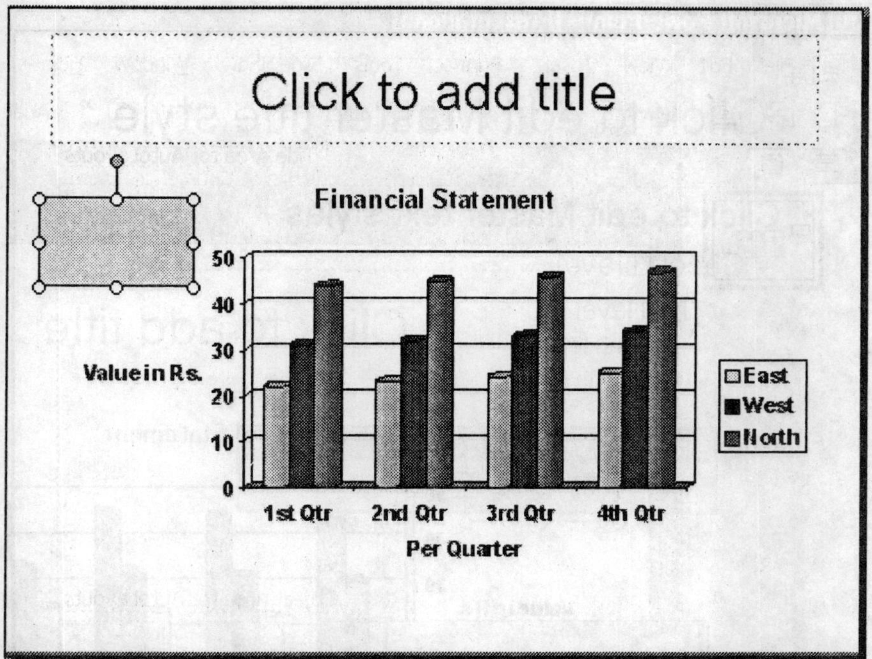

1. **AutoShapes** button is available on the drawing toolbar.
2. Clicking on it will lead to the various other options on the menu. It has Lines, Connectors, Basic Shapes, Block Arrows, Flowchart, Stars and Banners, Callouts, and Action Buttons. More AutoShapes will lead you to more shapes.
3. Select one of the menu, in this case, I have selected **Stars and Banners**, as can be seen on the next page.
4. Position the mouse pointer at one corner of an imaginary rectangle that would contain the shape, hold down the mouse button, drag to the opposite corner of the rectangle, and release the mouse button.
5. The shape will be created as shown on the next to next page.

Adding Text Box

Supposing on a slide you want to add some text in the form of some

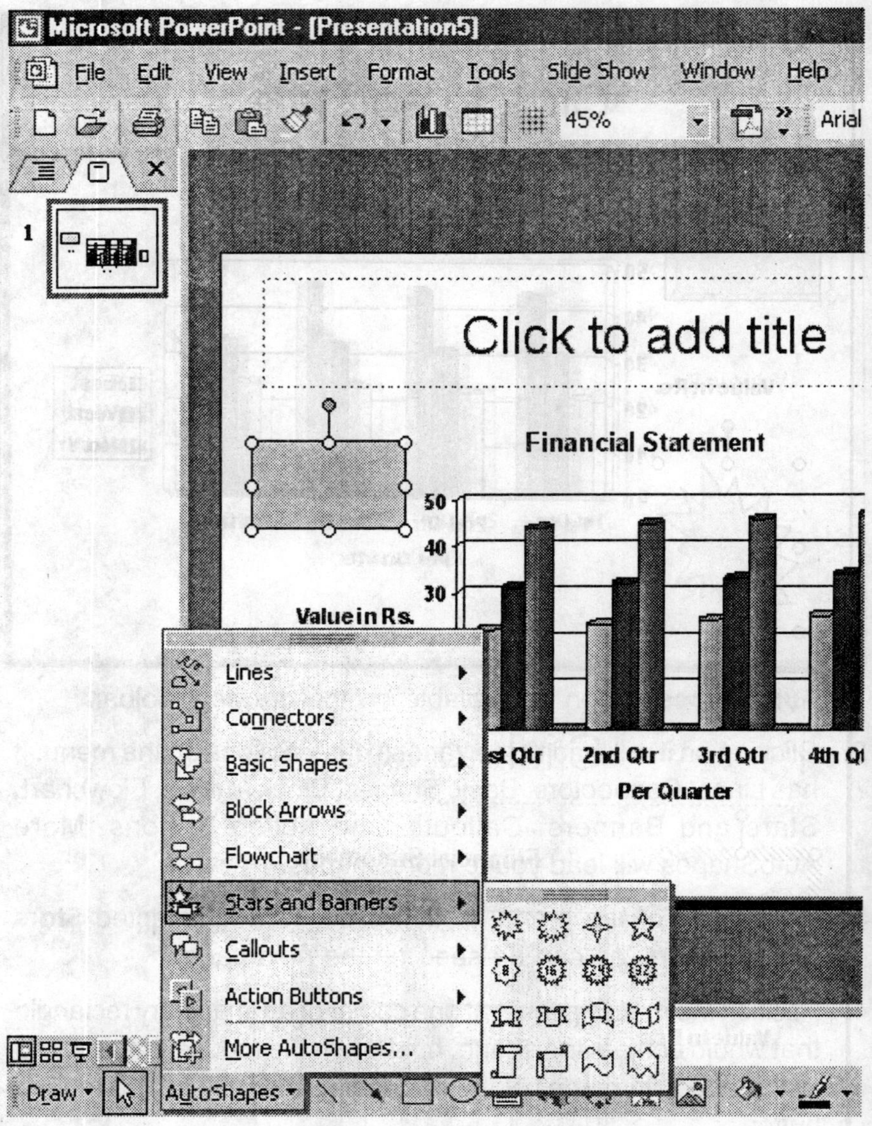

message or an afterthought. You can always do so by adding a text block on the slide.

1. Select **Text Box** from the Insert menu.
2. Click in the slide where you want the text box to appear.

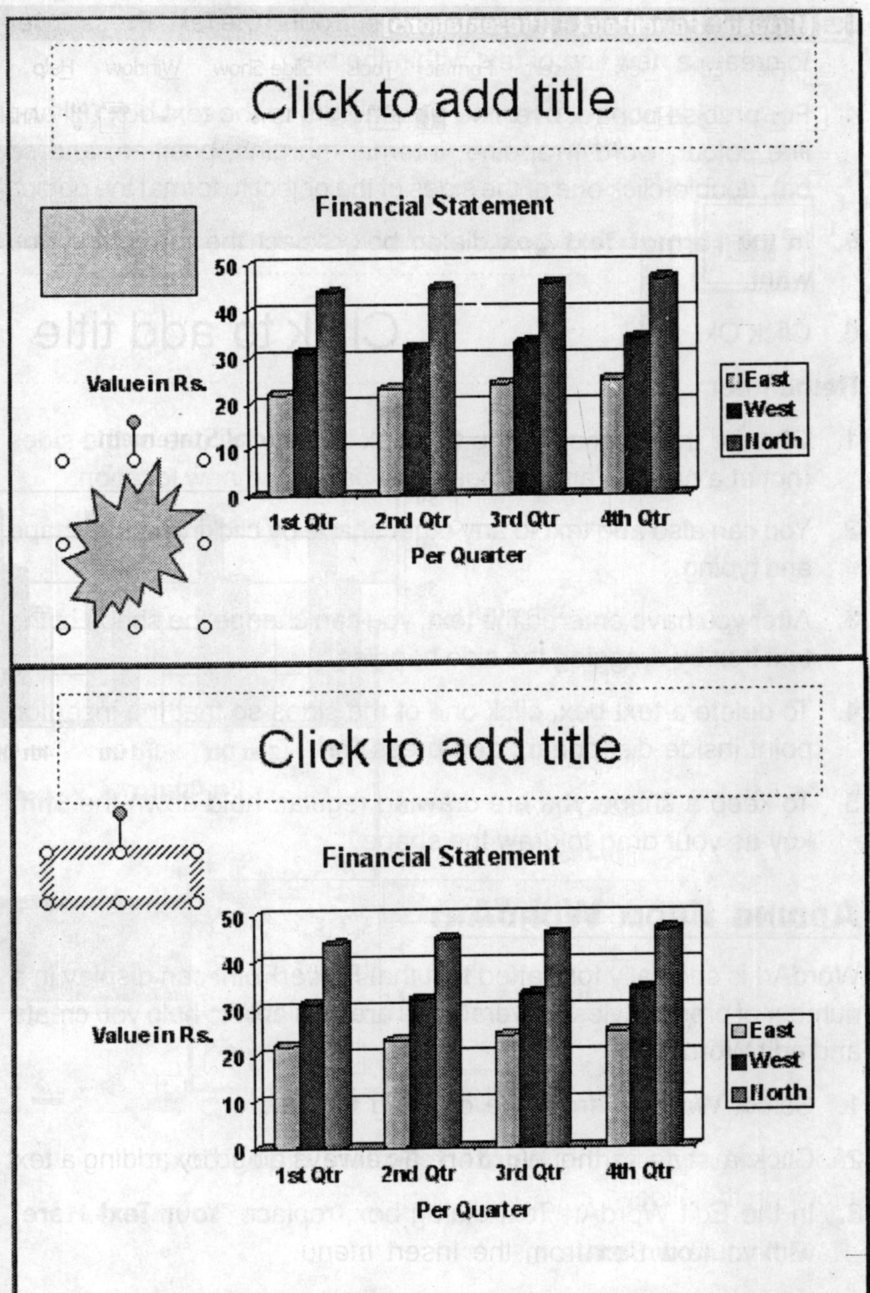
Click to add title
Financial Statement
Value in Rs.
50
40
30
20
10
0
1st Qtr
2nd Qtr
3rd Qtr
4th Qtr
Per Quarter
East
West
North
Click to add title
Financial Statement
Value in Rs.
50
40
30
20
10
0
1st Qtr
2nd Qtr
3rd Qtr
4th Qtr
Per Quarter
East
West
North

3. Type the text. The box expands to surround the text. Press **Enter** to create a new line of text within the box.
4. For precise control over the parameters of the text box (fill and line colour, word wrapping, internal margins, position, and so on), double-click one of the sides of the object to format the object.
5. In the **Format Text Box** dialog box, select the formatting you want.
6. Click Ok.

Remember

1. Change the location of the text box by clicking one of the sides (not at a handle) and dragging the box to the new location.
2. You can also add text to any other shape by clicking in the shape and typing.
3. After you have entered the text, you can change the shape of the text box by dragging the side handles.
4. To delete a text box, click one of the sides so that the insertion point inside disappears and press **Del**.
5. To keep a shape you are drawing regular, hold down the **Shift** key as your drag to draw the shape.

ADDING FROM WORDART

WordArt is specially formatted text that PowerPoint can display in a number of preset styles. Several tools are available to help you create and edit WordArt.

1. Select **WordArt** from the drawing toolbar.
2. Click a style in the **WordArt Gallery** dialog box.
3. In the Edit WordArt Text dialog box, replace "**Your Text Here**" with your own text.
4. Set the font, size, and style you want.

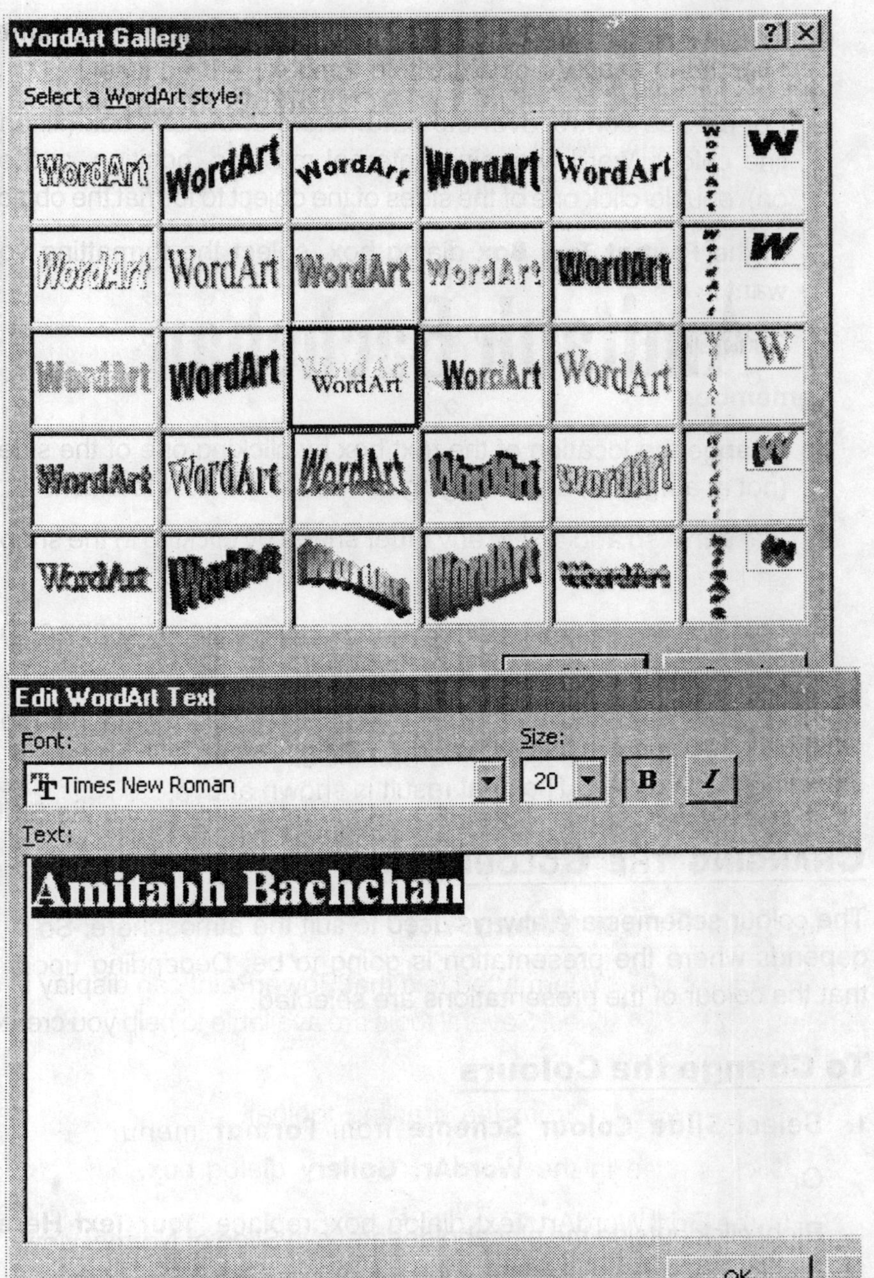
WordArt Gallery
Select a WordArt style:
Edit WordArt Text
Font:
Times New Roman
Size:
20
B
I
Text:
Amitabh Bachchan
OK

Click to add title

Amitabh Bachchan

5. Click Ok.

On the these page you see the various dialog boxes which appear in selecting the WordArt. The final result is shown above.

CHANGING THE COLOUR

The colour schemes are always used to suit the atmosphere. So it depends where the presentation is going to be. Depending upon that the colour of the presentations are selected.

To Change the Colours

1. Select **Slide Colour Scheme** from **Format** menu.

   Or

   Right click outside the placeholder areas in Slide or Normal view and format object from the shortcut menu

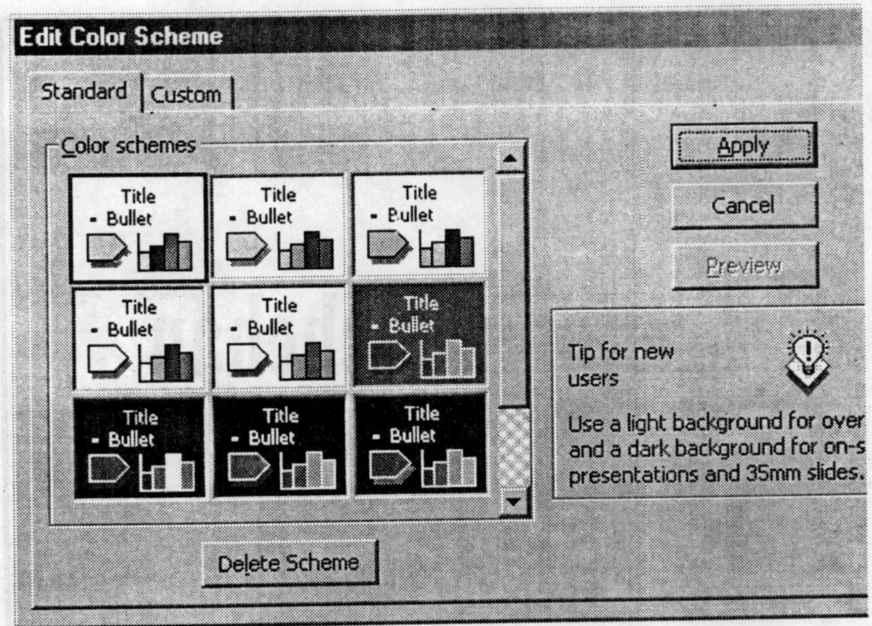

2. There are two options in Color Scheme dialog box, **Standard** and **Custom**.
3. Standard colour scheme allows you to choose from one of the standard colours.
4. Custom colour scheme allows you to create a custom colour of your own.
5. In both the cases you can either apply to the single slide or apply the colour scheme to all the slides by choosing the options **Apply**.

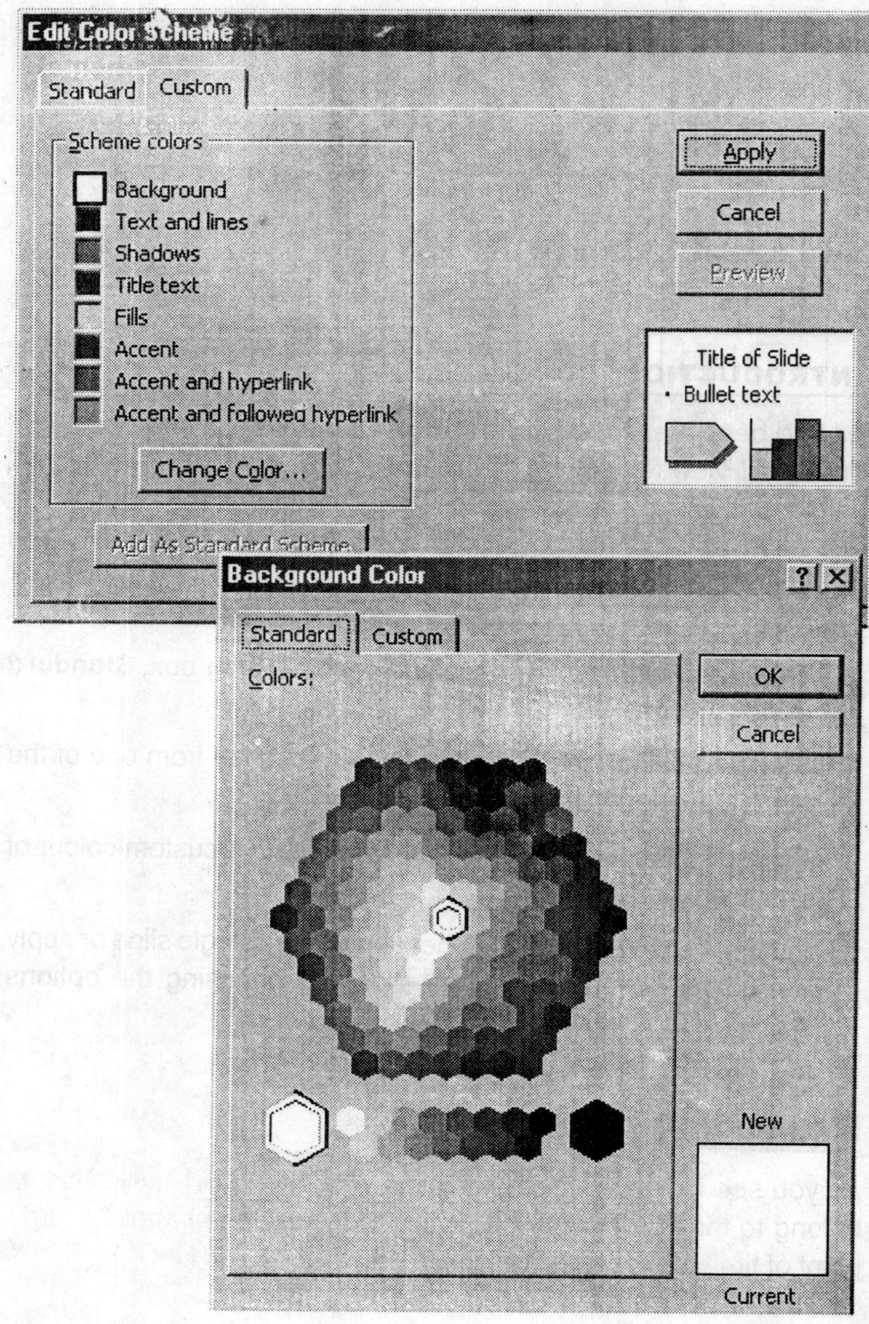
Edit Color Scheme
Standard
Custom
Scheme colors
Background
Text and lines
Shadows
Title text
Fills
Accent
Accent and hyperlink
Accent and followed hyperlink
Change Color...
Add As Standard Scheme
Apply
Cancel
Preview
Title of Slide
• Bullet text
Background Color
Standard
Custom
Colors:
OK
Cancel
New
Current

20

Working in Slide Sorter view

Introduction

As had been mentioned earlier, Slide Sorter view displays rows of thumbnail views of slides. In this view, you can rearrange slides, delete or duplicate slides, and change the template to change the look of the presentation.

For this I would refer to the **Marketing Plan** mentioned in the earlier chapter using the **AutoContent Wizard**.

To Switch to Slide Sorter view:

1. Click the Slide Sorter View button.

   Or

   From the View menu, choose Slide Sorter.

   You can see the presentation in the Slide Sorter view on the next page.

There are lots of things which can be done in this view mode. Let us discuss few of them.

Reordering Slides

As you see from the view, each slide is numbered. These number belong to their order of display. This order can be changed at any point of time in the presentation.

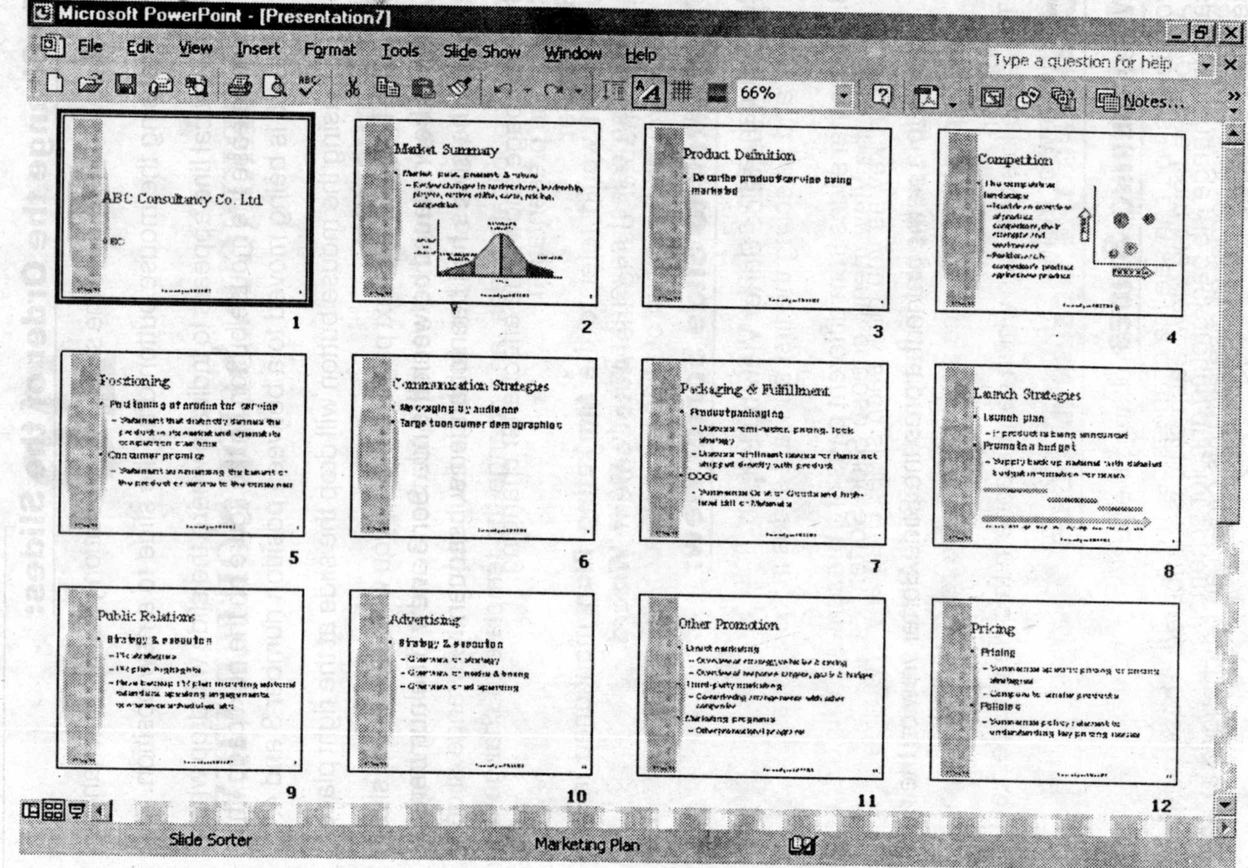
Microsoft PowerPoint - [Presentation7]
File Edit View Insert Format Tools Slide Show Window Help
Type a question for help
66%
Notes...
ABC Consultancy Co. Ltd
1
Market Summary
2
Product Definition
Describe product/service being marketed
3
Competition
4
Positioning
Positioning of product or service
Consumer promise
5
Communication Strategies
Messaging by audience
Target consumer demographics
6
Packaging & Fulfillment
Product packaging
7
Launch Strategies
Launch plan
Promotion budget
8
Public Relations
Strategy & execution
9
Advertising
Strategy & execution
10
Other Promotion
11
Pricing
Pricing
Policies
12
Slide Sorter
Marketing Plan

To Change the Order of the Slides:

1. Click with the mouse the slide whose position you want to change.
2. Pressing the mouse button drag the slide to a new position.
3. A vertical line appears to indicate where the slide will drop when you release the mouse button. In the figure on the next page, the slide 6 is being moved to a between position number 3 and 4.
4. Releasing the mouse button will drop the slide at the right place.
5. In the figure on the next page (bottom), you will see that the slide 6 has been placed between the number 3 and 4. The numbering of all the slides has been changed subsequently.
6. Next page shows the effect after changing.

Remember

1. You can select several slides to move by drawing a selection box around the group of slides and then dragging the group to the new position.
2. You can also select several slides by holding down the **Shift** key and selecting the first and last slides in the series.
3. To gather slides from different parts of a presentation, hold down the **Ctrl** key as you click each slide. Drag any one slide in the group to a new point in the presentation. All the selected slides will appear in sequence and in the same relative order at new position.

CHANGING THE DESIGN IN SLIDE SORTER VIEW

While still in this view, you can change the design of the slides. When you do this you can see the changes been done on the slides. You can also change the background or color scheme for all sides or for selected slides.

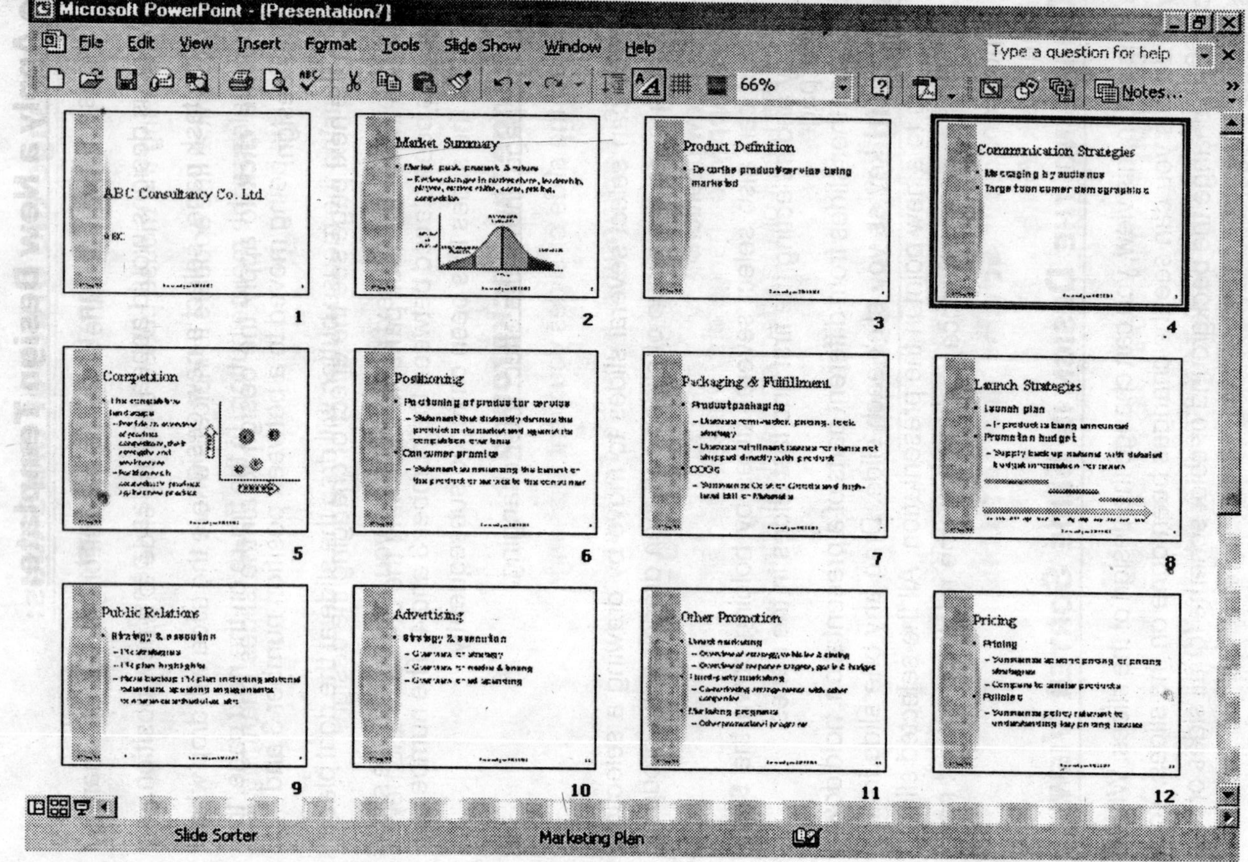
Microsoft PowerPoint - [Presentation7]
File Edit View Insert Format Tools Slide Show Window Help
Type a question for help
66%
Notes...
ABC Consultancy Co. Ltd
Market Summary
Product Definition
Communication Strategies
Competition
Positioning
Packaging & Fulfillment
Launch Strategies
Public Relations
Advertising
Other Promotion
Pricing
Slide Sorter
Marketing Plan

To Apply a New Design Template:

1. Choose **Slide Design** from the **Format** menu.
2. Various designs would appear in the task pane.
3. In the task pane, select a new design.
4. **Double click** to apply the design to all the slides changing to this design.
5. On the next page see the effect of changing the design.
6. Notice that in the task pane, it is showing the previous and new design.

To Change the Background

1. Select the slide or slides you want to change.
2. Choose **Background** from the **Format** menu.
3. Make the change in the Background dialog box.
4. Click **Apply** to change only the selected slide or slides.
5. See the result of the effect on the slide number 2 on the next to next page.

To Change Colour Scheme

1. Select the slide or slides you want to change.
2. Choose **Colour Scheme and Edit Colour Scheme** from the **Task Pane**.
3. Make the change in the Colour Scheme dialog box.
4. Click **Apply** to change only the selected slide or slides.
5. See the result of the colour scheme as applied to the slide number 2 on the next to next page.

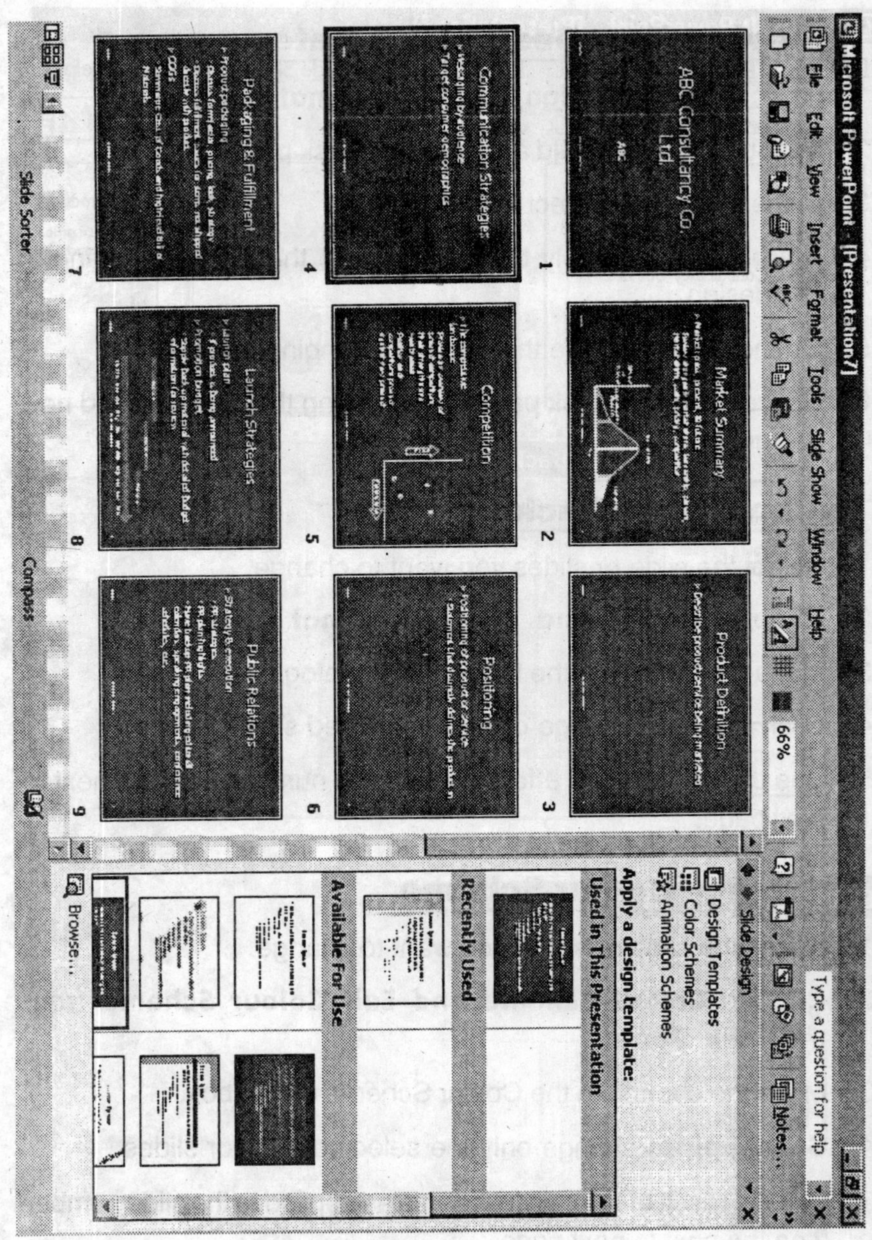
Microsoft PowerPoint - [Presentation7]
File Edit View Insert Format Tools Slide Show Window Help
Type a question for help
66%
Notes...
ABC Consultancy Co. Ltd.
Market Summary
Product Definition
Communication Strategies
Competition
Positioning
Packaging & Fulfillment
Launch Strategies
Public Relations
Slide Design
Design Templates
Color Schemes
Animation Schemes
Apply a design template:
Used in This Presentation
Recently Used
Available For Use
Browse...
Slide Sorter
Compass

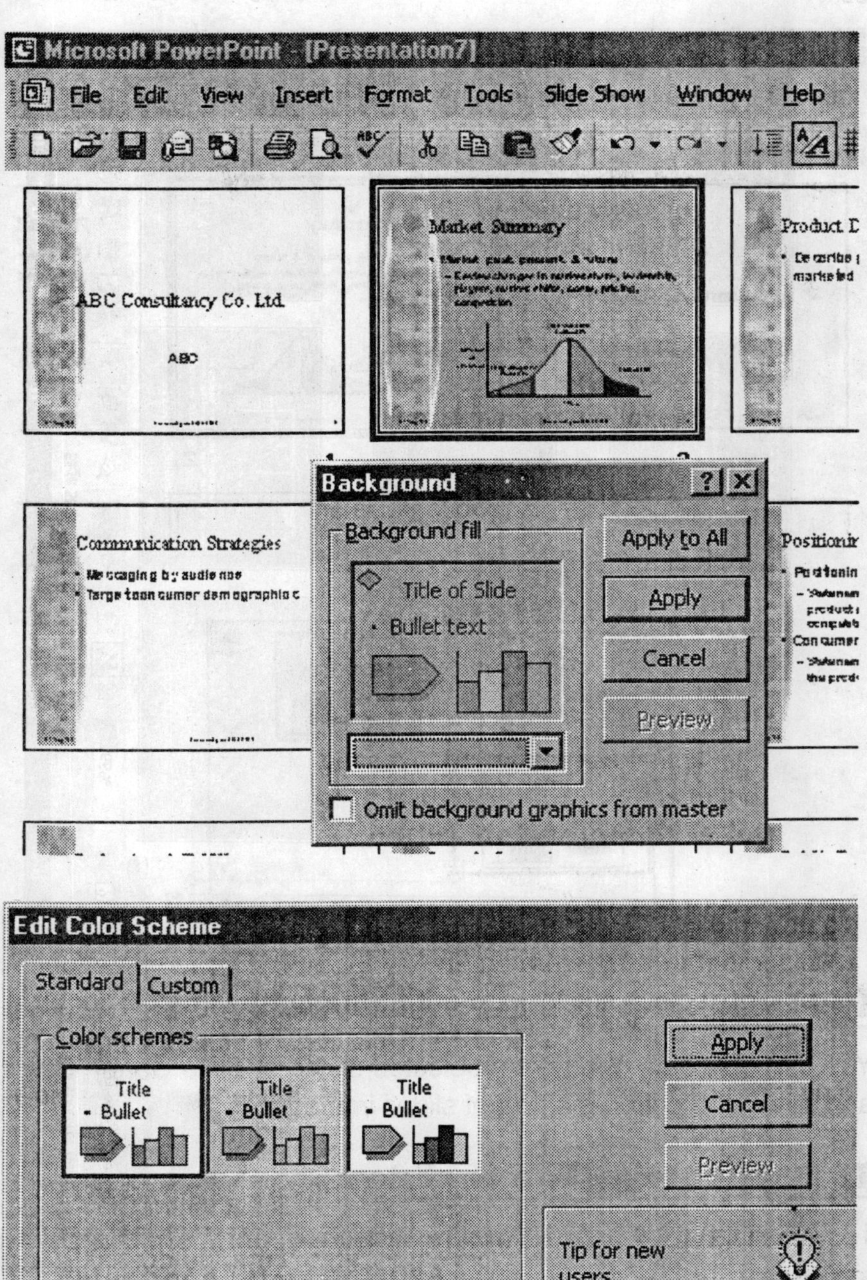
Microsoft PowerPoint - [Presentation7]
File Edit View Insert Format Tools Slide Show Window Help
ABC Consultancy Co. Ltd.
ABC
Market Summary
Product D
Communication Strategies
Positionin
Background
Background fill
Title of Slide
Bullet text
Apply to All
Apply
Cancel
Preview
Omit background graphics from master
Edit Color Scheme
Standard
Custom
Color schemes
Title
Bullet
Apply
Cancel
Preview
Tip for new users
Use a light background for over

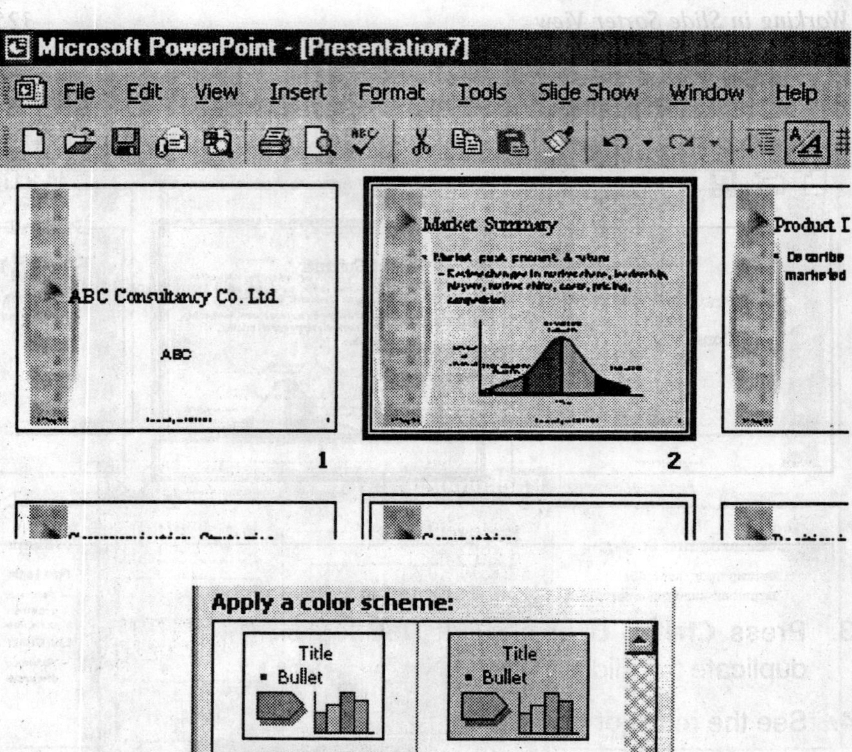

DUPLICATING AND DELETING SLIDES

You can duplicate and delete selected slides in Slide Sorter view and see the effect on the flow of slides immediately.

To Duplicate a slide or slides:

1. Select the slide or slides you want to duplicate.
2. Slide number **2** has been selected in figure next.

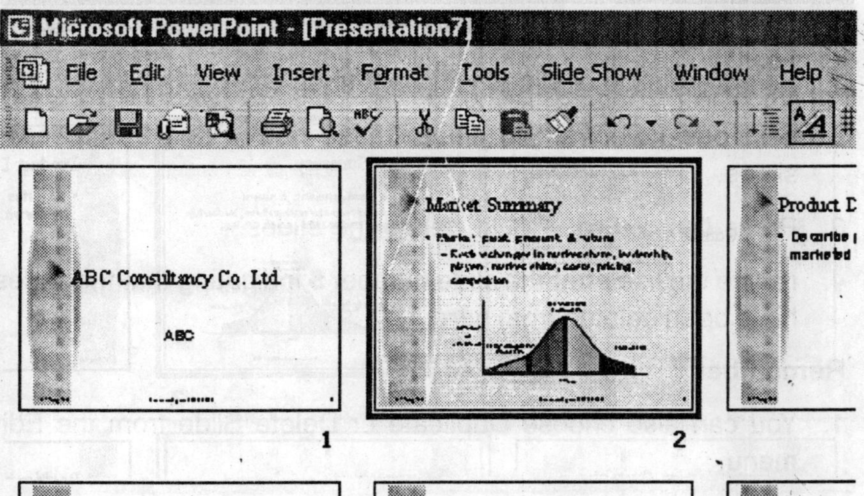

3. Press **Ctrl + D** or click at **Duplicate** in the **Edit** menu to duplicate the slide.
4. See the result of this below.
5. Slide number **3** is the duplicate of **2**.

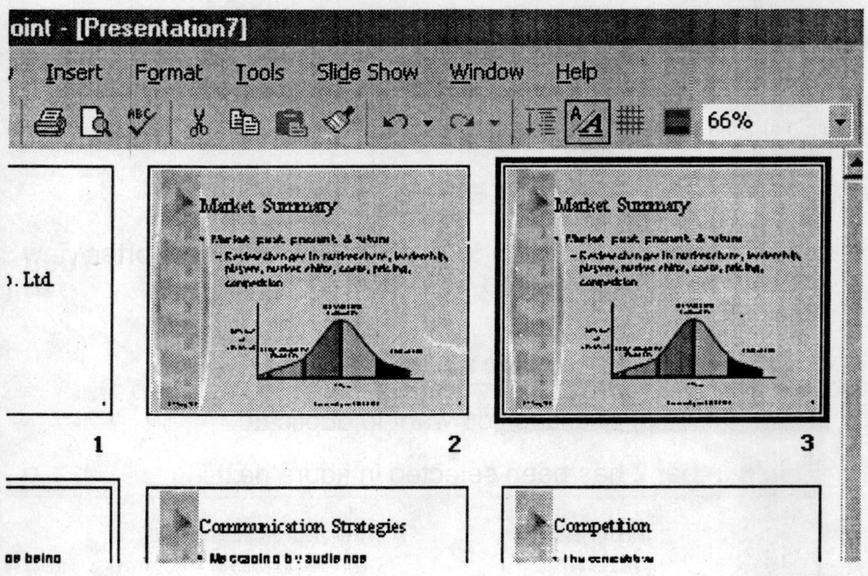

To delete a slide or slides:

1. Select the slide or slides you want to delete.
2. Supposing we want to delete these new **6** and **7** numbered slides.
3. Press **Del** or **Ctrl + X** to delete the slides.
4. Notice the line after the slide number **5** indicating that the slides have been deleted from here.

Remember

1. You can also choose Duplicate or Delete Slide from the Edit menu.

21

Making Slide Shows

Introduction

This effect shows all the hard work you have put in making the slides. It shows one slide after another, stopping in between for a set time on either the monitor of your screen or on the projector which may have been attached to your computer. It is also possible to add animated effects on the slides and show them in a sophisticated manner. It is also possible to add audio, video, narration, music, etc., to your slides.

Adding Effects

These effects can be of the form of wipes, splits, dissolves, etc., which you usually see in the film show. For this you have to work in the Slide Sorter view.

To Add a Transition View

1. Choose the slide on which you want to put this effect.
2. Click at **Slide Transition** in the Slide Show menu.
4. In this task pane, choose a transition effect from the drop-down list, a speed (slow, medium, or fast) and the advance option (on mouse click or after a period of time).
5. Click **Apply to All Slides** to apply this transition effect to all slides.

6. To apply the same transition effect to multiple slides, hold down the **Shift** key while you click the slides and then choose a transition effect.
7. To preview the transition effect in Slide Sorter view, click the transition icon that appears below each slide that has a transition effect.
8. A small icon can be seen on all the slides in the **Slide Sorter** view of the slides on the next page.

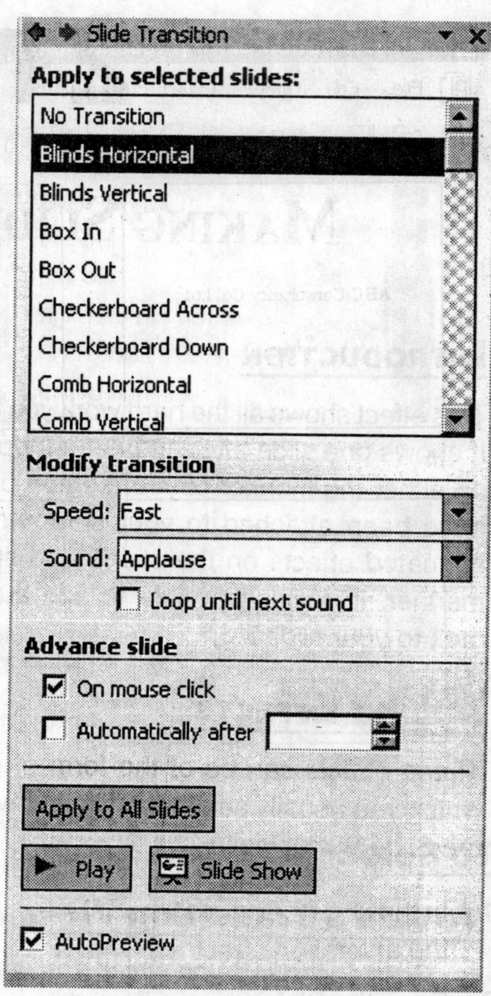

ADDING ANIMATION

As had been mentioned in the beginning of this chapter. You can add animation to the slides which are going to displayed. This helps in presenting a slide with special effects. You can choose from the various animations available.

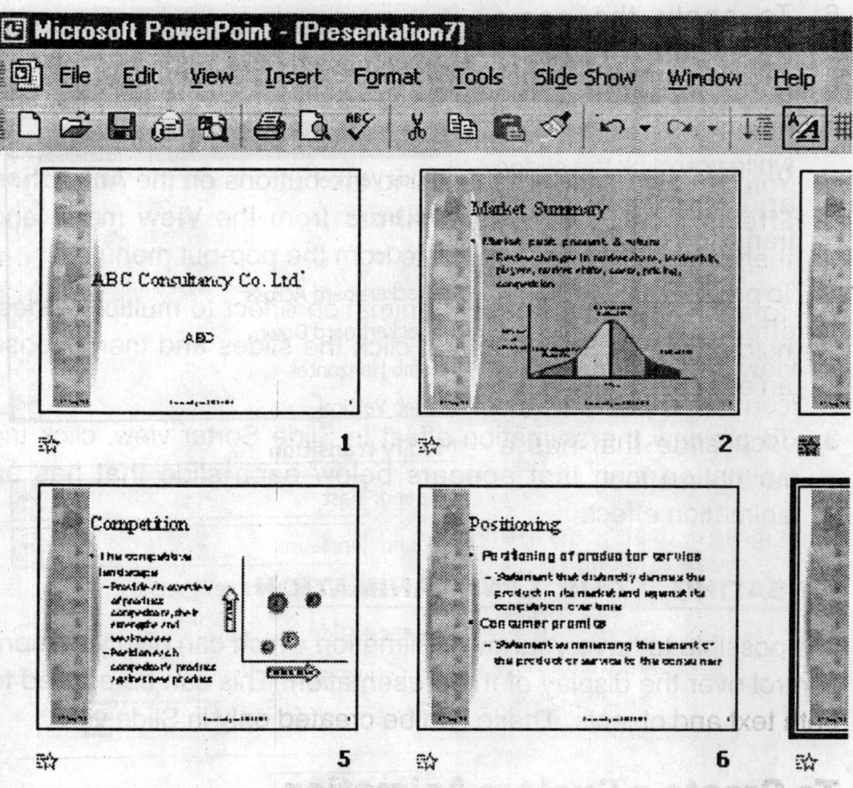

To Select an Animation

1. In the Slide Sorter view click at the slide to which you want to add the animation effect.
2. From the Slide Show menu, select Animation Schemes to have them in the task pane.
3. Select the one which you want to apply to the slide/slides.
4. Once it has been applied, you can see the small icon being put under the slide to show that this slide has an animation effect.
5. You can see the preview of this animation effect by clicking at the preview button.

6. If you want you can apply different effects on various slides and see the whole presentation having the different effects.

Remember

1. You can also apply effects using the buttons on the **Animation Effects** toolbar. Choose **Toolbars** from the **View** menu and then choose Animation Effects from the pop-out menu.
2. To apply the same present animation effect to multiple slides, hold down the **Shift** key and click the slides and then choose an effect.
3. To preview the animation effect in Slide Sorter view, click the animation icon that appears below each slide that has an animation effect.

Creating Your Own Animation

It is possible to have your own animation which can give you more control over the display of the presentation. This can be applied to both text and objects. These can be created only in Slide view.

To Create a Custom Animation

1. Select the slide where you want to put this animation and display it in the Slide view.
2. Select **Custom Animation** from the **Animation Effects** toolbar.
3. In the Custom Animation dialog box, check the items you want to animate and set the order and timing, as shown on the next page.
4. Click at **Effects** panel to select the effects from the drop-down list.
5. Select the options here according to your liking or choose the ones selected in the dialog box shown on the next page at the bottom.

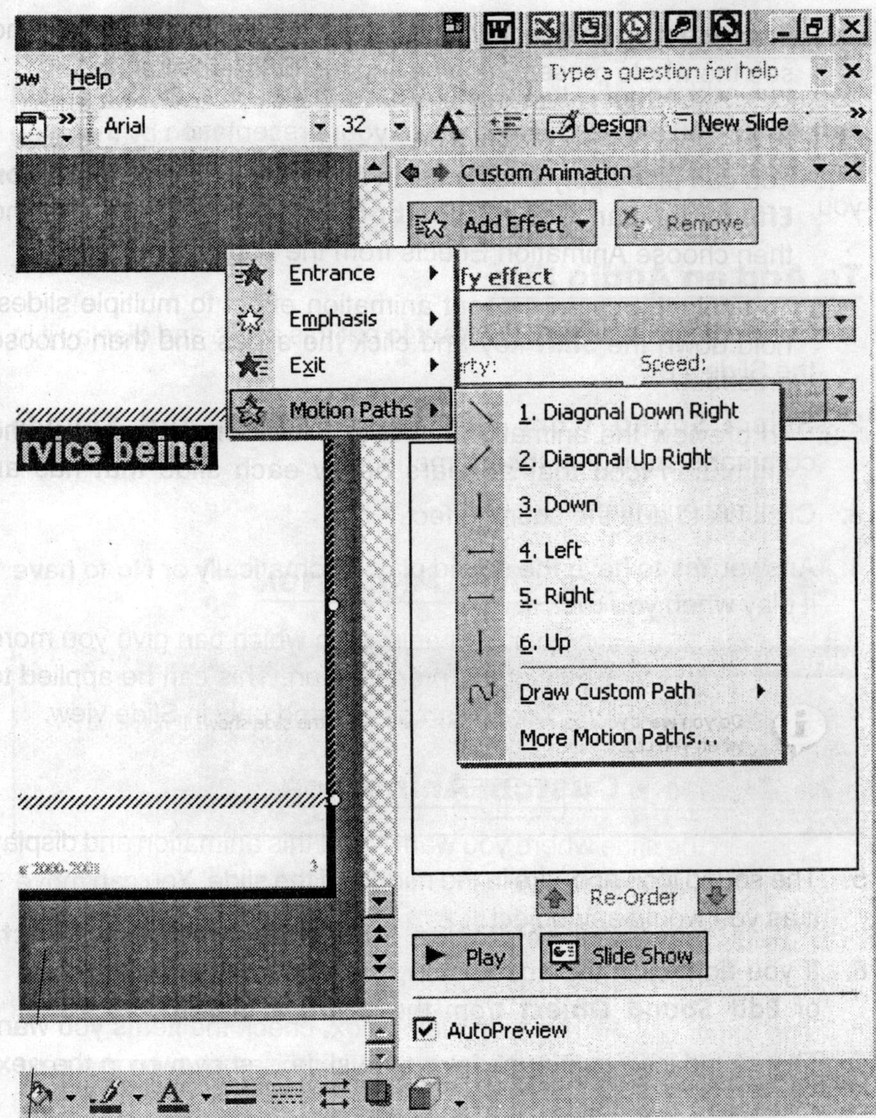

6. Click at **Preview** to see the effect of the animation.
7. You can also preview an animation by clicking the **Animation Preview** button on the Animation Effects toolbar.

Adding Audio Effect

You can add sounds to the transition effects and to the preset animation. You can also add audio to your presentation by inserting files from the **Clip Art Gallery** or from other folders available to you.

To Add an Audio File

1. Select the slide where you want to put this audio and display it in the Slide view.
2. Select **Sound from File** in the **Movies and Sounds** command from the **Insert** menu.
3. Click Ok to add the sound effect.
4. Answer **Yes** to have the sound play automatically or **No** to have it play when you click it.

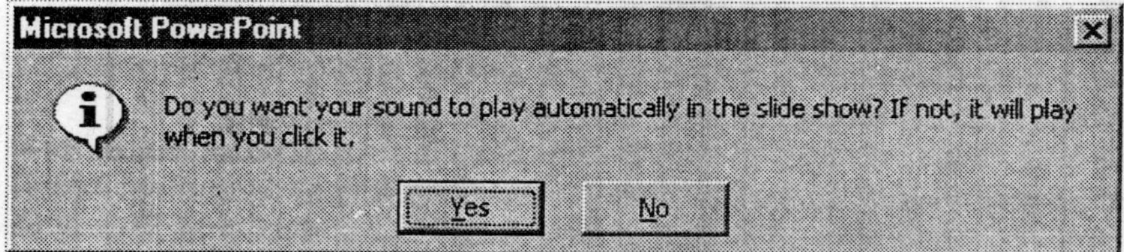

5. The sound icon appears in the middle of the slide. You can move it as you would any object.
6. If you right-click the sound icon, you can choose **Play Sound** or **Edit Sound Object** from the shortcut menu.
7. The sound icon as it appears on the slide is shown on the next page.

Adding Video Effect

Like sound, you can add video effects too. The steps are quite similar to the ones used in the case of Audio.

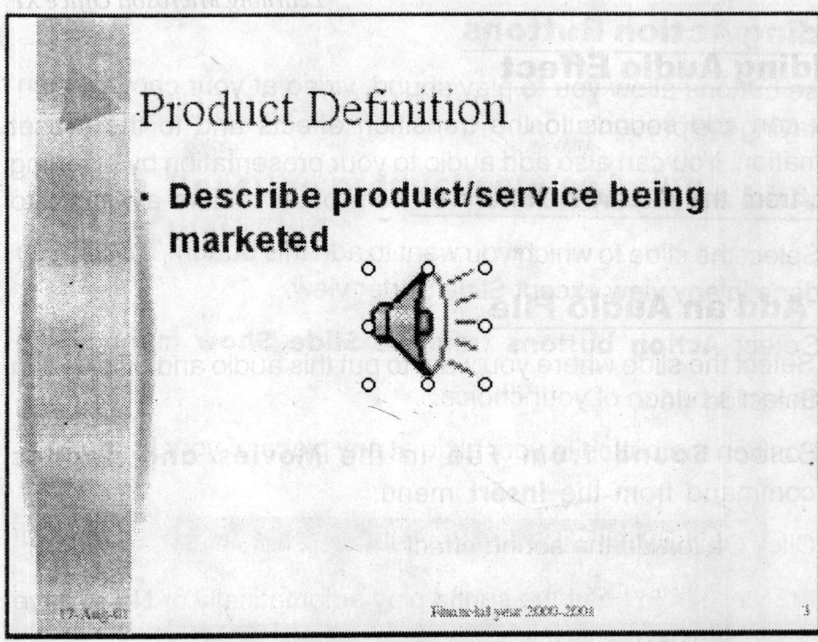

To Add an Video File

1. Select the slide where you want to put this video and display it in the Slide view.
2. Select **Movies from File** in the **Movies and Sounds** command from the **Insert** menu.
3. Click Ok to add the video effect.
4. Answer **Yes** to have the sound play automatically or **No** to have it play when you click it.
5. The video icon appears in the middle of the slide. You can move it as you would any object.
6. If you right-click the video icon, you can choose **Play Video** or **Edit Video Object** from the shortcut menu.
7. The video icon as it appears on the slide.

Adding Action Buttons

These buttons allow you to play sound, video at your choice when displaying the presentation.

To Add an Action Button:

1. Select the slide to which you want to add this button. This can be done in any view except Slide Sorter view.
2. Select **Action buttons** from the **Slide Show** menu.
3. Select a button of your choice.
4. Position the button in your slide at any place of your liking.

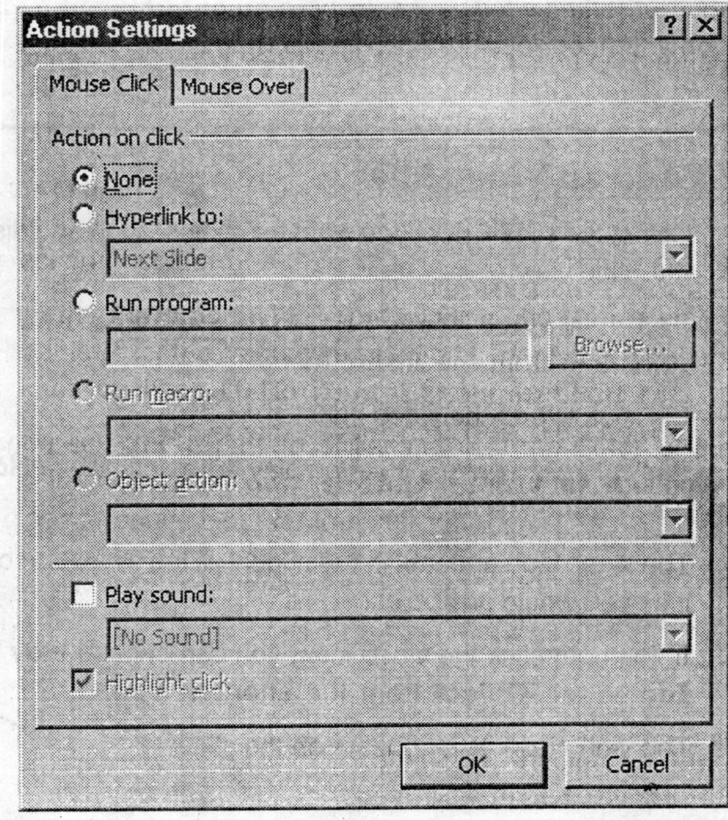

5. On clicking the button PowerPoint will give rise to a new dialog box called **Action settings**.
6. Make the necessary settings and click Ok.
7. You action button is now properly placed in the slide.
8. You can add actions to other objects simply by selecting them and then choosing Action settings from the Slide Show menu.

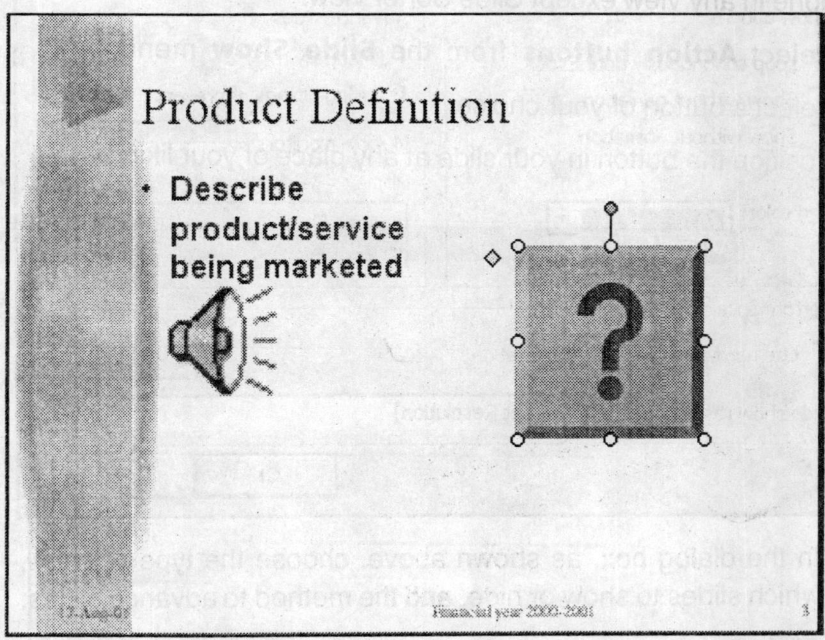

SETTING THE SHOW

Now comes the most important part of the software where you are going to setup the whole show of presentation to run without your help.

You can choose to hide few slides for not displaying.

To Set Up the Slide Show:

1. From the Slide Show menu, choose **Set Up Show**.

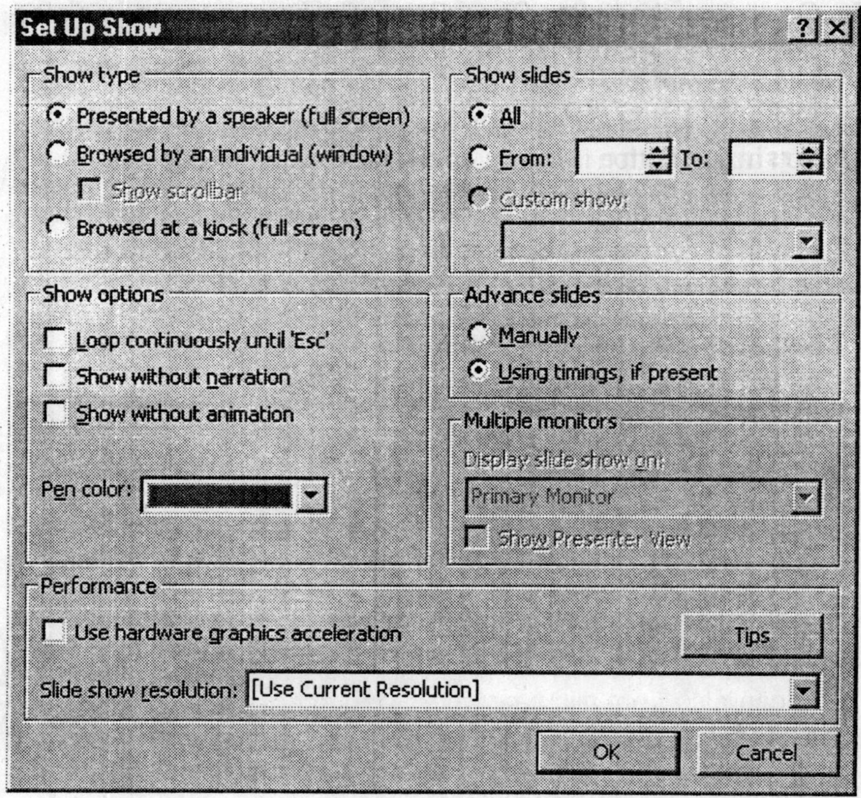

2. In the dialog box, as shown above, choose the type of show, which slides to show or hide, and the method to advance slides.

3. Click Ok.

4. Click the **Projector Wizard** button in the Set Up Show dialog box for help connecting your computer to a projector.

5. Choose **Custom Shows** from the Slide Show menu to add slides from this presentation to a custom show.

6. Even though a slide is hidden, you can display it by clicking a hyperlink or an action pointing to it.

Rehearsing the Show

As we see the preview of the page before printing. PowerPoint also allows you to do the same. For this you have what is called the **Rehearsing of the Show**.

You can run the show from any view.

To Rehearse the Slide Show:

1. From the Slide Show menu, choose **Rehearse Timings**.
2. You can click the Rehearse Timings button on the Slide Sorter toolbar too in the Slide Sorter view.
3. The show begins with the timer set at the top left hand corner of the screen, as shown on the next page.
4. To use these timings, choose **Use Slide Timings** in the Set Up Show dialog box.
5. To advance through the slide show, click anywhere on the slide. You can also right-click anywhere and choose as action from the shortcut menu.

   You can also use keystrokes given below:

Slide Show	*Keystrokes*
Next Action	Spacebar, Enter, N, Page Down, Right Arrow
Previous Action	P, Backspace, Page Up, Left Arrow
Go to slide number	number + Enter
Black/White screen	B or W (press again to return to show)

Setting Timings Manually

You can set timings manually for the exact amount of time that you want each slide to remain on the screen. To set slide timings manually:

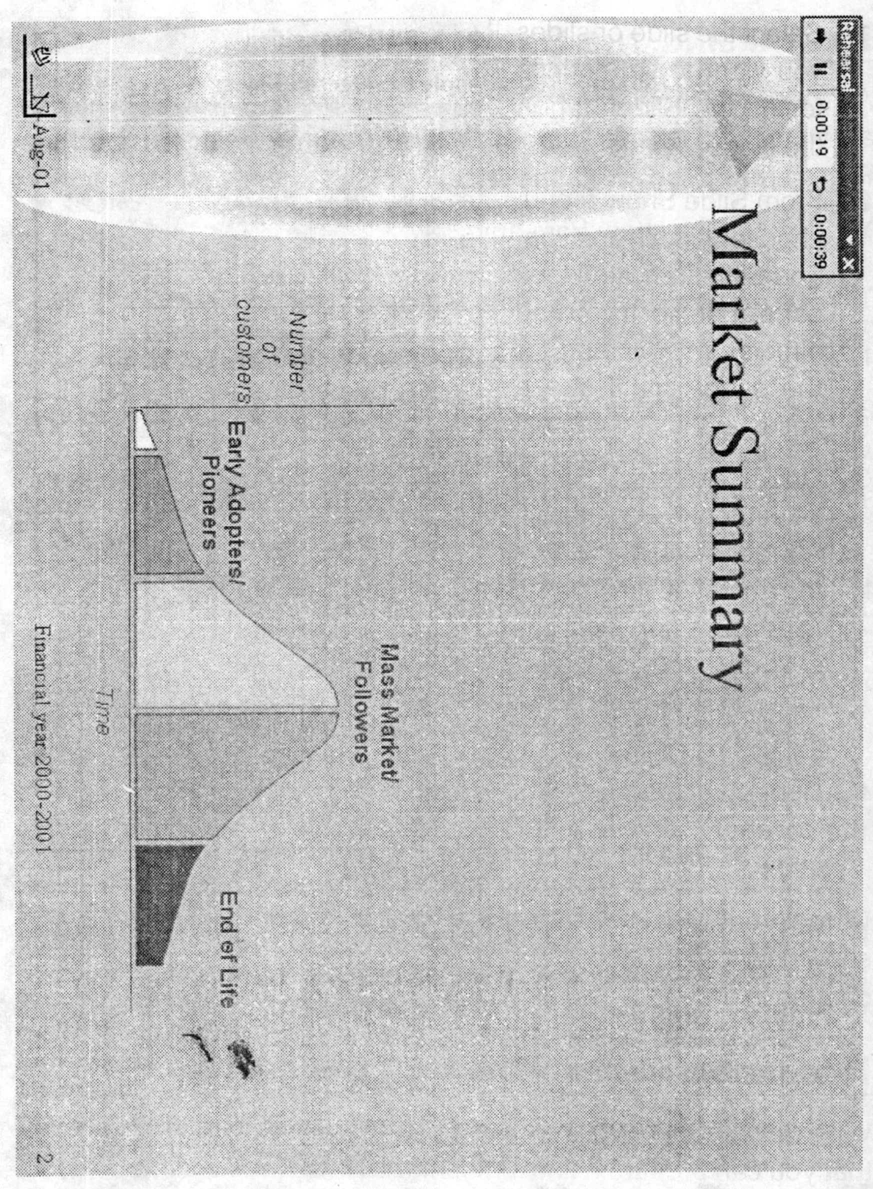
Rehearsal
0:00:19
0:00:39
Market Summary
Number of customers
Early Adopters/ Pioneers
Mass Market/ Followers
End of Life
Time
Aug-01
Financial year 2000-2001
2

1. Select the slide or slides you want to set timings for on the Slides tab in the Normal view.
2. From Slide Show menu, choose Slide Transition. The Slide transition task pane appears. If you had already set a timing for the slide, you'll see a timing in the task pane.
3. Under Advance Slide, select the Automatically After check out and use the arrows in the list box to enter the time in seconds that you want the slide to remain on the screen.
4. Repeat the above steps for each slide in your show.

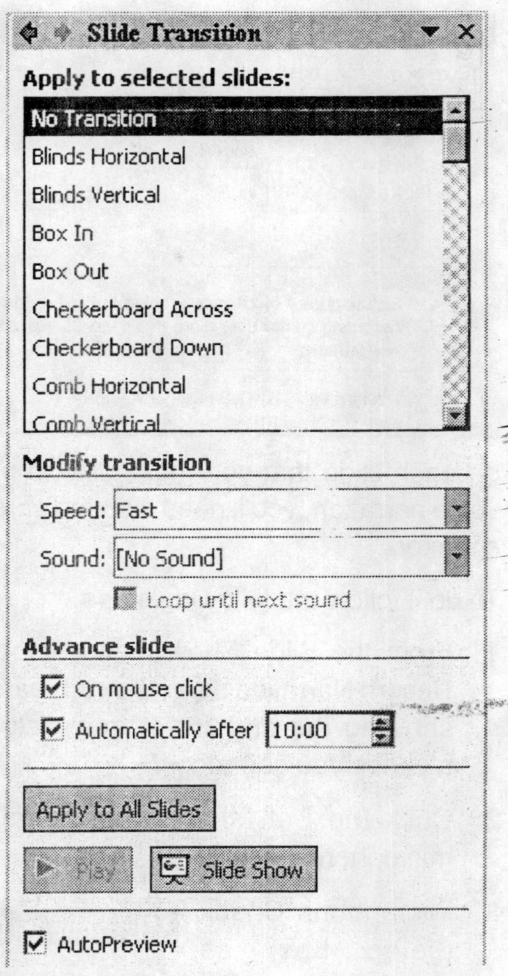

When you run your slide show now, you will notice the change in timings as entered by you.

Recording Narration

With PowerPoint, you can add voice narration to a slide show so that you can prepare a final presentation in advance, complete with recorded material in your own voice. If you want to record narration or comments for single slides, you can do so, but PowerPoint treats these as individual sound (.wav) files, displayed with a sound icon

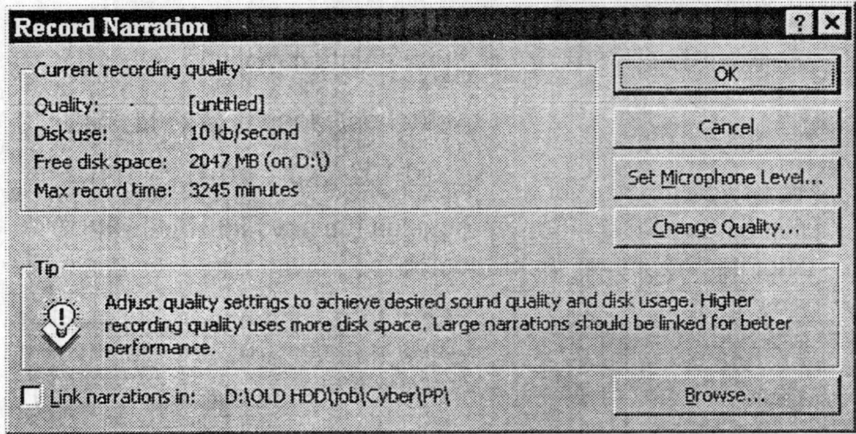

on each slide that you must click to play the sound. To record a voice narration, you'll need a sound card, a microphone and a set of speakers.

To do it follow the following steps.

1. From the Slide Show menu, choose Record Narration. The Record Narration dialog box appears, as shown above appears, showing the amount of free disk space and the number of minutes you can record.
2. Click the Set Microphone Level button to calibrate your microphone.
3. Microphone Check dialog box, as shown here, would appear. Use it to customize the recording or playback.

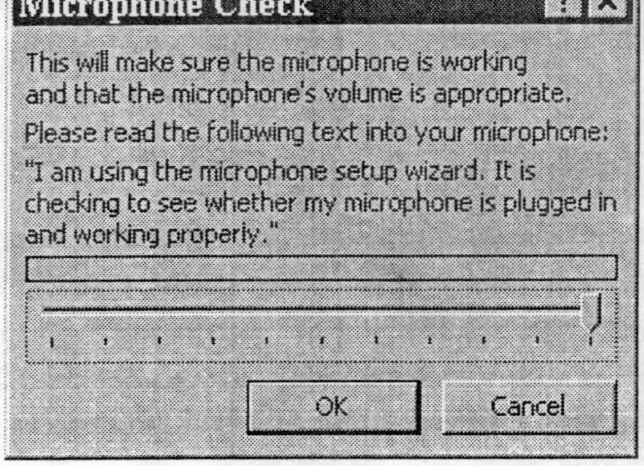

4. To begin recording, click OK.
5. Record voice

content for each slide in your presentation, clicking to move from one slide to the next. PowerPoint records the narration with timings for each slide.

6. When you're finished with the recording, PowerPoint displays a dialog box asking whether to save your narration with your slide timings. To do this, click Save.

7. To save the narration only, click Don't Save. Your presentation will then open in Slide Sorter view with a sound icon displayed in the lower right corner of each slide.

Pen to Mark Slides

You can use the Pen feature during the slide show, just as you would use a marking pen.

To use the Pen feature during a slide show:

1. Right-click to get a short submenu.
2. Click at Pointer Options
3. From the submenu select Pen.
4. Using the pen under the mouse, write or draw whatever you want to on the slide.
5. Press Enter or the spacebar to move to the next animation or slide.
6. To change the pen color, right-click a slide, point to Pointer Options, point to the pen Color submenu and a click at a new color of your choice.
7. To return to the regular mouse pointer, press Ctrl+A.
8. To erase the pen markings, press E.

Using Meeting Minder

Use Meeting Minder to record the minutes as the meeting progresses,

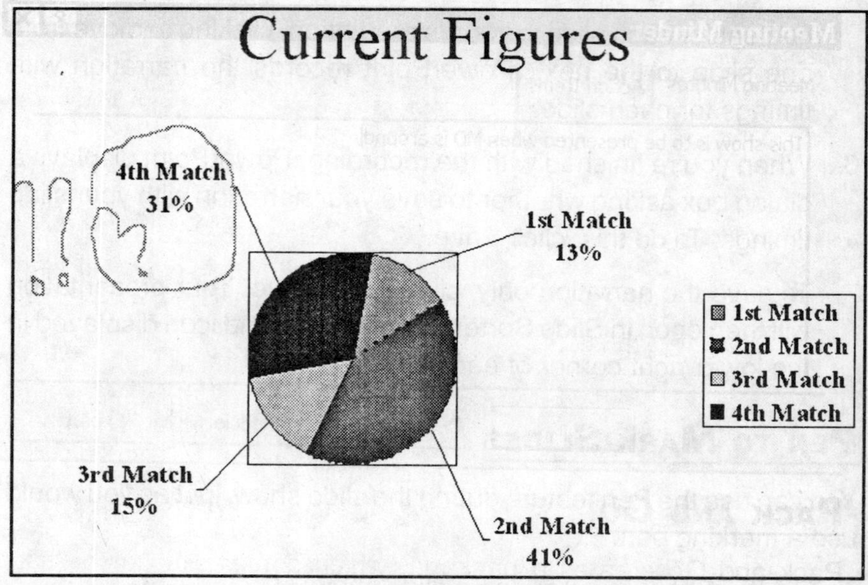

typing up the important points items to be acted on. After the meeting, transfer your minutes to you note pages or to a new Microsoft Word document. From there, you can print them and distribute copies to all the attendees and to those people who couldn't attend.

Follow these steps to work with Meeting Minder:

1. During the slide show, right-click a slide and choose Meeting Minder from the shortcut menu.
2. Click the appropriate tab that indicates what you'd like to do or click Schedule to start Outlook.
3. If you're adding an action item or meeting minute, type it in the space provided as shown in the dialog box, on the next page.
4. To export action items and meeting minutes to a Word document, click Export. Edit the text in word, if necessary, then save the document and exit Word.
5. When you are finished with the Meeting Minder, click OK.

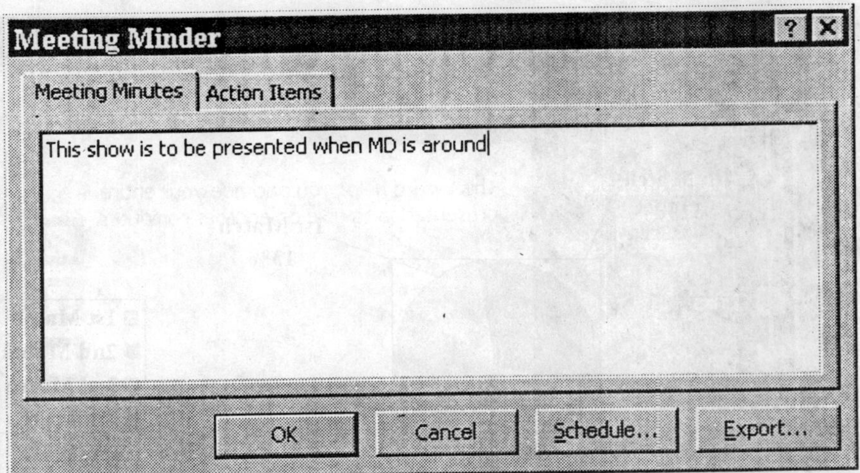

Pack and Go

Pack and Go creates a package, which contains a compressed copy of your presentation, along with all its multimedia files that you copy to disks, as well as the PowerPoint Viewer. It allows you to run the slides even if the computer does not have PowerPoint loaded into it.

To Pack up your presentation to Go, follow the following steps.

1. Open the presentation that you want to compress and save to disks.
2. Choose from File menu, Pack And Go. The Pack And Go wizard opens.
3. This wizard will take you through the 6 different steps before creating a compressed copy of the presentation.
4. On the next page, you see all the steps.
5. At the end you would return to the presentation.

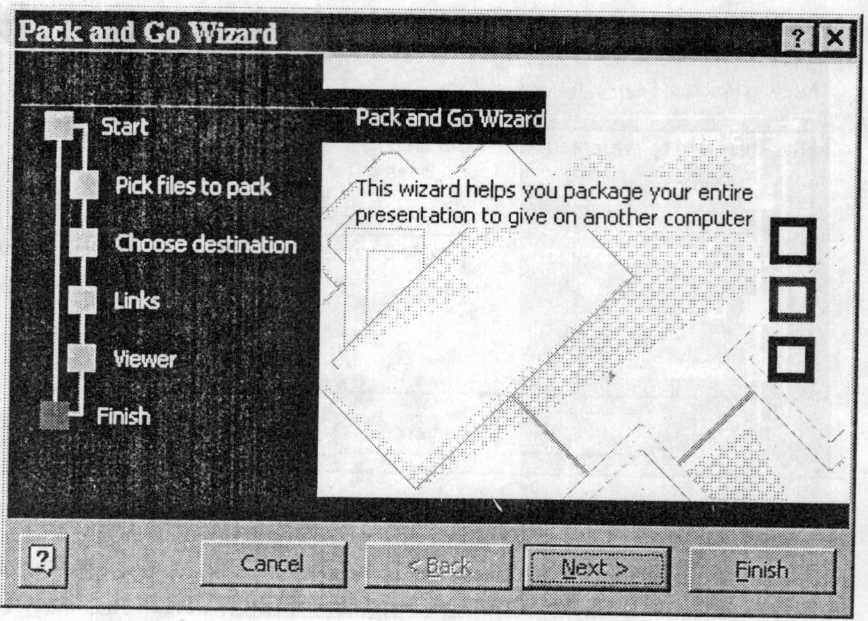
Pack and Go Wizard
Start
Pick files to pack
Choose destination
Links
Viewer
Finish
Pack and Go Wizard
This wizard helps you package your entire presentation to give on another computer
Cancel
< Back
Next >
Finish

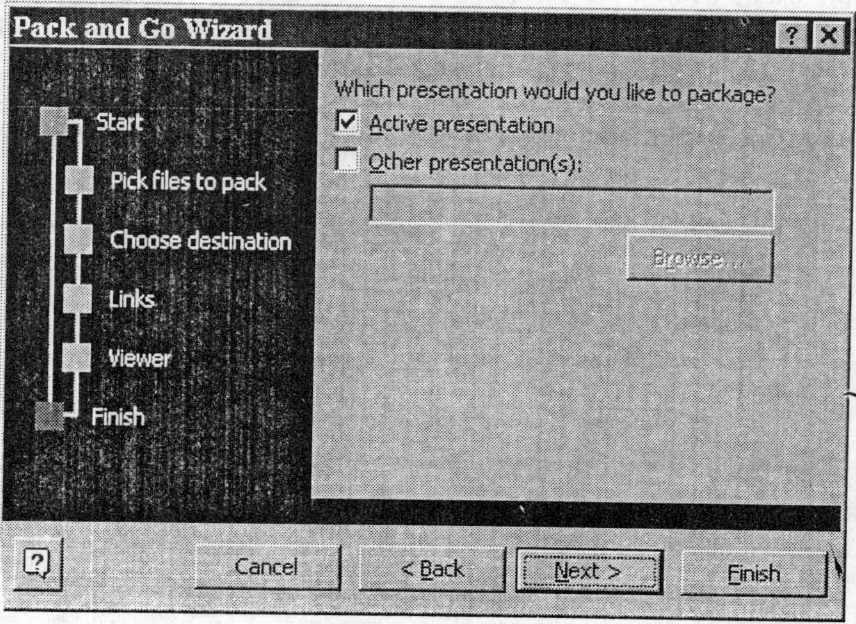
Pack and Go Wizard
Start
Pick files to pack
Choose destination
Links
Viewer
Finish
Which presentation would you like to package?
Active presentation
Other presentation(s):
Browse...
Cancel
< Back
Next >
Finish

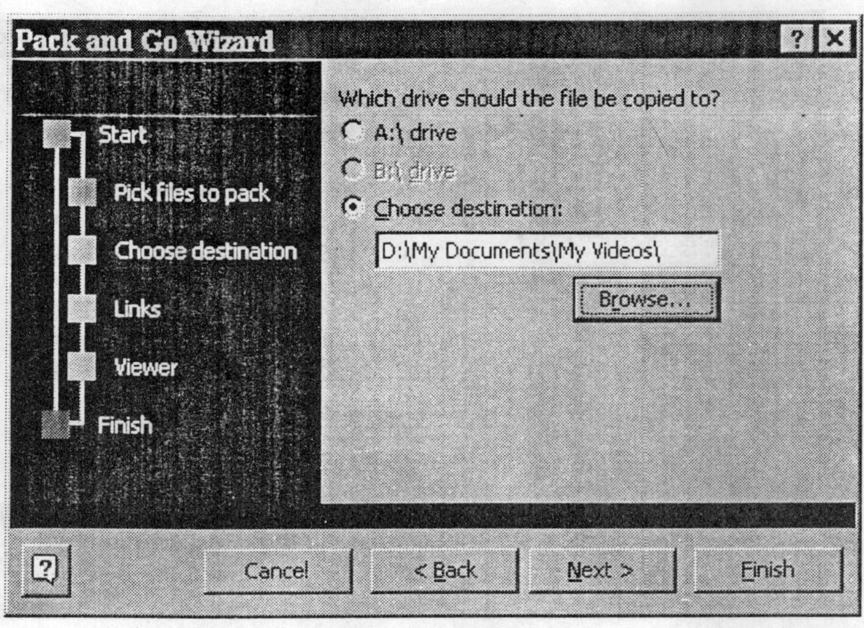
Pack and Go Wizard
Start
Pick files to pack
Choose destination
Links
Viewer
Finish
Which drive should the file be copied to?
A:\ drive
B:\ drive
Choose destination:
D:\My Documents\My Videos\
Browse...
Cancel
< Back
Next >
Finish

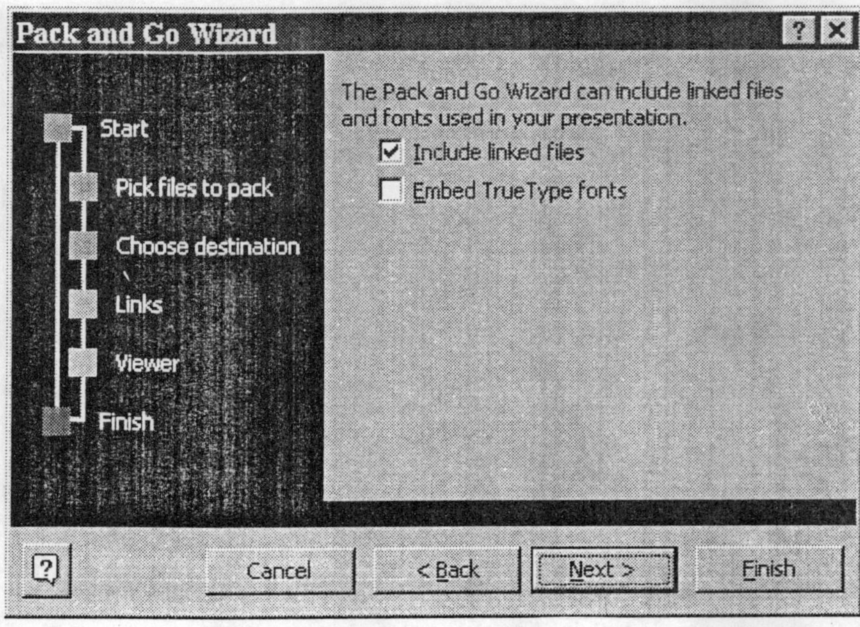
Pack and Go Wizard
Start
Pick files to pack
Choose destination
Links
Viewer
Finish
The Pack and Go Wizard can include linked files and fonts used in your presentation.
Include linked files
Embed TrueType fonts
Cancel
< Back
Next >
Finish

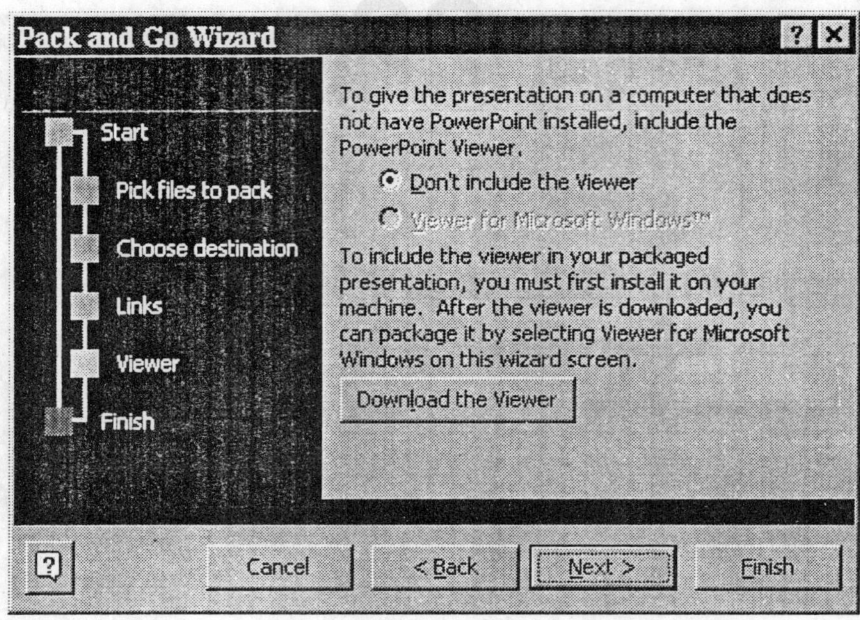
Pack and Go Wizard
Start
Pick files to pack
Choose destination
Links
Viewer
Finish
To give the presentation on a computer that does not have PowerPoint installed, include the PowerPoint Viewer.
Don't include the Viewer
Viewer for Microsoft Windows™
To include the viewer in your packaged presentation, you must first install it on your machine. After the viewer is downloaded, you can package it by selecting Viewer for Microsoft Windows on this wizard screen.
Download the Viewer
Cancel
< Back
Next >
Finish

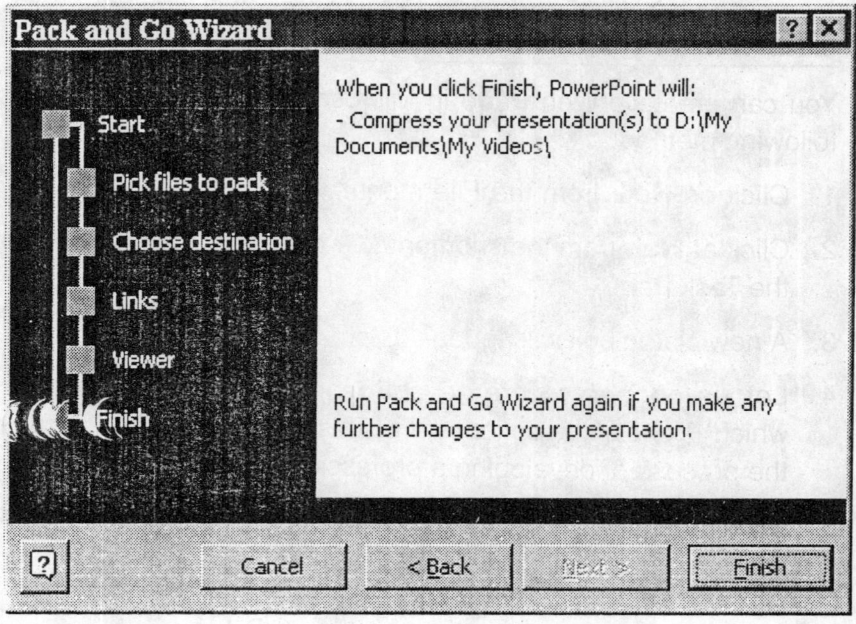
Pack and Go Wizard
Start
Pick files to pack
Choose destination
Links
Viewer
Finish
When you click Finish, PowerPoint will:
- Compress your presentation(s) to D:\My Documents\My Videos\
Run Pack and Go Wizard again if you make any further changes to your presentation.
Cancel
< Back
Next >
Finish

22

Creating a Web Page using Wizard of FrontPage 2002

Introduction

FrontPage 2002 provides you a complete sit back type of Wizard which allows you to just sit back and allow FrontPage to create the Web Page for you. Only thing that you have to do is to answer few of the queries of the software.

FrontPage has two type of wizard; one which creates the **web site** and the one which creates a **single page**.

Creating a Web Page using Wizard

You can create a Web Page in Microsoft FrontPage 2002 by the following method:

1. Click on **New** from the File menu.
2. Click at **Web** from the submenu. Or choose Web templats from the Task Pane.
3. A new dialog box will appear, as shown on the next page.
4. Let us choose to create a **Corporate Presence Wizard** which is one of the options here. This wizard guides you through the process of developing a professional Web.
5. Click at the icon of the Wizard to start it.

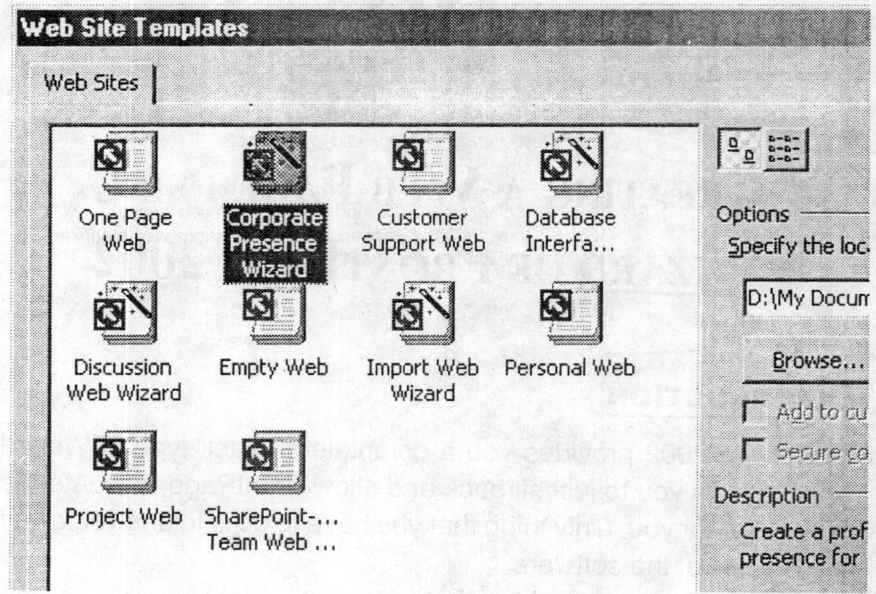

6. It has numerous features that make it easier to establish a company's Web.
7. When you select this wizard, you will have to fill information in a series of 13 different dialog boxes, as shown on the following pages.
8. Fill up the data known to you.
9. To be able to fill the data in the dialog boxes, I suggest you keep the following information ready with you:
   - The products or services that will be promoted on the Web.
   - Whether feedback is required from the visitors or not.
   - Whether the feedback is to be saved, if yes, how.
   - Whether the Web needs to have its own search engine.
   - The company's information to be displayed on the Web page.
   - All the relevant company information like e-mail address, etc. and the Web related inquiries.

9. In case of any doubt leave the box as it is, since you can always come back to old box by pressing Back.

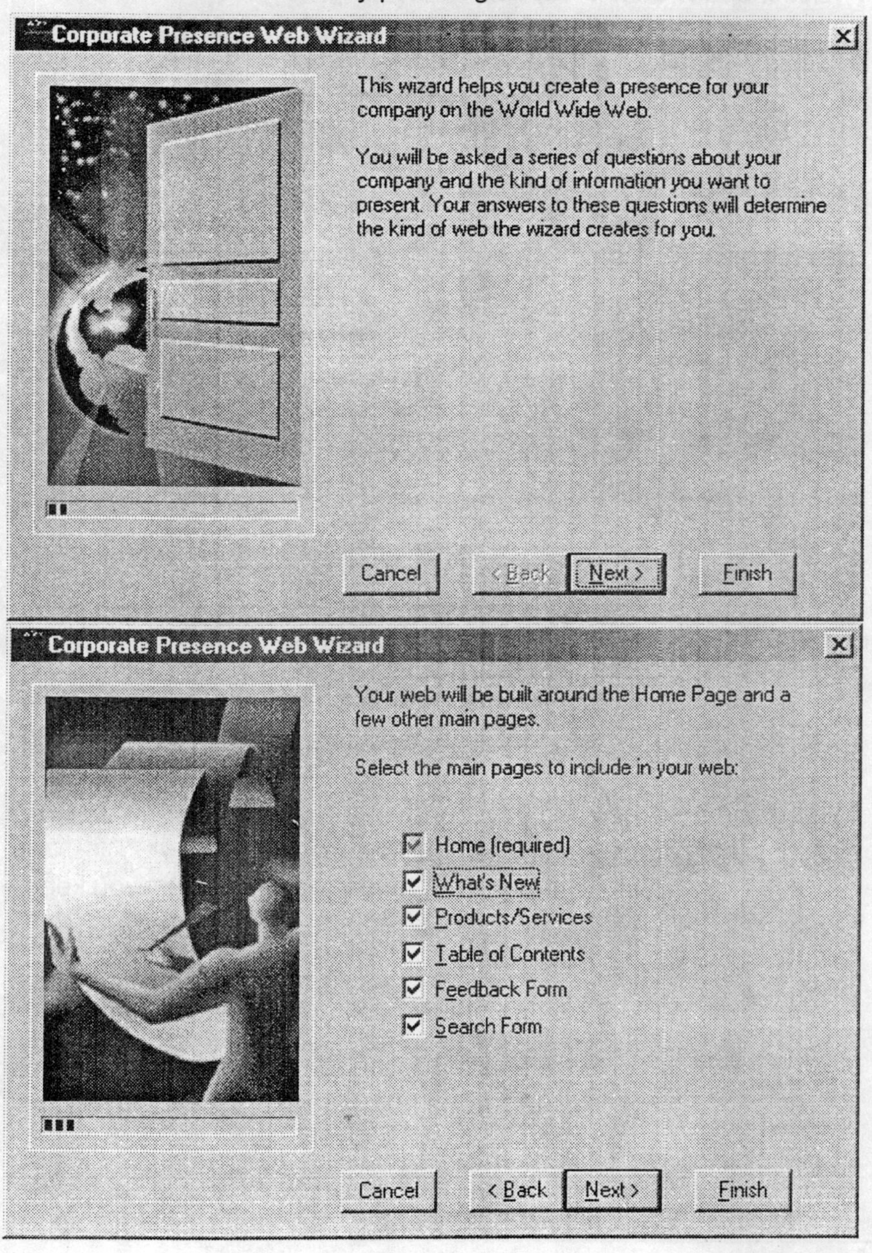

10. The Corporate Wizard includes a lot of explanatory text that describes what it is capable of creating.

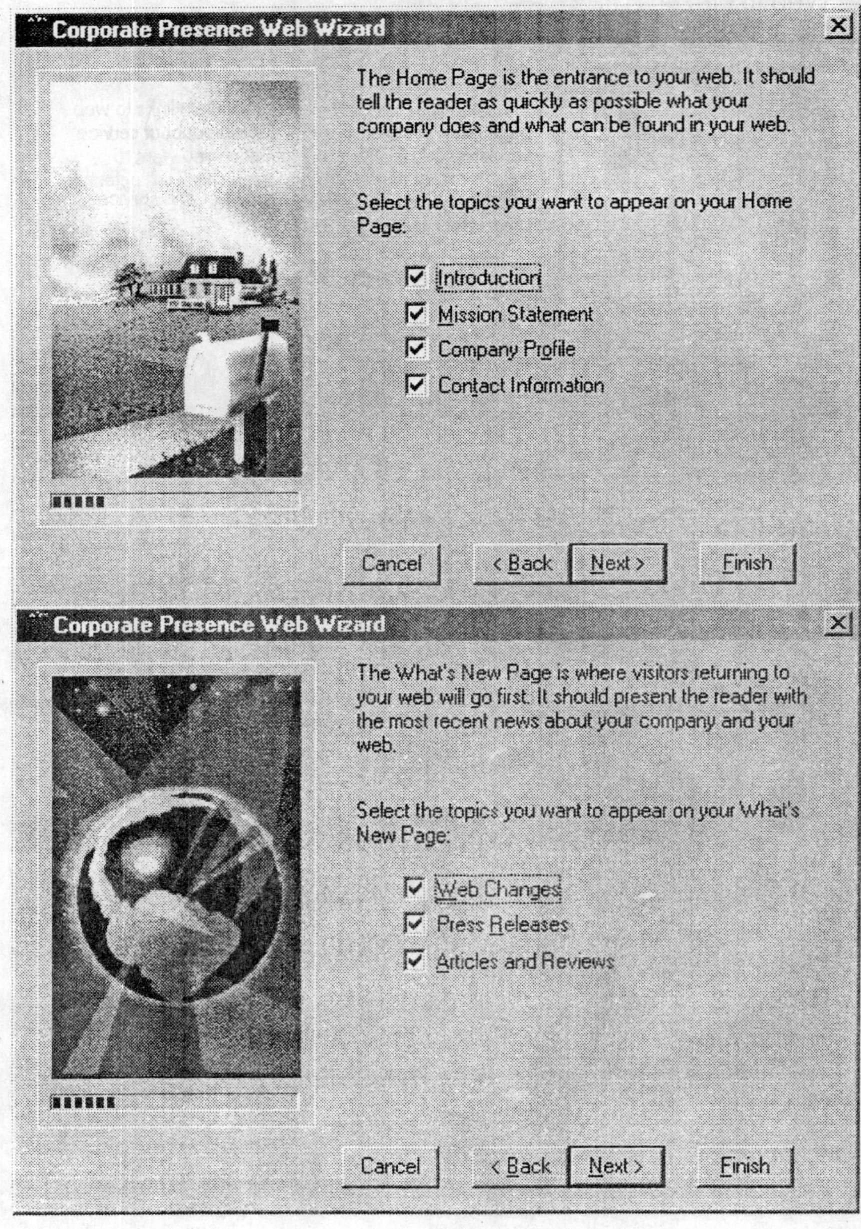

11. After you answer all the questions on all 13 dialog boxes, the Corporate Presence Wizard is finally ready to create the actual Web itself.

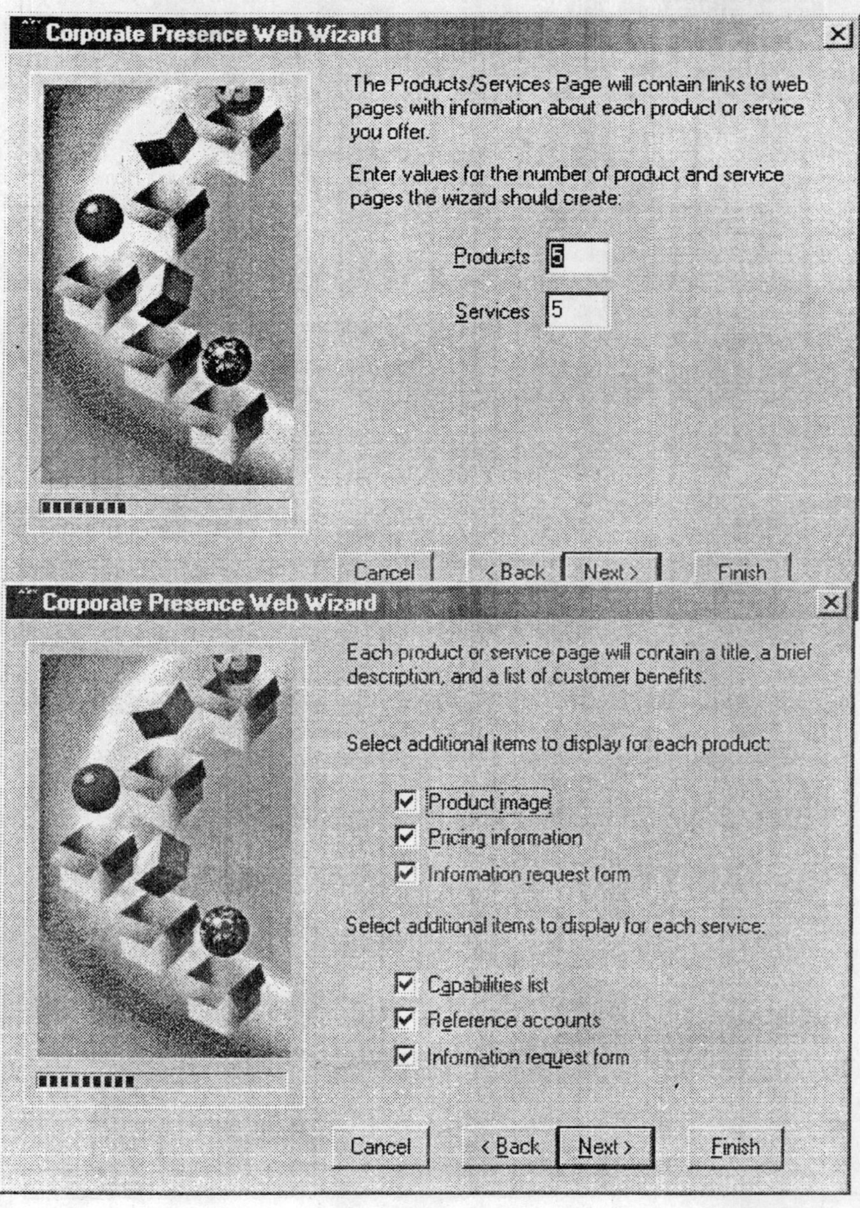

Corporate Presence Web Wizard

The Feedback Form lets readers tell you what they think about your web, your company, and your products.

Choose the information you want to collect from rea when they submit comments:

- [x] Full Name
- [x] Job Title
- [x] Company Affiliation
- [x] Mailing Address
- [x] Telephone Number
- [x] FAX Number
- [x] E-mail Address

Cancel | < Back | Next > | Finish

Corporate Presence Web Wizard

The Feedback Form stores the information it collect from readers in a file on your web server.

Do you want the feedback file to be compatible wit database and spreadsheet programs?

- (•) Yes, use tab-delimited format
- ( ) No, use web-page format

Cancel | < Back | Next > | Finish

Corporate Presence Web Wizard

The Table of Contents Page displays a set of links every page in your web, using a format similar to the Hyperlinks View in FrontPage.

Choose from the following presentation options:

- [x] Keep page list up-to-date automatically
- [x] Show pages not linked into web
- [x] Use bullets for top-level pages

Cancel | < Back | Next > | Finish

Corporate Presence Web Wizard

What should appear at the top of each page?

- [x] Your company's logo
- [x] Page title
- [x] Links to your main web pages

What should appear at the bottom of each page?

- [x] Links to your main web pages
- [x] E-mail address of your webmaster
- [x] Copyright notice
- [x] Date page was last modified

Cancel | < Back | Next > | Finish

Corporate Presence Web Wizard

Many web authors like to identify pages that aren't quite finished. Would you like to mark each unfinish page in your web with the Under Construction icon shown below?

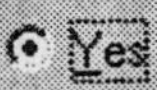

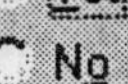

Cancel | < Back | Next > | Finish

Corporate Presence Web Wizard

The Web Wizard uses your company's long name (example: ACME Industries Incorporated) and short name (example: ACME) in many places throughout web.

What is the full name of your company?

Netraffic Integrated Marketing

What is the one-word version of this name?

NIM

What is your company's street address?

B-17, Nizamuddin East, New Delhi -1100

Cancel | < Back | Next > | Finish

Corporate Presence Web Wizard

The following contact information for your company \
be available to any page in your web.

What is your company's telephone number?

91 11 4353877

What is your company's FAX number?

91 11 435 6454

What is the e-mail address of your webmaster?

mayank@netraffic.org

What is the e-mail address for general info?

info@netraffic.org

Cancel | < Back | Next > | Finish

Corporate Presence Web Wizard

You can select a theme to coordinate the graphics, colors, and fonts used in your web.

Press the button below to bring up a dialog that lets select from a list of available themes. If you don't choose a theme now, you can still apply one later to the pages generated by the wizard.

Choose Web Theme

Cancel | < Back | Next > | Finish

Choose Theme
Apply Theme to:
All pages
Selected page(s)
(Install Additional Themes)
(No Theme)
Axis
Bars
Blank
Blends
Capsules
Cascade
Checkers
Copy of Straight Edge
Edge
Vivid colors
Active graphics
Background picture
Apply using CSS
Sample of Theme:
Banner
Button
Button
Heading 1 Style
Bullet 1
Bullet 2
Bullet 3
Heading 2 Style
OK
Cancel

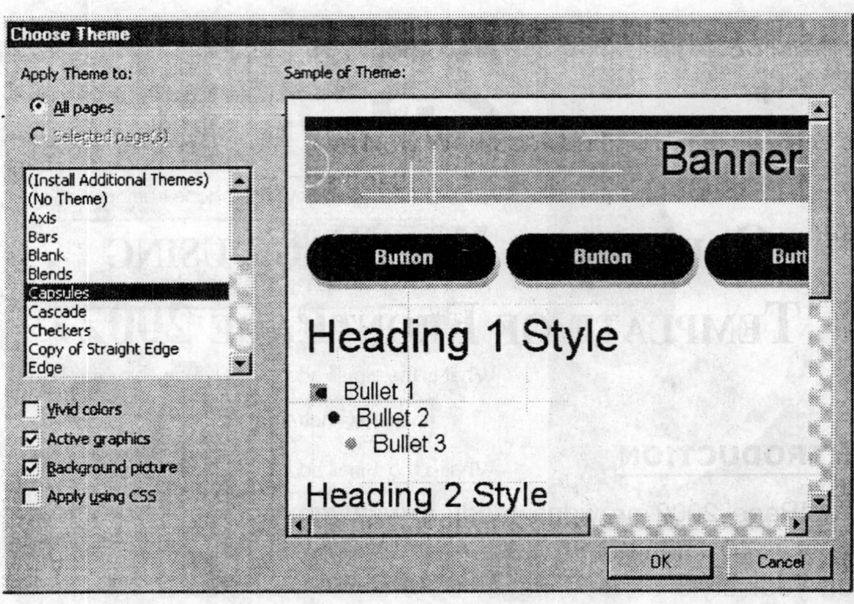

Corporate Presence Web Wizard
Those are all the answers the wizard needs to creat
your Corporate Presence web!
You can finish customizing the web pages after they
are uploaded to the server. The wizard will add som
tasks to the Tasks View to help you remember to ec
them.
Show Tasks View after web is uploaded
Cancel
< Back
Next >
Finish

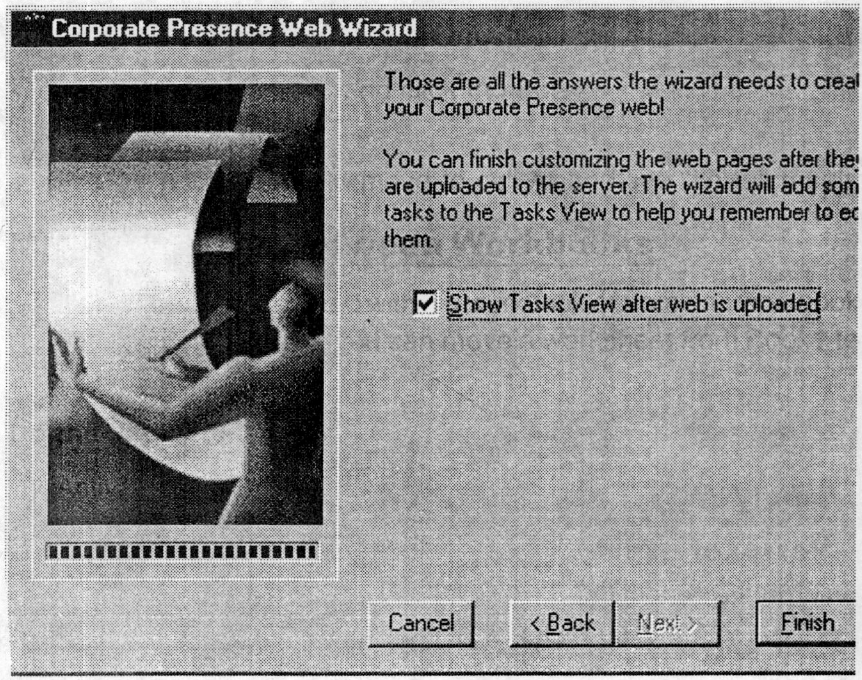

23

Creating a Web Page using Template of FrontPage 2002

Introduction

FrontPage 2002 provides ready to use **templates**. There are as many as 48 different templates, I am sure at least one of them would suit your style of Web page. Before you can create a page in FrontPage 2002, you must create a Web that will contain that page.

Selecting a Web Template

1. Click at **Empty Web** from the task pane.
2. A new dialog box will appear, as shown on the next page.
3. You can choose here one of the following:

One Page Web	A Web with a single page
Customer Support Web	A 19-page Web that enables a company to offer customer support for one or more of its products
Empty Web	A Web containing no page
Personal Web	A Web for personal information
Project Web	A 23-page Web devoted to a collaborative project, with pages

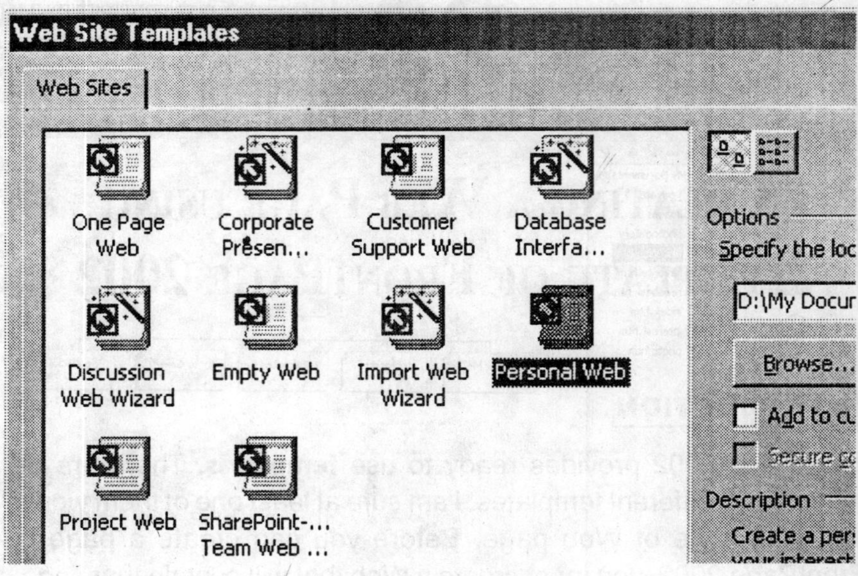

for member information, project status, a schedule, group discussions, and an archive.

4. You will have to inform the location of the Web page in the hard disk too.
5. Choose **Personal Web** from here.
6. You will get your personal web page as shown on the next page which does not have any task.
7. You can add task by choosing Add task from the Edit menu/Task
7. A **navigation view** of the same page will look like the one shown on the next page (bottom).
8. As can be seen there are 4 main pages on this:
   - A main page called Home page for all the information
   - A page to describe your interests
   - A page to display your photos

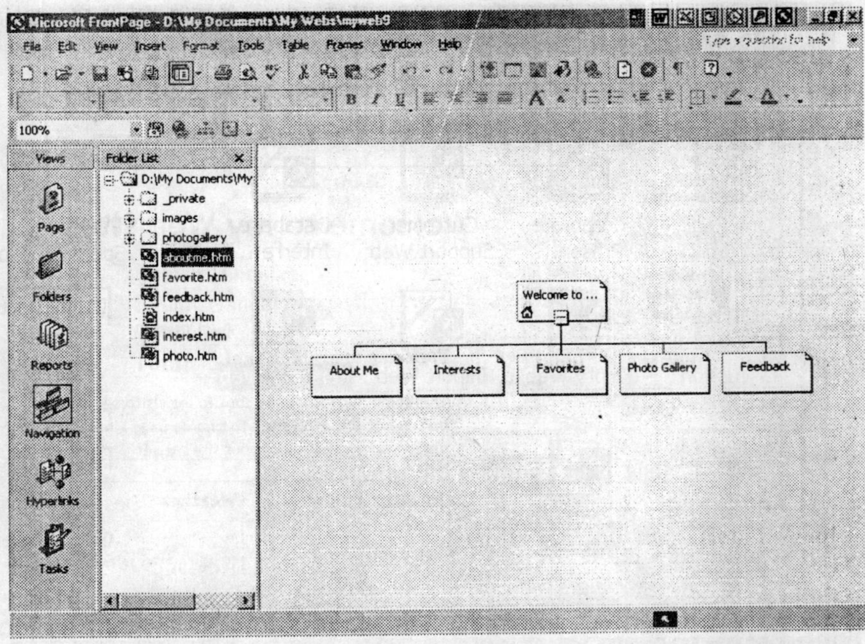
Microsoft FrontPage - D:\My Documents\My Webs\myweb9
Folder List
D:\My Documents\My
_private
images
photogallery
aboutme.htm
favorite.htm
feedback.htm
index.htm
interest.htm
photo.htm
Page
Folders
Reports
Navigation
Hyperlinks
Tasks
Welcome to ...
About Me
Interests
Favorites
Photo Gallery
Feedback

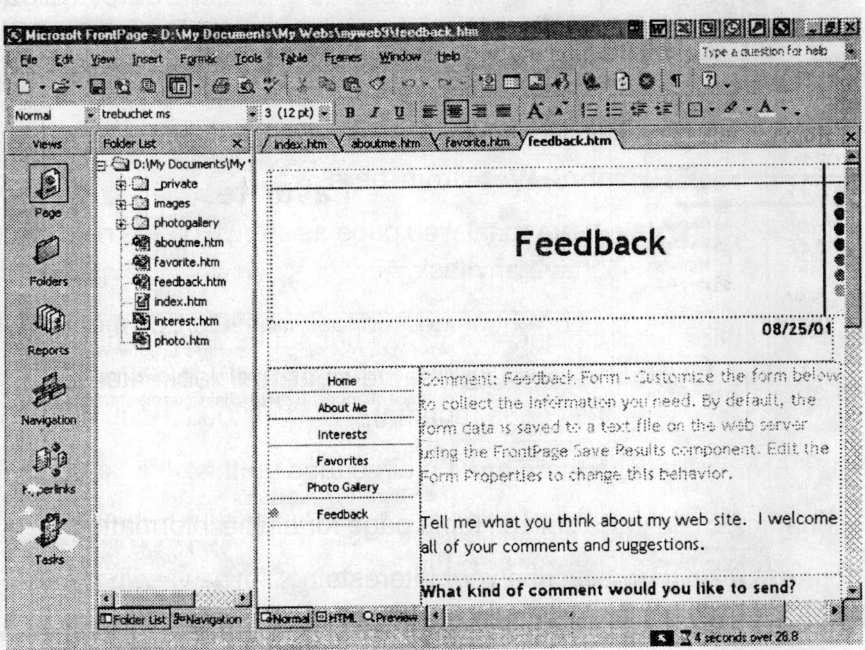
Microsoft FrontPage - D:\My Documents\My Webs\myweb9\feedback.htm
index.htm
aboutme.htm
favorite.htm
feedback.htm
Feedback
08/25/01
Home
About Me
Interests
Favorites
Photo Gallery
Feedback
Comment: Feedback Form - Customize the form below to collect the information you need. By default, the form data is saved to a text file on the web server using the FrontPage Save Results component. Edit the Form Properties to change this behavior.
Tell me what you think about my web site. I welcome all of your comments and suggestions.
What kind of comment would you like to send?

Microsoft FrontPage - D:\My Documents\My Webs\myweb9\index.htm
File Edit View Insert Format Tools Table Frames Window Help
Type a question for help
Normal
trebuchet ms
3 (12 pt)
Views
Page
Folders
Reports
Navigation
Hyperlinks
Tasks
Folder List
D:\My Documents\My
_private
images
photogallery
aboutme.htm
favorite.htm
feedback.htm
index.htm
interest.htm
photo.htm
index.htm
aboutme.htm
favorite.htm
feedback.htm
Welcome to my Web site
08/25/01
Home
About Me
Interests
Favorites
Photo Gallery
Feedback
Welcome to my Web site!
The home page is a good spot to let visitors know the purpose of this Web site. The home page gives visitors an impression of your site's style.
Favorite Links
Weather
Comment: This space
Comment: This space can
Folder List
Navigation
Normal
HTML
Preview
6 seconds over 28.8
Microsoft FrontPage - D:\My Documents\My Webs\myweb9\favorite.htm
Favorites
Make a list of your favorite sites from the World Wide Web. You can add hyperlinks to other Web Sites, or replace an existing links, by selecting the text and choosing the Hyperlinks command from the Insert menu.
The Microsoft Network
Write a description about the hyperlinks you are adding, so visitors will know what the site contains.
3 seconds over 28.8

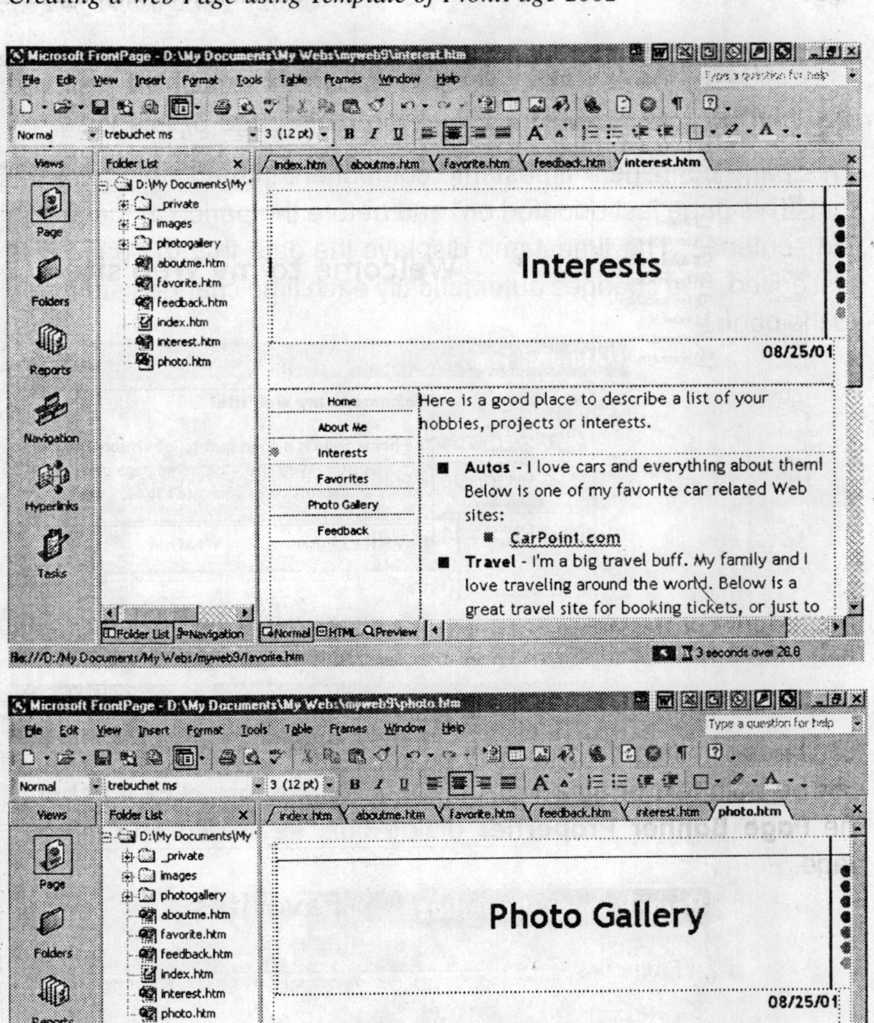
Microsoft FrontPage - D:\My Documents\My Webs\myweb9\interest.htm
File Edit View Insert Format Tools Table Frames Window Help
Type a question for help
Normal
trebuchet ms
3 (12 pt)
Views
Page
Folders
Reports
Navigation
Hyperlinks
Tasks
Folder List
D:\My Documents\My
_private
images
photogallery
aboutme.htm
favorite.htm
feedback.htm
index.htm
interest.htm
photo.htm
index.htm
aboutme.htm
favorite.htm
feedback.htm
interest.htm
Interests
08/25/01
Home
About Me
Interests
Favorites
Photo Gallery
Feedback
Here is a good place to describe a list of your hobbies, projects or interests.
Autos - I love cars and everything about them! Below is one of my favorite car related Web sites:
CarPoint.com
Travel - I'm a big travel buff. My family and I love traveling around the world. Below is a great travel site for booking tickets, or just to
Folder List
Navigation
Normal
HTML
Preview
file:///D:/My Documents/My Webs/myweb9/favorite.htm
3 seconds over 28.8

Microsoft FrontPage - D:\My Documents\My Webs\myweb9\photo.htm
File Edit View Insert Format Tools Table Frames Window Help
Type a question for help
Normal
trebuchet ms
3 (12 pt)
Views
Page
Folders
Reports
Navigation
Hyperlinks
Tasks
Folder List
D:\My Documents\My
_private
images
photogallery
aboutme.htm
favorite.htm
feedback.htm
index.htm
interest.htm
photo.htm
index.htm
aboutme.htm
favorite.htm
feedback.htm
interest.htm
photo.htm
Photo Gallery
08/25/01
Home
About Me
Interests
Favorites
Photo Gallery
Feedback
My Photo Gallery
Use a photo gallery to put pictures on your Web Site yo
like to exchange with friends and family. Photos of new
graduations, weddings, baby pictures, or anything else
placed here.
Folder List
Navigation
Normal
HTML
Preview
23 seconds over 28.8

- A page to list your favourite Web sites.

You can click at **index.htm** to get the main page of this Web.

This page contains a timestamp component immediately after the text “This page last updated on” and before the period at the end of the sentence. The timestamp displays the date that the page was last edited, and changes automatically each time changes are made to the page.

Date and Time

Display:

Date this page was last edited

Date this page was last automatically updated

Date format: 08/25/01

Time format: (none)

OK Cancel

Each page in the personal Web template has a banner at the top. It can be both text or graphics. To change it, **double click** it to bring the **Page Banner Properties** dialog box, as shown on the next page.

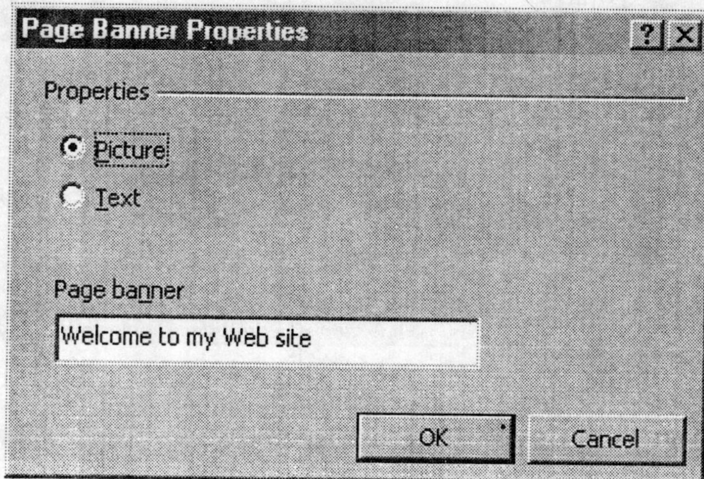

Now come back to the **Page view** and click at **favorite.htm** to get the figure as shown on the next page.

This page contains three hyperlinks. Each one of them leads to different search engines.

They are:

Microsoft Network

Expedia.com

MSNBC

If you want you can change these hyperlinks.

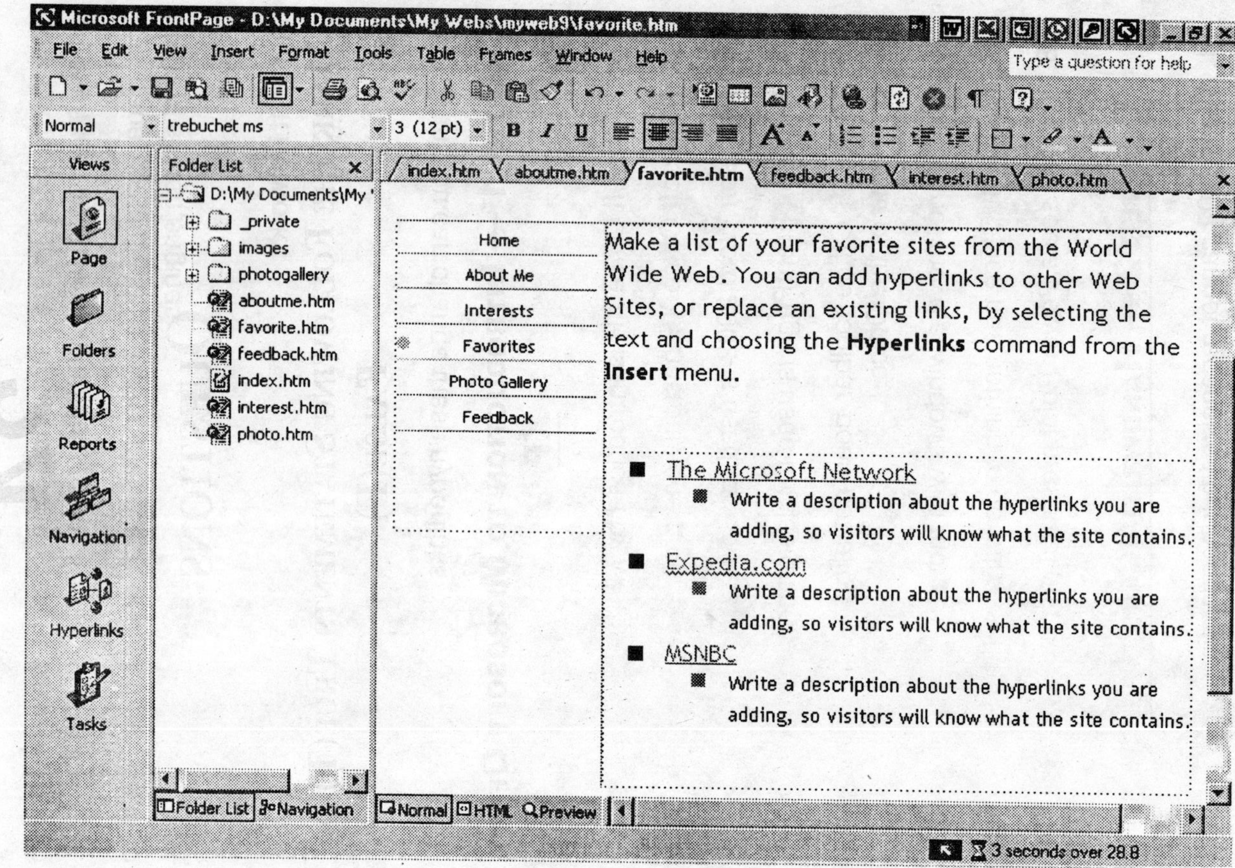
Microsoft FrontPage - D:\My Documents\My Webs\myweb9\favorite.htm
File Edit View Insert Format Tools Table Frames Window Help
Type a question for help
Normal
trebuchet ms
3 (12 pt)
Views
Page
Folders
Reports
Navigation
Hyperlinks
Tasks
Folder List
D:\My Documents\My
_private
images
photogallery
aboutme.htm
favorite.htm
feedback.htm
index.htm
interest.htm
photo.htm
Folder List
Navigation
index.htm
aboutme.htm
favorite.htm
feedback.htm
interest.htm
photo.htm
Home
About Me
Interests
Favorites
Photo Gallery
Feedback
Make a list of your favorite sites from the World Wide Web. You can add hyperlinks to other Web Sites, or replace an existing links, by selecting the text and choosing the Hyperlinks command from the Insert menu.
The Microsoft Network
Write a description about the hyperlinks you are adding, so visitors will know what the site contains.
Expedia.com
Write a description about the hyperlinks you are adding, so visitors will know what the site contains.
MSNBC
Write a description about the hyperlinks you are adding, so visitors will know what the site contains.
Normal
HTML
Preview
3 seconds over 28.8

24

QUESTIONS

MARK THE FOLLOWING STATEMENTS TRUE(T) OR FALSE(F)

CHAPTER 1 — INTRODUCTION TO MICROSOFT OFFICE XP

1. Microsoft Office XP is introduced by Microsoft.
2. Microsoft Office XP has only one program.
3. Microsoft Word 2002 is used for Spreadsheets.
4. Microsoft FrontPage is used for designing Web page.
5. Microsoft Office toolbar does not allow you to run various programs of the Office.
6. You cannot move a windows with mouse.
7. Microsoft Office has nothing to do with the Web.
8. You can see a Power Point presentation on the Web.

CHAPTER 2 — HANDWRITING AND SPEECH

1. Word 2002 cannot recognize your handwriting.
2. Word 2002 can recognize your speech.

Chapter 3 — Creating Document in Word 2002

1. You can highlight the text by mouse only.
2. You cannot right align the text in Word 2002.
3. While spell checking you can add new words to the dictionary.
4. You can put border across a selected text in Word 2002.
5. In Word 2002, you close the file using Close command.
6. There is no difference in Save and Save As command.
7. You can print a number of copies of the document in Word 2002.

Chapter 4 — Proofing Your Document

1. Cutting and Copying of the data is similar to Moving the text in Word 2002.
2. AutoCorrect corrects your mistakes while you type.
3. AutoFormat formats the document for you.
4. Using Find and Replace you can find a word and replace with another.
5. Header are put on the top of the page.
6. You cannot open two document files simultaneously in Word 2002.

Chapter 5 — Working with Longer Documents

1. Table of Contents appear at the end of the book.
2. An entry is first marked for printing as part of Table of Contents.
3. An index appears at the end of the page.

4. An index has the word and the page number where it appears in the book.

5. Bookmark cannot be put in a document in Word 2002.

Chapter 6 — Creating Documents using Wizards

1. You cannot create a memo using wizard in Word 2002.

2. You cannot create a resume in Word 2002.

Chapter 7 — Additional Commands of Word 2002

1. Break command allows you to put a page break in the document.

2. You can number the paragraphs using Bullets and Numbering.

3. Once type you cannot change the case of the typed matter in Word 2002.

4. You can have unequal columns in Word 2002.

5. You cannot create and print envelopes using Word 2002.

6. Letter Wizard command helps you in creating a letter.

7. You cannot count the number of words in a document.

Chapter 8 — Using Drawing Tools of Word 2002

1. You cannot draw your own drawings in Word 2002.

2. You cannot modify pictures in Word 2002.

3. There are no ready made arrows on drawing tool.

4. You cannot use Callouts in Word 2002.

Chapter 9 — Using MailMerge in Word 2002

1. In MailMerge you cannot use spreadsheet.

2. MailMerge is useful for sending same letter to different people.

Chapter 10 — Creating a Worksheet in Excel 2002

1. You cannot copy a formula in Excel.

2. For copying etc. you can take the help of menu on the right click of the mouse.

3. Before printing you can see a Preview of the worksheet too.

4. You cannot print a range of a worksheet.

Chapter 11 — Advance Techniques of Excel 2002

1. You cannot insert a comment in the worksheet.

2. You can have the logical formulas in Excel.

3. Header is put on the top of the Worksheet.

4. You can group a number of rows for outlining it.

5. It is possible to print labels on the rows and columns on every page.

6. You can lock a worksheet so that others cannot access it.

7. You cannot name a particular range of cells.

8. You can set a value goal for a cell.
9. A name cannot be given to a sheet.
10. You can work between two workbooks.

Chapter 12 — Working with Charts in Excel 2002

1. Charts are usually created using Chart Wizard.
2. Once created you cannot modify a chart.
3. You can add more data to the chart after making it.
4. You can modify the chart type.

Chapter 13 — Creating a Database using Wizard in Access 2002

1. You can create a database using the Database Wizard.
2. Main Switchboard is like a main menu.

Chapter 14 — Working with Tables

1. A table wizard allows you to create a table.
2. You can enter data in a table directly.
3. You cannot edit data in the table.
4. You can store more than 300 characters in the text field of the database table.

Chapter 15 — Working with Reports

1. You cannot print a report on printer.

2. AutoReport is the easy method of creating a report.
3. You can create a report using Report Wizard.
4. You cannot AutoFormat a report.
5. A report cannot have the charts in it.

Chapter 16 — Creating Presentation using AutoContent in PowerPoint 2002

1. AutoContent command is part of the New Presentation command.
2. You cannot create 35mm slides with PowerPoint.

Chapter 17 — Creating New Presentation

1. A New slide helps you in creating a presentation.
2. Clip Art can be added into the presentation slides.

Chapter 18 — Creating Presentation from Template

1. You can see your presentation in 5 different views.
2. A Template is a ready to use design with text and colours.

Chapter 19 — Working on Presentations

1. You cannot change the background colour of a slide.
2. Header information is displayed at the bottom of the slide.
3. You cannot add a logo to your presentation.
4. You can add text from WordArt into the presentation.

Chapter 20 — Working in Slide Sorter View

1. You cannot change the order of the slides.
2. You cannot change the format of the slide.

Chapter 21 — Making Slide Shows

1. You cannot add animation to your presentation.
2. You can add sound and video to your presentation.

Chapter 22 — Creating a Web Page using Wizard of Front Page 2002

1. Wizard is easy way of creating a Web page.

Chapter 23 — Creating a Web Page using Template of Front Page 2002

1. You have to create a Web page for putting the template.

Answer the Following Questions

Chapter 1 — Microsoft Office XP

1. Describe the various new constituents of Microsoft Office XP.
2. Describe the function of Microsoft Office Bar.
3. Explain the icons on the Microsoft Office Bar.
4. Describe in brief the working with mouse.
5. What all changes have been made for the Web in various Office constituents?

Chapter 2 — Handwriting and Speech

1. What sort of system you require for speech?
2. How would you install handwriting feature?
3. How would you install speech feature?

Chapter 3 — Creating Document in Word 2002

1. Describe the various alignments of the text in Word 2002.
2. Describe what the red and green lines in the document signify and how you get rid of them.
3. How are Styles used? Describe.
4. Describe the process of putting Borders and Shades.
5. How do you close the Word document?.
6. Describe the difference between Save and Save As commands.

7. Describe the various options of printing in Word 2002.

Chapter 4 — Proofing Your Document

1. What all editing tools you can use in Word 2002?
2. Describe the working of AutoCorrect command.
3. What does the command AutoFormat do? Explain.
4. Explain how would you find a word and replace it with another in Word 2002.
5. Describe the method of putting page numbers in a Word document.
6. Describe how Header and Footer are put in the Word document.
7. What are Endnotes and Footnotes? Explain.
8. Describe how does it help by using the Split command.
9. What do you mean by tiling of the document? Explain.
10. How would you animate the text in the document? Explain.

Chapter 5 — Working with Longer Document

1. What is Table of Contents? How is it created in Word 2002?
2. Describe the method of creating index in Word 2002.
3. What is a bookmark? How is it created in Word 2002?

Chapter 6 — Creating Document using Wizards

1. Describe how would you create a resume in Word 2002?
2. Describe how would you create a memo in Word 2002?

3. Describe how would you create a business label in Word 2002?

4. Describe how would you create a fax cover letter in Word 2002?

CHAPTER 7 — ADDITIONAL COMMAND OF WORD 2002

1. Describe how would you insert a page break in a word document in Word 2002?

2. What all you can change by using the Change Case command?

3. Describe how would you put bullets and numbers in a word document using the Bullets and Numbering command in Word 2002?

4. How would you create a newspaper like columnar text in Word 2002?

5. Describe the process of putting a comment in the Word document in Word 2002.

6. What is Insert, File command used for? Explain.

7. Is it possible to see the full screen of the word document? If yes, how?

8. Write a letter using Letter Wizard.

9. Describe the various options of paragraph spacing and alignment in Word 2002.

10. Describe how would you protect your document?

11. Is it possible to count the number of words in a word document? How?

12. What are Hyperlinks? How are they created in Word 2002?

13. How would you keep track of the changes done in your document using the Tracking commad of Word 2002?

Chapter 8 — Using Drawing Tools of Word 2002

1. Which are the various tools on the Drawing toolbar?
2. How would you modify images?
3. How are different ready made arrows, callouts, etc., are used?
4. Describe the process of WordArt.
5. What are Watermarks? How are they created in Word 2002?

Chapter 9 — Using Mail Merge in Word 2002

1. Describe the process of MailMerge in Word 2002.
2. Create a letter using MailMerge command of Word 2002.

Chapter 10 — Creating a Worksheet in Excel 2002

1. Describe the working of the copying formula.
2. Describe the process of saving a worksheet.

Chapter 11 — Advance Techniques of Excel 2002

1. How would you audit a worksheet? Explain.
2. Describe the process of inserting a comment in the worksheet.
3. Describe how the logical functions work in worksheet.

4. Describe how would you put Headers and Footers in a worksheet.
5. How would you merge two worksheets?
6. Describe the method of putting Outlines to worksheets.
7. How would you put labels on your rows and columns of the worksheet?
8. How would you protect your worksheet?
9. How would you name a range of cells?
10. Describe the various type of references.
11. Describe the command Goal Seek.
12. Describe the process of naming sheets.
13. How would you create a style?
14. How would you copy entries between workbooks?
15. What do you understand by Consolidation of Worksheets? How is it done in Excel 2002?
16. What are Scenarios? How are they used Excel 2002?

CHAPTER 12 — WORKING WITH CHARTS IN EXCEL 2002

1. Describe how would you insert a chart in the worksheet?
2. Describe the working of Chart Wizard.
3. Describe the process of modifying chart.
4. How would you add data to the chart?
5. How would you add a trendline to your chart?
6. Describe the process of creating a PivotTable Report.

Chapter 13 — Creating a Database using Wizard in Access 2002

1. Describe the process of creating a Access database using the help of Wizards.

Chapter 14 — Working with Tables

1. Describe the process of creating a table using the Table Wizard method.
2. How would you add a field to a table?
3. How would you enter and edit data in a table?
4. What do you mean by indexing?

Chapter 15 — Working with Reports

1. Describe how would you create various reports using the AutoReport method?
2. Describe the process of creating report using Report Wizard.
3. What do you understand by Sorting and Grouping Records? Explain.
4. How would you add chart to your report?

Chapter 16 — Creating Presentation using AutoContent in PowerPoint 2002

1. Describe the process of creating a presentation using the AutoContent Wizard.

Chapter 17 — Creating New Presentation

1. Describe the process of creating a presentation using the method of New Presentation.

Chapter 18 — Creating Presentation from Template

1. Describe the process of creating a presentation from the design templates.
2. Describe the various view available for seeing the presentation on screen.

Chapter 19 — Working on Presentations

1. Describe how would you change the background colour of the slide?
2. How would you change the information of Header and Footer?
3. Describe the process of inserting a Text box in a slide.
4. How would you add text from the WordArt into your slide?

Chapter 20 — Working in Slide Sorter View

1. How would you change the order of slides in Slide Sorter view?
2. How would you duplicate a slide?
3. How would you delete a slide?

Chapter 21 — Making Slide Shows

1. Describe the process of adding audio and video to your slides.

2. What animated features can be added to the slides?
3. Can you create your own animation? How?
4. What are the functions of Action buttons? Explain.

Chapter 22 — Creating a Web Page using Wizards of Front Page 2002

1. Describe the process of creating a Web page using Wizard.

Chapter 23 — Creating a Web Page using Template of Front Page 2002

1. What do you understand by the term Template?
2. Describe the process of creating a web page with templates.

Titles in the Learning Series

1. Windows 98
2. Word 2000
3. Excel 2000
4. PowerPoint 2000
5. Access 2000
6. FrontPage 2000
7. Office 2000
8. PageMaker 6.5
9. Photoshop 5.5
10. CorelDRAW 9.0
11. Internet and e-mail
12. DOS 6.0/6.22
13. Outlook 2000
14. FrontPage 2000
15. Flash 4
16. JAVA
17. HTML 4
18. C++
19. Windows ME
20. JAVA Servlets
21. UNIX
22. JavaScript
23. Visual Basic 6.0
24. Tally 5.4
25. AutoCAD 2000
26. XML/XHTML
27. Flash 5.0
28. Photoshop 6.0
29. Oracle 8i
30. CorelDRAW 10
31. e-commerce
32. Word 2002

33. Excel 2002
34. Access 2002
35. PowerPoint 2002
36. FrontPage 2002
37. Microsoft Office XP
38. Computer Fundamentals
39. C#
40. C
41. Dreamweaver 4.0
42. Red Hat Linux 7.1
43. Windows XP
44. Networking
45. Tally 6.3
46. HTML (Rev.)
47. Photoshop 6 (Rev.)
48. PageMaker 7.0
49. Illustrator 9.0
50. Flash 5 (Rev.)
51. SQL Programming
52. JavaScript (Rev.)
53. Multimedia
54. PC Hardware
55. Internet & e-mail (Rev.)
56. Unix (Rev.)
57. C++ (Rev.)
58. Microsoft Office 2000 (Rev.)
59. Visual Basic (Rev.)
60. Java 2 (Rev.)
61. Visual FoxPro (Rev.)
62. Photoshop 7
63. Illustrator 10
64. Visual C++
65. AutoCAD 2002
66. Microsoft Office XP (Rev.)

Forthcoming Titles in the Learning Series

Active Server Pages

Java Beans

Java Networking

Java Swings

Java Graphics

Java Server Pages

Oracle 9i

Microsoft Windows 2000

Flash MX